Better Homes and Gardens.

NEW COMPLETE GUIDE TO
LANDSCAPING

Better Homes and Gardens. Books
Des Moines, Iowa.

Better Homes and Gardens® Books
An imprint of Meredith® Books

New Complete Guide to Landscaping
Contributing Project Editor: Cathy Wilkinson Barash
Contributing Editor: Kate Carter Frederick
Copy Chief: Terri Fredrickson
Copy and Production Editor: Victoria Forlini
Editorial Operations Manager: Karen Schirm
Managers, Book Production: Pam Kvitne,
    Marjorie J. Schenkelberg
Contributing Copy Editors: Sharon McHaney, Barbara Feller-Roth,
    James Stepp
Contributing Proofreaders: Kathy Roth Eastman, Beth Ann Edwards,
    Fran Gardner, Sandra J. Siedel, Barbara Stokes, JoEllyn Witke
Contributing Technical Editors: Raymond L. Kast, Aaron Christensen
    of Livable Landscapes
Contributing Technical Reviewer: Nancy Beckemeyer
Indexer: Donald Glassman
Electronic Production Coordinator: Paula Forest
Editorial and Design Assistants: Kaye Chabot, Mary Lee Gavin,
    Kathleen Stevens

Book Development Team: Steadman and Associates
Writer: Todd A. Steadman, ASLA
Designer: Robert Morse
Copy Editor: Caroline Haas
Proofreader: Bob Sounder
Illustrator: Tom Rosborough

Meredith® Books
Editor in Chief: James D. Blume
Design Director: Matt Strelecki
Managing Editor: Gregory H. Kayko
Executive Editor, Home Improvement and Gardening:
    Benjamin W. Allen
Executive Editor, Gardening: Michael McKinley

Director, Sales, Special Markets: Rita McMullen
Director, Sales, Premiums: Michael A. Peterson
Director, Sales, Retail: Tom Wierzbicki
Director, Book Marketing: Brad Elmitt
Director, Operations: George A. Susral
Director, Production: Douglas M. Johnston

Vice President and General Manager: Douglas J. Guendel

Better Homes and Gardens® Magazine
Editor in Chief: Karol DeWulf Nickell
Deputy Editor, Gardens and Outdoor Living: Mark Kane

Meredith Publishing Group
President, Publishing Group: Stephen M. Lacy
Vice President-Publishing Director: Bob Mate

Meredith Corporation
Chairman and Chief Executive Officer: William T. Kerr

Chairman of the Executive Committee: E. T. Meredith III

Thanks to: Janet Anderson, Colleen Johnson, Sandra Neff,
Lyne Neymeyer, Sherry Rindels, Mary Irene Swartz, Marcia Teter

All of us at Better Homes and Gardens® Books are dedicated to
providing you with information and ideas to enhance your home
and garden. We welcome your comments and suggestions. Write
to us at: Better Homes and Gardens Books, Garden Editorial
Department, 1716 Locust St., Des Moines, IA 50309-3023.

If you would like to purchase any of our gardening, cooking,
crafts, home improvement, or home decorating and design books,
check wherever quality books are sold. Or visit us at:
bhgbooks.com

Photo Credits:
Cathy Wilkinson Barash: 22T, 37L, 37TR, 47, 96TC, 97T,
118T, 120T, 122TL, 122TLC, 122BLC, 129R, 139, 161T,
162BR, 164, 175TR, 176BL, 182T, 184L, 186, 192B, 193TR,
196L, 200BR, 224, 228, 230, 231, 234BR, 240T, 243TR, 247,
249TC, 251, 259TR, 259BR, 260TL, 265TL, 265BC, 270,
274T, 277, 280, 281, 282BL, 282BR, 284, 298BL, 301T, 305C,
305B, 307T, 314TR, 314BL, 314BR, 315, 323, 328, 330, 331,
338T, 342L, 343, 344TR, 344CL, 344BL, 346, 348, 350, 351,
352, 353, 354, 355, 356, 357, 358, 359, 360, 361, 362, 363,
364, 365, 366, 367, 368, 369, 370, 371, 372, 373, 374, 375
David Cavagnaro: 194TC, 194TR, 194BL,194BC, 194BR,
195TL, 195TC, 195BL, 195BC, 195BR, 254L
Rosalind Creasy: 314TL
Derek Fell: 234BC, 344BR
Dency Kane: 9, 21T, 22BL, 45, 81L, 98B, 99, 112T, 117TR,
117B, 122BL, 131L, 137B, 146T, 218T, 219, 236T, 237, 244BR,
246T, 253TR, 254C, 254R, 258T, 258L, 259CL, 261TR, 278,
294B, 306T, 325
Michael Landis: 11, 25T, 54R, 58, 78, 79, 80T, 80BR, 81B,
102B, 103T, 107, 128L, 131CR, 134L, 158T, 161C, 167T,
169B, 253BR
Dayna Lane: 56
Charles Mann: 20, 22BR, 23T, 24T, 25BL, 80BL, 119L, 128BR,
129B, 131CL, 131R, 135R, 137T, 142TR, 142BR, 147BL,
148BL, 153BR, 158BR, 161B, 208R, 232BR, 248BR, 259TL,
286T, 296T, 301B, 302
Sylvia Martin: 15, 23BL, 55B, 103TC, 106, 114T, 135T, 145,
162TR, 162BL, 163T, 183, 214T
Jerry Pavia: 241T, 241BR
Todd Steadman: 103BC, 109, 119R, 125, 130B, 136T, 181,
200BC, 201BC, 260TR, 260BL. 260BR, 261TL, 261TC, 261BL
Charles Thomas: 194TL

CONTENTS

CHAPTER 1

PLANNING & DESIGNING

Lay a path to success with a master plan

GETTING STARTED

If your home is your castle, what does that make your landscape? Gone are the days of building a moat around the property to protect it from intruders. Modern landscapes are meant to be more aesthetic and purposeful. As a conscientious homeowner, you want the landscape to serve the family's needs, in addition to extending your home's charm and beauty. The ideal landscape provides your family with recreation, privacy, and pleasure. Yet it's adaptable to change as your family evolves. What's more, the landscape should—and will—add to your home's value and its curb appeal in all seasons, especially fortunate at selling time.

See the big picture

Think of designing a landscape for the bare lot surrounding your new home as an adventure in creativity. Perhaps your property needs only a few small, easily doable projects to make it more attractive. Either way, it's important to consider how each change will relate to the big picture. Stand back from time to time to see the entire landscape and how each part fits into it.

Begin at square one, whether you seek to perform landscaping magic by transforming a new site or you are refreshing an established one. Starting at square one means that you first see what you have to work with. Look at your

▲ **Knowing your site and knowing what you want, then developing several preliminary designs before settling on your favorite, can result in a landscape that is as attractive and functional as this one.**

landscape as if through a giant magnifying glass—scrutinizing every detail. Then allow yourself to dream. Soon you'll be conjuring up all sorts of ideas and sketching out some rough plans. By gradually working through the initial stages, you'll move on to planning and eventually have a finished design.

Develop a master plan

Landscape professionals will tell you that a master plan is the key to any landscape project or solution. A master plan is more than a drawing or a design—it's a well-thought-out plan of action that includes a design. It enables you to feel confident that you're on the correct path toward building the landscape that's right for you and your property.

Any project becomes more attainable when you're willing to accomplish the plan in stages. Be realistic about how much you can accomplish each year. Many people like to work—and budget—on the basis of a five-year plan.

If followed step-by-step, the process outlined in this book's pages will lead you to a complete landscape design. Although detailed and complex, the process can be enjoyable if taken a little at a time. You won't regret spending the time to do it right. When you've finished, you'll have a master plan—or a masterful design—to show for your efforts. In the event the words "master plan" seem set in concrete, you may find the idea of "long-range plan" less fixed though no less useful in accomplishing the small and large goals that add up to a satisfying landscape.

Follow that dream

Before putting pencil to paper or planting flowers, spend some time figuring out what you want to accomplish in your landscape. Much of the planning and designing will occur in your head as you consider ideas and think about what appeals to you most. Brainstorm and take notes on paper. As you proceed with each step in planning and design, be sure to adapt the plan to your particular conditions and desires instead of trying to follow lots of rigid rules.

Before you spend money on materials or contractors, explore different ways to reach your goals. Learn new skills by volunteering to help a friend build a deck. Watch a professional pour concrete or build a retaining wall at a new homesite. Be inspired rather than intimidated by opportunities to learn.

At any step in your decision-making, don't hesitate to ask for expert advice from landscaping professionals. When you reach the final design and are ready to begin the actual work, continue to ask for help when you need it.

After all, landscaping is a practical yet personal process, and you want the outcome to be wonderful. What could be more rewarding than designing your home's landscape, transforming your plans into reality, and enjoying the results for years to come? Trends such as butterfly gardening, heirloom vegetables, old roses, and ornamental grasses can be the icing on the cake in keeping the whole process fresh, appealing, and exciting.

▲ **A pleasing mix of trees and flowering shrubs, textured paving, and attractive outdoor furniture creates an intimate landscape that invites relaxation.**

Map and Measure

If you begin with a simple drawing of your existing landscape, known as a base map, you lay the groundwork for an organized approach to more doable and affordable landscape improvements.

Take your time with this important step. Subsequent drawings—the site analysis and the conceptual, preliminary, and final designs—all use the base map as a starting point. The accuracy of the base map makes it a dependable tool, which in turn helps ensure the success of any project, large or small.

Base map preparations

First, obtain a map that shows the exact size and shape of your property. This may be the plat, a deed map, the architect's or builder's plans, or a topographical plan with contour lines showing the site's elevation or gradations. The map should include the fixed structures and hardscape—the house, driveway, sidewalks, fences, walls—and their measurements.

Plats are useful for locating easements on a property, but not every state plats lots. Depending on where you live, a plat may have been included in the papers you acquired when purchasing your home. If not, you may be able to obtain it from the city or county assessor's office. There may be a fee for this service. While you are asking for a plat of your property, also ask for a copy of all local ordinances regarding easements, height restrictions, and any other regulations that may have an effect on your landscaping project.

Make several copies of the plat; label and store the original in a safe place.

Then get ready to create your base map by gathering a few materials that will make the task easier: a 100-foot tape measure, plenty of sharp pencils, graph paper, and tracing paper. As you measure your property, follow the tips on page 11.

Make sure the measurements on your map are accurate; mark any changes on a copy of the plat map. Measure the outside dimensions of the lot, house, garage, and any other major structures or hardscape areas. Record the measurements.

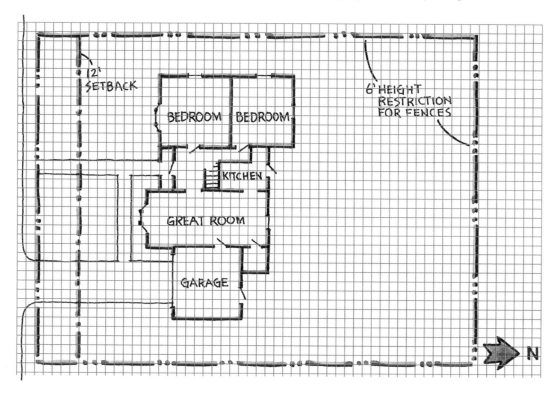

HOW TO MEASURE

- To accurately locate the house on the map, measure the property lines, then measure from each corner of the house perpendicular to the nearest property lines.
- Similarly, locate other structures by recording the distances between them and other objects. For example, to plot the location of a tree, choose two fixed points, such as two corners of the house, and run the tape measure from each of these two points to the tree. The illustration (right) shows how to take one of the two measurements.
- If you're working alone and need to measure a straight line, use a large nail that can fit through the clip at the tape's end. This will secure the tape while you pull it taut and take a measurement.
- To measure a curved bed, you need a straight line to measure from. If the bed has no wall or fence

Measuring from a known point

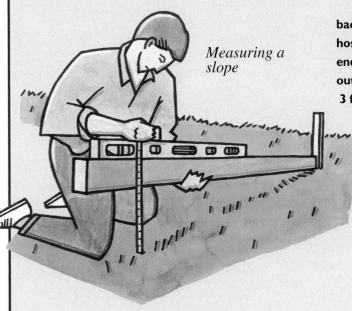

Measuring a slope

backing it, create a line with string and stakes, a hose, or another measuring tape. Starting at one end of the bed, measure from the line to the outside edge of the bed. Repeat this process every 3 feet until you have measured the entire area.

This will result in a series of dots on your base map that reflects the curving edge of the bed. Connect the dots to determine the general shape of the bed.

- Measure a slope or simple grade change in increments. To do this, extend a board out from the top of the slope. Make sure it is level, then measure the distance between the board and the ground (left). Mark the location of the slope and note its grade on the base map. For more information on measuring slopes, see page 51.

Personal Inventory

An important step in landscaping your yard is knowing what you expect from the finished project. Think about how you plan to use your yard and how its design might enhance its use. Then assess your current landscape to learn what works and what doesn't. At first, focus on what you like and don't like about the existing landscape; then start identifying your family's wants.

Make landscape planning an enjoyable process that includes everyone's ideas. Hold a family meeting to discuss the questions on page 13 and brainstorm the possibilities. These questions will help you in creating a complete assessment of your current landscape, leading you to discover the best landscaping solutions for your home.

As you discover your yard's assets and shortcomings, list them in a notebook or on a computer. Take notes as you identify your needs and desires. Start a wish list and let the ideas flow—don't worry about costs or labor at this stage. If an idea seems muddled at first, jot it down anyway; the details likely will become clear in time.

Keep an open mind and wait until later to make specific decisions. Your landscape's problems and your household's needs will change with time. Both people and trees mature; lifestyles and tastes change, so consider the pros and cons of all the ideas.

The view from within

Think about where you spend the most time in the house. Consider the view from your bedroom window, your favorite chair, the kitchen sink, or your seat at the dining room table. When you look out windows and doors, think about what you see, as well as what you would like to see. As you make landscaping plans, take advantage of existing views and consider how your proposed changes will alter the view.

▶ **A landscape assessment guides your decisions. As a result, you will know the size and location of a pool, and whether the existing lawn suits your needs.**

Landscape assessment worksheet

Use the following questions and checklists to assess your existing landscape and dream about the future's possibilities.

✔ FAMILY

- **Who is the family?** List all current and prospective household members, from children to older relatives.
- **How do you live?** Ask each family member: Where and how do you spend most of your time indoors and outdoors? How does this change seasonally?
- **Are pets part of the picture?** What are the current or foreseeable needs of a pet?
- **How do you see the future?** How long do you plan to live in this home? Do you plan to make any structural additions or major changes?

✔ LIFESTYLE

- **How do you use the yard?** List your favorite activities as well as any desired forms of recreation. Do you have places to exercise as well as relax? Is there room to store furniture and outdoor gear?
- **How much time do you spend outside?** How many hours, on average, do you spend monthly on yard maintenance, gardening, and outdoor fun?

- **Is company coming?** How often do you entertain outdoors? How many people are involved? What activities are included?
- **How do you play?** Is there ample room for the activities that typically occur in your yard?
- **Do you grow your own food?** Is there adequate space for enough fruits, vegetables, and herbs to supply your household? Are these spaces located conveniently near the kitchen?

✔ TRAFFIC ZONES

- **Is there enough parking?** How many vehicles must be accommodated daily? (Include guest parking.)
- **Where do you enter?** Which entryways are most commonly used by family members and guests?
- **Where are the pathways?** How do you circulate in and out of the house, onto and off the property? Think in terms of all kinds of traffic: foot, bike, and vehicle.

✔ PRIVACY & SECURITY

- **Do you feel safe?** Are there areas of the property where you don't feel secure? If the yard is not entirely fenced, is fencing feasible? Is there adequate lighting?

Is it safe to pull out of the driveway and use the sidewalks? Would thorny shrubs bolster security?
- **Do you have privacy?** Is privacy adequate, especially in areas where you want it most? What might your neighbors or the city do that would change that?

✔ PRACTICALITIES

- **Is your landscape easily maintained?** Is there enough room to use and store maintenance equipment?
- **Does the landscape suit your region's climate?** Do the plants and structures work together to create a beautiful landscape that withstands the weather?

LANDSCAPE CHECKLIST

Basic features

___ lot lines	___ septic tank
___ house	___ terrain, slope
___ driveway, street	___ soil, drainage
___ garage	___ existing trees/shrubs
___ parking area	___ good views
___ sidewalk, boulevard	___ poor views
___ deck	___ sun exposure
___ patio, terrace	___ summer winds
___ sewer/water lines	___ winter winds
___ power/phone lines	___ easements, ordinances
___ well, cistern	___ deed restrictions

Structural features

___ garden beds	___ other buildings
___ fence, wall	___ pet runs
___ paths	___ air conditioning unit
___ gazebo, pergola	___ fuel storage tank
___ greenhouse	___ garbage cans, recycling area
___ play structure	___ compost pile
___ pool, spa	___ barbecue grill
___ toolshed, storage area	___ lighting

Decorative features

___ lawn, groundcover	___ vines
___ flowers	___ container plantings
___ herbs	___ arbor
___ vegetables	___ trellis
___ fruits	___ garden art, statuary
___ bulbs	___ pond, waterfall, fountain

SITE ANALYSIS

Once you have inventoried your landscape, it's time to take a more in-depth look. Use the checklists on pages 17 and 19 to analyze the environmental aspects and structural features of the site in terms of pros and cons. Note what you like and don't like— what works and what doesn't.

Record your findings on copies of the base map. Make separate maps to study the various sun and shade, wind, and drainage patterns of the landscape, if necessary. Whether you're analyzing the entire site or seeking to improve only part of it, this process helps you understand how all the parts work together.

Pros and cons of your landscape

In time, you'll get to know the lay of the land, as well as how each of the landscape's elements fits or whether it needs to be remodeled or replaced. You'll start to see problems and opportunities in a new light. Maybe you can turn a drainage problem into an attractive feature. You might reconsider planting fruit trees at the back of the lot, for example. Or perhaps dwarf trees would fare best along the sunny west side of your house where they would provide a space-saving way to improve privacy, add evening shade, create year-round interest, and provide fruit for the family.

If possible, evaluate the site over a year before you start to change any of it. Note, for instance, how the sun moves over the property, where shade occurs or water collects, if areas lack privacy or lighting, and where you'll find the best sunset views or the most convenient spot to store your gardening tools.

Gather ideas

Ideas abound in other people's yards. Tour local gardens, taking notes and photos as you see design ideas that might work in your garden. In addition, stroll through the home and garden shows that occur in most cities. You'll find everything you need for a landscaping project, from professional services and building materials to plants to scores of adaptable ideas.

◀ Knowing how water drains allows you to convert a problem into an asset. For example, a low spot where water collects can be turned into a dry creek.

THE VALUE OF TREES AND SHRUBS

In addition to having aesthetic and functional value, trees and shrubs have monetary value that can be measured by competent appraisers.

Considerations
- Trees are the most valuable plants in a landscape because they are the most useful. For example, they may function as energy savers, air-conditioners, or wildlife havens.
- Shade trees can reduce the cost of heating and cooling your home by 10 to 50 percent.

Values
Landscape appraisers use these criteria to determine how much trees and shrubs are worth:
- Size: A mature oak is more valuable than a fast-growing poplar because it is more difficult to replace. Generally, large trees provide more benefits (and have more value) than small ones.
- Type: Some kinds of trees have a higher value due to their hardiness, durability, adaptability, and overall desirability (sturdy, low-maintenance, or attractive). Japanese maples and dwarf conifers are among the most highly valued trees.
- Condition: Healthy, well-formed trees and shrubs have more value than malformed, poorly maintained, or storm-damaged plants.
- Location: The plant's value to the property arises from both functional and aesthetic considerations. Trees and shrubs that form a focal point, frame the house, or stand in a hedgerow represent high-value specimens.

Replacement
- Have your trees and shrubs appraised; take pictures of them. Keep the records for insurance, legal, and income tax purposes. Insurance formulas take into account how easily a plant can be replaced.

▲ A site analysis helps you identify hardscape and plantings on your property and allows you to determine each item's monetary value.

- Become well-informed about the value of what you have before digging it up or cutting it down. It would be a shame to remove a valuable plant.
- Consider moving plants before removing them completely. Ask yourself whether removing the plant will cost more than the plant is worth.
- Once you know the value of a plant and have decided that it doesn't fit your overall landscape, contact local nurseries, botanical gardens, arboretums, or garden clubs—you may find someone who will adopt the plant. Someone may even pay for the privilege.

Additions
- When adding a tree or shrub, always visualize its mature size and shape. Will it outgrow its location or become tangled in utility wires?

The Environment

Your region's climate affects your landscape in more ways than you might think. The level of activity in your yard, the quality of your outdoor life, your choice of plants and building materials, and the success of plantings all depend on the weather and its extremes.

When planning a landscape, you need to be aware of a number of elements that influence the conditions in your area every day. These include patterns of sun, shade, wind, and precipitation. Keep in mind that these climatic patterns change subtly with time of day, season, plant development, and addition or removal of structures.

Understand microclimates

Depending on the region where you live, the weather can change constantly. In addition, conditions can vary from yard to yard within the same neighborhood and even within your own yard. These variations are known as microclimates. For example, a spot in your yard may be cooler or warmer, wetter or drier, and quicker to freeze or thaw than others. Most yards have several microclimates, which are determined by sun exposure and other factors.

By taking advantage of the warmer microclimates of your yard, you may be able to grow tender plants that would ordinarily succumb in an exposed spot.

You can also change microclimates. For example, you can build raised beds in an area where soil drains poorly. This not only fixes the drainage problem but gives you a bed that warms up earlier in the spring. You could bring in the first crop of leaf lettuce and radishes days or even weeks ahead of in-ground plantings.

Use the checklist on page 17 to explore the conditions in your yard and the way they're affected by climatic elements. Then use the drawing below as a guide for creating your own site analysis on a base map. Make up your own symbols and add to the list, if you like. Take the time to be thorough because you will refer to your site map many times, as you will see in the pages ahead.

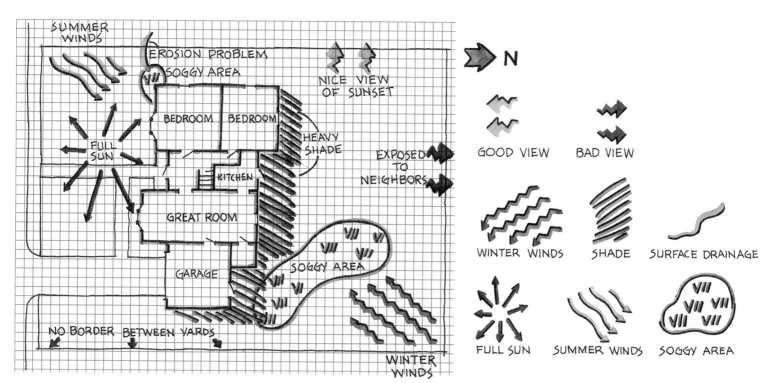

Site analysis checklist No. 1

☑ RAIN, SNOW, & DRAINAGE

- **Rain** As the main source of water for plants, rain is vital to their survival. Contact your county extension service or a local weather service to determine the average annual amount of precipitation in your area. It's also important to know when your area is typically wet and dry. You want to be prepared to provide supplemental watering.
- **Snow** Snowfall contributes to soil moisture. A heavy blanket of snow insulates soil and can keep it warmer.
- **Surface drainage** It's important to know what happens when rain falls in your yard. It may seem silly, but the best way to do this is to walk around the yard the next time there's a heavy rain and watch how the water moves. Note what happens around gutter downspouts, ditches, and any low spots.
- **Soil drainage** Soil's ability to allow water to percolate through is essential to good drainage. After a heavy rain, note any areas where water puddles or soil remains soggy for some time.
- **Irrigation** Note the location of irrigation lines, heads, and spigots.

☑ SUN & SHADE

- **Sunlight** Note the number of hours of sun exposure received by each part of the property. An area receiving six hours of sun or more is in full sun. Anything less than that is shade.
- **Shade** There are several degrees of shade, from light to dense. Light shade is the brightest; densely shaded areas receive little sun. An area of partial shade receives about four hours of sun per day, either directly or indirectly. On the base map, mark the areads of sun and shade along with the amount of sun each receives throughout the day, particularly in the afternoon. Repeat this procedure during each season and note the changing angles of sun (see illustration below).

☑ WIND

- **Summer breezes** The same sources you used to learn about annual rainfall can identify the prevailing wind directions in your area. Notice how existing plantings or structures work for or against channeling breezes where you want them to go.
- **Winter wind** Blocking winter winds can reduce your fuel bills. Windbreaks, which double as privacy screens, can also minimize snowdrift development.
- **Odors** Unpleasant odors that come from off-site need to be noted in conjunction with the wind patterns. This also applies to your own trash bins or compost pile.
- **Noise** Consider noises you want to block or buffer.

☑ VIEWS

- **Good views** Draw arrows toward appealing views from various spots in the yard. A view can be of an object in your own yard or your neighbor's, or of something on the horizon.
- **Poor views** Do the same for unpleasant views. Consider seasonal changes.
- **Views from within** Include what you see from inside the house as well.

☑ TERRAIN

- **High or low** It's more revealing to walk around the grounds and note high and low spots, as well as any steep or eroding areas, than to look at a drawing. Moisture and frost may settle in low areas. Elevated places will be exposed to winds.

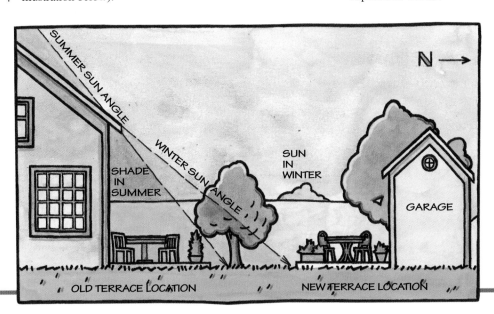

Structural Elements

Once you are armed with the knowledge of your year-round climatic patterns, it's time to consider the existing structures on your property and how these elements relate practically and aesthetically.

At this stage, you'll analyze the physical elements, from plants to paved areas and from storage space to utility locations. The checklist on page 19 provides a guide to various fixed objects in a typical landscape. Although your base map may already include many of these elements, this is the time to make a comprehensive map. Use the symbols below or develop your own set of symbols.

To create a true map of your existing landscape, you'll need to accurately locate all of the structural elements on your site analysis. Double-check all measurements once you have them on your drawing. This step can save you time and money during construction.

Go back to your list of pros and cons. Chances are, by now you've become much more aware of what works and what doesn't work in your landscape, as well as what you like and don't like. This is the perfect opportunity to make note of any additional insights.

Discover landscape solutions

The variations of climate and terrain across the continent provide some difficult landscaping challenges. It helps to remember that each challenge presents opportunities, whether you must deal with a steep slope and erosion issues or harsh weather and poor soil. Perhaps you'll discover that terracing the slope would make room for the patio you've always wanted or that the flat expanse of mucky soil offers just the spot for the water garden of your dreams.

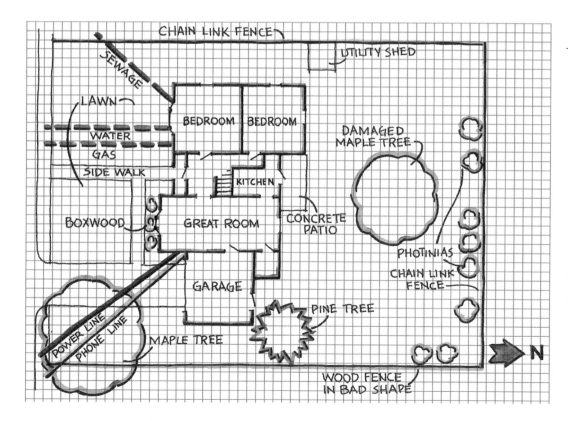

Site analysis checklist No. 2

✓ PLANTS

- **Trees** Mark each tree on the site analysis. Indicate the spread of the branches. Envision the trees' mature dimensions. Note the condition of each tree and its relation to other features—leaves dropping in the pool or branches hanging over the neighbor's driveway.
- **Shrubs** Mark all shrubs on your map. For these and other plants, note any special features, such as bark, bloom, or fragrance, and the seasons they're most prominent.
- **Flowers** Use the baseline method of measuring described on page 11 to outline flower beds. Note what is currently growing as well as what blooms at other times of the year. Also mark any areas with container plantings.
- **Groundcovers** Outline turfgrass areas, as well as locations of other groundcovers, including creeping or low-growing perennials, annuals, and shrubs.

✓ STRUCTURES & HARDSCAPE

- **House** Your home and most of the other fixed structures and hardscape should already be included on your base map. Label the floor plan and indicate the location of windows and outside doors.
- **Other structures** This includes freestanding buildings, such as a gazebo, pergola, shed, playhouse, or doghouse. Think about these structures in terms of their use, condition, and potential. Use the checklist on page 13 to add other features to your map and to make sure you have not forgotten anything.
- **Privacy and security** Note the location and condition of fences, walls, gates, or entryways. Check that they are within the guidelines established by your easements (legal restrictions on your property or that shared with other property owners) and zoning or building codes.

- **Paving** Note all walks, steps, drives, and parking areas, along with materials used, their condition, and any design features.
- **Entertainment areas** Measure decks, patios, and terraces and add them to your drawing. Note the materials used and any drainage problems.
- **Play areas** Whether this means a simple swing, a sandbox, or an intricate play structure, note its location, condition, and potential safety hazards.

✓ UTILITIES

- **Underground utilities** Know where the electric, gas, water, phone, cable, and sewer lines are located. Look in the front of your phone book for the listing of a service to mark utility lines for you. Be there when the utility workers do the job, and make sure the mark for each utility is labeled. Ask for the depth of each line and any restrictions regarding planting on top of them.

- **Overhead utilities** Identify these on your own. Check with utility companies regarding access rights. Note the heights of the utility lines.
- **Meters** Locate all power, gas, and water meters. Be sure you know the guidelines regarding accessibility.
- **Air-conditioning** Draw in the location of the unit and its measured size.

✓ PRACTICALITIES

- **Maintenance** Locate space for storage of seasonal tools, maintenance equipment, and furniture. This includes equipment for maintaining a pool and other outdoor features that may require service.
- **Weather resistance** Note where plants and structures work together to create weather screens, such as shade during hot summers and late afternoons. Mark these and other places that you wouldn't change. Indicate whether the plants and hardscape work well together and are particularly attractive.

GARDEN DESIGN BASICS

Like a trowel and a spade, the basic elements of garden design provide you with ever-dependable tools for making the best garden possible. Rely on these artistic principles to take the mystery out of garden design. Choose and combine your plants and other landscape features on the basis of these elements—just as a professional designer would—for the most beautiful scheme imaginable.

Even if you work with a professional to develop your garden design, understanding these principles helps you speak the pro's language and contributes more to the final results.

Line

Line is one of the most important and useful of all design elements. Everything in the garden involves line. Think about the trunk of a tree, the distant horizon, the line created when a lawn ends and the adjacent woods begin. A sidewalk, driveway, or fence is a clear and readily accessible line in the landscape. As you plan and design your garden, always consider the line that is created by whatever you are adding.

There are four main ways to describe lines: curved, straight, horizontal, and vertical. None is more important than the others—each has different effects.

▶ **Lines leading away from you tend to pull you along. The strong line of this walk leads the eye down the path and into a patio area.**

Curved lines shape informal garden beds and add interest to pathways. Straight lines evoke a sense of order and a crispness that is more formal.

Soothing horizontal lines create a sense of stability. Think of the ocean and how its wide expanse meets the sky, creating an irrefutable sense of peacefulness and majesty. Vertical lines project a sense of strength and movement.

No matter which types of line you use, be aware that lines lead the eye. Lines going away from you on the ground draw you forward. Horizontal lines on the ground slow you down. Vertical lines lead the eye up and out of the garden. Curving lines take the eye on an intriguing journey. All are desirable. It's up to you to know where the lines will lead you or your eye and what you will see when you get there.

Light

What could be more lovely than early morning or evening in the garden, when plants virtually glow from warm backlighting? Who can deny that light gives plants life?

Light and shade change the way colors look and how they work together. Although you can't control natural light, you can play up its effects. Bright light has the same impact as warm color—it advances visually, making an object or area feel closer than it really is.

Keep in mind that light can be either natural or artificial. It is easy to add a low-voltage lighting system to extend your garden enjoyment into the evening hours. Various fixtures and their positioning create different effects. Frontlighting a dark area highlights a

▼ **When thinking about ways to use light in the garden, remember the value of the patterns created by shadows.**

particular feature. Backlighting silhouettes a sculpture, tree, or shrub. Sidelighting, which can also produce dramatic effects, is used mostly for safety along walks and paths.

Texture

Texture evokes emotional responses. Both tactile and visual textures invite you to touch. Use texture to contrast plants in groups or minimize architectural lines.

The characteristics of texture divide plants into three basic groups: coarse, medium, and fine. Coarse-textured plants, hardscaping materials, or garden structures have large or boldly tactile components, such as the leaves of rhubarb or an arbor made with rough-cut 8×8 posts. Fine-textured materials include many ferns and grasses or a delicate structure such as a bent-wire trellis or arbor. Medium textures fall in between.

Changes in texture can be subtle; the textures of various plants (and objects)

▲ **Combine a range of fine-, medium-, and coarse-textured plants to achieve balance and a bit of drama.**

are relative to one another. An ornamental grass, when viewed alone, may seem a fine-textured plant. However, when compared with zoysiagrass, which is much more finely textured, it may appear more coarse-textured.

You'll find lots of textures—smooth or prickly, ripply or frilly—and endless ways to combine them to achieve repetition, contrast, balance, and unity. All are found in a successful garden.

Often, the textural appeal of plants is found in their leaves. Dainty-leaved plants make a staccato of dots; grasses, irises, and daylilies paint pleasant, smooth stripes. Smooth hostas paired with astilbe's feathery flowers and serrated foliage make a classic combination.

GARDEN DESIGN BASICS
continued

Form

A landscape without strong, contrasting forms becomes as confusing as a melody without rhythm. The form and shape of plants and other objects in the garden work to divide space, enclose areas, and provide architectural interest. Grouping plants displays their shapes and creates various effects.

Round forms, such as boxwood or barberry shrubs, for instance, add definition and stability to a mixed border. A series of mounded forms creates an undulating rhythm.

Repeated, narrow verticals also add stability. Alone, an upright arborvitae or a thin cactus looks awkward. Clustered, they appear well-placed. The strong uprights of a fence add a sense of security and completeness.

◄ **Before choosing a plant, picture its mature size, shape, and overall presence.**

Pattern

Pattern is the repetition of shapes in order. Pattern creates rhythm, as well as charm. It reinforces texture and contrast.

When creating patterns, think of light and shadow as part of the palette. Use pattern to draw attention to an area; be careful not to overdo bold patterns, which can overwhelm. Also apply this principle when creating backgrounds. Lay a brick herringbone pattern in walkways, patios, entryways, and driveway borders to unify your hardscape, for example. Employ pattern as a way to direct people through the garden too.

Scale

Scale, or proportion, is the size relationship of one object to another. A 30-foot tree is out of place in the middle of a small patio, but a dwarf tree makes sense. Conversely, a massive house overpowers a narrow front walk lined with strips of flowers.

▲ **Whether the landscape is large or small, it is important to have perspective on the scale of the elements. Note that in this well-conceived setting, the circular pads get smaller as you approach the small statue.**

▲ **Sprinkle bold patterns here and there, especially in dark or dull spots, for visual excitement.**

Balance

Visual balance is achieved when the elements on each side of a real or imaginary axis are equal.

If too much emphasis is placed on one side of the garden, your eye will be drawn more readily there and not to the garden as a whole.

There are two basic types of balance: symmetrical (formal) and asymmetrical (informal). When establishing balance, you need to determine a central reference point from which to draw an axis. It could be the front door, a tree in the backyard, or any other object.

Symmetrical, or formal, balance is the easiest to see and understand: The elements on either side of a real or imaginary line are mirror images. The pool garden below is a good example of this kind of balance.

Formal balance doesn't always suit a home or garden style. You may prefer informal, or asymmetrical, balance. For

example, a large tree on the left can be balanced by three smaller ones on the right. Or a large mass of cool colors on one side can balance a small mass of hot colors on the other side.

Unity

Unity results when all of the basic garden design principles come together in a balanced, harmonious whole. Focusing on harmony will help as you choose from an exciting and sometimes bewildering array of plants and other landscaping materials.

◀ Unity is the harmonious blend of different elements of design—in this case, color.

Make simplicity a guidepost as well, and you likely will achieve a unified design that gives you a sense of completeness. Good structure in the overall design, combined with hardscape that meets your needs for service and enjoyment, creates the perfect setting into which you can place favorite plants–trees, shrubs, groundcovers, flowers, and seasonal containers.

▼ Informal or asymmetrical balance is achieved by using different but equally weighted objects in a design.

▲ Symmetrical or formal balance is accomplished when one side of a setting is balanced by a mirror image on the other side.

GARDEN DESIGN BASICS *continued*

Contrast

Contrast emphasizes the difference between a plant or an object and its surroundings. Using contrast is the best way to avoid predictability in a garden. It also adds a pleasing sense of tension between elements. Like most garden design principles, in moderation contrast is good, but too much can be confusing and unrelaxing to the eye.

You can create contrast by manipulating various elements such as form, texture, and color. Achieve a distinctive look by planting the contrasting forms of horizontal 'Bar Harbor' juniper in front of red-twigged dogwood, for instance.

You can contrast textures by varying hardscaping materials, such as bricks and gravel, or plant textures, such as a leathery leaved magnolia next to a finely needled cedar or juniper shrub.

▲ **The contrast of the blue door set in a natural wood fence draws attention to itself. The door's dramatic color is accentuated further by the contrasting yellow flowers.**

Color

Color seduces the eye, evokes mood, and reflects the seasons. As a powerful and unifying tool, color has predictable effects. Cool blues, purples, and greens soothe and recede, whereas warm reds, oranges, and yellows enliven and advance.

Single-color schemes enchant with their simplicity. The real fun comes in expressing your personality by combining colors. Some colors compete for attention; others harmonize.

Although flowers are the jewels of the garden, too many different colors look chaotic. Remember that a balance of subtly different colors creates a pleasing effect.

◄ **Color contrast adds variety and interest. Colors opposite each other on the color wheel, such as purple and yellow, create strong contrast.**

Rhythm

Rhythm and repetition come about when you correctly position or contrast features. Rhythm avoids monotony.

Gardens that may be complete in almost every sense may seem ordinary until rhythm is introduced—for instance, a stately procession of shade trees along a drive or the reptetition of pavers or the pickets in a fence. These elements create a clear sense of movement.

Rhythm doesn't necessarily require literal repetition. It may be achieved by the use of line. The path shown below undulates with similar—although not exact—curves. In addition, the consistent use of the vertical lines of the bamboo helps create a sense of rhythm.

Another example of rhythm is the gradual change along a planting bed of warm colors and coarse textures to cooler colors and finer textures, and then back to warm and coarse. As different plants come into bloom and then recede, to be replaced by others, there will still be a satisfying sense of visual rhythm.

◄ **The rhythm of repeated shapes—such as the curves of the undulating path—leads the eye and suggests movement.**

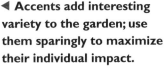

◄ **Accents add interesting variety to the garden; use them sparingly to maximize their individual impact.**

Variety

Just as you choose your guests for a dinner party with concern for their interests and personalities, so can you combine a variety of plants for compatibility.

Similar shapes and colors reinforce a theme. But certain focal points, by virtue of their interesting character, deserve major attention. These focal points should stand out from the rest of the garden. Occasional accents, such as an arbor, a sculpture, or a specimen plant, help create balance in a garden between the reference points and the background.

The photo (above) shows how color, form, and texture all combine in a captivating scene. The terra-cotta statue stands out against the blue-gray concrete, immediately drawing and holding the eye. Stone in the foreground provides a contrasting texture in a similar form. Plants soften the overall effect.

◄ **Repeating a form helps unify a garden. Even if these arbors were placed throughout the garden rather than in a line, a sense of unity would result.**

A THREE-STEP PLAN

Step 1: The conceptual plan

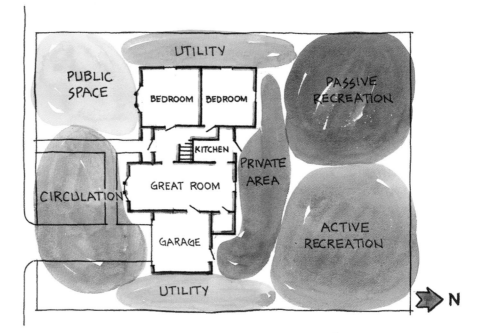

At last, it's time to start combining realities and fantasies. With a site analysis and personal inventory in hand, you've already accomplished a large part of the design. Now take it a step further by thinking of your yard as a whole and drawing a conceptual plan. Here you'll identify general use areas that you need or want.

Define use areas

First, make a list of the basic ways you use different parts of your property and the unique requirements of each. The following general use areas should spark your thinking:

Recreation Play areas for children, volleyball, croquet, horseshoes, and other active sports, as well as passive recreation such as reading and relaxing.

Entertainment Outdoor cooking areas, places to sit, rooms with a view.

Utility Areas for storage, garbage, recycling and composting.

Circulation The main traffic areas, including parking, driveways, and entryways to the house.

Private space Areas that you want to be secluded. These may overlap with entertainment and recreation.

Public space Areas that may not be used much by you or your family but are seen by your neighbors or passersby.

Establish relationships

Look at your list of use areas and think about how the concepts relate. For example, you don't want to locate the garbage can near an entertainment area.

Lay tracing paper over your base map and shade rough areas—or bubbles—as shown in the illustration above. Within each bubble, note the parts of your personal inventory that could occur in that area. Draw as many of these rough, conceptual plans as you need to work out various scenarios until you find one that includes as many elements as you need.

USING LANDSCAPE SOFTWARE

Landscaping software allows you to create a landscape and watch it grow, all without leaving your chair. Various software programs offer a wide range of options to help you trade your pencil and graph paper for a mouse and a computer screen.

Choose a program

Most programs are designed with do-it-yourselfers in mind. Some software allows you to scan a photo of your site and superimpose plants and hardscape features on a digital version of it. Other programs let you create an electronic base map and make infinite changes as you choose plants and features and move them around.

Look for a program that guides you through a survey of your property, then lets you define and map the site. An accompanying tutorial helps with this process.

The software you choose might also include a growth feature that enables you to see what plants look like as they mature, and a shadow caster that shows where tree and building shadows will fall any time of day throughout the year. Growth and shadow affect the placement of gardens, decks, and swimming pools. Three-dimensional viewing gives you a real-life view of the landscape and even takes you on a virtual tour.

A cost-estimating feature helps you plan and track costs at every stage. A sprinkler system installation feature simplifies this

project by formulating a workable plan, complete with flow rates and a shopping list of pipes and emitters.

Other software features include plant encyclopedias with photos, botanical names, and plant care guides; a search feature that helps you identify plants appropriate for your region's climate; demonstrations of common gardening and building tasks; and troubleshooting guides.

Internet options

Search the Internet for an ever-growing world of gardening resources. You'll find websites that offer everything you need, from expert advice to garden planning options. Order plants and products to arrive on your doorstep, or get the information you need within minutes.

◄ Once you are comfortable using landscape design software, you will probably find it easier to experiment with different design ideas.

Step 2: The preliminary plan

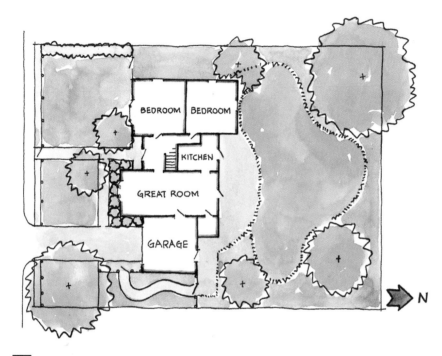

◀ **Make several preliminary designs, such as the one at left, to sketch out as many ideas as possible. Then pick the best ideas and blend them into one final design.**

Try out different designs now by using copies of your base map, or by laying tracing paper over it, to sketch out variations. As you dream up alternative plans, read the relevant parts of this book. Start comparing prices for materials, then start making decisions.

You needn't be an artist, but do draw to scale, making the relationships on paper as they will be in reality. Completing a perfect design will take more than one or two tries. Plan on doing at least three different preliminary plans, and enjoy developing the process.

Each preliminary plan will bring you closer to the final design. With each scheme, you'll learn a little more about how all the pieces fit together and

discover that there are many different ways to accomplish what you want.

Fitting everything into a satisfying scheme takes patience. You may have to set the design aside and give it time to evolve. You'll jump-start the creative process by coming back to the design later with fresh ideas.

With several drawings that reflect different approaches, you'll end up with a smorgasbord of design ideas from which to make your final choices.

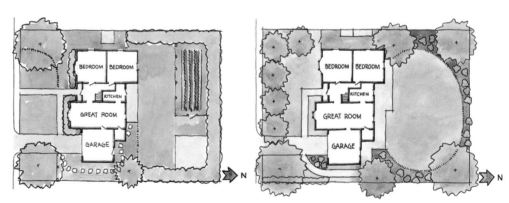

▲ **Each preliminary plan yields a different look. The plan (above left) uses more rigid lines and fewer trees than the plan (above right), making the front yard more open and sunny. The plan (top left) creates more of a sense of privacy and uses more naturally flowing lines. When you look at the final design on page 29, you can see that aspects of all three preliminary designs were used.**

Step 3: The finished plan

The beauty of having a plan is that you know where the project is going. Even if it takes years to get there, all of your work and expense will be taking you in the right direction. Savor the pleasure of this accomplishment and carry it with you as you build your dream landscape.

Review all your preliminary designs, pulling from each the components you like most and compromising if necessary. Make the final plan as accurate as possible. It will be the guide to determining costs. Make copies to give to the contractors you hire to do the work.

Finally, ask yourself: Have I resolved the existing problems? Does the plan meet building codes and easement restrictions? Have I provided for the use and pleasure of everyone in the family? Does the plan suit our lifestyle and our home's style? Is the plan realistic in terms of the time and cost needed to implement it? Will the landscape be pleasing, accessible, and safe year-round?

At this stage you don't have to be too specific about plant types, structure design, or materials. Employees at home and garden centers can help you make final choices.

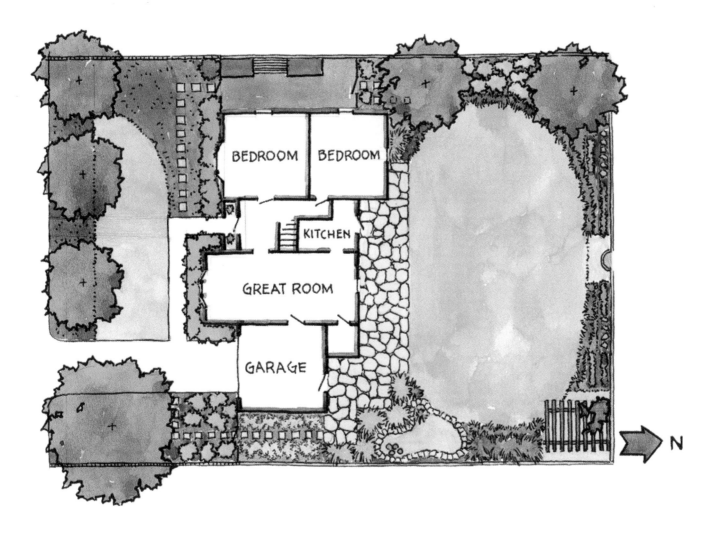

PRACTICAL MATTERS

Until now, it has been paramount to dream and scheme rather than worry about costs or who will do the work and when. Now is the time for wise planning, which includes comparing costs as well as scheduling the work, whether you tackle it yourself or hire someone else to do it.

Set a budget

Using your final design, make a list of every major component. Most plans call for some work that's beyond your capability, time, or desire to do it yourself. Start contacting landscaping professionals (see page 33). Also do comparison shopping for materials.

To devise a budget for landscaping, compare what you think you can spend (what your resources allow) and what you think you should spend (what the best quality materials cost). On average,

budget 15 to 25 percent of your new home's price to install your dream landscape. Budget 5 to 15 percent of your home's value to renovate an established property. If you keep your expenses within this range, your landscaping efforts are most likely to boost the value of your property.

To help finalize your budget, make a chart that has room for each item on your list followed by three columns, labeled A, B, and C. Fill column A with the cost of your ideal choice for each particular feature or task. When you are finished, add up all the numbers to see if you are within your budget.

If that number is too high, go back through the list and make changes to the amount or quality of materials, or even delete some items. Put those numbers in column B. After adding that up, if you are still over your desired budget, repeat the process in column C.

you can save half the cost of a hired job if it is within your skill level to do it yourself. If you plan to stretch out the installation over several years, keep in mind that the cost for some products and services may increase over time.

As you figure costs for each item on your plan, start thinking about your priorities. First, do the things that would most likely increase the resale value; such as the construction of a deck, front entry, and retaining walls or the purchase of trees and shrubs. Also include costs for the essentials that will be scheduled first, such as tearing out old landscape features, site grading, drainage system installation, and bed building. Add in the costs of other basics, including paving, lighting, and plants. Be realistic about the cost of maintenance, and include it in the budget.

As you figure costs for each item on your plan, a project and priority list will take shape. Stick with your plan. Think twice if a contractor pushes you to install a waterfall when you want only a pond. It's your landscape and you have the final say.

LANDSCAPE FEATURE	COST-A	COST-B	COST-C
PATIO	$1600	$1200	$800
DECK	$3200	$2750	$1400
ROSE GARDEN	$400	$300	—
PATCH LAWN AREA	$350	$50	—
NIGHT LIGHTING	$900	$750	$400
IRRIGATION SYSTEM	$1300	$300	$150
VEGETABLE GARDEN	$350	$75	—
RETAINING WALL	$1400	$1000	$500
NEW FRONT WALK	$600	$400	$200

Landscaping dollars and sense

Stretch your landscaping budget by following some of these tips:

- Formulate a plan. A well-thought-out design and a plan of action save money and time and reduce stress.
- Get bids. If you work with contractors, get at least two itemized bids for each project and compare them. Ask for a written guarantee of the work. Set start and finish dates.
- Don't skimp on the quality of materials or contractors. Flimsy construction will cost more in time and money to correct mistakes or replace materials.
- Salvage as much as possible in an existing landscape. Before you dig up plants or tear down structures, first think of ways to preserve them. Even a crumbling concrete sidewalk can see new life as a stepping-stone path or garden edging.
- Move existing trees and shrubs, if necessary, to protect them during construction or to allow them to thrive in a better location.
- Prepare and improve the soil by working in lots of organic matter, such as compost, rotted manure, and chopped leaves. This is one of the wisest landscaping investments possible.

▲ **Ask neighbors and friends for their best money-saving tips, referrals for good contractors, and resources for materials.**

- Do some of the work yourself, not only to save on the cost of installation but to invest personal pride in the project. Hire teenagers to help you shovel gravel or lay sod—to save your back and your pocketbook.
- Buy the largest trees that your budget allows. They require the most years of any plant to mature but add the most value to the landscape.
- Weigh the advantages of sod, grass seed, and groundcover. Sod provides an instant lawn but at a premium price compared to grass seed.
- Grass seed requires at least six months to become established, but it germinates and grows easily; it's one of the best ways to save money. Increasingly popular lawn alternatives, such as low-growing wildflowers or

groundcovers cost more than turfgrass up front with little maintenance expense. Gravel is another affordable, carefree alternative.

- Ask an expert for help at any stage in the planning or installation. See page 33 for more information.
- If you're running water or power lines to a new area of the garden, install more water spigots and electrical outlets where they may come in handy.
- Get expert advice from your county extension service or a garden center when selecting the best plants for your garden. Learn what they will need to survive and thrive. Native plants, already adapted to the climate, generally need less water and attention.

- Avoid impulse buying. Keep a copy of your garden plan handy and take it along to the garden centers. Make sure plant purchases fit the plan.
- Consider more than just cost when selecting materials. Free wood chips may seem like a good deal for a path, but concrete won't wash away in a hard rain, and it looks tidy for years with little care. In addition to quality and maintenance factors, compare energy savings, comfort, safety, and other aesthetic qualities.
- If space is tight, choose features that do double duty, such as benches that open for storing cushions or play equipment or an arbor that supports a swing.
- Rent or borrow expensive tools that you won't use much, such as a rototiller, power washer, or paint sprayer. Go together with several neighbors to purchase a pricey tool that you can all share, such as a chipper/shredder, snowblower, or chain saw.
- Use your landscape to save on grocery bills. Grow the fruits, vegetables, and herbs that your family enjoys most.

A Plan Of Action

Make patience and flexibility your steadfast partners in any landscaping venture. Continue your step-by-step approach to landscaping by determining a plan of action now. Just as you must budget the costs over time, determine what needs to be done and the order of projects.

Whether your plan is large or small—entailing weekends or years—it's always worthwhile to think things through and take your time when making decisions. For example, it's better to wait a month after installing a patio before planting around it. In that time, you may realize that you overlooked a good view or miscalculated the angle of the summer sun. Instead of planting a few shrubs, you decide that an arbor would be more suitable. Moral of the story: Don't

▲ **When you begin to implement your landscape design, start by building fixed structures, such as fences and arbors, that frame the garden, and then proceed with planting beds.**

rush the work. Set a pace that allows you to enjoy the process.

If you're anxious to get started, however, you'll hardly go wrong by planning to do the following projects first (because you'll see huge improvements

before long). Deal with drainage and soil improvement issues. Proceed with construction of a deck, a patio, a privacy fence, a pool, or an outdoor living area. Make exterior repairs on the house before you start working on any of the surrounding landscape. Clean up the lot, remove dead plants, and pull weeds.

Remember, landscaping is an ongoing process. As yards and gardens continually evolve, there's always another project—more fun and challenge—on the horizon.

◄ **Plant the turf last to prevent potential damage caused by other construction, such as stone walls and garden beds.**

As you plan, design, and build your landscape, you may need professional assistance. Familiarize yourself with the roles of landscaping pros. Ask for references and call to verify the quality of the work. Choose someone who listens and seems open to your ideas. Build a relationship with your contractor or landscaper. Contract for one section or phase of the work at a time; try the contractor out before you commit to the next section.

Landscape architects These professionals are trained and licensed (in most states) to practice. They are generally the most qualified to guide you through planning and design. Costs for their services range from hourly consultation fees to flat fees for the entire project. Choose a landscape architect to review your design and plan before you begin construction.

Landscape designers Landscape designers are not regulated or accredited. If you are interested in working with a landscape designer, check references carefully. There are some extremely gifted designers with extensive plant knowledge. Usually they are more adept at formulating planting plans than master planning or designing permanent garden structures.

Landscape contractors They are not governed by any licensing agency or state regulations—only standard business practices. Landscape contractors are often hired to install the projects of landscape designers and landscape architects who do not install their own. There are some highly skilled and professional contractors in the marketplace and others who aren't. Discuss who will furnish the materials. Ask for samples of materials that will be supplied by the contractor.

Garden centers A garden center is an ideal source for plants and expert local advice. Most staff members are not skilled in planning and design, but a landscape designer may be available. Many garden centers offer a discount on plants if you work with their design service in compiling a landscape plan.

Government Call the main county or city planning office and ask about submitting your landscaping plan for building and land disturbance permits. Contact your subdivision office or neighborhood association to submit your plan for approval, if need be.

QUESTIONS TO ASK WHEN HIRING LANDSCAPE PROFESSIONALS

- What is your professional title and training?
- Are you licensed or certified?
- What references can you provide?
- Do you have a portfolio of your finished projects?
- Do you have a specialty?
- What style are you most comfortable working with?
- Would you explain how you will do the job?
- How much is the project going to cost?
- When is payment expected?
- Do you accept installment payments?
- What can I do to help cut costs?
- Do you have proof of insurance and bonding?
- Are your materials and workmanship guaranteed?
- What is your contingency plan in case of problems or additional costs?
- When can you start and finish the project?
- How soon can you provide the written contract?

CHAPTER 2

DRAINAGE & SLOPES

Have soil and water where you want them

SOIL

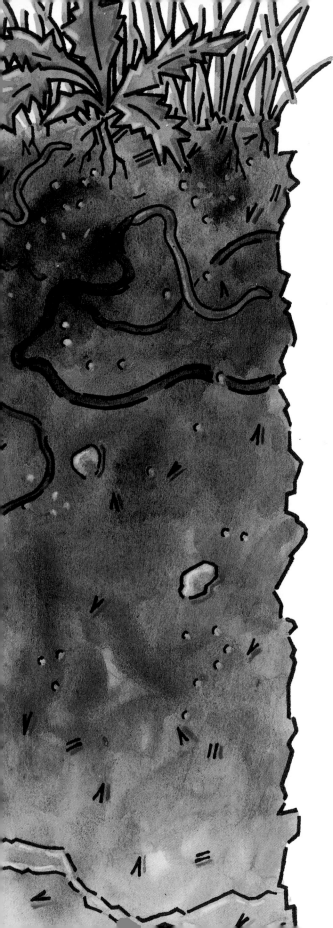

The importance of drainage cannot be overestimated; it affects every aspect of the landscape. Because soil structure plays a crucial role in drainage—at both the surface and subsurface levels—it pays to take a close look at it.

The value of soil

Soil has three main functions: as a growing medium, as a foundation for building, and as a conduit, over and through which water passes.

A good growing medium is essential for successful gardening. It's easier to know your soil and build it to be healthy before you plant rather than trying to amend soil around existing plantings. Once it's prepared—and prepared right—maintaining the soil is easy.

If there are any permanent structures or construction that will be set in mortar, the soil must provide a good foundation. If it is prone to shifting, whatever is on top of it will shift as well. Before investing in any construction, thoroughly investigate soil that is loose and crumbly for stability.

Soil drainage is covered in detail on pages 38-45. You can eliminate potential problems if you take the time now to learn all you can about how water drains on your property.

◀ As this profile shows, healthy soil has many different layers and is filled with organisms. Knowing how to build a healthy soil is essential to creating a healthy garden.

Soil science

You can study soil science for years and still have a lot to learn. The typical homeowner needs to know only the basics of nutrition and texture.

Soil is more than the dirt in which you grow plants. Think of good, healthy soil as an organism teeming with life and constantly evolving.

Soil nutrition depends on the micro- and macronutrients that are present and available. Due to the behavior of certain nutrients at the molecular level—especially nitrogen—there may be plenty of a given nutrient in the soil, but if the pH (a measure of the relative acidity or alkalinity of the soil) is too low or high, the nutrients become insoluble and cannot be taken up by the plant roots. Most plants prefer a pH around 7 (neutral). Soils with a pH of 1 to 6.5 are acid, and 7.5 to 10 are alkaline. Most soils are between 5 and 8. A soil test reveals the pH and what nutrients are present. Soil test results from a laboratory often suggest amendments needed to maintain a good balance of nutrients and the proper pH.

Soil texture is an important aspect of the soil. It affects drainage, root growth, and plant stability. To test texture, squeeze a handful of lightly moistened soil. Soil with good texture forms a ball that can easily be broken apart with your fingers. Very sandy soil will not form a ball. Clay soil forms a sticky ball that does not readily break apart.

How to test your soil

Here are some simple steps to determine the makeup of your soil.

STEP 1 Identify the number of tests you need to make. On a property that is fairly uniform, one soil test is usually enough. Varied properties may need more tests. For example, changes in native vegetation or problem spots where plants have trouble growing may indicate changes in soil. Slopes and low, poorly drained areas often have a different type of soil. Soil next to concrete and brick-and-mortar foundations, walls, or driveways may have a different pH. Each noticeably different area should have a separate soil test.

STEP 2 Take the samples. You'll need 8 to 10 samples per 10,000 square feet of yard. Collect them randomly from around your property. Scrape off surface debris and dig down 6 inches, using a trowel, spade, or soil probe. The tool should be made of steel; other materials affect the results. Avoid touching the soil, too. The natural oils in skin can alter pH. Put the samples into a clean plastic bucket and thoroughly mix them together. Measure 1 cup of this soil blend into a clean, sealable container, such as a plastic bag or margarine tub to send to the testing laboratory.

STEP 3 Test the soil. Send the container to your country extension service if they provide soil testing services, or to a private testing laboratory. For a minimal fee, the lab will test the soil, provide you with the results, and make recommendations for correcting any deficiencies the results point out. A wide range of do-it-yourself testing kits are available as well in nurseries, garden centers, and home centers. Follow their directions exactly.

SOIL AMENDMENTS

Compost Called black gold by gardeners, this decayed organic matter is the best soil amendment there is. Any type of soil will benefit from the addition of compost. It is loaded with nutrients, retains moisture, and creates air spaces. See pages 224–225 to learn how to make your own compost.
Peat moss Canadian sphagnum peat moss improves soil structure and helps retain moisture. It is somewhat acidic and will lower pH.

Topsoil This is available from a variety of sources, but looks can be deceiving. Just because it is dark doesn't mean it's good. Ask for a soil test analysis or do one yourself before you buy.
Worms Worms loosen soil and break down organic matter into nutrient-rich castings. Worms are available from garden-supply catalogs.

Compost

Good garden soil

DRAINAGE

ood drainage is as important to a garden as good plumbing is to a house. A properly drained garden near the house actually helps prevent water from getting into the basement. It also eliminates unwanted boggy areas and reduces plant stress and the loss of soil caused by erosion.

Just as plumbing is installed before a house is finished, drainage needs to be considered before you build your garden. It is much easier to determine how your garden handles rainwater runoff—and how to deal with it—before developing the landscape than it is after you add structures and planting beds. In addition, as you go about creating your landscape, your modifications to topography will affect drainage. For example, if you want a level area for outdoor entertaining, you may find you need to terrace that part of the lawn, which will affect how the area drains.

The basics of drainage

Garden drainage is divided into two basic types: surface and subsurface. Surface drainage is the easiest to observe and, in most cases, the easiest to manage.

The best way to learn about your surface drainage is to wait until a heavy rain; then walk around your property, noting any problem areas. As you observe how runoff behaves on your property, keep three questions in mind: How does water run off hard surfaces? Where is water being channeled through the garden? Where does water leave the property or where does it collect?

First, pay attention to water draining off the roof of the house. Is the water captured and channeled adequately? Also pay attention to water from the roof or any other structures, such as sheds or garages. What happens to water that lands on your driveway, walks, or other paved areas? What about the surrounding areas? Does any water from the street, neighboring paved areas, or nearby structures come onto your property?

The second step is to understand where water goes once it leaves the paved areas. Also note what happens to water that falls on the planted areas of the garden. Are there any natural drainage channels? Are there signs of erosion?

Finally, you need to know what happens to that water. Does it gather in one or more areas of the property? If so, is it suitable for water to collect there? If the water leaves the site, where does it go? Does the runoff affect your neighbors—and if so, how? Check local ordinances. Some towns don't allow drainage onto neighboring land.

Subsurface drainage is a bit harder to monitor and control. Perform the percolation test on page 43 to see how quickly water moves through the soil. Another way to help determine subsurface drainage is to walk around your property an hour after a heavy rain and note whether there is any standing water—if there is, the subsurface drainage is inadequate. Also look for signs of bare spots in the lawn, spindly plants, or plants that can't stay erect—signs of "wet feet."

◄ **Creating good garden drainage is a two-part process: identifying what occurs naturally, then modifying the drainage to suit your needs and style.**

Drainage as an asset

Be creative when channeling water. It can be an attractive addition to the garden if you view it as an opportunity. Here a loose-stone walkway is also a drainage channel.

Use the water

Use your drainage system to create water and bog gardens. Or simply grow plants that like the abundant moisture found along a drainage channel.

Prepare for the worst

When assessing your drainage, check with the local county extension service to find out the average rainfall. Also ask for statistics on the 50- and 100-year rains, which are the highest rainfalls on record.

Rooftop Runoff

When it comes to directing rainfall that lands on your property, begin at your house. Whether your house has gutters and downspouts or water drains freely from the roof, you need to manage that water before it hits the ground. As the photos (right and below) show, utilitarian features need not look boring as long as they transport water where you want it.

Wherever water leaves a gutter or falls to the ground, make sure the water drains away from the house. This is especially important if your home has a basement. Poor management of the runoff from a roof is the main reason for a wet basement. Even if the house is built on a slab and you don't have a basement, make sure the soil slopes away from the structure. Standing water against a house can breed insects that range from a nuisance (such as mosquitoes) to a genuine threat (such as termites).

▲ **A custom-made gutter system—using a length of bamboo cut in half—captures and channels rooftop runoff. The drip chain provides a track for the water to run down into a dry well (see pages 44–45).**

If you suspect that you have a drainage problem around the perimeter of the house, you may need to use the subsurface techniques discussed on page 43 to move water away. But before digging drainage trenches, consider adding gutters, improving the carrying capacity of existing gutters, or repositioning them to allow water to be gathered and channeled where you want it to go. Then you can attach fixed or retractable downspout extensions to drain the roof runoff a safe distance from the house. Extending the outlet of a downspout by as little as 6 feet can eliminate the risk of water backing up into the basement.

Subsurface drainage will typically take care of even the heaviest rains. However, depending upon the volume of water, you may want to have the downspouts feed into a dry well (see pages 44–45). Drainage lines leading from a dry well can be connected to a system designed to drain the garden or run onto the driveway or street.

◄ **Use the vertical lines of your home drainage system as clues for design ideas, such as training a vine parallel to the downspout.**

▶ **Horizontal headers of brick slow the flow of water along this pathway; the gravel allows the water to be absorbed.**

Pavement Drainage and Drainage Swales

Once you have directed water away from your house, the next concern is how to drain water from any hard surfaces, such as walks, driveways, and parking areas. Unless these surfaces are made of gravel or some other water-permeable material that will allow water to percolate through, the water that falls on them has to drain off. The volume and velocity of water that collects there can be significant. If you do not provide adequate pavement drainage, erosion is likely to occur.

If built properly, walks, driveways, and parking areas slope or tilt in two directions. The first angle of the slope follows the terrain, such as a sloped driveway. In most cases, the lay of the land determines this angle. The other angle—called pitch—measures the tilt of the driveway or walk to one side. Sloping in this manner allows water to run gradually off to one side instead of rushing down to the end of a driveway before it is captured in a catch basin or storm drain, or channeled out onto the street.

Properly designed pavement poses few drainage problems. However, you might inherit paving that does not drain well. In such a case, you should identify where the water leaves the pavement and, if the volume is significant during a heavy rain, consider adding a dry well. An alternative is to plant a thick, matting groundcover, such as lily turf or myrtle, to slow down the flow of water enough to allow the soil to absorb it.

Drainage swales

Whether called a drainage swale, dry creek, or ditch, this feature is the workhorse of surface drainage. Used to channel surface water, it can be an attractive landscape feature in its own right.

There are three types of drainage swales (see page 42 for how to build them). A dry creek resembles a rock-lined streambed but functions as such only when draining the site. It is the best approach when regular, heavy volumes of water are expected. A grass-lined ditch also serves as a water channel, handling a large volume of water infrequently. The third type is a combination of the first two. Stones slow the flow of water and prevent erosion, and a mixture of grasses and other water-loving plants are planted in the swale to absorb water.

▲ This natural-looking creek is actually artificial and is designed to handle site runoff. Equipped with a pump, it doubles as an attractive water feature.

▲ A striking river of stone channels runoff from a property, across the sidewalk, and into a storm drain.

How to make a drainage swale

MATERIALS
Shovel
Landscape fabric (dry creek)
Gravel
Decorative stones
Large stones
Sod (grass swale)
Sturdy, clumping plants
  (combination swale)

DRY CREEK
A dry creek can accommodate frequent and large volumes of water. The meandering path the water travels among the stones slows the flow, thus reducing erosion. This feature gives the illusion of having a creek in the yard, even though it only runs during and shortly after a downpour.

Although the width and depth of a dry creek are largely a matter of personal taste, a good choice is at least 24 inches wide and 12 inches deep. Even though water can move freely along the smooth stones, sloping the bottom of the ditch at least 3 percent ensures optimum drainage. For tips on how to calculate a slope, see page 51. Depending upon the amount of rain and the topography of your property, it may be necessary to gradually increase the depth of the bottom of the swale to keep the water flowing. You can fill the swale evenly with stone to have the surface level look the same from one end of the swale to the other.

Once the ditch is dug, run water from a hose into the dry creek to make sure there is an even flow from beginning to end. Before adding gravel, line the ditch with landscape fabric to keep soil from working its way into the gravel. Add gravel to within 3 to 4 inches of the surrounding soil; then top it with decorative stones. Place a few large stones along the edge to help hold the smaller stones in place and to create a more natural appearance.

GRASS SWALE
This is the easiest drainage feature to create. It is well-suited for large volumes of water—but only on an occasional basis. Repeated flooding makes it hard for turfgrass to stay healthy.

To create a grass swale, prepare the ditch the same way as described for a dry creek. If you want to mow the grass planted in the ditch, keep the swale wide and shallow enough for a mower. If you have to deepen the ditch to maintain a 3 percent slope, increase the width proportionally so the swale is easy to mow. If this alternative is undesirable, consider using subsurface drainage.

After you have dug the ditch, line it with sod. Seeding and sprigging will not work as well; the new plants are likely to erode before the roots become established. An alternative is a low-growing groundcover.

COMBINATION SWALE
There isn't a technical name for this swale—it combines the looks and slowing effects of a dry creek with plants for added texture and color.

Dig a ditch with a 3 percent slope. It won't need mowing, so you can make it steeper than a grass swale.

Place large stones along the sides and bottom of the ditch, digging out notches to set the stone along the sides. Place the stones randomly; occasionally pile two or more stones on one another. Once you have arranged the stones aesthetically, start planting sturdy, clumping plants between the stones. Extend the planting for a few feet on either side of the top of the bank for a more natural look. See page 47 for recommended plants that can withstand the force of the water.

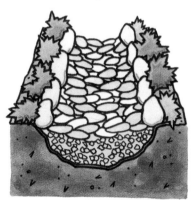

Dry creek

Grass swale

Combination swale

Subsurface Drainage

A subsurface drainage system takes away the water that surface drainage can't handle. Soil absorbs a certain amount of water; once it is saturated, water puddles on top of the ground or runs off. In some cases, the soil is so dense that water does not penetrate it. A gravel-topped subsurface drainage system will help gather and channel the water. Even well-drained, loamy soils benefit from subsurface drainage, especially if the site doesn't have the slope necessary to handle surface drainage.

The gravel-topped drainage (below) is a good way to handle runoff around the foundation of a house. Position the drainage so water from the roof drops onto the gravel and is carried away. This solves the problem of trying to get plants to grow under falling water. It also eliminates soil splattering onto the house.

The key to a good subsurface system is water flowing freely from one drain line to another—connected by Y couplers—then

Percolation test

to an exit. Plan all the drain lines and their depths before you purchase any material or start digging. If you need an extensive drain field, have a landscape architect or contractor check your design.

Percolation test

A simple percolation test determines how quickly soil drains. Dig a hole 12 inches deep and 12 inches wide; fill the hole with water. If the water drains out within four hours, you can get by with surface drainage. If it takes longer than that, consider a subsurface drainage system.

How to install subsurface drainage

The turf-topped method handles only subsurface drainage. The gravel-topped method feeds surface drainage into a drain line.

MATERIALS
Shovel
Stakes
Landscape fabric
Builder's sand
Gravel
4-inch-diameter perforated drain line

STEP 1 **Plan it on paper.** Use a base map and draw where you want to gather and direct water. Be aware that a 4-inch-diameter drain line can handle the drainage for 25 feet of soil on either side. Plan to connect any intersecting drain lines at 60-degree angles.

STEP 2 **Determine the depth.**
Determine the distance the drain line needs to drop from the highest point (usually against the house) to the exit point. Plan to drop the bottom of the drain line 3 inches for every 25 feet of distance.

STEP 3 **Lay the pipe.** Dig a trench 24 inches deep and 12 inches wide. If the ground is level, slope the bottom of the trench. To do this, place a stake every 8 feet. As you reach each stake, dig the trench another inch deeper. Smooth out the "steps" when you are done.

Line the ditch with landscape fabric; then pour 4 inches of sand on the bottom. Lay the drain line with the holes facing down; use stakes or bricks to keep the line in the center of the ditch. Cover the line with 6 to 8 inches of gravel. Fold the landscape fabric over the gravel. Fill the rest of the trench with soil and sod, or with gravel only, depending on which type of drainage channel you are installing.

If using gravel, edging the trench with bricks or other material will help hold the gravel in place.

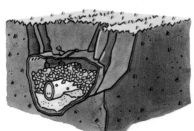

Turf-topped drainage

Gravel-topped drainage

Dispersing the Water

Once you have collected water from your site and channeled it where you want it, you need to dispose of it. This may be as simple as running it to an existing natural drainage area or feeding it into a storm sewer. However, in some cases, the topography of the property may dictate managing the runoff (or at least part of it) on-site. There are several methods for doing this: catch basins, dry wells, holding basins, and detention ponds.

Catch basins

A catch basin is a prefabricated structure built into paving, such as a driveway or parking court, or in a low spot in the yard. It is designed to catch surface water. Water falls into the basin, which is usually a large plastic box, then is channeled into a subsurface drain system.

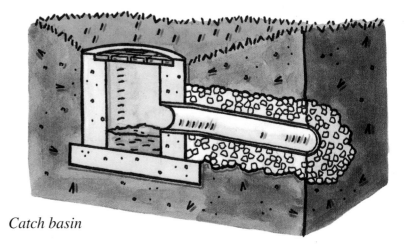

Catch basin

The catch basin is covered with a grate to prevent large debris from entering. The bottom of the drain lines that exit the basin should be about 4 inches above the bottom of the basin so debris can settle to the bottom of the basin instead of clogging the drain lines. Still, a catch basin will need periodic cleaning. Catch basins in a variety of sizes are available at most home improvement centers.

Dry wells

A dry well earns its name because most of the time it is dry. At other times, it serves to gather water like a well. It collects excess water and allows it to drain slowly into the surrounding soil.

A dry well can be large or small, depending upon the volume of water it must handle. You can make a simple dry well to hold a relatively small volume of water: the runoff of a garden spigot or the overflow of a downspout.

To handle a larger volume of water, you'll need a larger dry well, such as the one in the right-side illustration on page 45. The one shown here—which is roughly 3 feet deep, 3 feet wide, and 4 feet long—can disseminate a large volume of water that has been collected by subsurface drainage pipes. The hole is lined with landscape fabric, filled with gravel, and then topped with a 2-inch-thick slab of concrete. Soil and sod can conceal the concrete, if desired.

It may be necessary to dig several dry wells to handle drainage from various parts of the yard. In fact, it may be easier to build several dry wells than to install an elaborate drain field emptying at a centrally located dry well.

▶ **A low-lying area is a natural collection spot for surface drainage from a garden. Rather than fight nature, create a water garden that doubles as a retention pond.**

▶ Create a bog garden from an existing soggy spot by channeling more surface or subsurface water to it. Dig a bowl-shaped depression and line it with vinyl sheeting. Punch a few small holes in the vinyl so the water will drain slowly.

Holding basins & detention ponds

The drainage solutions offered thus far are all belowground. A holding basin is an attractive aboveground alternative. This can be as simple as a natural depression, or it may be a hole dug specifically to hold excess runoff that slowly percolates into the ground.

A holding basin has several virtues. It is a lot easier to turn a low spot into a holding basin than to build a dry well. A holding basin can become another garden feature and add a new growing environment to the overall design, enabling you to grow new and different plants.

If the basin is located in an area with sandy to loamy soil and drains quickly, you can turn it into a bog garden. Line the depression with vinyl and cut 1-inch-diameter holes every few feet for drainage. Add about 12 inches of soil and snake a soaker hose across the top of the soil. Plant bog plants in the depression. During periods when the natural runoff is inadequate to sustain bog plants, turn on the soaker hose.

If the basin is in an area with clay soil, which doesn't drain quickly, allow it to overflow and expand in size during heavy rains. Or, if the terrain is sloped, create a place for excess water to run off. Make a spillway (a low area on one side of the basin) that allows excess water to flow down into another drain field or holding basin and be carried away. In this case, the basin is now detaining water on its way to someplace else and is called a detention pond.

Dry wells

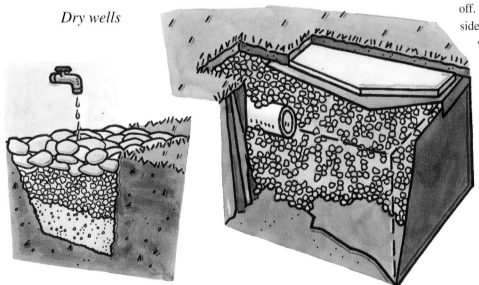

EROSION CONTROL

One good reason for putting time and thought into managing your drainage is to control erosion. The movement of or loss of soil—primarily due to water moving across it—affects your property in several negative ways. It can kill existing plants by robbing them of soil, and it prevents plants from establishing themselves. It washes away precious topsoil and can actually change the shape of the garden. Erosion can even undermine a structure—including your house. If for no other reason, erosion should be prevented because it is unsightly.

Addressing surface and subsurface drainage on your property helps to control erosion. However, those drainage solutions focus on moderate terrain and deal mainly with runoff. The two main causes of erosion in the garden are steep slopes and shallow soil. Simply put, the steeper the slope, the greater the risk of erosion.

Pages 50–59 offer a variety of ways to manage slopes—from building a retaining wall to terracing or adding steps. All of these methods involve construction, which may be expensive and labor-intensive. Before altering the actual shape of the garden, you might consider alternative ways to prevent erosion.

▲ Control erosion on a slope by blocking the flow of water, covering the slope with landscape fabric, adding plants, or a combination of all three. Staking a length of 1×4 flush with the ground is a quick and temporary method of erosion control and can be used anywhere erosion is a problem. For a more lasting solution, spread landscape fabric over the area that is eroding and hold it in place with large metal staples. Cut holes in the fabric and set groundcover plants in place. The plant roots will help keep erosion to a minimum.

Planting

Adding plants is the best way to control erosion. Although turfgrasses slow down erosion, the roots of many herbaceous and woody plants (some of which are listed on page 47) do a far better job of holding onto soil.

Once the plants become established, their root systems hold the soil firmly in place. Roots also absorb the water that percolates into the soil, so there is less subsurface drainage. In addition, the leaves of the plants—trees, shrubs, perennials, or groundcovers—act as a buffer between the rain and the soil. The foliage takes the brunt of the force of the rain, saving the soil from the impact and reducing erosion.

In most cases, a planted slope looks more natural than a retaining wall. A notable exception is a retaining wall that is built to be a rock garden. Several tips for planting on a slope can be found on page 48.

The only limitation to planting on a slope is its angle, or steepness. Unless the slope is greater than 60 degrees, you can grow almost anything on it. Trees and large shrubs may require more planting preparation (such as individual mini-terraces) and care than perennials. Planting turf on a steep slope is not advised because of the hazards associated with mowing.

Landscape fabric

Landscape fabric is one of the best man-made materials available for controlling erosion. Landscape fabric provides a protective covering for the soil, keeping it from eroding. Used properly, it will not slip or wash away, yet it serves many of the same functions as a mulch. Organic mulch works fine on a gentle slope, but it tends to wash away too easily on a steep grade.

The modern fabrics (as opposed to the once-popular black plastic sheeting) allow water to flow into and transpire out of the soil. Because the sun's rays don't reach the soil, it is less likely to dry out. Without the benefit of sunlight, weed seeds in the soil will not sprout—making the fabric a good weed preventive too.

One of the best uses of landscape fabric is as a quick cover-up for a freshly dug or graded slope. Cover the soil with fabric and hold it in place with long metal staples. Later—when the season is right for planting or you have the time—cut slits in the fabric, place plants through the slits, water thoroughly, and let them grow. Cover the fabric with an attractive stone or organic mulch. By the time the fabric breaks down (in some cases, up to 20 years later), the plants will be well-established.

◀ A length of 1×4 staked horizontally into the base of a slope provides a quick but temporary fix to control erosion while waiting for plants to establish.

Blocking

Blocking is a remedy for temporary and isolated erosion problems. Set a length of 1×4 into the soil to block water (or soil) from passing beneath it. Stake the 1×4 into place. The soil that is washed down the slope will build up behind the barrier, providing an area to plant. Once the plant roots take hold, remove the 1×4 and replace it with decorative stone or mulch.

PLANTS FOR EROSION CONTROL

Choose plants whose root systems become established quickly. Consider plants with deep (4 inches or more), fibrous root systems that can grab onto the soil.

AVOID these thugs that take over more than the slope:

- Evening primrose, sundrops (*Oenothera* spp.)
- Five-leafed akebia (*Akebia quinata*)
- Japanese honeysuckle (*Lonicera japonica*)
- Porcelain berry (*Ampelopsis brevipedunculata*)
- Ribbon grass (*Phalaris arundinacea*)

RECOMMENDED PLANTS

- Bugleweed (*Ajuga reptans*)
- Catmint (*Nepeta* spp.)
- Daylilies (*Hemerocallis* spp.)
- English ivy (*Hedera helix*)
- Fountain grass (*Pennisetum* spp.)
- Moss phlox (*Phlox subulata*)
- Cape leadwort (*Plumbago auriculata*)
- Purple moor grass (*Molinia caerulea*)
- Bush cinquefoil (*Potentilla fruticosa*)
- Wintercreeper euonymus (*Euonymus fortunei*)

Juniper

Cotoneaster

Blue fescue

TAMING SLOPES

Depending on how you view it, land that varies in topography is both a blessing and a challenge. On one hand, changes in grade add interest to the garden, help create microclimates, offer more square footage of garden in the same lateral space as a level area, and can create or block a view. On the other hand, a sloped area of the garden can be difficult to establish, may require substantial construction to make it usable for anything other than planting, and is far more prone to erosion than a flat area.

Decide how you intend to use the slope. If you need the space for an outdoor room or another use requiring a level area, you will have to terrace. You will also want to make terraces if you need a cutting or vegetable garden. (Terraces and how to build them are discussed in detail on pages 50–51.)

If you don't plan to carve a level area out of the slope, another choice is to cover the slope with plants to prevent erosion. There are several considerations to keep in mind when planting on a slope: adapting your design to accommodate steepness, creating safe and easy access to maintain plantings, and dealing with the microclimate created by the slope.

▲ **Several small terraces in a steeply sloped yard are easier to build and tend than one big one.**

Designing with slopes

Get the most from designing a sloping area by taking advantage of these suggestions.

Views If your house is at the top of the slope, it—or any other structure in that location—becomes the dominant element in the landscape. Even a normal-sized home may appear imposing from below. Create a meandering walkway up to the house and use a mix of plantings to create visual interest along the way.

If the entry to your house is at the high side of a hill and the garden flows down and away from the house, there is an opportunity for good overall views of the garden and sights beyond the property. The slope can be used to block or frame a view, as well.

Perspective A slope is not always viewed from above or below. Be sure your design works from the side as well. One trick to designing the side view of a slope is to plant taller objects at the low end of the slope. The natural topography already leads the eye from the top of the slope to the bottom. Planting something tall, bold, or bright has a way of stopping the eye and leading the vision back up the slope.

Creating rooms To break up the expanse of a slope, you can terrace the area and create a series of outdoor rooms. Tips on terracing and how to build retaining walls are given on pages 50–59.

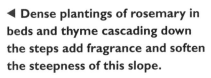

◀ **Dense plantings of rosemary in beds and thyme cascading down the steps add fragrance and soften the steepness of this slope.**

◀ **Stairs that cut across a slope at an angle make the climb to this house longer but less steep. They also make the house less imposing.**

Planting on a slope

No matter what planting design you come up with when dealing with a slope, take note of these practical considerations.

Microclimates Heat and moisture follow certain patterns—warm air rises, cold air sinks—causing a difference between the climatic conditions at the top of a slope and those at the bottom. These variations, called microclimates, are most likely to occur if the base of the slope is part of a longer, low-lying slope or ridge that runs through a neighborhood. The direction the slope faces can also create a microclimate. For example, a north-facing slope is significantly colder than a south-facing one. A site analysis will help determine what, if any, differences in temperature exist along a slope.

Establishing plants Amend soil well and cover the entire area to be planted with landscape fabric before planting. This prevents erosion and suppresses weeds. Cover the fabric with mulch.

The key to planting trees and shrubs on a slope is to provide a sufficient area for each plant so the roots can take hold. For larger plants, dig the uphill side of the hole a little deeper and mound up soil on the downhill side to keep the slope from eroding as the plant becomes established. Holes for perennials, groundcovers, and bulbs can be dug flush with the slope.

Maintenance and safety Turfgrass is the least desirable plant in terms of maintenance and safety. It accentuates the severity of a slope and can be dangerous to mow. Manufacturers suggest not mowing slopes that exceed a 3 to 1 ratio (1 foot in height for every 3 feet of lateral distance).

Whatever you plant, you will need to be able to reach the plants for routine maintenance. Even if you're covering a slope with woody and herbaceous plants, build pathways perpendicular to the slope or angled across it for easy maintenance. To move straight up and down a slope, build steps.

▶**Avoid mowing on a steep bank by planting a flowering groundcover. Shown here is ajuga.**

Terracing

Terraces allow you to get more useful space out of a slope. It can create a level area around the entryway of a home to expand the entry landing and provide a place for company to spill over when needed. Further out in the yard, the level area you create can be used for growing flowers or vegetables; playing games such as horseshoes or boccie ball; relaxing on a bench, chair, or chaise lounge; eating meals al fresco; or entertaining guests. The level areas created by terracing also slow surface drainage and allow more water to be absorbed by the soil.

Terracing is an effective way to draw attention to and accentuate the slope. Terraces on a steep slope will require retaining walls to hold them in place, as seen in the photo below. On a more gentle slope, you can get by with one or two steps constructed of stone or wood, as shown in the photos at right and on page 51.

▼ **For a stable and erosion-free terrace on a steeply sloped site, incorporate a retaining wall at each level.**

Moving earth

If you think of your favorite yard and garden areas, they probably have one thing in common—they are not completely flat. During the early stages of construction, some of the soil needed to be moved.

Before starting a major garden project, refer to your master plan. Determine any areas that need to be built up, leveled, or smoothed out. This overview of your needs for cut (soil to be removed) and fill (soil to be added) should indicate whether you have enough soil to do what you want. It should also tell you where you will need to haul any excavated soil. If you need to store excavated soil temporarily, cover it with plastic so that it doesn't wash away. Hold the plastic in place with bricks or large stones. Storing soil on a firm surface (such as plywood or concrete paving) makes it easier to move later on.

Moving earth to build retaining walls and terraces can often be done by hand—cutting deep into a slope, building the wall, and replacing the soil behind the wall. However, it is worth

▲ **The vertical change from terrace to terrace can be as little as one foot.**

looking into the cost of having someone come with a small, pneumatic-wheeled tractor designed for landscape grading. The light weight and maneuverability of this machine enables an experienced operator to move the same amount of earth in one afternoon that would take an average person several days to move.

This step in the process underscores the importance of a master plan. Most contractors have half- or full-day minimums. It would be a shame to have someone come out to do a few hours' work on one project, and then six months later need something else when, with a little planning, all the work could have been done at the same time.

▲ **In addition to solving problems, terracing can be used to accentuate whatever slope you do have. Without the wood steps, this slope would hardly be noticed.**

How to calculate percent of slope

Accurate measurements are needed for drainage lines and steps. This method calculates slope easily and accurately.

STEP 1 **Rent a builder's level.** Also called a rod and transit, this equipment is readily available at rental stores. With it and a master plan in hand, you have all the tools required to measure the relevant slopes on your property.

STEP 2 **Choose a starting point.** Select a central spot in the garden and set the level on the tripod. Look through the telescope. Whatever aligns with the horizontal line of the crosshair is level with the instrument. Ideally, you can see all the points you want to measure from one location. If not, measure in increments.

STEP 3 **Start measuring.** When you rent the level, you will also get a measuring rod that extends up to 20 feet. Have a helper place the rod on a known point (such as the footing of the house) and aim the telescope at it. Record the number you see on the

rod. Have your helper go to where you want the drain line to come out and take another reading. The distance above or below the first reading is the height above or below the fixed point.

Steps

Steps are an almost indispensable part of slopes. Eventually you will have to get from one point to another, and unless you have planned a zigzagging path (which can be fun and functional) you will need to add steps. The three keys to successful steps are comfort, safety, and attractive style.

Comfort

You have probably walked on steps that forced you to alter your normal stride so much that it felt awkward. You also may have ascended a long flight of stairs without a landing to break up the climb. To find the right stride for your steps—before building them—pay attention to any stairs you climb. If you find a set that feels comfortable and natural to you, measure the distance from the top of one step to the top of the next. Then measure the depth of the step from front to back to use as a guide.

The ideal rise is 5 to 7 inches. The ratio of rise (height of the step) to run (depth of the step) is the major factor in comfort. Multiply the rise by two and add the run. If the result is between 25 and 27, the step is suitable.

Safety

Comfort and safety go hand in hand. Steps that relate to a natural stride reduce the risk of tripping or falling. Use railings on any steps if the slope is steep. Even a light railing, such as the rustic bentwood twig railing at left, provides a handhold. Check local ordinances before you build steps. If you plan to use the steps at night, illuminate them in some fashion.

Style

The steps shown on this page are but a few of the styles you can build. When choosing design and materials, match the rest of the garden. This attention to detail makes the garden yours.

▲ **Generously wide steps made of 4×4s are simple to build. Using gravel instead of concrete or soil eliminates drainage problems.**

◄ **Railings are important on steep steps. They needn't be fancy or expensive. This recycled wood from the garden provides a rustic look.**

◄ **Steps should be wide and inviting. These steps were cut to blend with the surrounding stone.**

How to build timber and paver steps

MATERIALS

Tape measure
String
Stakes
Masking tape
Plumb line
Shovel
Level
6×6 timbers
Drill with ½×8-inch bit
12-inch spikes
2-foot lengths of ½-inch rebar
Gravel
Landscape fabric
Builder's sand
Screed (use a 1×2 cut to fit)
Brick pavers (Another option: fill the step frames with gravel or stone)

STEP 1 Determine the number of steps and their dimensions. Measure the total rise and run (see page 52) of the set of steps. Calculate the number of steps needed by dividing the total rise of steps by the ideal rise for each step; round off to the closest whole number. To find the run for each step, divide the total horizontal distance of steps by the number of steps. Adjust the steps so they fit 6×6s and an even number of pavers.

STEP 2 Stake and excavate. Mark the width and length of the set of steps with stakes and string. Attach tape to the string every place a new step begins. Hang a plumb line from the string to mark the four corners of each step. Dig a smooth, level hole the width of the step and 6 inches longer than the step (to allow room for the next riser).

STEP 3 Set the frame in place. Cut 6×6 timbers to form a box. Drill ½-inch holes through the timbers 8 inches from each end. Level the timbers and secure with spikes. Drive rebar through the holes and into the ground to anchor the first step.

STEP 4 Lay the frame for the next step. Make another frame exactly like the first one. Place the front timber on the back side of the first step. Attach with 12-inch spikes, then secure to the ground with two lengths of rebar. Repeat as needed.

STEP 5 Prepare the base. Add 1½ inches of gravel to each step and tamp down. Lay landscape fabric over the gravel. Add a 2-inch layer of builder's sand on top of the fabric. Using a screed, smooth the sand so it forms a level layer 2 inches from the top of the timbers.

STEP 6 Put pavers in place. Lay pavers in the desired pattern and sweep sand over them for a snug fit.

RETAINING WALLS

When dealing with a slope, you may need to hold back part of it to create the garden area you want. This is where a retaining wall is needed. These structures can be an attractive asset to the garden, often becoming a powerful design feature.

Siting considerations

The first step in adding a retaining wall is deciding exactly where to place it. This is determined by a combination of your needs and what the site offers.

When designing a wall, remember that retaining walls hold back a tremendous amount of soil and the water contained in it. An improperly built wall can collapse. In most areas a homeowner can build a retaining wall up to 40 inches high. Anything higher than that will probably require a licensed contractor. Before starting the project, check local building codes. If you want to do the work yourself, you might choose to build two staggered low walls rather than a single high one.

If it is the right height, all or a portion of the wall can serve as bench seating. Or the wall can be curved inward to allow space for a seating area in front of the wall (see photo on page 55).

If the wall will be near a walkway or drive, leave at least 18 inches for a planting strip, or build the wall right up to the paving. If the paving already exists and you want the wall to be flush with it, be careful not to disturb the foundation of the paving when preparing the wall base.

Retaining wall styles

There are several different styles of retaining walls, each requiring various levels of skill. If you are building the wall yourself, remember that all styles require a fair amount of muscle just to move the soil around.

Mortared wall A mortared wall can be made of brick, concrete block, or stone fixed in place with mortar. This rigid structure cannot withstand the heaving of soil during winter freezing and thawing. In cold-winter areas, a mortared wall requires a footing below the frost line (up to 4 feet deep in some areas). Be sure to add weep holes—openings in the wall—to allow water to drain through. These special requirements make mortared walls the most difficult to build. For step-by-step instructions on building masonry retaining walls, see pages 56-57.

▲ The spaces between the stones of this dry stack wall allow water to pass through, avoiding the buildup of water pressure.

▲ Sometimes a series of retaining walls works better than a single high one. These walls were built from pressure-treated landscape timbers.

◄ Consider building a retaining wall low enough to double as seating. Use large, smooth stones for the top course.

Soften the impact

A retaining wall is a large expanse of wood, stone, brick, or masonry. Although this may be desirable and attractive, you might want to soften the look by adding plants. You can plant trailing or weeping forms in the soil behind the wall or between the stones atop the wall. Also, plant along the base of the wall, letting vines or other plants grow up to mask the wall or training them against the wall in a set pattern.

When planting and training plants, be sure to avoid blocking weep holes. If water pressure builds up behind the wall and causes it to lean, it will be next to impossible to repair. Be sure to follow the directions carefully for installing drain lines behind a wall.

Dry stack wall A dry stack wall is made by carefully stacking stones on top of one another and gently sloping the wall back toward the slope. Dry stack walls are attractive and blend into a natural setting better than other walls. These walls don't require a footing because the individual stones can shift with the soil. Although this shifting may require an occasional readjustment to the wall, the trade-off is the relative ease and low cost of building. Because there is no mortar between the stones, water can pass through freely, and little or no water pressure builds up behind the wall. See pages 132–133 for step-by-step directions for building a dry stack wall.

Wood wall Typically made of landscape timbers, a wood retaining wall is affordable and relatively easy to build. It is also the most versatile for adding

seating, decorative finials, or other features. Use pressure-treated lumber for construction; regular lumber decomposes too quickly in contact with moist soil. Since a wood wall is relatively light, you may need deadmen—timbers that are attached perpendicular to the wall and extended back into the soil—to hold the wall stable against the weight of the soil behind it. The addition of deadmen results in a solid wall but requires a lot of digging.

► **This handsome brick retaining wall is within the skill level of most do-it-yourselfers.**

How to build a masonry retaining wall

▲ Add pizzazz to a masonry wall by finishing it with stone veneer. It's less costly than building a stone wall.

MATERIALS

Shovel
Concrete
Chalk line
⅜-inch plywood spacer
Concrete blocks
Rubber gloves
Goggles

Mortar
Masonry trowel
Level
Rubber mallet
Cap blocks
Gravel
Drain line

STEP 1 **Prepare the footing.** Dig a 2-foot-wide trench to just below the frost line. Fill it with concrete until level with the surrounding soil. If the frost line is deep where you live, you can pour concrete footings below the soil line, then build a foundation wall up to the soil level. Mark the footing with a chalk line to indicate where you want the front of the wall to be.

STEP 2 **Dry-lay the first course.** Use a piece of ⅜-inch plywood as a spacer. Lay out the first course of blocks without any mortar. If the wall is straight, use a half block for each end (2a). If the wall will tie back into the soil, use a full block for each corner (2b).

STEP 3 **Mortar the first course.** Once you are sure the first course fits the way you want it, mix a batch of mortar (mix only one batch at a time). Spread 1 inch of mortar on the footing; set the first three or four blocks in place. Use about ⅜ inch of mortar between blocks. Tamp the blocks into place with a rubber mallet or the trowel handle. Scrape off and remove any excess mortar.

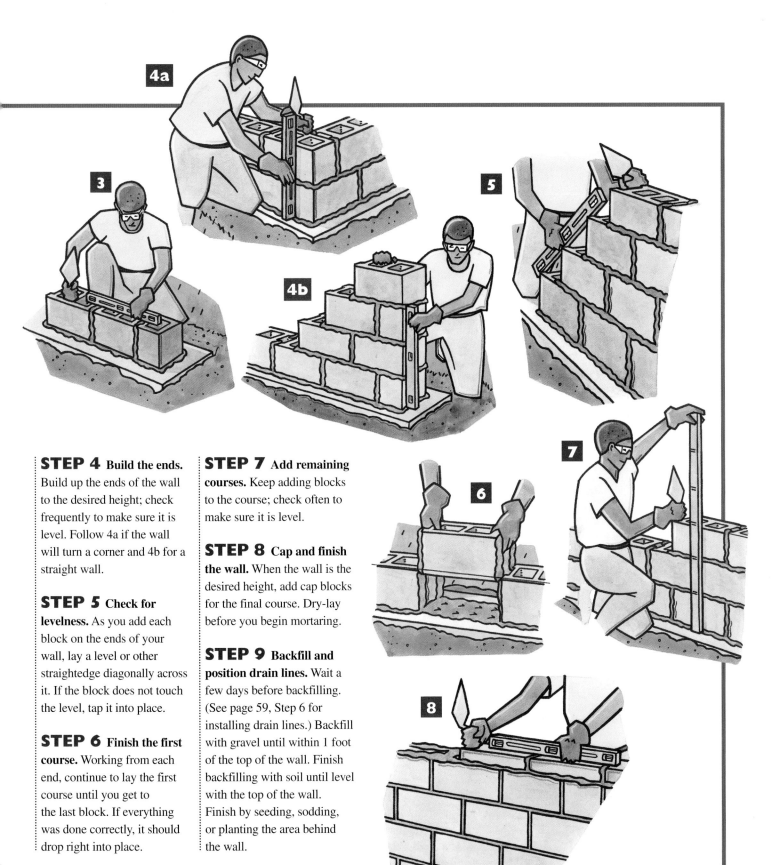

STEP 4 Build the ends. Build up the ends of the wall to the desired height; check frequently to make sure it is level. Follow 4a if the wall will turn a corner and 4b for a straight wall.

STEP 5 Check for levelness. As you add each block on the ends of your wall, lay a level or other straightedge diagonally across it. If the block does not touch the level, tap it into place.

STEP 6 Finish the first course. Working from each end, continue to lay the first course until you get to the last block. If everything was done correctly, it should drop right into place.

STEP 7 Add remaining courses. Keep adding blocks to the course; check often to make sure it is level.

STEP 8 Cap and finish the wall. When the wall is the desired height, add cap blocks for the final course. Dry-lay before you begin mortaring.

STEP 9 Backfill and position drain lines. Wait a few days before backfilling. (See page 59, Step 6 for installing drain lines.) Backfill with gravel until within 1 foot of the top of the wall. Finish backfilling with soil until level with the top of the wall. Finish by seeding, sodding, or planting the area behind the wall.

How to build a wood retaining wall

Retaining walls made of wood are affordable and easy to build, mainly because they don't need a footing. An alternative method for building is described in the caption for the photo below. The following directions are for the wall shown in Figure 1; it is made from 6×6-inch landscape timbers.

MATERIALS

Shovel
Tamper
Landscape fabric
Gravel
6×6 landscape timbers
Drill with ½×8-inch bit
Sledgehammer
Builder's level
Builder's square
3-foot lengths of ½-inch rebar
12-inch metal spikes
4-inch drainpipe
Topsoil

STEP 1 Lay out the wall and prepare the base. Use stakes and string to mark where the wall is to be built. Dig a trench 6 inches deep and 18 inches wide, then tamp it firmly to compact the soil. Line the trench with landscape fabric and top with 2 inches of gravel.

STEP 2 Lay the first course. Cut the timbers to the desired length and drill holes through the timbers near each end. Set timbers into place. Pound each one into position with a sledgehammer, check for level, then anchor each timber with pieces of rebar driven through the predrilled holes and into the ground. Use a builder's square to ensure corners are at 90-degree angles.

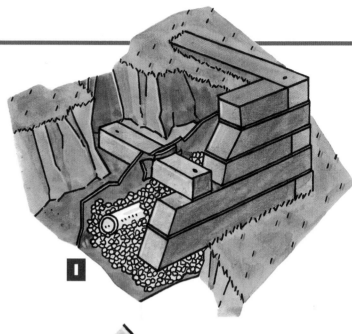

Alternate method

The photo shows another type of wood retaining wall. Set 4×4 posts at least 2 feet into the ground, spaced 8 feet apart. Stack landscape timbers behind the posts and secure with 10-inch carriage bolts that go through the post and timbers. Line the back side of the wall with landscape fabric and lay gravel and a drain line before backfilling (see page 57).

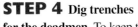

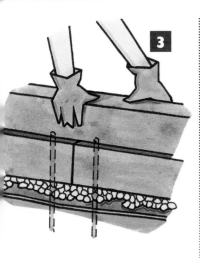

STEP 4 **Dig trenches for the deadmen.** To keep the wall vertical over time, you will need to run pieces back into the slope. These pieces, called deadmen, tie the wall into the soil. Every 8 feet along the third course, dig a 4-foot-long, 6-inch-wide trench perpendicular to the wall. At the rear, dig a 2-foot-long trench to handle a crosspiece under the deadman.

STEP 3 **Lay the second course.** Position the next course of timbers so the joints are staggered and the ends overlap on the corners. The second course should be ½ inch closer to the slope. This setback is essential for wall stability. Attach these timbers to the first course with spikes driven through predrilled holes. Avoid drilling into a piece of rebar.

STEP 5 **Secure each deadman.** Cut a hole in the landscape fabric and slide the deadman through the hole so one end of the deadman is in the trench you dug and the other is resting on the second course of the wall. Once the deadman is level, use 12-inch spikes to secure it to the wall.

Use a piece of rebar to secure the other end of the deadman to the crosspiece under it.

STEP 6 **Install drain lines.** Before completing the third course, lay a piece of drainpipe (with holes down) on top of a 4- to 6-inch gravel base along the back side of the wall so that it exits at one end. Be sure the drain line slopes to one end of the wall at the rate of about 1 inch every 4 feet.

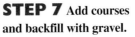

STEP 7 **Add courses and backfill with gravel.** Continue adding courses, remembering to set each one back toward the slope by ½ inch and securing them. When the last course is positioned, backfill behind the wall with a 6- to 12-inch-wide layer of gravel to within 1 foot of the top of the wall. Fold over the edges of the landscape fabric and cover with topsoil. Level the area for planting.

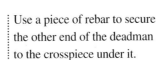

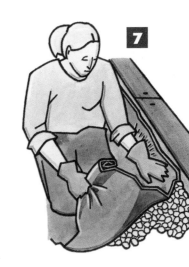

CHAPTER 3

LAWNS

Carpets for the garden

DESIGNING THE LAWN

A large carpet of lush grass has come to symbolize a well-designed landscape. Lawns and lawn care account for a vast majority of the time, money, and resources spent on home landscape. The lawn has, in many ways, become an icon of the American garden, almost expected and usually desired.

Or is it? The growing desire to be less petrochemically dependent in home yards has led to rethinking earlier concepts about what amount and kind of lawn might be appropriate. The rough-and-tumble grasses suited to a playing field aren't likely to need the high maintenance of a putting green's refined blades, such as frequent mowing, fertilizing, and doctoring with pesticides, herbicides, and fungicides. On the other hand, there are places in almost every home landscape where a sward of perfectly manicured lawn is the key to a more beautiful home and garden. Concentrating efforts where the payoff is greatest can be both personally satisfying and environmentally friendly.

A healthy lawn begins with a good design, and good design begins with a clear idea of what you are trying to accomplish.

Reasons for a lawn

The desire to have a nice lush lawn runs deep. So asking yourself why you want a lawn may at first seem obvious. Consider, however, the amount of time and money you will spend on the lawn, and the reasons for thinking it through become more logical.

The most common reason for having a lawn is aesthetic. It serves as a foreground for the house, a flower bed, or a neighboring woodland. In most cases, the turf is the finest visual texture in the garden, against which all the rest of the plants are measured. Depending upon how the soil beneath the turf is sculpted, the effect can be dramatic, especially when the turf is laid out in a smooth, even plane like a green carpet leading to a focal point. Or it can be relaxing when the grass gently hugs rolling earth, weaving in and out of shrub and flower beds. This kind of lawn is where bed preparation pays off.

▼ Lawns make ideal overflow areas when you entertain large groups. A level lawn such as this one supplements the patio space.

▲ As you plan and design, shape your lawn to form an outdoor room. This one can be used as a private area.

Another popular reason for a lawn is recreation. There is no substitute for grass when it comes to having a place for children or adults to play. A play lawn will suffer wear and tear and not be as lush as the ones shown here. Therefore, you may not want a play lawn in a part of the garden reserved for show.

A lawn is also good for entertaining. You may have to invest more care in the preparation stages of a lawn used for entertaining to create a level surface. It makes sense to have the lawn near a patio or terrace.

Sometimes a lawn is the best all-around solution when you have a large area that needs to be covered quickly. Other groundcovers require less maintenance once established, but they cost more to plant and take longer than turf to get full coverage. Before committing to turf, though, you may want to explore the alternatives on pages 78–81.

The size and shape of the lawn

Once you know how you will use your lawn, you can decide on its actual size and shape. If it is to be used for outdoor entertaining, refer to page 145 for the spacing required for various types of patio furniture. For just about everything else, size is a matter of taste. As you design, keep in mind the time and the costs required for lawn maintenance.

When determining the shape of the lawn, take clues from the location, sun, and style of the garden. If the existing site has clear, open spaces, a lawn may thrive. If the site is steep or sloping, or has many trees and shrubs, you may want to carve out a smaller lawn area that matches sun patterns.

If your garden style is formal, geometric shapes might suit; flowing curves lend themselves to more natural gardens. For more on lawn shapes, see page 67.

Avoid squiggles

If the lawn has curves, make them bold. For the best impact, use large S-shape curves. A series of small curves will look timid and indecisive.

DESIGNING THE LAWN
continued

The impact of lawn shape

The impact that lines have on design is readily apparent when you look at the edge of a lawn. Equally important to your lawn design are any other lines that exist in the garden or that you plan on adding. Ensure that all the lines are compatible. If you are adding or reshaping a lawn in an existing garden, note how the shapes vary from different viewpoints. What looks good from the patio might look completely different from the living room. Take these factors into account when developing your master plan.

Use the shape of the lawn to trick the eye. In the photo above, the eye is drawn to the farthest bed, where the lawn splits. The lawn appears to extend beyond or around the bed. The truth is, the lawn ends just out of view. The design creates the illusion that the lawn continues beyond that point.

▲ The lines of this lawn lead out of sight, giving the impression that the lawn is bigger than it really is.

Avoid planting individual trees or shrubs in the middle of the lawn—they block light and compete for water. They also break the plane of the lawn and are hard to mow around. The same is true for birdbaths and fountains.

If there is already a tree in your lawn or you want to add one, surround it with a bed that is wide enough to mow around without having the mower wheels dig into the grass.

Lawn edging

The perimeter of the lawn forms a line. Emphasize that line with a visible edging. Whether made of stone, brick, wood, or metal, edging marks a clear line between the lawn and whatever is on the other side. Even if this line is as simple as a shallow trench, it serves as a permanent marker to help you maintain the shape of the lawn. As you choose an edging material, make certain that it is in keeping with materials you have used elsewhere in the garden. For more on installing edging, see pages 232–235.

Edging also serves some practical purposes. It is a barrier to weeds that infiltrate from surrounding beds or wooded areas, and it keeps grass from invading beds. In some cases, edging doubles as a mowing strip, making maintenance easier.

▼ Gently curving lines are relaxing to the eye and create a natural atmosphere, even in a formal setting.

► Be sure to make any island beds big enough to easily mow around, and keep them neat with some type of edging.

Keep the lawn clear

Avoid planting individual trees or shrubs in the middle of the lawn. A solid plane of green emphasizes the shape of the lawn and is easy to mow.

Add mystery

Have parts of the lawn curve out of sight. This draws the eye and adds a sense of intrigue as you walk across the lawn. Add a focal point at the end of the lawn.

Have a crisp edge

Use an appropriate edging and keep the grass trimmed. A beautiful lawn is marred by a jagged edge. A crisp edge compensates for a rough spot in the center of the lawn.

Lay out the lawn

After deciding on the purpose and shape of your lawn, the next step is to lay it out. There are several methods for doing this, and they all start with a drawing. For tips on measuring and transferring ideas to paper, see page 11.

As you decide the exact placement of the lawn, consider the location of underground utilities. In most cases, turf is a perfectly acceptable planting over utilities, but a show lawn is best located elsewhere. It would be a shame to have to dig it up to repair a clogged sewage line. Be sure you know the depth of any utilities to avoid damaging them when preparing the soil.

Consider the impact of trees. You need to know their shade patterns throughout the seasons, and the range and depth of their roots. This information will keep you from damaging shallow tree roots when tilling the soil and help you avoid planting grass in heavy shade.

The method you use to mark the borders of the lawn depends on the lawn shape.

▲ Geometric shapes such as this arc need to be laid out precisely. Page 88 shows you how to get the desired effect.

Rectangular shapes are easily laid out with stakes and string. Use the method shown on page 88 to make circles and arcs. If you want natural, flowing lines, use a long garden hose or heavy rope. Toss the hose outside the area you want to turn into lawn, then pull the hose into curves. This results in more graceful curves than if you tried to arrange the hose in the desired shape.

Examine the shape of the lawn from all appropriate viewpoints. Then do one last test: Push or drive your mower around the perimeter. If there are any areas where you have to back up, rearrange the hose until you have an edge you are able to mow along in one pass.

Now use a can of spray paint, or dribble sand from a milk jug or bucket, to mark the line made by the hose. Remove the hose, and use a spade to dig a line to define the shape of the lawn.

▲ Edging would make this curve between the lawn and the garden easier to mow.

▲ Plants that are allowed to spill onto the lawn give a natural appearance to the landscape.

How to choose a lawn shape

The shape of your lawn is determined by its use, the landscape, appearance, and your desired maintenance level.

Use is an important factor in determining lawn shape. If the lawn will be used for recreation and entertaining, it should have a large, open area, such as that provided by circular and rectangular shapes (right). Most lawn sports, such as croquet, badminton, volleyball, putting, and boccie ball, also require an open space; most need a playing area.

The landscape also plays a role in the shape of the lawn. Some of the most interesting lawn designs trace the shadow patterns of the house and trees during the growing season. Although some types of grass tolerate shade, most require at least six hours of sun a day. In boggy or rocky areas or those with shallow roots from nearby trees and shrubs, the soil and terrain can be modified to handle turf, or the lawn should be located elsewhere.

If your primary concern is appearance, the site itself will present the primary limiting factors. You might choose a geometric shape to project a strong sense of order, control, and formality. Open or free-flowing shapes are more playful, relaxed, and natural.

Considerations when estimating maintenance are the total number square feet to mow and the total number of linear feet to edge. Undulating lines increase the amount of edging and trimming that is required.

CIRCULAR The most formal lawn shape. Circular lawns make strong visual statements. Level circular lawns are well-suited to entertaining. When laying out a circular lawn, it is worth taking the time to get the circles perfect. If this style appeals to you, you might also like ovals and half circles.

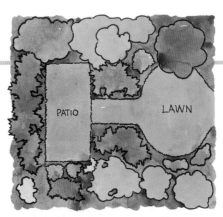

RECTANGULAR Lends itself best to recreation. A rectangular lawn can be seen in one glance. This lawn shape is more suited to a formal than a natural garden. Ease of maintenance makes rectangular shapes an attractive choice. Different mowing patterns add a creative touch (page 77).

OPEN The most relaxed lawn shape. Gently flowing lines have a soothing effect on the eye and the mind and fit well with an informal garden. This type of lawn often results when you allow the shade patterns of trees to determine the shape of the lawn. Open-shape lawns are suitable for recreation and entertaining.

FREE-FLOWING Ideal for creating pocket gardens. This free-flowing lawn provides five different garden areas. This shape has the added benefit of illusion; not allowing the eye to see all the lawn at once draws a person into the garden, adds mystery, and may make the garden appear larger. Be aware of how much edging is required with this shape.

Choosing a turf type

A successful lawn depends on choosing the appropriate grass. You have several options, but usually one is best suited. These are some considerations to keep in mind:

Light Most grasses need at least six hours of full sun a day during the growing season to thrive. Fine fescue and St. Augustinegrass are exceptions, but they have other cultural limitations. If there isn't enough light, thin the tree canopy. Plant a shade-tolerant grass, or grow a ground cover instead of grass.

Climate Average summer temperatures and average winter temperatures are critical in the selection of turf. Know the limits of the turfgrass you choose for your yard.

Water Know the water requirements of the turf you are considering. Although you can water a lawn during a drought, you may not be able to avoid excessive rain, so proper drainage is a must.

Use Bermudagrass is a good general-purpose grass and makes a good recreational surface. Ryegrass is a lush, fine-textured grass but is not resilient to foot traffic. St. Augustinegrass is great for hot, sunny areas but is springy to walk on and tends to build up thatch. Zoysiagrass is refined-looking but doesn't handle foot traffic. Although buffalograss is low-maintenance for high and dry places, it tends to clump and therefore has an uneven surface.

Maintenance Determine the amount of mowing, watering, and fertilizing the grass requires. Also consider how prone the grass is to disease and weeds, how often you need to dethatch or aerate it, and how easy the grass is to install or patch.

Fescue

Tall fescue is a drought-tolerant cool-season grass. It grows well in sun or light shade and can take heat well. Avoid mixing it with other grasses; it can "clump out." Fine fescue includes several grass species—chewings fescue, hard fescue, and creeping red fescue. They are often included in seed mixes because they are so shade tolerant.

Kentucky bluegrass

Kentucky bluegrass is best suited to full sun in areas with cool summers; it grows throughout North America, except southern regions. It is one of the most cold-hardy grasses and is often used in public parks. It requires regular watering to look good during periods of drought. Kentucky bluegrass is prized for its thick, dense turf and fine texture. Some of the best new cultivars, unlike the old standards, are disease-resistant and may require less maintenance: 'America', 'Blacksburg', 'Blue Star', 'Eclipse', and 'Julia'.

Ryegrass

Perennial ryegrass is one of the main components of cool-season grass mixes. It germinates quickly and wears well. In the South, annual ryegrass is used to overseed dormant warm-season grasses in winter. Neither annual nor perennial ryegrass tolerates extreme heat or cold, and neither is very drought-tolerant. Both do best when given plenty of sun.

Bermudagrass

Bermudagrass is a warm-season grass. Though it is fairly drought-tolerant, this grass thrives when it receives abundant water. It wears well, staying green longer than other warm-season grasses. Bermudagrass is common in the mild-winter West Coast, southern regions, and parts of the Midwest. Some varieties can be started from seed; others are grown only from sod or sprigs. Regardless, it establishes itself rapidly.

St. Augustinegrass

St. Augustinegrass is a coarse warm-season grass that is well-adapted to the humid coastal areas of the South. It is not tolerant of freezing temperatures but stands up to shade and high traffic. It is the coarsest of all the turfgrasses.

Zoysiagrass

Zoysiagrass is a warm-season grass grown mainly in the Central United States. It grows best in hot weather and becomes brown and dormant when temperatures dip to freezing. Zoysiagrass is the most winter-hardy of the southern grasses. It stays brown all winter in cooler climates and is slow to green up in spring. It is a dense grass that is somewhat tolerant of shade.

Buffalograss

A warm-season grass, buffalograss grows to just 4 inches tall and can go without mowing. Its fine-textured gray-green blades make a handsome (but not manicured) lawn. A native American grass—one that dominated the Midwestern prairies—it does best in the Plains States east of the Rockies. It looks attractive from spring until frost. Like zoysiagrass, it turns a pale straw color from late fall through winter. It is not fussy about soil and does well in clay.

Bahiagrass

Bahiagrass is the low-maintenance choice for warm coastal areas of the United States. It is tough, growing even in poor, sandy soil, wears well, and is coarse-textured. However, it is susceptible to dollar spot, brown patch, and mole crickets. It is a warm-season, heat-tolerant grass. It establishes itself at a moderate speed and requires frequent mowing.

CREATE A HEALTHY LAWN

Whether you sod, sow, or sprig your lawn, the best way to ensure a healthy lawn and to get it off to a good start is to prepare the planting area correctly. A healthy lawn is easier to maintain than a struggling one.

Each method of establishing a lawn has merits. Sodding is the fastest method; it is similar to laying carpet. At the end of the day, you have a green lawn. Unfortunately, it is the most expensive way to start a lawn, and it is no substitute for thorough soil preparation at the outset. The best sod in the world cannot take hold and become self-reliant turf unless the ground bed on which it is laid is first cleared of debris, cultivated, and leveled.

Seeding is the easiest and least expensive way to start a lawn. As with sodding, a smooth, even, nutrient-rich bed is essential for success with this method, and it yields a lush, healthy lawn.

Sprigging a lawn is a good choice if you are using a grass that spreads by runners, such as bermudagrass or zoysiagrass. Sprigging also costs less than sodding. However, depending upon the turf you choose and the site conditions, one to three years may be required for full, even coverage—and you will spend quite a bit of time fighting weeds.

How to prepare an area for lawn

STEP 1 **Get rid of the vegetation.** Do this regardless of the method you use to install new grass. Killing existing vegetation eradicates weeds, allows you to loosen the soil and add nutrients, and makes it easier to level the site.

Use a nonselective herbicide, such as glyphosate, or rent a sod cutter for large areas. A sure, safe, but slower method of killing an existing lawn is to smother it. Mark the perimeter with a shallow trench 4 to 6 inches wide. Take soil samples and submit them for testing (page 37). Lay newspapers three sheets thick over the area. Cover with black plastic, overlapping the seams by 6 inches (illustration 1, below left). **Hold down the plastic.** Place 2×4s along the edge of the plastic and across it. Weigh down the boards with bricks (illustration 2, below).

The time it takes for the grass to die varies with the type and amount of existing vegetation and the temperature. Allow three to six months.

STEP 2 **Prepare the bed.** Once all vegetation is dead, remove the plastic. Pick up any large pieces of paper. The rest will decompose. Till the entire area at least 8 inches deep—paper, plants, and all.

STEP 3 **Add amendments.** Review the results and recommendations of the soil test and add the appropriate amendments. Till them thoroughly into the soil. Use a rake to smooth the ground, eliminating low spots and breaking up large clumps of soil.

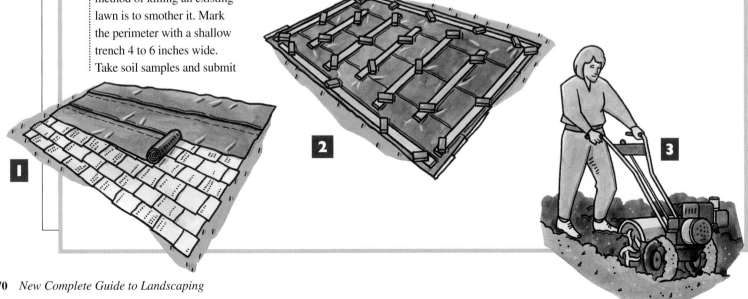

How to sod a lawn

Sod during the grass's period of active growth, which is summer and early spring for cool-season grasses and late spring to summer for warm-season grasses. There is less stress caused by heat and drought. Have the soil fully prepared before the sod is delivered or before you pick it up. Put the sod in place as soon as possible. When purchasing, add about 5 percent to the exact square footage you want to cover. This allows for any odd-shape pieces.

Getting started. Use the steps outlined on page 70 to prepare the soil.

STEP 1 Lay the sod. Begin against one edge of the lawn and work your way across. Lay a piece of sod flush with the edging and press it firmly into place. Lay the next piece flush with the long side of the first piece. Use a sharp butcher or utility knife to trim the sod to fit where it overlaps. Cut the sod gently to avoid knocking loose any more soil than necessary.

STEP 2 Piece the sod together. For the next row, return to your starting point. Lay down a section of a 2×12 board to disperse your weight over the freshly laid sod. Use a half piece of sod to start the next row. This staggers the seams. Continue until the area is covered. Expect some odd-shape pieces as you go along, but try to avoid pieces smaller than 1 square foot.

STEP 3 Rake and roll. Rent a drum roller, which looks like a barrel with a handle, and fill it halfway with water. Roll this over the newly sodded area to press the sod into place. Then gently rake the area to remove debris. If the rake snags on any uneven seams, trim or press the sod into place. Water thoroughly, especially the seams.

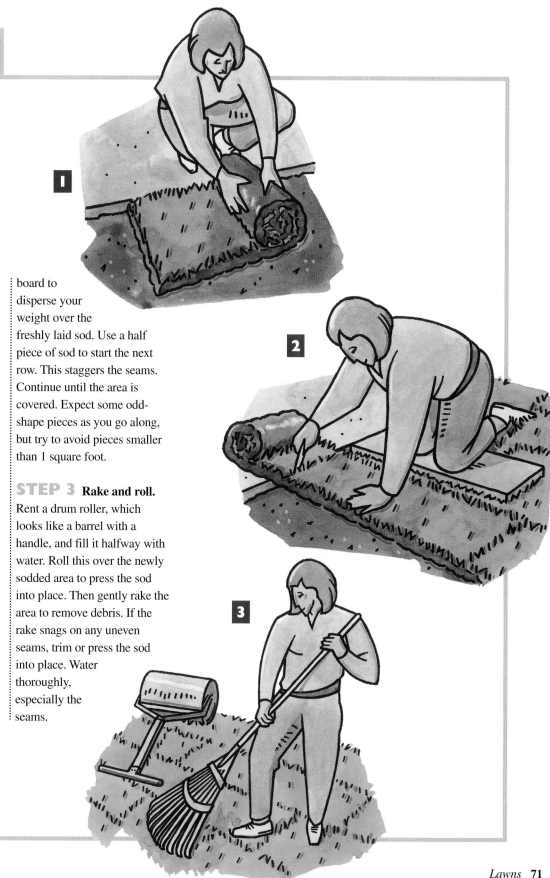

How to seed a lawn

Seeding is the most affordable and easiest way to create a lawn. Late summer is the best time to seed cool-season lawns, with spring the second best time. Seed warm-season grasses in late spring. The drawback to seeding is waiting for the grass to become fully established. Until established, the lawn is susceptible to weeds and erosion. The steps outlined here ensure fast coverage and the fewest weeds.

STEP 1 **Prepare the bed.** Follow the procedure described on page 70. For the best-looking lawn, eliminate all existing grass. You can overseed existing grass, but you risk creating a mottled look due to the mixed grasses.

STEP 2 **Sow the seed.** Seed bags include recommended rates of seeding. Too much or too little causes problems.

Seed can be sown by broadcast or drop spreaders, or by hand broadcasting. Both types of spreaders work equally well, provide uniform coverage, and are ideal for large areas. They are typically found at the same places that sell seed. To calibrate a spreader, measure a large area of clean paved driveway and run the spreader over it. Sweep up the seeds and weigh the amount to gauge the rate of spreading. Adjust the rate using the directions that come with the spreader. After you achieve the proper calibration, gather and reuse the seed.

It is difficult to broadcast seed evenly by hand; use this method in small areas only.

STEP 3 **Water, mulch, and wait.** As soon as the seed is on the ground, use a gentle spray from a hose to thoroughly moisten the seeds and the soil. Strong blasts of water knock seeds around, resulting in bare spots or dense clumps.

Mulch the entire area with a light layer of coarse material, such as straw. This protects the seed from heavy rain, direct sun, and hungry birds. It also helps to maintain evenly moist conditions around the seeds and, therefore, encourages uniform sprouting and the quickest cover possible. Block off the area with stakes and string. Water daily until you start to see the grass emerge. After that, water every other day for three weeks. Begin mowing as soon as the grass reaches the typical mowing height. Mow with a well-sharpened blade, and remove no more than one-third of the grass blade at any one time.

How to patch a lawn

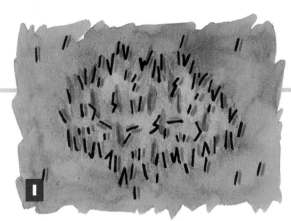

STEP 1 **Identify the area to be patched and why it needs patching.** Many times an existing lawn needs repair. The first step is to understand why there is a problem. It could be physical damage done by an animal, a piece of equipment, or heavy foot traffic. Or it could be caused by dense shade, a soggy spot, root competition, or a disease.

It is essential for you to know and remedy the cause for the damage. Otherwise, your repair is only temporary.

STEP 2 **Clean the "wound."** Use a butcher knife, spade, or sharp trowel to dig out all the damaged turf. When you finish you should have an area with smooth edges and no damaged or diseased turf showing. Smooth and amend the soil if necessary.

STEP 3 **Set the patch in place.** To make a patch, find an area of your lawn that can spare a piece of turf the size of the area you dug. This ensures an even match. If this is not an option, the next choice is to purchase a roll of sod and cut it to match the area to be patched. If that is not available, use plugs. As a last resort, use seed.

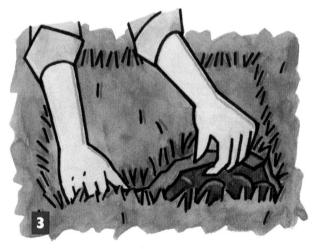

STEP 4 **Press the patch into place.** Lay the sod in position. Trim as necessary with a sharp knife to attain a tidy fit. Roll a piece of PVC, a wood rolling pin, or a 1-liter bottle filled with water over the patch to ensure good contact with the soil. Water in place thoroughly.

PLUG A LAWN

Plugging is a slow but affordable method of establishing a lawn. Prepare the bed as shown on page 70, then use a trowel to set plugs of grass in place. Space them at the recommended distance—usually 6 to 8 inches apart. Expect full coverage in one to two growing seasons.

LAWN CARE

There are several steps to lawn care, whether you do it yourself or hire a lawn care service. The first steps are choosing the right turf for the site and purpose and getting the grass off to a good start with proper installation. There are also ongoing tasks to ensure that the lawn stays healthy.

Lawn fertilizing is big business. However, most people fertilize the lawn too much. Despite what you may have heard, well-prepared soil and a properly selected, planted, and maintained lawn require little supplemental feeding. Before you convert your lawn into a nitrogen junkie, give it a year or two with one annual feeding. Leave the clippings on the lawn and see how it does. Once you get a lawn dependent on fertilizer, it is hard to go back. For more on fertilizer, see pages 340–341.

Other lawn maintenance issues covered here and on the following pages include watering (there is a right and a wrong way), weeding, and mowing.

As you follow through with each lawn task, the goals of your master plan will begin to materialize.

How to fertilize

A properly established and maintained turf needs only one or two annual applications of fertilizer.

METHOD A
Spreader. If you are using granular fertilizers, a drop or broadcast spreader ensures uniform application. Calibrate the spreader to apply the fertilizer at the rate recommended on the product label. The same method described on page 72 for seeding calibration works for fertilizer too. Depending on the type of fertilizer, you may need to water immediately after application to prevent the fertilizer from burning the grass.

METHOD B
Hose-end sprayer. Water-soluble and liquid fertilizers are applied using this method. Screw the hose end into the sprayer, fill the canister with the fertilizer, set the dial at the recommended rate, and spray the lawn.

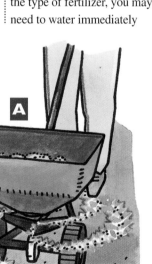
Broadcast spreader

A

Hose-end sprayer

B

How to water

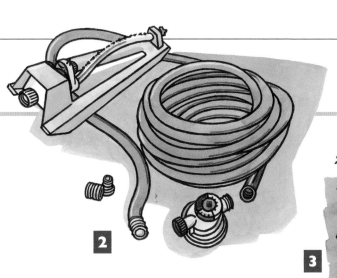

Watering is the most frequent lawn maintenance task, yet it is often done improperly. It pays big time to learn how to water correctly.

STEP 1 Determine when and how to water. The golden rule in watering the lawn is to do it infrequently and deeply. As the root profile illustrations below right show, the way you water influences the way the roots grow. Moreover, the way the roots grow determines the drought tolerance of the turf, which, in turn, has a direct effect on how much—and how often—you need to water.

Watering deeply and infrequently results in a deep and broad root system (1A), which can withstand periods of drought. Make sure you give the lawn at least an inch of water each time. If you only lightly sprinkle the lawn every day or so, you will have shallow-rooted grass (1B). These roots have never had to go deep for moisture, but when the surface soil dries out, the roots are nowhere near water.

STEP 2 Set up a system. You can have an adequate lawn irrigation system without spending a lot of money. You need a hose long enough to reach the areas you want to water. Use quick couplers to move the hose easily and attach it to different sprinklers. Choose sprinklers that can be adjusted to cover the area you want. A simple timer is surprisingly affordable; it screws right onto the spigot and turns water on and off automatically.

STEP 3 Calibrate the system. Adjust your sprinklers to completely cover the lawn area. This may require moving the sprinkler at least once during each watering, depending on the size of the lawn. Impact sprinklers can be adjusted and left in the ground at their proper place. Most blend nicely into the lawn. Using quick couplers makes this method of watering the lawn extremely easy.

Once you have complete coverage, calibrate how long it takes to apply an inch of water. Do this by placing a series of equal-sized containers (such as margarine tubs or coffee cans) around the lawn and run the sprinkler, timing how long it takes for all the tubs or cans to have an inch of water. During the active growing season, most grasses need 1½ inches of water every 10 days to thrive, and stay green and grow strong enough to fend off weeds.

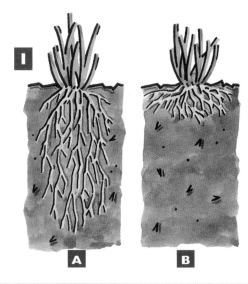

How to weed

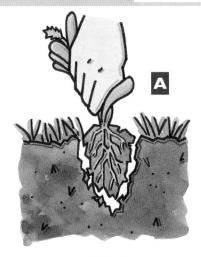

METHOD A Pull.

Unless you get the roots when you pull a weed, the weed comes back even stronger.

Always grasp the weed as close to the soil as possible and pull on it gently. Avoid yanking it. Pulling is the quickest and easiest way to weed, especially if you have well-prepared soil. It is easier to pull weeds after a rain.

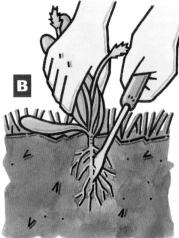

METHOD B Dig.

Digging is required for weeds with tough root systems, thorny stems, or deep roots. Use a tool such as a dandelion digger to make this a quick job. Insert the narrow, forked blade several inches into the soil and pop out the plant. If you see evidence of broken roots, dig into the resulting hole to remove the rest.

METHOD C Paint.

For some broad-leaved weeds, application of an herbicide eliminates the weed without leaving a hole in the lawn. It is also the best way to avoid accidentally harming anything other than the weed. Painting the herbicide on the weed reduces its impact on the environment. Wear rubber gloves and use a small paint brush to apply.

WEED CONTROL

Lawn weed control has three important aspects. The first is how weed-free do you want your lawn to be? If you don't have a show lawn, you might find that a few weeds are easily removed when they get out of hand, or the lawn can be mowed on a regular basis. Some people even encourage weeds such as dandelions because of the carpet of yellow they provide in the spring. If you are willing to accept a few weeds here and there, your maintenance requirements will be substantially less.

If you want the lawn free of all weeds and are willing to spend the time and other resources to accomplish that, you will have to be diligent. This approach relies on keeping the lawn healthy (to make it difficult for weeds to get a toehold) and being able to identify weeds and the proper control. These two factors are important regardless of your weed tolerance.

Keeping the lawn healthy is your first line of defense. Dense grass provides little room for weed seeds to find a place to germinate. Should a weed germinate, a healthy, vigorous lawn with a good, deep root system (encouraged by watering slowly and deeply rather than quickly and shallowly) has an advantage when competing with a weed for food and water.

If a weed persists despite your pulling, digging, and countering with vigorous turf, you may need to use an herbicide. First you'll need to know the name of the weed and whether it is an annual or perennial. Early in the growing season, preemergent herbicides can be applied against a range of weeds and weedy grasses that grow from seeds. Later, postemergents can be applied directly on the leaves of offending plants.

What is a weed?

A man moved to a new city and the following spring found dozens of beautiful yellow flowering plants in the garden. They thrived in drought and bloomed all summer. He tried several sources to identify the flower so he could get more. He finally asked his neighbors (natives to the region), and they said, "Oh, that's a weed."

Following a few simple tips will help you get the most from your mowing. The idea is to make mowing easier and also to encourage a healthy lawn.

Height Most grasses have an optimum height. It is based on how the root system develops, how quickly leaf blades break down when cut, how fast the grass grows, and how dense the grass gets. Know the recommended height and mow no more than one-third of the blade surface at one time. If the grass has grown too high, mow it once to remove one-third of the height, wait a few days, cut it back by another third, and continue until you achieve the recommended height.

Frequency Frequency should be regulated by how long it takes the turf to exceed the optimum height by one-third. For example, if the optimum height for your grass is 2 inches, cut it to 2 inches each time the grass reaches 3 inches in height.

Pattern Alternating the direction in which you mow a particular swath of lawn promotes healthier grass. Mowing the lawn in a pattern also creates an interesting look and makes mowing more fun.

Mulching Turfgrasses have a lot of leaf surface and are filled with nutrients. Consider using a mulching type of mower that chops leaf blades into fine pieces and deposits them on the lawn. This enriches the soil, saves fertilizer, and avoids your having to rake later.

Timing Mow when the grass is dry; wet grass doesn't cut well. And mow late in the day to prevent freshly cut leaf blades from being exposed to the sun.

Mower type There are two basic mower types: reel and rotary. Reel mowers (including push mowers) are quieter and produce a scissors type of cut. Although using them is good exercise, they are impractical for large areas.

Rotary mowers cut with a sharp blade that cuts the grass at a high speed. They are the fastest and easiest way to mow the lawn. To assure clean, efficient cutting, plan on sharpening the blade of a rotary mower after every 10 hours of use.

Edging and trimming The efforts and impact of a perfectly mowed and maintained lawn are enhanced by a finished edge. Use a permanent edging material. If the edging does not double as a mowing strip, use a string trimmer or vertical edger to trim the perimeter of the lawn each time you mow. Because of their tendency to scalp the grass plant right to the ground, string trimmers are more difficult to use well than any other edging tool. Lawn shears give a more refined edge but require considerable physical exertion. Mechanical lawn edgers give a clean, professional appearance—but also require an investment for the equipment, storage space, and routine upkeep.

LAWN ALTERNATIVES

ulches and groundcovers can be ideal alternatives to a lawn. They're worth considering if you'd rather not spend time and money maintaining lush grass. Although most groundcovers cost more to install than turf, their subsequent care costs far less than that required by a lawn. You can start to realize savings in less than three years.

There is a wide range of groundcovers, including ornamental grasses, low-growing evergreen and deciduous shrubs, perennials, and ferns. You can even establish a wildflower meadow in a sunny area. Here are some of the virtues and drawbacks of mulches and groundcovers.

Mulches

The quickest and easiest alternative to a lawn is a mulch. Although not suited for every setting, mulch, where appropriate, can be attractive.

Mulches can be organic or inorganic. Organic mulches, made from once-living material, include pine straw, chipped or shredded bark, pecan or cocoa shells, and compost. Inorganic mulches include stone, lava rock, gravel, and even glass.

▲ An area of stone mulch reduces the resources required for lawn care and fits well into this contemporary landscape.

▲ This solid mat of lily turf tames a slope that would be difficult to mow if covered with lawn. This groundcover is virtually maintenance-free.

Organic mulches look natural in settings other than the arid Southwest, where stone and gravel are in keeping with the indigenous landscape. If you want to use an organic mulch to cover an area, keep in mind that the material breaks down over time and needs to be replenished. For this reason, it is best to use a material readily available in your area or even from your own property. There is a benefit to the decomposition—it enriches the soil.

Organic mulches are relatively lightweight and easy to spread, but they can be washed out by rain and blown around by wind. Inorganic mulches, such as lava rock and pea gravel, are heavier and not as easy to spread, but once in place they stay put. They do not break down over time, so they rarely need to be replenished.

For both types of mulch, put down a barrier such as landscape fabric between the soil and the mulch to discourage weed growth. It is much easier to pull weeds from loose mulch or gravel than from soil. Be sure that the barrier material is permeable to water to prevent the mulch from washing out.

Shade-loving groundcovers

Most grasses require six hours of sun a day to stay healthy and full. If all or part of your garden does not receive that amount of sun, do not despair. There are many options for carpeting the earth in shady areas. Besides mulches, there are wonderful low-growing plants that, once established, require little maintenance other than spring cleanup and the occasional removal of a weed.

The first step is to assess the amount of light an area receives. This information comes straight from your site analysis, if you have one, or simply track the amount of sun throughout the day. Consider how shade patterns shift from the beginning of the growing season to the end.

Besides the duration of the shade, also consider the density. Conifers and other evergreens cast deeper shade than deciduous shrubs and trees, which also permit more sun early in the season and may facilitate growing wildflowers as groundcover.

Once you know how much sunlight you have to work with, determine the effect you want. Ask yourself if the area needs to withstand foot traffic. Only a few groundcovers withstand even moderate

▼ A lawn alternative is mixed pavers and groundcover such as this bugleweed.

traffic. Next determine the color and texture you are interested in. Then decide whether you want the groundcover to bloom. With this wish list in hand as a starting point, turn to page 362 and review the list of suggested groundcovers. There are many possibilities for both warm and cold climates and dry and moist situations.

While lack of sun and an abundance of shade may dictate mulch or groundcover as a better choice than grass for carpeting basically flat or level ground, where steep slopes are concerned, deep-rooted groundcovers are a more likely satisfactory solution. Proper soil preparation at the outset is a must, along with a basin created around each plant to hold enough water to assure that the roots can take hold to sustain healthy growth and also to stabilize the ground.

▲ A large swath of vinca (periwinkle) is more practical than turfgrass. Besides needing less water and fertilizer, it requires no mowing and offers violet blooms in late spring.

▲ Many sun-loving groundcovers have the added benefit of blooming in bright colors, such as this flowering thyme.

LAWN ATLERNATIVES
continued

Sun-loving groundcovers

Many homeowners would like to have more bright, sunny areas. If your potential lawn area is suitable for a garden, you might broaden your definition of groundcover to include other types of plantings that thrive in sun.

You could turn the area into a flower bed with a mixture of low-growing perennials, annuals, and bulbs (selected from the lists on page 350–363). They can be as low or high maintenance as you

▲ This black mondograss is an attractive, low-maintenance alternative to turfgrass.

choose for them to be.

One alternative is a wildflower meadow. Choose a mixture of low-growing varieties suited to your region, or accept plants that grow slightly higher as a trade-off for lower maintenance.

▲ Some people fight it, but here, moss makes a natural substitute for lawn in a place that lawn would never thrive.

Another idea for covering sunny areas is to plant herbs or vegetables, even in the front yard.

If you are looking for a more traditional, low-growing alternative to a lawn and you have plenty of sunshine, there are many choices. Readily available sun-loving groundcovers include creeping juniper, creeping thyme, Asian jasmine, any of the creeping sedums, Persian catmint, and many others.

Keep in mind that dark colors such as plain green pachysandra or English ivy absorb light more readily than variegated or bright-colored foliage and tend to slow down the eye. This is a factor if you want the eye to be drawn over and past the groundcover to a setting, structure, or planting beyond. Use light-colored groundcovers such as a silver-leaved or multicolored ajuga to direct vision beyond them.

Planting and caring for groundcovers

Good soil preparation helps make up for the slower growth of most groundcovers and ensures full coverage as fast as possible. Approach the planting of a groundcover in the same way you would prepare a bed for lawn.

Pay special attention to soil quality and the results of the soil test. Recommendations for amending soil for a lawn can be different than for a groundcover. Amending the soil before planting a groundcover is more important than with a lawn, because it is harder to enrich soil after it is covered with groundcover than it is to fertilize the lawn.

Smoothing the soil is less important with a groundcover than with grass, because the foliage masks all but the biggest "bulges."

The process of planting a bed of groundcover varies depending upon the plant you use and its ultimate spread. To determine the number of plants you need, divide the square footage of the bed by the number of square feet an average plant will cover when mature. Resist the temptation to set the plants too close together. You may gain faster coverage but at the expense of an overcrowded bed.

Once established, most groundcovers require little more than watering during drought. Plants grown in sun and in warm climates require more watering than those in the shade or in cool climates.

Some groundcovers need to be cut back every few years. This can be done by adjusting a rotary mower to the highest setting and making a pass over the bed, or by using a string trimmer. Edging helps keep the borders neat.

If the bed becomes covered with leaves in the fall, blow or rake them off or work them in between the plants as mulch so they don't block the sunlight. Keep fallen leaves and other debris off groundcover for appearance's sake and also to keep from smothering desirable growth.

▲ Use walls and fences to give height to your garden and let groundcovers or vines scramble over them.

Regional Lawn Maintenance Schedule

	SPRING	SUMMER
Cold-winter climates	• Service the lawn mower. • Sharpen mower blades, if not done during fall or winter. • If the soil under the lawn is compacted, aerate it. • Top-dress the lawn with a ½-inch layer of compost or humus. • Spread slow-release fertilizer on the lawn, if not done in fall or winter.	• Set out a rain gauge so you can accurately measure the amount of rainfall. • When there is little or no rain, wait 10 to 14 days before watering in dry weather. • Set the lawn mower blade higher—raise it to 3 inches or more. • Patch any bare spots. • Remove weeds as soon as they appear.
Mild-winter climates	• Sharpen mower blades, if not done during fall or winter. • Spread slow-release fertilizer on the lawn. • Put in new lawns with sod, sprigs, or seed. • Aerate the lawn if necessary. • If there is more than ½ inch of thatch, dethatch the lawn.	• Set out a rain gauge so you can accurately measure the amount of rainfall. • When there is little or no rain, water every 7 to 10 days in dry weather. • Adjust the mower blade to the correct height for the specific grass in your lawn. • Repair any bare spots in the lawn with sprigs or plugs.

FALL

- If the soil is compacted, aerate the lawn.

- In early September, overseed existing lawns, and seed or sod new lawns.

- Top-dress the lawn with compost or humus. Or shred fallen leaves with the mower and spread on the lawn.

- When mowing for the last time of the season, lower the blade one-half inch or so. This keeps the grass from matting under snow.

- If the soil is acidic, add lime. Wait at least two weeks after application to fertilize.

- Work off Thanksgiving dinner by fertilizing the lawn. This promotes strong root growth during winter.

- Sharpen the lawn mower blade to prevent it from tearing the grass.

- Plant sprigs or plugs where there is evidence of insect damage or where weeds have been removed.

- For a green lawn all winter long, overseed warm-weather grasses with annual ryegrass.

WINTER

- Drain the gas from string trimmers and lawn mowers before putting them away for the winter.

- Indicate the edges of the lawn with 3-foot markers or stakes with reflectors if your lawn abuts an area that is plowed or cleaned with a snowblower.

- Use a nonsalt deicer on walkways that are adjacent to lawns.

- Keep off snow-covered lawns.

- Service the lawn mower and string trimmer.

- If you overseeded the lawn with annual ryegrass, mow it as needed.

- Consider installing an irrigation system. It can be especially beneficial in sandy soil.

CHAPTER 4

WALKS & PATHS

Getting around in your landscape

WALKS

A walk is the usual route from the street or parking area to the front door. It creates a first impression and sets the tone for the house and garden. Comfort, safety, and a clear choice of direction are the three hallmarks of a well-designed walk.

A walk is generally more formal than a garden path. As a rule, a walk is at least 3 feet wide and rarely more than 4 feet wide—enough so two adults can stroll comfortably side-by-side without either

▲ The stone in this walk echoes the stone in the wall, unifying the whole area. Crisp edging along the walk simplifies lawn chores.

of them running into plant material adjacent to the walk at ground or shoulder level.

For safety, a walk needs to be well-lit, level, and made of a firm material that is not slippery when wet. Materials to avoid include gravel, which can be difficult to walk on, and glazed ceramic tile, which can be slick when wet.

The walk should be obvious to visitors. The direction of the walk and its destination should be easily visible—whether the walk begins at the street, driveway, sidewalk, or guest parking area.

Determine the purpose

Although the primary purpose of most walks is to lead the way to the front door, a walk can also be the route from the parking area to another entrance of the house. A walk can ensure easy access between the house and heavily trafficked areas of the garden such as a swimming pool or terrace.

In the garden, a walk is the route that wheelbarrows and garden carts can traverse. The width and firm surface make it easy to transport heavy loads of soil, compost, or tools and supplies between a compost bin or garden shed and the vegetable or flower garden.

Choose a style

A walk can be either straight or curving. Because most walks begin or terminate at the house, the design style should fit its architecture. The material you use to build the walk is a matter of style. A discussion of walk materials is found on pages 96 and 97.

A straight walk appears more formal than a curved walk. It is a no-nonsense means to get you quickly to a destination, and it is less expensive and easier to build than a curved walk.

A gently curving walk lends itself to less formal settings. It is appropriate only when there is enough room for gentle, sweeping arcs. When there is only a short distance to travel—20 feet or less—curving a walkway results in small, tight

◀ A gently curving walk creates a relaxed approach to the front door of the house.

◀ **Make a long, straight walk exciting by flanking it with a multilevel planting bed. Add interest by edging the walk with a contrasting material.**

arcs that are too angular for comfortable walking.

A walk creates a transition from one area to another, so it's important to think about the experience people will have as they move along it. A straight course through an expanse of lawn is not very exciting; a walk that passes beneath an arbor, near ornamental trees, or along a flower bed is more enjoyable. The placement of the walk should take into account the views approaching the house and those leading away.

Proportion is an important consideration. A short straight walk of 20 feet or less rarely needs to be more than 3 feet wide. Longer, curving walks can be 4 feet wide, or may be made to appear wider when flanked with an undulating 3- to 4-foot-wide flower bed.

Plants alongside a walk often feel and look right at about 3 feet tall. Taller plants can evoke a closed-in feeling, and they require more maintenance to keep them pruned out of the way.

▶ **Large concrete pavers set in a bed of gravel create a comfortable yet formal walk from a parking area to a patio.**

How to lay out a walk or path

METHOD A

Flowing lines. Toss a garden hose or heavy rope beyond the outside edge of the proposed walk. Gently drag the hose into position. This creates more natural curving lines than positioning the hose precisely. It might take several tries before you get the look you want.

Cut enough ¼-inch dowels to a length equal to the width of the walk so you can place one every 2 feet along the hose. Position them perpendicular to the hose and hold them in place with large staples. Use the dowels as a guide to lay a second hose to mirror the line of the first.

Using a spade, dig carefully along the outside of each hose to mark the lines of the walk. Or mark them with sand or lime.

METHOD B

Straight walk, right angle. Measure the width and approximate length of the walk with a tape measure. Temporarily stake each corner of the walk and run string between all four stakes.

For an exact outline (and to help in measuring right angles), use batter boards. To make batter boards, lay two 1-foot lengths of 2×4 on the ground 4 inches apart. Nail a 16-inch length of 1×4 flush with the top of the 2×4s, allowing 2 inches of 1×4 to extend out on each side.

Center one batter board 2 feet beyond each line formed by the temporary strings and stakes. Use a hand sledge to set one batter board at the end of each string marking the edge of the walk (below). Tie the string to the center of each 1×4. Repeat at the other end of the string.

Slide the strings along the 1×4s to form two parallel lines the length of the walk. Take measurements every few feet to be sure the width of the walk is even. To ensure the angles are true right angles (90 degrees), use the triangulation method shown on page 120. Use sand or lime to mark the outside edges of the walk.

METHOD C

Arcs and circles. Use batter boards to mark the edges of the walk, as in Method B. Measuring from point C below to pivot point A, B is the midpoint. Mark A with a stake. The distances from C to D and C to E are both twice the width of the walk. From point C, measure point D along one outside edge of the walk and point E along the other. Stake points D and E.

Cut a string the length of A to D. Tie one end to the A stake and the other to an open bottle filled with sand. Swing an arc from D to E; the spilling sand marks the outer curve. Shorten string by the width of the walk to mark the inner curve.

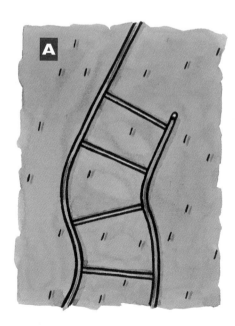

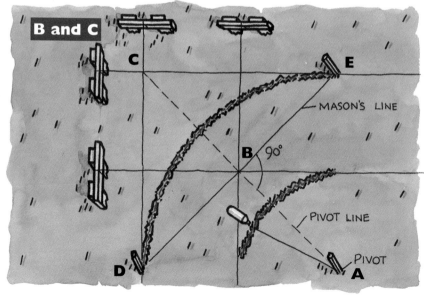

How to build a stone-on-mortar walk

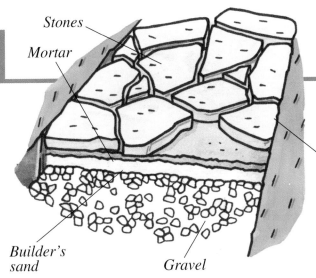

Stones

Mortar

Edging

Builder's sand

Gravel

This walk requires a sturdy bed to hold the base in place and mortar to keep it all together.

MATERIALS

Stakes and string or sand
Shovel
Edging (prescored 1×4s, plastic, or metal)
Medium or fine gravel
Plastic sheeting (optional)
Paving stones
Gloves and goggles
Builder's sand
Broom or rake
Hand sledge and brick chisel
Type M mortar
Rubber mallet
4-foot length of 2×4
Soil

STEP 1 **Build a bed and lay the base.** Mark the outer dimensions of the walk with string or sand. Dig a bed

6 inches wider than the finished walk and at least 8 inches deep. Set the edging about 3 inches in from the side of the bed to allow space to work. Stake the inside and outside of the edging every 2 feet to prevent bowing as gravel and sand push against it.

If the paving stones are 2 inches thick, lay a 3-inch layer of gravel; if the stones are thicker or thinner, adjust the depth of the gravel accordingly so that the finished walk will be flush with the edging. If your soil is soggy, place a piece of heavy plastic on top of the gravel to protect the masonry from excess water.

Add 2 inches of builder's sand on top of the gravel. Sweep or rake the sand along the length of the walk. Be sure the space from the top of the edging to the top of the sand is consistent.

STEP 2 **Place the stones.** Set the stones on the sand; start along one edge and work your way to the center.

You might have to break some stones to fit. The thinner the stone, the easier it is to break. Be sure to wear gloves and goggles. Set the stone to be broken on top of the adjacent stone. Mark the

desired shape on all four faces with a pencil or knife. Score all four faces with gentle taps of a hand sledge on a brick chisel. Prop the stone on top of another stone and hit the part to be discarded with the sledge.

STEP 3 **Set the stones in mortar.** Once the stones are in place, mix a batch of mortar thick enough to cling to a trowel turned on edge. Starting at one end of the

walk, remove three or four stones and spread a 1-inch-thick bed of mortar. Set the first stone and tap it into place with a rubber mallet. Repeat the process along the length of the walk.

Check for high or low spots as you go; rock a 4-foot 2×4 on the stones. Add or remove mortar as necessary. Let the walk cure for two days, then fill the joints between the stones with mortar. Sponge off excess mortar. Remove the edging and fill the resulting trench with soil.

How to build a paver- or brick-on-sand walk

Border pavers

Pavers

Builder's sand

Gravel

Landscape fabric

MATERIALS
- Shovel
- Gravel
- Builder's sand
- Border pavers or bricks
- Landscape fabric
- Rubber mallet
- 6-foot length of 2×4
- 6-foot length of 1×4
- Hammer and nails
- Pavers or bricks
- Broom

STEP 1 **Build a form and base.** Mark the shape and location of the walk (see page 88). Choose the paving pattern you want and lay out a portion of the walk on a firm surface such as the driveway. Include border pavers in the pattern. Measure the exact width of the laid-out walk with the pavers fitting snugly.

Dig a bed as wide as the walk and deep enough to accommodate 3 inches of gravel, 2 inches of sand, and the thickness of the paver.

You might have to dig a trench for the border pavers so they will be flush with the rest of the walk. For added stability, lay landscape fabric in the border trench. Line the edge of the path with border pavers (top right). Use a rubber mallet to tamp the border pavers into place.

Spread 3 inches of gravel. Lay landscape fabric over the gravel and spread 2 inches of builder's sand.

STEP 2 **Level the sand.** Build a screed by cutting a 2×4 a foot longer than the width of the walk. Cut a 1×4 the exact distance between the border pavers. Center the 1×4 on the 2×4 so the 1×4 extends below the edge of the 2×4 a distance equal to the paver thickness. Nail the 1×4 in place. Starting at one end of the walk, drag the screed to form a uniformly deep and smooth surface.

STEP 3 **Place the pavers in place.** Starting at one end of the walk, set the pavers in place. Follow the order and pattern of the pavers exactly as they were laid out in the driveway. Any other pattern might not fit between the border pavers.

Set the pavers so they fit together snugly and are flush with the top of the border pavers. Use a rubber mallet to tamp the pavers into place.

If you have difficulty fitting a paver into the pattern, a previously laid paver was set wrong. If that happens, remove the pavers until you find the one that was misplaced. Start over from that point.

STEP 4 **Sweep sand over pavers.** With all the pavers or bricks in place, spread a ½-inch layer of dry sand on the walk. Sweep the sand back and forth over the pavers. Repeat the process until all the spaces between the pavers are filled with sand. Wet the walk with a fine spray of water from a hose.

Spread sand, sweep, and wet the walk several times over the next three weeks and whenever the walk feels wobbly. Over time, it may become necessary to remove pavers to add sand.

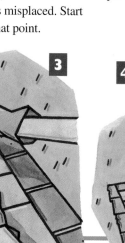

PATHS

▲ A casual garden path surfaced with mulch blends well in a meadow setting. Make the edging higher than the path to keep the mulch in place.

A path guides people through a garden, putting them in close contact with plants and other landscape features. Often built for sheer fun, a path is a more leisurely route and has fewer guidelines than a more heavily trafficked walk.

A path may not connect with the house or even be visible from it. Unlike a walk, the design and materials of a path can be a reflection of the garden rather than the style of the house. Using path materials that complement adjacent features in the landscape allows the path to blend with its surroundings and create a harmonious setting.

Reasons to have a garden path

Practicality A practical path defines a route that people walk routinely. Look for trodden footpaths in the grass; these are "desire lines" that show where a path should be laid. If you have an existing path that nobody uses, remove it and locate a path where it will be used.

Install a practical path even if the need is occasional. For example, if you drag hoses to a specific part of the garden several times a week, a path will make the chore easier. Use hose guards around any curves in a path to protect the plants.

Use the path to direct guests from the garden to the back door or to special areas within the garden.

Aesthetics A path can be an art form; consider it horizontal sculpture. Whether it's a strong, sweeping line or a gentle curve that meanders through a series of beds, a path leads the eye. When you lay out a path, think about where it will lead and what people will see as they stroll along it. The choice of paving material itself can contribute to a pleasing appearance.

Pleasure Have fun with paths. They can go anywhere you want. Dead-end a path at a shrub bed, or make one that goes in a big circle. Wind a curving path among trees and bend it out of sight.

Make your path with unusual materials. Homemade stepping-stones embedded with found objects, pieces of pottery, or your family's handprints in the concrete personalize the path. For instructions on making personalized stepping-stones, see page 92.

◀ In a low-lying or soggy area, elevated decking keeps your feet high and dry.

◀ A combination of aged brick and concrete pavers forms an informal path through a lush garden.

How path materials affect design

The design of a path influences the choice of material. Knowing the effects and best uses of different materials helps you select the most appropriate one.

Stone Stone is versatile and widely used. Set in mortar or sand, mixed with other materials, or used alone, stones mark footfalls along the path. When possible, use indigenous stone, which blends with the landscape better than anything else.

Brick Brick is second only to stone in popularity. Many homes are made of brick, so a brick path ties these homes and gardens together well. Old brick is desirable. Its aged appearance makes any garden seem well-established. Like stone, brick can be set in sand or mortar or mixed with other materials.

▼ A grass path is casual and inviting but cannot handle a great deal of foot traffic.

Pavers Pavers are available in a range of styles, shapes, and colors. From the inexpensive, plain concrete squares readily found at home centers to high-end ceramic tiles, such as the ones in the photo (below right), there is a paver style to fit any budget. When designing a path with pavers, experiment with the pattern, especially when using small pavers (4 to 6 inches across). The broad choices of colors make it easy to create a woven patchwork design.

Stepping-stones A variety of stepping-stones—ready-made in many styles and sizes as well as do-it-yourself kits—is available at garden and home centers. Experiment with different materials to create your own. Two-inch-thick discs cut from the base of a felled tree set the tone for a woodland path.

Concrete stepping-stones are easy to make. Build a form from 2×2s; pour concrete into the form, let it set, then remove the form. To personalize the stepping-stones, press large leaves, coins, handprints, pottery shards, or other found objects into the concrete as it hardens.

Grass A path is the reverse of the usual role of grass; usually a path made of a solid material cuts through a lawn. A strip of grass leading through a paved or

planted area can look dramatic. Design a grass path so one or two quick passes of a mower will keep it trimmed.

Mulch A mulch path has a casual look. Organic mulch is as easy on the garden. It allows water to pass through to the soil below, and it slowly breaks down into nutrients. Replenish the mulch at least once a year as it decomposes. Set the edging 1 to 2 inches higher than the path to keep the mulch in bounds. Some types of mulch are easier to walk on than others. Bark nuggets are too coarse for comfort.

Gravel Gravel is elegant to look at and easy to work with, and it costs less than many materials. Use it to create the appearance of a dry stream, enhanced by a few large stones along the path. If one of the purposes of your path is a peaceful place to walk, you may not like the crunching sound that gravel makes when it is walked on.

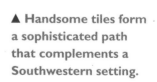

▲ Handsome tiles form a sophisticated path that complements a Southwestern setting.

◄ Pine needles that drop from nearby trees are an ideal surface for use on a woodland path.

How to make a gravel or mulch path

MATERIALS

Shovel and mallet
Prescored 1×4s (or other
   edging material)
12-inch stakes
Landscape fabric
Construction-grade gravel
Decorative gravel or mulch

STEP 1 Build a deep and sturdy bed. For a gravel path, dig a bed 4 inches deep and as wide as the path. Line the sides with prescored 1×4 edging. Pound stakes 8 inches into the soil every 3 feet along straight portions of the edging and every 6 inches along curved portions. Keep the top of the stakes flush with the edging. The stakes will protect the edging from bowing when you fill the form with gravel and create lateral pressure against the sides.

For a mulch path, dig a bed 4 inches deep on the edges, sloped to a depth of 6 inches in the center.

STEP 2 Line the bed with landscape fabric. For either a gravel or mulch path, lay landscape fabric as a liner on the soil. Make certain it comes halfway up the inside of the edging. The fabric separates gravel and mulch from the soil. It prevents erosion and provides a weed barrier between the path and the soil.

STEP 3 Add gravel or mulch. For a gravel path, carefully spread a 2-inch layer on the bed. Use additional stakes to reinforce areas that show signs of bowing. Drive all of the stakes ½ inch below the top of the edging. When you are sure the form will hold, slowly spread the rest of the gravel until it is ½ inch from the top of the form.

To economize, use construction-grade gravel for the bottom layer, then spread decorative gravel on top. With time, some construction-grade gravel will work its way to the surface. To prevent this, lay landscape fabric between the gravel layers.

For a mulch path, fill the center of the bed with 2 inches of construction-grade gravel to form a drainage channel. Cover it with landscape fabric, then spread the mulch. It should be no higher than ½ inch from the top of the form.

Wet down the mulch, then walk back and forth on the path several times to pack it. In a week, add more mulch as it settles, then periodically as the mulch breaks down.

ground every 5 feet. When you reach the end of the path, turn around and walk back to the beginning. Change the path if you want. Walk the path in both directions several times and make adjustments as you go. Pay attention to the terrain; avoid steep slopes, roots, or other obstacles. Direct the path to the special features of the garden. Focus on views above eye level; take advantage of the good views and avoid the poor ones.

Once you have the centerline of the path laid out, mark the side boundaries. If you are using individual stepping-stones, walk the path in your normal gait. Mark exactly where to center each stone for a comfortable pace. When placing the stones, keep in mind the stride of others using the path; arrange stones closer together for children.

A multiuse path

A path that doubles as a patio is a good use of limited space. Make the path at least 4 feet wide and as long as you want; avoid a long, straight line. Stagger a straight path (above left) so you don't see it all at once. The result is a large area for outdoor entertaining that still feels intimate.

Mixing materials on a combination path and patio allows the area to look and feel like both. Break up the paving with gravel, mulch, or low-growing herbs and groundcovers. Or set stepping-stones or pavers into an existing lawn path or other narrow strip of grass.

PATHS *continued*

Lay out a path

Laying out a path is easier than laying out a walk because a path is more informal and less exact, and the width can vary along the way. Imperfection is part of the charm of a path.

A walk is designed to get you quickly and comfortably from one place to another, whereas a path can meander through the garden, letting you take your time along the way. The path can even weave among trees, shrubs, and other garden features.

Once you know the starting and ending points, you can lay out the path exactly. Walk the desired route and mark the centerline of the path with stakes or pieces of coat-hanger wire with brightly colored cloth tied to one end. As you walk the route of the path, insert a marker into the

▲ Moss hugs concrete pavers, making a path that doubles as a patio for outdoor dining.

▲ Set individual stones into an existing path for a route that is both solid and water-permeable.

How to set stones or pavers in grass

Make a handsome path in a day and walk on it that night.

MATERIALS

Stones or pavers
Sharp knife or trowel
Spade
Builder's sand
Rubber mallet

STEP 1 Determine the spacing.
Walk the desired path in a normal stride. If your stride is significantly longer or shorter than average, take that into account. Place the stones in their approximate position. Walk the path in both directions until you are comfortable with the stones' placement.

STEP 2 Mark the exact location of the stones.
If the stones are not uniform, turn each one until you get the desired effect. Using a sharp knife or trowel, make a clean, straight cut 2 inches into the grass to mark the outline of each stone. Be as exact as possible to ensure a snug fit.

STEP 3 Dig a base for the stones.
Move the stones aside one at a time. Cut straight down through the grass and at least an inch into the soil. Use a spade to remove the entire patch of grass with the roots and soil intact. Remove the grass carefully if you will be using it to repair areas elsewhere in your lawn. Lightly water the grass patch if you cannot transplant it immediately.

As you dig the base for each stone, take care to ensure that the hole maintains the shape of the stone. Check several times for fit. Dig the hole 2 inches deeper than the thickness of the stone. Remove any rocks or roots that are in the way.

Spread a 2-inch layer of sand in the hole. Set the stone in place and tamp it with a rubber mallet. Walk back and forth on the stone a few times to settle it so it is flush with the surrounding soil. Eliminate wobbling and stabilize the stone by adding or removing sand.

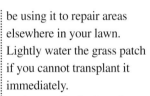

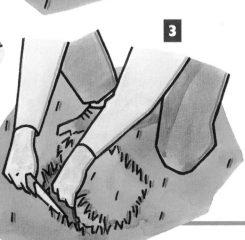

Materials for Walks and Paths

Brick

Before deciding on brick, remember that unless you want to cut bricks to fit, the line of the walk or path must be straight or uniformly and gently curved. Brick is a durable and refined material that is relatively expensive and time-consuming to lay. Old brick costs even more unless you find someone who is tearing down an old brick structure. Most salvaged brick has clinging mortar that you have to chip away. New brick is available in a range of colors and finishes. The only potential maintenance on brick is removing a white residue (alkaline salts) that may appear; scrub the brick with a fiber brush dipped in muriatic acid.

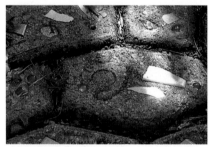

Custom paving

A walk or path can have aesthetic value all its own. Using concrete (an easy, affordable, and readily available material), you can create one-of-a-kind pavers decorated with materials such as marbles and porcelain. Mix a batch of concrete; add dye or stains if you choose. Pour the concrete into a form made of a plastic-lined 12-inch-wide indentation in the soil, a pizza box, or 2×2s fashioned into a shape. Press decorations (buttons, coins, pebbles, or porcelain shards) into the drying concrete. Remove the form and you have a custom paver.

Exposed aggregate

Exposed aggregate—concrete with a high percentage of uniform, pea- to marble-sized stones mixed in or added to the finished layer—is durable if properly installed by a professional. When the concrete is poured, the very top layer of masonry is washed or brushed off to expose the aggregate. Only 20 to 30 percent of the top layer of aggregate is exposed. Stone used for exposed aggregate is available in shades of brown to gray. It costs more than plain concrete but less than stamped concrete or pavers. Unless you use very coarse aggregate, this material can be slippery when wet.

Grass

The ease of installation and the relative low cost of materials make using a strip of grass to form a walk or path an attractive option. However, grass is the least durable path material and requires regular maintenance. Avoid using grass for a path that is traversed more than five times a day. If you make frequent trips on the walk with a full wheelbarrow or garden cart, the grass will wear and become thin. Make a grass path wide enough so that it can be mowed with one or two passes of a mower. Use a crisp edging of brick, wood, or stone flush with the lawn to clearly mark the borders of the path. The edging makes mowing easier.

Gravel

Gravel allows water to percolate through, so the path drains better than any other type. You will find a range of gravels from which to choose; you do not need a professional to make a gravel path. Crusher-run is a granite mix containing medium and small stones as well as granite dust, which helps bind the materials together. River rock and pebbles are more expensive and have a refined look. Gravel maintenance is limited to keeping the material in place and replenishing it occasionally. Avoid gravel where fully laden wheelbarrows or people wearing high heels regularly travel.

Mixed media

Making a list of the building materials used in your hardscape and building your walk with a mix of materials on that list is a useful way to unify building materials found throughout the garden. It can be challenging to come up with a mix that looks good. Brick and concrete are a common combination; stone and concrete also work well. A stone and brick mixture is less common and can be hard to blend. The cost, availability, and durability of this type of path will vary with the materials used.

Mulch

Use mulch for a quick and easy path. Depending upon the availability of the type of mulch you choose, this can be the least expensive path to make. Durability depends on the material you use. Pine straw breaks down quickly, whereas bark nuggets take much longer to decompose and tend to feel coarse underfoot. Maintenance is limited; keep the mulch within the desired boundaries and replenish the mulch as required. Edging defines the path and keeps the mulch in place. Mulch is not recommended for a path that needs to handle a wheelbarrow or garden cart.

Stained and stamped concrete

Concrete can be more than a plain gray slab. Stained, painted, or textured concrete looks attractive. You can stain it yourself; add color to the concrete during mixing or curing. Painting is an option that requires regular touch-ups every two to three years, depending on how much the walk is used.

Stamped concrete is made by pressing a metal form into damp concrete. When it dries, a single slab of concrete looks as though it is made of many individual stones or pavers. Stamped concrete is highly durable. The tools needed to stamp concrete are cost-prohibitive for small amounts.

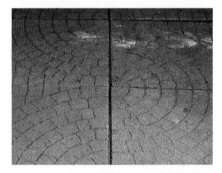

Stone

Refined stone, such as slate and marble, is more uniform, durable, and costly than fieldstone. Fieldstone is a more forgiving medium. It is imperfect in its natural state, so slight variances from a level or straight line don't stand out. Slate, marble, and fieldstone are virtually maintenance-free. Sandstone, although attractive, has a tendency to chip, shatter, and flake from physical damage, freezing, and thawing.

Stone prices and availability vary depending on location and regional geography. Keep an eye out for renovation and construction projects; they often unearth mounds of stone that must be disposed of or sold as salvage.

DRIVEWAYS

Automobiles are a dominant element in American culture, as evidenced by the money spent and space devoted to accommodating cars as part of the home. Driveways, carports, parking bays, and garages have a major impact on the landscape.

Driveways and parking areas—necessities in this culture—are often afterthoughts. Careful planning of these features is worth the effort, whether you are redesigning an existing landscape or designing a new one.

More material will probably be used to surface a driveway and parking area than in the rest of the landscape combined. Choose the material carefully, with appearance, cost, and durability in mind. For more information about materials, see pages 102–103.

▲ **A combination of grass and paving has a softer appearance, is more economical, and conserves more rainwater (has less runoff) than paving alone.**

Plan ahead

Review the master plan for your landscape (see page 10), which shows your current and anticipated parking needs. Strive to design and build with future needs in mind. You'll save money by building all the parking you need now, rather than adding more in five or 10 years. As long as the design and construction are sound, you'll recover the cost of parking improvements when you sell the house. See page 101 for more information on planning your driveway.

Driveway concerns

The driveway must be clearly identifiable from the street. Use a mailbox, house number, reflector, or other marker to avoid any confusion about where the entrance is—day and night.

Turning the car into the drive from the street should be an easy maneuver with good visibility. The driveway itself should be an easy ride—smooth and at least 10 feet wide. When you pull out of the driveway into the street, an unobstructed view in both directions is essential.

If you have a steep site, angling the drive across the property instead of heading it straight up the slope allows you to maintain a safe and legal grade. Check local building codes for specific requirements in your area.

Provide ample space along the driveway so people can walk without rubbing against parked cars. Make a path that parallels the driveway. Define it with a material different than the drive. For safety, keep the walk flush with the driveway and free of steps.

◀ **The lines of a driveway are dominant in the landscape. Accentuate them with plantings along one or both sides.**

Remember the doors

When adding a parking bay for family or for visitors, be generous with the spacing so that people will have an easy time getting in and out of the car—on both sides.

Keep safety in mind

Be sure there is an unobstructed view in both directions at the street end of the driveway. If the drive is on a curve, install a mirror that allows you to see oncoming traffic around the bend.

Consider drainage

Rain that lands on impermeable driveways and parking areas rarely finds its way into the garden soil. Consider paving with a permeable material, such as gravel, turf pavers, or dry-laid brick or stone. Or slope the drive to keep water on-site.

Driveway styles

Most homeowners don't have the option of choosing their driveway; it often comes with the house. If you have the opportunity to build a house or decide to improve the value of your home by modifying the existing driveway, you should know your options. It is important to take the time to understand the site, your needs, and the choices open to you.

Straight drive A straight drive is usually the least expensive and easiest style to add. It is the most common approach taken by builders of new properties.

A straight driveway can be as attractive as any other drive if you take full advantage of the opportunities its simple lines offer. Plant a row of ornamental trees along one or both sides of the drive. The trees accentuate the strength of the line created by the paving, and they cast shade for parked cars. If there is a path along the driveway, a row of trees with their lower limbs (any branches less than 8 feet above the ground) removed makes the approach to the house more pleasant, while allowing you a view beyond the trees.

Minimize the impact of a long, straight drive by breaking the expanse of paving with headers. Headers are rows of brick or other pavers set perpendicular to the line of the driveway. They are made of a material that contrasts with the drive.

If your drive goes straight into a garage, consider adding a turnaround. Although this requires additional space, it is well worth the added safety; you won't have to back down the drive and onto a busy street.

Curved drive A curved drive is elegant leading through a big property. You can build a curved driveway that winds through the landscape, perhaps to avoid removing or damaging any trees.

Construct a curved driveway slightly wider than a straight drive (12 feet instead of 10 feet) to make it easier to keep all wheels on the pavement. Any groundcovers and low-growing plants bordering the driveway should be hardy enough to withstand being run over by the occasional tire of an errant vehicle.

Molding a circular driveway to the contours of the land requires less grading and reduces the speed of rainwater runoff (which in turn cuts down on erosion). Following the contours of the land can produce a more graceful driveway than a straight path.

▲ Break up a straight driveway by passing it through a walled entryway into an auto court.

Circular drive A circular drive is ideally suited for a large formal landscape on level land. It requires a minimum diameter of 40 feet, which makes it an expensive option.

Having a circular drive often results in cars parked right in front of the house. Make the driveway at least 18 feet wide so a car can park in a line along the edge of the drive with ample room for another car to drive past.

If space in the front yard is limited, consider a semicircular drive. Although the design bisects the front yard, it makes an easy approach for visitors.

▼ An elegant circular drive is easy to maneuver, shows off a large tree or planting at its center, and requires a lot of space.

Planning your driveway

The four main considerations when planning a driveway are the entrance to the property, destination, route across your property, and dimensions and materials. They are interdependent and should be addressed before you start to build.

ENTRANCE

The entrance to the property is dependent on the route of the drive and the destination.

Before deciding where the drive will meet the street, familiarize yourself with any local ordinances or guidelines. In some localities a driveway must be at least 10 feet from the neighboring property line.

Identify the location of any underground utilities and find out if there are any building restrictions that apply. Even if you are allowed to build over or under utilities, if repairs become necessary, the driveway might be damaged.

Safety is a key factor. When determining where the drive will meet the street, choose an area with maximum visibility. A cleared space at least 5 feet in from the street and 15 feet to either side of the drive provides unobstructed views.

DESTINATION

A driveway can have another destination besides a private parking or service area. It can also lead to visitor parking. To accommodate visitors, a pullout along the driveway is a good option. For details about planning for parking, see pages 104–105.

ROUTE

Once you have determined the location of the driveway entrance and where the parking area(s) will be, you are ready to lay out the route for the driveway.

The lay of the land, the cost, and the desired appearance all help determine the route. Try to follow the contours of the land. Keep the drive at least 10 feet from the base of small trees and 20 feet from the base of trees that are 30 feet or taller; this prevents damage to the tree roots. It also reduces the risk of tree roots breaking up the paving.

DIMENSIONS

Although your driveway is on private property and you have flexibility in how it is designed and built, the standard dimensions that have been developed over time are good guidelines to follow. The diagram below illustrates the minimum dimensions for a semicircular driveway. You can double these dimensions to determine the amount of space you need for a circular drive.

Other standard driveway widths are:
Straight drive: 10 feet
Straight drive with room to pass parked cars: 18 feet
Curved drive: 12 feet
Two-way drive: 16 feet
Minimum turning radius for drive entries: 15 feet

A discussion of materials is on pages 102–103.

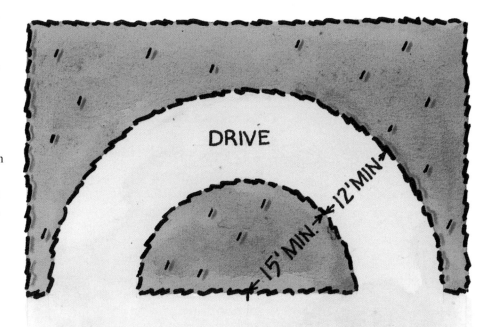

DRIVE

15' MIN. — 12' MIN.

STREET

Choosing Driveway Materials

One of the most important choices you can make about the landscape is the material for the driveway. This decision has a major impact on cost, appearance, maintenance, and durability.

Select a material in keeping with the overall setting, especially the architecture and building materials of the house and any visible garden structures. A complementary driveway material unifies these components even more than a walk or path does. A brick drive blends with a brick home more than a cobblestone drive. If the cost of building a brick drive exceeds your budget, edge a concrete drive with bricks or use brick headers.

Cost is a major factor in deciding how the drive will be built. Although you may design the driveway yourself, you are likely to have a professional build it. It's not that the actual work involved is any more difficult than building a terrace; it's a matter of how much work there is to do. It's one thing to excavate, prepare a base, and build a 3×20-foot walk and quite another to go through the same process for a driveway that is 10 feet wide and 100 feet long. If time is not a factor, you might want to do it yourself. If you have it built by a contractor, you need to know the dimensions and square footage of the drive before asking for bids. For more on working with professionals, see page 33.

The base for the driveway is just as important as the surface material. A good base starts with grading that forms a level surface. A minimum of 4 inches of gravel is required to disperse the weight of the cars; an even deeper base is necessary if heavy vehicles, such as delivery trucks, will use the driveway.

The last consideration in driveway paving is drainage. Driveway materials are often impermeable, so rainwater runoff has to be channeled where you want it. Use a city drain or build a catch basin to capture the water once it runs off the driveway. Otherwise, water running down the drive may cause erosion.

Asphalt

Asphalt has many virtues as a driveway material. It can be molded easily to fit almost any shape without the installer having to build a form; it is somewhat flexible, so if a tree root beneath the driveway starts to press up on the asphalt, the paving won't crack the way concrete does. Although the root can push through the asphalt, this material is easy to repair with patching material that is simply scooped from a bucket and pressed into place. Repairs may be required when asphalt gets soft in very hot weather or when a heavy vehicle drives along the edge of the driveway. A solid base and edging help prevent this type of damage.

Brick

Brick is an elegant-looking driveway material. It lasts a long time and stands up to a lot of traffic. Because of the cost, it is seldom used for a driveway. The only material more expensive than brick is refined stone. If brick appeals to you yet cost is a concern, use brick for part of the drive. Build the entry and the first 10 feet of the driveway with brick, then pour a concrete drive with brick edging and brick headers every 10 feet. Pave the arrival or parking area with brick as well.

The best method for laying a brick driveway is to set it on a bed of concrete. Although brick on sand costs less, the driveway may become uneven over time.

Cobblestone and river rock

Cobblestone and river rock are often set into a bed of concrete that rests on a base of gravel. These materials are attractive, but may be cost-prohibitive and difficult to find. From a purely visual standpoint, the color and texture of cobblestone and river rock allow them to blend into the landscape. However, they may clash with the style of your home. These stones are best suited for cottage-style homes or others evoking a past era.

These are two of the bumpiest paving materials to drive on, so they are best used on short driveways. Depending upon the surface of the stones, they can be slick when wet. These materials are not suited to cold-winter areas; it is difficult to remove snow from them with a snowblower, shovel, or plow without nicking the stones.

Concrete

This is the most common building material in North America. It is affordable, available, and—when installed properly—durable. Of all driveway materials, concrete requires the most preparation. A level bed, solidly built form, expansion joints, and a layer of packed gravel are essential for long-term success. Proper pouring and finishing of the concrete also contribute to an enduring drive.

You can add interest to an otherwise dull-looking drive by breaking up the solid expanse of concrete with headers. The rows of contrasting materials also serve a useful purpose. Concrete expands and shrinks with heat and cold. Adding headers allows room for the concrete to expand and contract, preventing seasonal cracking. Expansion joints (asphalt or wood strips) are another option.

Grass and concrete

There are several products available that are made with a pattern of concrete that has 50 percent or more open space in which grass can be planted. The driveway is built using modular panels that come in various sizes from 2 feet square to 4 feet square. Once the panels are in place and level, the open spaces are filled with soil, and grass is sown or plugged. Once the grass is established, the surface is solid enough to drive and park upon. It has the appearance of turf and is water permeable. Tire treads and engine leaks may affect the health of the turf. Although tire marks may be visible for a short period of time, a tough grass (such as Bermudagrass) is resilient enough to handle it. This material is ideal for overflow parking areas.

Gravel

A gravel driveway is easy to install. Because water can move easily through it, potential drainage problems are avoided. Gravel drives are especially handsome when made with decorative gravel. Gravel is suited only to sites that are fairly level; even then the edges must be contained to hold the gravel inbounds. The only maintenance necessary is to add gravel periodically to replenish loss that occurs due to normal use. An often overlooked aspect of gravel is the sound it makes. The telltale crunch can alert you to arriving cars. It is nearly impossible to walk on gravel when wearing high heels, so if you decide on a gravel drive, plan for a landing or an arrival area with a solid surface.

PARKING

arked cars visually dominate many residential landscapes. Having invested time and money in your home and garden, you may not want to have the landscape marred by a cluster of automobiles parked directly in front of the house.

For most homeowners, providing ample parking is a challenge. They not only must find a spot for multiple family vehicles, but visitors also need a place to park. Although parking on the street or in the drive is functional and typical, with a little effort you can find a way to handle all your parking needs on-site.

Determine your parking needs

To determine whether your current parking needs are met, consider the following questions:

- Do visitors have to park on the street?
- Do visitors frequently use the wrong entrance to your home?
- If all the cars in the household are parked, do any of them block others from passing?
- Do you frequently run off the driveway and onto the lawn or plants while performing basic driveway maneuvers?
- Do you have to back up more than 50 feet to reach the street?

- Will the household change in the near future in a way that affects any of your answers?

If you answered yes to any of these questions, you need to solve some parking problems. Some solutions include curbside, off-street, and on-site parking.

Curbside parking—parallel to the curb—is one way to provide the parking you need without taking up any space on your own property. But it can put visitors too far from the house and some localities do not allow curbside parking or limit it to certain times or sides of the street.

Off-street parking is another option. It applies the various parking solutions shown on page 105, except parking is accessed directly off the street instead of the driveway. This is not permitted in many towns, because it can interfere with a sidewalk.

If curbside or off-street parking are unavailable, consider on-site parking. Parking is contained on your property and is accessed by your driveway. The discussion and illustrations on page105 provide a starting point for planning parking. No matter which type of parking you choose, you should consider the issues of privacy, security, and safety.

◀ **A buffer of vegetation can almost hide a parking area. Locate the area on the side of the house so it is a less dominant feature.**

Planning your parking

Locate parking as close to the house as possible. If the front door and front walk are clearly visible from the guest parking area, people will know how to get to the house. When possible, avoid having a parking area directly in front of the house. If it is unavoidable, plant a screen to help hide parked cars.

Identify any existing level areas suitable for parking. Using one of these can save the cost of grading.

Think about how the parking area looks without cars. Remember, parking areas can have recreational, entertaining, and other uses.

PARALLEL

Parallel parking is ideal when space is limited and only one or two additional spaces are needed for parking. The recommended area for parallel parking one car is 20 feet long and 10 feet wide. If you need parallel parking for two cars, extend the length of each space to 22 feet or more. The width remains 10 feet.

Parallel parking is the most difficult for drivers to use. Unless there is a turnaround at the end of the drive, parallel parking necessitates backing out of the driveway.

ANGLED

Even though angled parking is the easiest to drive in and out of, it takes up the most amount of yard. The spaces can be angled at 60 degrees or 30 degrees from the line of the drive. The two methods are about the same in cost and ease of use. As with parallel parking, the driver has to back the car down the driveway.

PERPENDICULAR

Perpendicular parking has many virtues that make it the most desirable type of on-site parking. It takes up only a moderate amount of room and is relatively easy to use.

The biggest advantage of perpendicular parking is that when leaving, the driver can back up and turn around in the driveway so the car can drive head-first into the street. A turning radius of at least 15 feet is needed for comfortable perpendicular parking.

Wheel stops (for angled or perpendicular parking spaces) show visitors exactly where to park. Wheel stops prevent the front of the car from blocking walks or paths leading from the parking area to the house. They also avoid **damage to surrounding plants.**

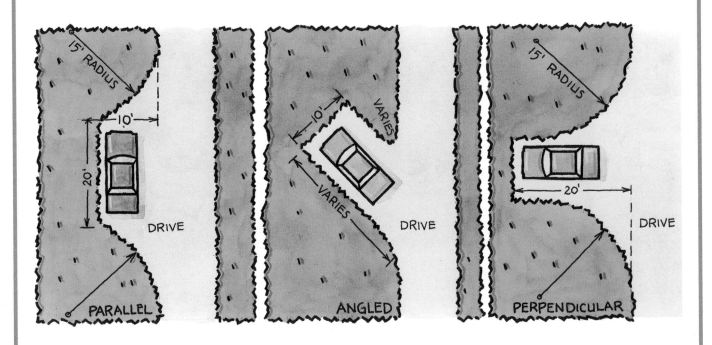

Privacy and Security for Parking

A parking area needs to be both private and secure. As with any landscape project, proper planning and design help accomplish both goals.

Privacy

Privacy for parking serves two purposes. First, the parking area should be hidden enough so you can enter and exit the car—or wash it on a sunny weekend—without feeling that you are on display. In the process of creating such privacy, you accomplish the second purpose—screening the parking from the street and other public areas. This minimizes any negative visual impact that cars, garages, and carports have for passersby.

One way to address privacy is to locate the parking behind the house, where it is less visible. If the backyard is fenced or hedged, the parking area has all the privacy you need. The main drawback is that it may place cars too close to a favorite garden spot. If that is the case, explore the various methods on pages 110 to 139 for screening to block the parking from view.

Parking in the front or side yard of the house requires a creative approach to privacy. When using a fence, wall, or hedge, strive for an aesthetic appeal that blends into the landscape. A structure or planting 5 feet high can screen most cars and give ample privacy, yet it doesn't have a feeling of total enclosure. It allows anyone behind it to see what is taking place on the other side of the screen.

A slight change in elevation could effectively screen parking and creates a sense of privacy without sacrificing security. The photo below demonstrates the impact of a modest grade on privacy.

If the drive runs straight from the street to a garage or parking area, it is difficult to have privacy. Screening or tall plants along one or both sides of the drive prevent passersby from seeing the cars unless they are at the end of the drive.

With some creativity—and enough room—you can have private parking for more than a single car if you have a straight drive that ends at a one-car garage with a door. Remove the back wall of the garage. Build a parking court and turnaround for two cars behind the garage. In effect, the garage becomes a covered driveway for loading and unloading, but no cars are parked there. The back side of the garage is open all the time, and the original garage door in front provides the privacy.

Security

A private parking area can be a hiding place for would-be criminals. You are vulnerable when you get in or out of the

► A change in elevation can minimize the visual impact of guest parking and a clearly marked, well-lit path and front door create a safe and reassuring entry to the home.

car and enter the house. Your arms may be full with bags of groceries or a briefcase. As you search for the house keys, you may be lulled into the sense of security that comes from being home. Although the odds are in your favor that you will never be the victim of such a crime, addressing three issues—lighting, visibility, and proximity to your entryway—will reduce the risk.

Lighting is the first line of defense for security. It enhances visibility in the parking area and contributes to your personal safety as you walk at night. You can see and be seen.

A quick and easy way to illuminate the parking area is to install motion detectors that activate existing lighting, or install a fixture that is a combination light and motion detector. These fixtures are inexpensive and readily available at home centers. Place one detector in the parking area. For additional safety, place another detector halfway up the driveway—before the garage or parking area. As you drive up, the area will flood with light. You can set the lights to turn off automatically any time from 30 seconds to five minutes. The timer prevents the lights from staying on all night after a neighborhood dog walks past the motion detector.

Use detectors to activate lights along any walks that lead to the primary entrance and to turn on a light over the door itself. A motion detector is a good security option even if you park in an attached garage with an automatic door.

Visibility is critical to security. Although planting shrubs to screen parking from the street is a good idea, make certain you can see from where the car is parked to the door you use. Avoid planting shrubs that are large enough for someone to hide behind close to the door of the house, along a path or walk, between the door of the house and the garage door, and by the garage door.

In addition to comfort and convenience, security is another reason to park as close to the house as possible. The fewer steps you have to take, the lower the risk.

▲ This enclosed parking court is attractive and spacious. Completely contained inside a walled area, it is also secure.

Parking that Doubles as a Terrace

If you ever need parking for three or four cars in addition to your own—even if only several times a year—think about creating a parking area that can double as a terrace. This idea is a more logical solution than you might first imagine.

In general, the requirements for a parking space are the same as those for an outdoor entertaining area. Both need a level open space, and a solid surface, and are best located close to the house. They are most attractive if built from materials that blend with the surrounding architecture.

▼ **An attractive terrace adjacent to the primary parking area provides overflow parking space when needed.**

Most homeowners are challenged to find enough appropriate places on their property for all of the elements in their master plan. Dual-purpose sites are ideal. When planning this kind of feature, decide which use is dominant. This choice helps you design and select the building materials. Generally, parking will dominate.

Although their requirements are strikingly similar, a parking area and a terrace are significantly different in scale. The amount of room needed to park and maneuver two cars is greater than the space needed for a typical terrace. You need an area at least 25 feet square to handle parking for two cars, plus another 10×20 feet for a turnaround. A comfortable terrace can be as small as 15 feet square.

Design the area for parking, then review the plan to see how it can be adapted to serve as a terrace. Although you might plan for a large concrete parking area, adding some bands of brick or painting or staining the concrete gives the area some sparkle for the times when it is used for entertaining.

Enclosing the parking area on at least two sides can create a courtyard feeling. You might even install a lightweight gate to limit access by cars, but leave one side of the parking area open. The remaining side becomes the transition to the garden.

The parking area can be enclosed by open and airy structures (below) or by more solid features, such as a tall hedge or high fence, for greater privacy. Allow a generous opening for breezes and people to move easily through the space. A formal entry covered with an arbor can minimize the openness of a terrace and can give a sense of enclosure.

Running bond

Straight bond

Modified herringbone

Brick is the ideal paving material for making patterns. Use the ones shown here or experiment with different shapes, sizes, and colors of brick and create your own pattern. Try using one pattern style for the edge or border of a drive and another pattern for paving down the middle.

Half-square

Pinwheel

Basketweave

Stagger step

Herringbone

◄ Be creative; go beyond the usual brick paving patterns and cut brick to fit specific shapes and dimensions. It's easy with the right tools and some experience.

CHAPTER 5

PRIVACY & SECURITY

Claim the garden as your own

PRIVACY

▲ **A sense of enclosure creates a truly private space. This intimate garden could be located a mile—or only 20 yards—from the nearest house and you wouldn't know.**

The garden makes a calming retreat, especially when everyday life moves at a frenetic pace. More people than ever desire an intimate setting where they can unwind without intrusions.

A successful garden should provide the same degree of privacy as your home. You need both open and intimate spaces. But as you plan your needs for privacy, be careful that you do not create a sense of isolation or of being within a fortress.

Types of privacy

Privacy is either complete or partial. No one can see into an area that is completely private from any vantage point short of an airplane or perhaps a neighbor's window.

A place for sunbathing or hanging a hammock might warrant complete privacy. In working to achieve privacy, avoid screening out desirable views.

Whatever method you use to create privacy, the ideal height for the barrier is at least 6 feet tall. This height is well above eye level for most people. If in doubt about the height, make it higher, because structures at eye level can make many people feel uncomfortable.

Partial privacy is just that. Passersby cannot see in, but a neighbor might. Screens and open-style fencing are frequently used when complete privacy is not required.

Creating private spaces

If a pool is already ideally situated, you can create privacy working with what exists. When creating a new spot for privacy, there are more options. Consider the views in and out of the area from all angles. Remember that deciduous vegetation creates privacy in summer but not winter.

Visit your neighbors and share your intentions. Design something that looks good from their perspective as well as yours. Not only is this neighborly, they may like your idea and share in the cost.

You need to know exactly where the property line is and be familiar with local ordinances and easements. Most communities have definite rules about fences, walls, hedges, or other screening that faces the street or divides properties.

◄ **Soften the impact of a tall privacy fence by painting it a muted color.**

Don't seclude yourself

Create privacy without isolation by adding gates or other openings to your structure for the times you want to open the garden.

Think of the overhead

A sense of privacy is linked to a sense of enclosure. Take advantage of the overhead canopy of any tall trees or other structures that provide a sense of enclosure.

1881

Use a two-sided fence

When building a fence for privacy, be a good neighbor and make both sides attractive. They do not have to be the same style. Consult with your neighbor in the planning stage.

SECURITY

Security is distinctly different from privacy. Privacy merely restricts the views into and out of an area, whereas security prevents entry. Although a dense hedge of thorny shrubs will thwart most trespassers, it is relatively easy to circumvent. For this reason, the best security measures are almost always built, such as a wall or fence, instead of planted.

Planning security

No fence or wall will keep out unwanted beings. Consider the structure as an important, frontline defense that is part of a complete security system that includes lighting and an alarm system. For more on lighting, see page 262.

The first step is deciding what or who you want to keep out. Hungry deer will jump all but the tallest fences, sometimes clearing up to 10 feet to feast on your garden. If the structure is to prevent unsupervised children from entering a swimming pool, 4 feet may be adequate (check local ordinanances). If the purpose of the fence is to keep out the neighbor's dog, the structure needs to extend at least a foot below the soil line. If keeping out people is your main concern, decorative pointed finials angled toward the outside of the wall or fence are an attractive and effective way to deter trespassers.

Unlike a fence or wall for privacy, a security structure needs to be seamless— it has to completely enclose the area being protected. Although you don't have to use the same type of structure for all sides, the styles should be compatible. For example, if an unseen part of the yard behind a garage is to be enclosed, you can get by with a less expensive but equally functional structure, such as chain link fence.

▲ Break up the expanse of a solid wall or fence with hanging plants or artwork mounted directly on the structure.

When planning a security structure, determine where a gate is needed. Depending upon the size and layout of your property, it may be smart to plan for at least one gate or opening large enough to allow a truck to pass through for times when you need to haul something big into the yard. If the need for this type of access is limited to rare or emergency situations, the opening doesn't have to be a gate. Instead, plan a fence with one or more panels that can be removed and replaced by screwing or bolting them together.

Security structures

To provide adequate homeowner security, a fence or wall needs to be at least 6 feet tall; 8 feet is even better. Anything solid and higher than 8 feet may be too costly and off-putting.

If privacy is not paramount, opt for an open security structure such as a wrought-iron fence. Nearly half of all security structures have an open design.

◄ The open design of a metal fence fades into the background.

Price is another consideration. An 8-foot-tall open structure costs less to build than a closed structure of the same size.

Often, in creating privacy or security features, you may block or channel wind and light. This can be a blessing or a curse. Either way, don't leave it to chance. Refer to your site analysis (see page 14) and plan accordingly. If your privacy fence blocks a cooling summer breeze, consider adding openings in the fence, having a solid bottom and an open top to allow air to move through, or using panels of shutters or lattice which allow breezes and privacy when you need them. These might be acceptable compromises between privacy and comfort.

One way to add height is to extend posts or pillars 4 feet above the finished structure and suspend canvas panels between them. The panels allow light and air to move through.

Refer to your site analysis (see page 14)

Security tip

Motion detectors can be used to turn on lights or sprinklers or sound alarms to scare people and animals from the yard. Be sure there is an easily accessible on-off switch.

Choose a style and color that will add pizzazz to the garden. The disadvantage to using canvas is that in most climates the panels will have to be replaced every 8 to 10 years.

▼ **If privacy is not essential, a combination fence allows plenty of light and air to pass through.**

FENCES

▲ A fence defines the boundaries of the garden and serves as a backdrop. Notice how this fence blends with the plantings to become part of the design.

Fencing has been a part of the landscape as long as there have been gardens. Fences are multipurpose. They create security and privacy, define boundaries, keep people and animals contained, and add to the aesthetics of the garden. The range of styles and materials, as well as the relative ease of building fences, add to their appeal.

Fence uses

Security and privacy Fences used for this purpose are typically large, solid, or otherwise imposing structures. To reduce the visual weight of such a structure, add vines, a wall fountain, plaques, or other artwork. Paint a trompe l'oeil opening to give the illusion of a passageway or an airy space. Use an open-style construction to reduce the visual impact of the structure and allow light and air to pass through.

Defining space One of the original reasons for fencing land was to claim ownership. The habit is still prevalent today. A fence does not have to be large in order to define space. A 2-foot-high fence clearly communicates that you want people to stay out of the area.

Fences are frequently used to surround a lot for no other reason than to mark the property line. When erecting a fence for this purpose, be aware of the exact property line and any required restrictions on placement, type of fence, or height.

Use a fence instead of a solid wall to create an outdoor room. It is much less expensive than most walls. As an added advantage, a fence is usually much more readily moved or expanded than a wall as

your garden grows or your design ideas or needs change.

Controlling traffic A fence—whether large or small—does a good job of directing people where you want them to go and avoid the places where you don't want them.

If using a tall fence, think about how it will feel to walk beside it. To soften the impact of all the wood or metal, consider putting a planting bed a few feet in front of the fence or training vines on it.

Aesthetic appeal Consider all aspects and impacts of a fence—appearances count a lot. Whether the pleasure is in forming a backdrop for a planting or in

▼ A metal fence combined with ornate concrete pillars is stately and elegant. Its austerity is tempered by the playful blue paint.

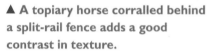

▲ **A topiary horse corralled behind a split-rail fence adds a good contrast in texture.**

the beauty of the craftsmanship and design, sometimes the best reason to have a fence is simply because it is attractive.

A solid fence serves as a backdrop to whatever is in front of it. Plant a specimen tree or shrub in front of the fence and use night lighting so it can be enjoyed at all hours. Consider how the color of the fence works with what is being planted in front if it. Should you be ready for a change, it is easily accomplished by painting all or part of the fence a different color.

Fence styles

There are many styles of fences from which to choose. The purpose of your fence will affect your choice. For example, if you want a decorative fence, you may choose a picket style. If privacy is your focus, you might choose a solid style such as a stockade.

▲ **A fence doesn't have to be costly. This simple fence uses small limbs from the property nailed to 2×4 rails as pickets.**

Traditional A white picket fence is the most traditional and the most common type of fence in many areas, yet it is one of the most diverse in design. There is virtually no limit to how you space and design the pickets, posts, and rails. The classic picket fence is painted white, but other colors may better suit your scheme.

The stockade fence is another option. This type of fence is made of panels of 1×8-inch pieces of wood placed shoulder to shoulder. Both picket and stockade fences are easy to build. Most home centers sell precut components or prefabricated panels.

▲ **Picket fences are one of the most popular fence styles, with virtually no limit to the design options.**

Formal or informal The most formal fences are made of wrought iron. They tend to be expensive but add an elegant look to a home. Informal fences include split-rail, lattice, bamboo, and woven wood, which work best in rural or wooded gardens. Funky, fun, or folk art fences are also in this category.

Functional Chain link is durable, affordable, and easy to install. It lets air and light pass through and can be made any height. Painting it a dark color helps it blend with the rest of the landscape.

Mix-and-match fences

Just as different parts of your landscape can have different looks, your fence style can vary throughout the garden. Fences can set a different mood for each area.

Fence Materials and Maintenance

With the purpose and style of your fence in mind, the next step is to determine the appropriate material. As you decide, be aware of the maintenance that each type of fence requires.

Wood Wood is the most affordable, readily available, and versatile material for fencing. It comes in uniform sizes, so you can easily plan, purchase, and build the fence yourself. Prefabricated wood fence panels are also available at most home centers. Use naturally rot-resistant wood such as redwood or cedar, or use treated lumber.

Some wood fences are made from unfinished wood. Split-rail fences and log fences can be made from store-bought posts and rails or from material found on your property. Making a fence

▲ Wrought iron fences lend an air of permanence to the garden. Maintenance is limited to rust removal and painting.

◄ The textural quality of this woven bamboo fence adds interest to a large expanse of fencing.

is a good way to recycle deadwood or wood from storm-ravaged or downed trees. The longevity of the fence depends on the wood used and your climate. As a rule, a fence made from fallen timber will last about half as long as one made from rot-resistant or treated lumber.

Metal Wrought iron implies permanence, order, and wealth. Historically, metal fences were custom-made of wrought iron. Because of the relatively low demand for it, wrought iron is now fairly hard to find. Estate sales are a good source.

The quality and pricing of aluminum fences make them an attractive alternative to iron. Aluminum fences come in a wide range of styles. They are easy to work with and lightweight. Aluminum fences do not rot or rust, so the paint lasts longer than on wood or iron.

Combination fences A fence can be made of more than one type of material. For example, masonry pillars instead of posts, with metal or wooden panels in between, achieve some of the permanence and elegance of stone without the massive feel of a solid wall. Coupling rustic posts with finished panels is a good way to tie together various aspects of the garden through building materials.

Freestyle This is a catch-all category for unusual fences that don't fit any other description. Usually reserved for the bold and adventurous homeowner, a freestyle fence can be made from almost any materials—metal car bumpers, old highway signs, vertical cross ties, bedsprings. A freestyle fence serves all the functions of a traditional fence while revealing more of the owner's character.

▼ Paint a fence a dark color, such as green, to help it fade into the background or blend with the garden.

Fence maintenance

The type and amount of maintenance a fence requires is based mostly on the material used to build it.

The combination of wood, paint, and weather conditions necessitates repainting a wood fence every four to five years. It may be necessary to do some touch-up painting between complete paint jobs. If you use a rot-resistant wood or treated lumber, you can prolong the life of the fence by applying a sealer or stain at the time of construction and prior to painting.

Any wood fence will last longer if you keep it clean. Spray it with a strong blast from a hose to wash away decaying leaves or other vegetation nestled in corners.

Training a vine to a fence can create an ideal condition for decay due to trapped debris, blocked light, lack of air circulation, and moisture retention. A vine-covered fence is difficult to paint. When it becomes necessary to repaint, gently remove the vine and lower it to the ground, paint the fence, then reattach and retrain the vine. In some cases, it is easier to cut back the vine to within a foot or more of the ground and allow it to regrow on the fence.

The only maintenance needed for a metal fence is occasional painting. When repainting metal (or wood, for that matter), it is best to scrape off all the old paint, remove the rust, and prime the metal before applying more paint.

FENCE FINISHES

NATURAL

Letting a fence age naturally is inexpensive and trouble-free.

- A natural fence blends well with informal or rustic surroundings.
- Even rot-resistant wood, such as redwood, cedar, or treated pine, will fade to gray over time. Adding a stain or a sealer will prolong its life and natural color.

PAINT

- You can use any color outdoor paint.
- A dark-colored fence seems to recede.
- Be sure the wood is completely dry before painting; otherwise, the paint will bubble as moisture escapes.
- Remove cracked or peeling paint before repainting.
- Always use a primer when painting a metal fence.
- Use a sprayer instead of a brush to save time.

STAIN

- A sealer or stain prolongs the life of the wood.
- Stain gives a natural look. Clear-stained wood ages the same color as untreated wood.
- A stain can make one wood look like another.
- Stain is thinner than paint. Apply stain liberally so the wood can soak it up.
- Brushes work better than sprayers.

VINYL-COATED

Some metal fences are available coated in vinyl.

- Vinyl-coated fences are virtually maintenance-free unless there is physical damage that breaks the vinyl coating.
- If the coating breaks, apply touch-up paint (a small jar is usually included with the fence).
- These fences are usually available in black, white, or green.

How to build a fence

MATERIALS

Stakes and string
Batterboards
Shovel
Gravel
8-foot 2×2 stakes
6-foot 4×4 posts
Concrete
Broom handle
8-foot 2×4 rails
Galvanized joist
  hangers and wood
  screws
Pickets

STEP 1 Lay out the fence. Know exactly where the fence will be before you

▼ A picket fence is easy to build and customize. This project allows you to choose the picket style.

start digging, cutting, or buying materials. Survey where you want the fence to go and lay out the length. Note any tree roots, drastic slope changes, underground utilities, or anything else that may cause problems.

The two most critical steps in the entire process are positioning the posts and creating right angles. Plan on a maximum span of 8 feet between posts—any longer and the rails may sag. Most lumber comes in 8-foot units. If the total length of a fence section is not evenly divisible by 8, make all the sections 8 feet long and finish with a shorter

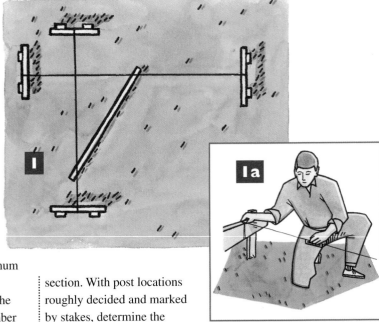

section. With post locations roughly decided and marked by stakes, determine the lumber, hardware, and other supplies needed for rails and pickets.

To make right angles, use the 3-4-5 triangle principle

shown in Drawing 1. Mark a point 3 feet along one string and 4 feet along the other. When the distance between

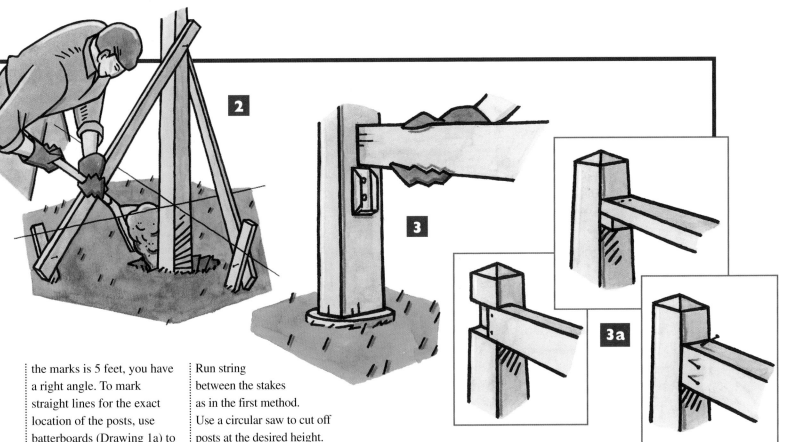

the marks is 5 feet, you have a right angle. To mark straight lines for the exact location of the posts, use batterboards (Drawing 1a) to hold guide lines in place.

STEP 2 Set the posts.

For each 6-foot post, dig a hole at least 30 inches deep. Add a few inches of gravel. Set the post in place. There are two methods for adjusting the posts to their proper height. Following the first method, hammer an 8-foot 2×2 stake in the ground at both ends of the fence line. Run a string between the stakes at the desired post height. Lift each post slightly and add gravel until the top of the post is flush with the line.

The other method uses 8-foot posts instead of 6-foot ones. Set them firmly in place.

Run string between the stakes as in the first method. Use a circular saw to cut off posts at the desired height.

Once the posts are in place, brace them as shown in Drawing 2. To make sure the posts are square with the line of the fence, set the two end posts first. Wrap string around one end post, pull it taut, then wrap it around the other end post. The face of all other posts should be flush with the line.

Fill each hole with concrete. Tamp it with a broom handle to remove any air pockets. Mound the concrete above the soil line so that water will drain away from the post. Let the concrete set at least 24 hours before you move on to the next step. Otherwise, you could easily bump the posts out of place.

STEP 3 Hang the rails.

The rails are the horizontal pieces that the pickets attach to. The easiest way to attach rails is to use galvanized joist hangers as shown in Drawing 3. Make a mark about a foot above the ground on one end post. Run a string to the other end post. Use a line level and adjust the string until it is level. Notice how far the bottom of the rail is from the ground. If needed, raise or lower the string an inch or two.

Center the first joist hanger on the inside of one of the end posts so that the bottom of the rail meets the line you have established. Fasten the hanger

in place using galvanized screws; predrilling makes this a lot easier. Repeat the process for the upper rail, the top of which should be about a foot below the top of the post.

The way the rails are attached affects the final look of the fence. Drawing 3a offers some alternative methods for hanging rails. Use a saw to make a dado joint—cut away part of the post so the rail is flush with the post (3a left). A block joint has the rail resting on a piece of 2×2 toenailed to the post (3a center). Or, you can use 6d nails to toenail the rail to the post (3a right).

How to build a fence (continued)

STEP 4 Attach the pickets. Picket styles are limited only by your imagination. Choose pickets that will make an appropriate visual statement. Consider whether that statement is consistent with both the theme of your landscape and the architecture of your home.

You can purchase precut pickets at a local home center. The average picket is 1×3 inches and 40 inches high.

Although it is a little more time-consuming, designing and making your own pickets saves money and can result in a unique fence. Use a jigsaw or other saw to make your own pickets from 1×2s, 1×3s, or 1×4s.

Once you decide on the right picket, you need to determine the spacing between pickets. This is usually equal to or slightly less than the width of the

picket itself. You can use any spacing you choose, but check local ordinances for specific guidelines if the fence will enclose a swimming pool.

A good way to decide on the spacing of your pickets is to lay two posts 8 feet apart on a flat surface, such as a driveway, then set two 2×4s on the posts where the railings will be. Play with the spacing of the pickets until you get a look that you like. As you

experiment with spacing, try staggering the height of the pickets so that every other picket, or every third picket, is longer than the ones beside it. As you do this, keep in mind the distance between posts; if necessary, adjust the spacing to avoid having a picket at the end of the rail that looks too close or too far from the post.

Before attaching pickets, make a spacer—a guide to keep all of the

◀ **Use a spacer to keep pickets even, and predrill holes before attaching the pickets.**

▼ **Wait until all pickets in a section of fence are up before setting the screws in all the way.**

4a

4b

pickets vertical and an equal distance apart (Drawing 4a). To make a spacer, cut a 1×2 or 1×4 to the desired width between pickets. Cut the spacer a little shorter than the pickets. Plan to place the first and last pickets exactly one spacer width from the post.

To attach the pickets, run a string between the posts at the desired height of the top of

◀ **Finials are crowning pieces attached to the top of fence posts. You can use traditional styles such as those pictured at far left, or be creative and use styles such as those shown in the photo near left.**

the pickets. Pull the string as taut as you can and use a line level to be sure it is level. If you are staggering the picket heights, run a separate line for each height. Butt the spacer flush against one of the end posts, then butt the first picket against the spacer. With each picket, check that everything is vertical and that the top of the picket is just touching the string.

Attach the picket with galvanized wood screws long enough to go through the picket and halfway into the rail. Drill two screws into each rail for a total of two screws per picket (Drawing 4b). Repeat the process for each picket. Frequently check to be sure that the string you are using for a height guide is still taut and level. Verify that the spacer and picket are vertical before you attach the picket. Avoid putting the screws in all the way until all of the pickets in a section are in place. Stand back and make sure you are happy with the look, then sink the screws in all the way.

STEP 5 Add the finishing touches.
If you are going to paint or stain the entire fence, it is best to add the post caps

◀ **A coat of white paint is the finishing touch to a traditional picket fence. Repainting it every few years will keep it fresh-looking.**

▶ **Be creative. Mix and match pickets. The photo (right) and drawings (below) show a range of shapes and styles.**

or finials before painting. If the finials are not going to be painted, or if you are using copper post caps, add them after you paint the fence.

Finials come in a wide range of styles, as shown in the photos on page 122. You can find finials at most home centers and in many mail-order garden catalogs. In addition to adding flair to the fence, finials prolong the life of the post by keeping out moisture.

Most finials screw into the top of the post. Make sure that the finial is centered. Drill a guide hole half the length of the screw into the top of the post, then screw in the finial. Even if you choose not to use a finial, you need a post cap of some sort.

Post caps come in a wide range of materials—from copper to galvanized metal to plastic. You can purchase them at the same places that sell finials. Post caps usually snap onto the top of the post; some are held in place by small screws that go into the side of the post.

You can design and make your own post caps by experimenting with various sizes and shapes cut from 1×4s or 1×6s. Or, in lieu of caps, try cutting angled pieces off the post tops.

Picket styles

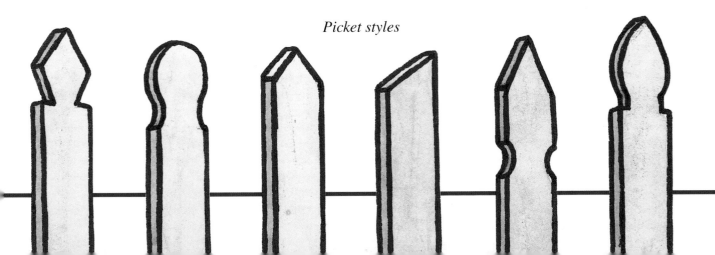

GATES AND HARDWARE

The entrance is the first impression many visitors have of a garden. Often the entrance is marked by a gate. The gate you choose, where it is placed, and the experience people have as they pass through it combine to make a first look at the yard and garden you have created. You may feel like breaking the mold, splurging, and investing in an imposing structure. If you do, be sure that other parts of the garden live up to the promise of its entrance.

Gate styles

There are as many choices of gate styles as gardens and gardeners. A glance at the ones shown on this page demonstrates just that. When it comes to gates, there are two schools of thought: Make it match or make it stand out.

The match-and-blend approach works well to tie the components of fences, gates, and walls together with the rest of the garden. It is the most suitable approach for those with conservative taste. The design clues for making the gate are found in the immediate surroundings. The fence photographs below left and below middle are good examples.

The opposite ideal is to make the gate stand out. The photos bottom right and above right are examples of fences that take on a sculptural quality. In the middle photo above, the gate is set in the middle of a hedge, making a contrast of color, texture, and design.

Gate locations

Clearly mark the gate location by placing it in a logical spot along the fence. This will make it easy for a guest to locate the gate in order to enter your garden. You went to a lot of trouble to get the style right, so why not call attention to it?

Make an exception to this rule when there is a utility area that needs to be accessed for service and is not a typical route for visitors to take into the yard or garden. In that case, design a gate that matches the rest of the fence and blends in.

The view you experience as you walk through the gate should be a determining factor in its location. Test the view by standing at the spot where you think you want the gate. Do you like what you see? Does it create a good impression and capture the theme of your garden? If so, that is the ideal location. If not, move a few feet along the fence until you find the appropriate spot.

Add vertical interest to the gate with an arbor or other structure over the top of the gate. It clearly marks the place you want people to enter and it frames the view.

Add to the appeal of an arbor or other vertical structure by planting annual or perennial vines, roses, or other climbing plants that will grow up and over it.

Gate hardware

Just as a clearly marked, handsome gate with a glorious view makes a good first impression, a sagging, sticking, squeaking, or rickety

gate also makes a statement about the garden and gardener.

Although a rustic look is appealing—and rusted metal is a current trend for garden objects—in most situations, galvanized metal hardware is preferable; otherwise, rust will stain the wood. If you splurge for wrought-iron hardware, it needs to be kept painted.

Strength is important. Some gates weigh more than 100 pounds—a lot of weight to hold on one side and have it swing freely. When in doubt about the holding capacity of a hinge, add more hinges.

Consider form too. Visualize the shape of the handles on a favorite piece of furniture or your kitchen cabinets and you'll know how important their form is. Adding a $20 handle to a $10 gate can elevate its stature significantly.

A good place to shop for garden hardware is at an antiques store. Other sources are estate or farm sales. Check the barn and other outbuildings. If you are willing to remove the hardware yourself and soak it in paint thinner or turpentine for a week, you might find just what you need.

Faux hardware

If you don't want to spend the money on antique hardware or can't find it, apply an antique finish to standard galvanized hardware.

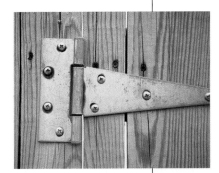

▶ **Galvanized -** Galvanized steel makes up in endurance what it may lack in looks. It is readily available and affordable.

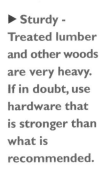

▶ **Sturdy -** Treated lumber and other woods are very heavy. If in doubt, use hardware that is stronger than what is recommended.

▶ **Faux finish -** If you find a sturdy but homely fixture, paint it to look like cast iron, or add a verdigris finish similar to old brass.

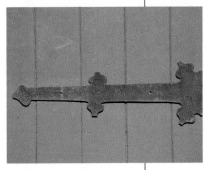

▶ **Ornate -** Dress up an otherwise plain gate or door with ornate hardware, as long as it is strong enough.

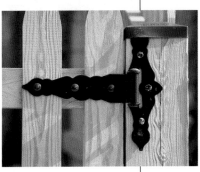

SCREENS AND BAFFLES

ometimes you don't need the full protection of a fence or wall. A screen or baffle may be all that is required to stop the eye and create a sense of protective enclosure.

These structures are usually free-standing single panels. They can be solid or open, depending upon whether or not you need to completely screen a view.

Screens can be used where a solid fence or wall might make you feel restricted, or when you are trying to achieve an open effect.

▼ What appears to be a fence panel is a free-standing screen used to create a sense of privacy.

right) are examples of constructed open screens. Although both of these are freestanding, screens can also be attached to a wall or other structure for stability. You can add charm by training vines to climb up the screen. A sparsely planted hedge at its base can provide the same effect.

Open screens

Create an open screen to allow breezes and sunshine through, while at the same time creating a sense of privacy. The two settings (left and above

Solid screens

A solid screen is more appropriate than an open screen when you want total privacy or need to completely block a view.

Think of a solid screen as a short fence. You can use the same principles discussed in the section on fences to determine the style of screen that is best in your garden. Anchoring endposts in poured concrete will be required in all but the most protected of places; otherwise a solid screen will be at the mercy of strong winds.

You may want to add some relief to a

▲ Almost completely covered with a vine, this screen is barely visible. This treatment is an ideal alternative to a solid plane looming over a garden setting.

solid screen by hanging art on it, such as a plaque or frieze.

Or you can install a wall fountain that will add the calming sound of trickling, playfully splashing water.

You can also view a screen as a blank canvas on which to paint a mural. Or you can train vines on it, provided there is enough light for the plants.

HOW TO TRAIN A VINE

Large, unbroken planes, such as those created by walls, solid fences, and other structures, beg for relief. One of the most appealing forms of relief is a vine (or vines) trained on the structure.

Training vines successfully means first choosing the right vine. The list on pages 364 and

365 will help.

You need to give the vine something to hang onto. You can hang chicken wire on L-brackets and let the vine climb up it. Or you can sink screws partway into the structure, stretch green nylon-coated wire

between the screws to create a pattern, and use twine to tie the vine to the wire.

MATERIALS

Two 12-foot 4×4 posts
One 4-foot 2×4
One 55-inch 2×4
Six 8-foot 1×2s
One 4×8-foot lattice panel
Two 3-inch metal braces
3-inch galvanized woodscrews
2 bags concrete mix

STEP 1 Assemble materials and prepare the frame.

This screen is about 8 feet tall and 4 feet wide and uses 4×4 posts for supports. You can make the screen any height you wish, but set at least 3 feet of the posts into the ground to make this project extra stable.

The size is variable, but for ease of building, this screen is designed to accommodate a prefabricated 4×8-foot panel of lattice.

Cut all the pieces to length. To make sure everything fits, lay the pieces of the frame on a solid surface before you assemble them.

STEP 2 Build the channels from the 1×2s.

Screw a pair of 8-foot 1×2s to each post, positioning each of the 1×2s flush with the outside edge of the post to create a

½-inch channel between them to accommodate the lattice. Keep one end of each channel flush with the top of the post. Cut the remaining two 1×2s into four pieces, each 46½ inches long. Position and attach these pieces in pairs to the two 2×4s, creating channels just like those on the sides of the posts. Pay close attention to spacing. On the 55-inch 2x4, mount the 1×2s 4½ inches in from each end of the 2×4. For the 4-foot 2×4, leave only ¾ inch of space at each end.

STEP 3 Set the posts.

Be sure that the channels are facing each other. Hold the posts exactly 4 feet apart by temporarily nailing scrap 1×4s to the posts at the top and bottom. Then plumb the posts and stake them in place.

STEP 4 Assemble the screen.

Secure the bottom 2×4 with metal braces. Next, have a friend help lift the lattice and slide it into place. Cap the screen with the 55-inch 2×4 and secure with more of the wood screws. Remove the scrap 1×4s, check for plumb again, and add the concrete. Allow it to set 24 hours.

WALLS

alls project a sense of permanence. This is for good reason. If built properly, they should last a lifetime or longer. Masonry walls have a visual weight stronger than most fences. Walls also help tie a garden to the architecture of the home.

As a general rule, a wall serves the same purpose as a fence. It provides privacy and security, and defines spaces. And it creates a mood in the garden.

There are three main ways to categorize walls: type, size, and material. Because of the expense and scale of this kind of project, be sure to think everything through before starting.

▼ **A brick wall surrounding a brick terrace ties together many different garden elements.**

Wall types

Your choice of wall type will be based on a combination of use, home and garden style, and budget.

Stone walls add a rustic feeling to the garden and are easier to construct than other masonry walls. The availability of stone will affect the cost.

Wall size and shape

Wall size and shape vary based primarily upon use. Security and privacy walls need to be 6 to 8 feet tall. A wall this size requires substantial footings and takes up a lot of space.

If you're building such a wall for security reasons, consider using a lattice-style brick design, which leaves open spaces for light and air to move through. You can do this only when using brick or cinder block because stone and poured concrete do not readily lend themselves to this. You can add strength to this type of wall by giving it a serpentine or undulating shape. This adds tremendous visual interest as well.

A large, solid expanse can be a little daunting, so

▲ **Capping a long or large wall with contrasting material is an attractive way to seal the wall.**

consider painting a mural on the wall, adding a window with shutters, or creating a mosaic. A wall also lends itself to having a tree, shrub, or vine espaliered to it or a vine growing up and over it.

◄ **Make use of a wall. Do some vertical gardening, such as training a climbing vine up and over the wall.**

▲ The formality of this stained stucco wall is accentuated by the symmetrical placement of plaster plaques on either side of the lamp.

◄ The height of this wall is extended, while the visual impact is lessened, by a hedge growing inside a planter built into the top of the wall.

This is best done by planting on the sunny side of the wall and having the plants drape over the top.

Another idea is to add a planter to the top of the wall. This is easy if you plan for it from the beginning, although most walls can be retrofitted to accommodate a planter. As with any container garden, a wall planter has specific and regular maintenance needs. The idea is most practical with a drip irrigation system. You will need to be able to easily and safely tend to the plants.

When it comes to large walls, the best bet is to work with a professional. There is nothing particularly hard about building a large wall, but errors could be costly.

This is especially true in areas where the frost depth exceeds a foot. In Zones 5 and below, foundation footings may need to be as deep as 4 feet, which involves moving a lot of dirt and mixing a lot of concrete.

Perhaps you need only a short wall to help guide people through the garden and keep them out of certain areas. Short walls are easier for the average homeowner to build.

There are also wall building systems, which are modular blocks designed to interlock. Most do not require mortar to hold them in place, so they can shift and heave as temperatures change and do not have the footing requirements of a wall set in mortar. As long as modular walls do not exceed 4 feet in height, they can be built by the average homeowner. Taller walls can sway, and a poorly built wall can topple.

Let the wall breathe

When building a solid wall, consider a cutout for air and light to pass through. It can even be used to frame a view. Shutters on the opening could be closed as needed.

Wall Materials

Two materials are most commonly used to build walls: stone and masonry. Masonry includes preformed materials such as brick, cinder block, and modular wall components. The choice of which to use is determined by cost and appropriate style.

Stone walls

Stone walls can be works of art. They instantly convey the look of an established garden. After all, stone is one of the oldest, if not the original, material used for building walls. Enhance the time-worn appearance of a stone wall with a covering of moss.

When considering a stone wall, it is important to know what materials are available locally. This is helpful in choosing a style that fits your setting. It also helps in reducing the cost of the wall. Stone is heavy and expensive to ship, so using local materials will usually cost less.

Most tall stone walls (more than 3 to 4 feet) are held in place by mortar and rest on a concrete footing just like a masonry wall. This is true whether the wall is made of solid rock or it is masonry faced with stone.

Large solid stone walls require a great amount of experience and time to create. They may best be left to experienced craftsman. But if you want to build one yourself, consider making a smaller wall or building a cinder block wall, then facing it with stone. This method of construction is easier and more economical, and it requires less stone.

To build such a wall, you must first prepare a footing. Check local building codes to determine the depth and width this needs to be. A footing typically begins as a trench dug to the proper depth and twice the width of the finished wall, followed by wood forms which are then filled with concrete.

Build the wall to the desired height, laying $\frac{1}{2}$ inch of mortar between each course of block. Place metal straps (called ties) about every 12 inches along the wall; they should protrude 4 to 6 inches on either side of the cinder block. These give the stone, and the mortar used to face the wall, something to hold onto.

Once the cinder block wall is built, start attaching the stone, using liberal amounts of mortar between the wall and stone and at least $\frac{1}{2}$ inch of mortar between stones.

▼ **Stone walls lend a natural look to the garden without sacrificing sophistication, as this elegant, well-laid wall illustrates.**

Masonry walls

Masonry walls, whether brick, cinder block, or modular block, are relatively easy to build once you have a good footing in place. With a level footing, it's just a matter of laying level courses.

Use sheets of fiberglass or metal mesh between courses to add additional strength.

Maintenance

You may need to remove discoloration or repair loose mortar. Efflorescence is the term for the powdery white mineral deposits that occurs on brick. To remove it, wet the wall thoroughly with a strong blast from a garden hose, then use a stiff-bristled brush to scrub the deposits off. (A wire brush will scrape the brick.) Remove recurring deposits by scrubbing with a mixture of 1 part muriatic acid to 12 parts water.

To repair mortar joints in stone or masonry, first remove all loose or damaged mortar with a chisel and hand sledge. Remove no more mortar than necessary. Go easy with the sledge to avoid further damage. Use a metal bar or mortar hook to scrape out old mortar and create a clean surface. Flush with a hose. Mix a batch of firm mortar and use it to pack the joints. Scrape away excess mortar so each joint is the same depth as the surrounding joints.

TIPS ON WALL MATERIALS

BRICK

- Brick is a common material for walls.
- It is readily available and uniform in size.
- A wide range of patterns can be created with brick.
- Brick walls are long-lasting—limited only by the craftsmanship of construction and the weathering of the mortar that holds it together.
- Brick is fairly costly.
- A tall wall takes skill to build properly.

CONCRETE

- Concrete is perhaps the most versatile material for wall building.
- It can be poured into prefabricated forms.
- An effective use of concrete block is to build a plain wall, then face it with stone or brick.
- Concrete block can be covered with stucco—plaster that can be textured and stained before it is applied or painted after it dries.

STONE

- Stone is the most natural-looking material for a wall.
- Sometimes you can find the material in or near your garden.
- It adds permanence and structure without being imposing.
- With a little practice, it is easy to use.
- Stones of different sizes are necessary because building a stone wall is like working a jigsaw puzzle.

COMBOS

- Sometimes enough of one material is not affordable or available.
- Combining materials can result in a unique structure.
- A combination of materials can unify various elements of the garden.
- A combination wall can utilize materials you might not have considered, such as bottles or odd-shaped pieces of metal.

Dry Stack Walls

Of the many different styles of walls you can add to the garden, none is easier or more charming than a dry stack stone wall. This type of wall does not use mortar; its stability comes from carefully stacking stones, and by gradually inching the wall inward so the top is narrower than the base. This kind of wall is usually not more than 3 feet tall, although you can make it taller, if you wish, provided the base is wide enough and city ordinances permit it. The 3-foot-tall wall (below) has a base that is 24 inches wide.

Once you know where you want to build your wall and how high it will be, assemble the materials needed and begin. Talk with the person supplying your stone to determine the quantity of stone you will need. Know the dimensions of your planned wall so it can be estimated as closely as possible.

Whether purchasing the stone or gathering it yourself, get a little more than you think you'll need, because you will use a wide range of sizes and shapes to make everything fit.

Have the stone delivered and set as close as possible to where the wall will be built, then start sorting it. Make six to eight piles of stones, each made up of stones of similar size and shape. Create a separate pile of flat stones that you can use for the top course. Sorting may seem like a lot of work now, but it will save you time once you start building.

How to build a dry stack wall

MATERIALS
Measuring tape
String and stakes
Spray paint (or sand)
Shovel
Gravel
Stone
Level
Rubber mallet

STEP 1 **Make a foundation.** A well-built wall rests on a carefully prepared foundation. To determine the center line for your wall, use the techniques described on page 120 for laying out a fence and making

▶ **This stone wall is not as hard to build as it looks. Allow plenty of time and plenty of stone, or hire it done professionally.**

right angles. Measuring from the centerline, use string and stakes to mark the outside line of each side of the base of the wall. Plan on a 2-foot-wide base for every 3 feet of height.

Use spray paint or sand to mark the borders of the base. Dig a trench 8 inches deep. A 4-inch layer of gravel in the trench supports the stone and provides adequate drainage.

STEP 2 Lay the base course. Anchor each end of the trench with a stone large enough to span the trench. Use a similar-sized stone to span the trench every 4 feet. Lay the beginning course of the front row of stones, then follow with the first course of the rear face of the wall in the same manner. Fill the space between with small stones, large gravel, or rubble.

STEP 3 Keep adding layers. To start the second course, place another large stone (about the same size as those used on the base) perpendicular to the large stone beneath it at each end of the wall. Continue placing medium-sized stones. Every 4 feet use a large stone that spans the width of the wall. Inch the wall inward, making it narrower as it goes up. The top should be about 2 inches narrower than the base for each vertical foot of wall. A 3-foot-high wall will have a 24-inch-wide base course and an 18-inch-wide top course.

As you build, frequently check to see that everything is level. Use a mallet to tamp stones into place; it is next to impossible to straighten a stone wall once it is built.

Plug vertical gaps between stones with small chunks of stone; tap them in place with the mallet.

Finish the wall with a layer of large, flat stones or make the top layer with a different type of stone to create a contrasting line.

Dry stack wall tip

Mix in a few stones of contrasting color or texture to add visual interest to the wall.

HEDGES

Hedges are rivaled only by stone walls as the oldest method of defining garden spaces. In addition to their historical precedent and pedigree, hedges provide privacy, control traffic, and direct the eye to and from views.

The fact that hedges are living structures gives them a special place in the world of gardening. Nothing else (short of topiaries) is trimmed and shaped into geometric forms. But not all hedges are pruned or otherwise forced into certain configurations. Sometimes they are left to their natural shape. Unlike a wall or fence, a hedge can bloom into a wall of color, offer rich autumn hues, or be a deep green all year long.

Uses for hedges

Privacy and security Hedges are ideal for creating privacy, but they have shortcomings when it comes to security. It is all but impossible to make a planting impassable to people or other animals. Thorny plants such as barberry, Burford holly, and shrub roses will discourage entry but not prevent it.

The amount of privacy provided by your hedge varies with the type of plant and spacing you use. Deciduous plants serve as organic shutters, blocking views and creating shade during the summer months when garden activity is at its peak, and allowing light in during winter months when outdoor areas are used less. Evergreen plants offer privacy all year long and are better suited for screening views into a house.

If you are planting a hedge for screening, consider the seasons you need screening and choose plants accordingly. Before planting a hedge of Lombardy poplars—which will grow to a height of more than 30 feet—for privacy in the front yard, check local ordinances. In some cases, the same height restrictions that apply to walls and fences will also apply to hedges.

As you choose plants for a hedge, think about their ultimate height, and weigh that against the maintenance that goes along with the plants. You may not want to teeter on a stepladder 8 feet above the ground to trim a hedge, which may be necessary depending on

▲ Growing hedges for the sheer fun of it is as good a reason as any. Before taking on a project like this, consider the time required.

▶ This tall, full evergreen hedge serves all the functions of a solid wall, but it has a much softer visual texture.

◀ A medium-height hedge forms a wall for an outdoor area around a pool. Although short, it provides a sense of enclosure when people are seated.

▲ Use a low hedge to outline a garden bed. Such a hedge can even take the place of edging.

▲ Marking a path with a low-growing hedge is an effective means of traffic control. The topiary rabbit is optional.

the plants you choose. As a starting point, review the list of hedge plants on page 139.

Hedges that control Use a low hedge to border a path and accentuate the lines of your garden while keeping people within desired boundaries. A hedge is a friendly way to mark property lines, separate yourself from your neighbors, or provide a buffer between your yard and the street. Hedges also create outdoor rooms. There is a softness to a living wall that can make a space feel friendly.

Using your site analysis as a guide, plant hedges to block harsh winter winds or channel cool breezes in the summertime. If you use hedges to block winter winds or snow, plant them within 30 feet of the house. Any farther away

and the winds will blow up and over them. Use evergreens at least 4 feet thick for wind control.

Hedges that define When most people think of a hedge, they have an image of a perfectly manicured row of plants. Knot gardens, labyrinths, and parterres are all created from hedges. These features may be different sizes and styles, but "hedges" defines them all. No other type of planting (other than topiary) can compare when it comes to showing dominion over the garden. Keep in mind the labor involved in maintaining a tightly trimmed hedge.

If this type of planting appeals to you, familiarize yourself with the planting options available in your area.

Know before you grow

Some localities have strict guidelines regarding the size and placement of any structure. In some cases, this includes dense plantings such as hedges.

Hedge Styles

▲ **A hedge offers a neighborly passage that connects two backyards. Just as when building fences, remember that there is someone living on the other side.**

Choosing a style of hedge for your garden depends upon what you want the hedge to accomplish and how much maintenance you are willing to do.

There are two basic hedge styles—informal and formal. As you ponder the right style for you and your garden, keep in mind that rules are made to be broken.

Formal hedges

A formal hedge uses one type of plant. It is designed with a specific size and shape in mind. Great effort is made to mold the planting to that shape, and even more effort is required to keep it there.

Formal hedges hold a unique spot in the garden world. They are elegant and stately. From a design standpoint, they can take the place of a built structure in a way nothing else can. A formal hedge takes on a form similar to what would normally be built of masonry or wood.

Formal hedges are best suited to gardens that have a definite order. An exception is a formal hedge used to form a border within which you allow plants to grow randomly, such as a cottage garden that uses hedges instead of a fence to define the borders.

Besides being composed of just one type of plant, formal hedges also have more rigid planting patterns and designs. Well-manicured plants are best complemented by right angles and straight lines. When laying out a formal hedge you may need to refer to page 88 or 120 for information on how to create perfect angles and lines.

When choosing patterns for laying out a formal hedge, refer to the tips on pages 236–239 for knot gardens and labyrinths. A good source for patterns for a knot garden is quilting books.

◀ **A formal stand of cypress provides total privacy for a seating area and serves as a contrast to the flower beds planted in front.**

▲ An evenly spaced planting of red-leaved Japanese barberry has an informal effect when it is left to grow in a looser form instead of being sheared into a specific shape. It also requires a lot less maintenance.

Informal hedges

An informal hedge is planted in a loose pattern and the plants are usually allowed to grow in their natural form. You can plant a hedge in a straight line or a formal pattern, then refrain from all but rudimentary pruning. More typically, an informal hedge is a type of planting that serves any of the usual purposes of a hedge but is not planted in a straight line or a definite pattern. The result is more about style than about function.

▶ As a variation on the traditional hedge, make a fence using twigs screwed or strapped to a simple wooden frame, then grow vines or other climbing plants on it.

You can create complete privacy by planting a staggered row of shrubs just as easily as you could a straight row. This is particularly useful if your garden has a natural, informal design. It is also a good way to handle the transition from the more well-tended areas of your garden to woods or natural areas that may abut your property.

Informal hedges offer the opportunity to use mixed plantings. You could select several different species or cultivars and repeat them either in a pattern or randomly along the length of the hedge.

If the plants don't need to be sheared into shape, you have a greater range of plants from which to select. An important advantage of an informal hedge is that it requires less maintenance than a formal hedge. Informal hedges still need pruning, but there will less of it. If you stagger your plantings, you will need 10 to 20 percent more plants than if they were set in a straight row.

Another approach is to create the appearance of an informal hedge by training vines to a framework (below).

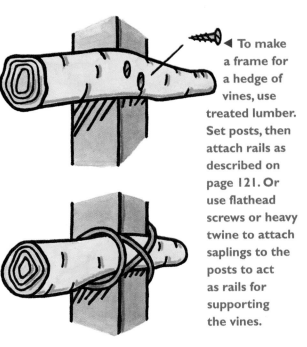

◀ To make a frame for a hedge of vines, use treated lumber. Set posts, then attach rails as described on page 121. Or use flathead screws or heavy twine to attach saplings to the posts to act as rails for supporting the vines.

Hedge Planting and Maintenance

The relative ease or effort of maintaining a hedge depends upon several factors. These include the intended use and style of the hedge, the plants you select, how you plant them, how the plants perform in your area, and the level of maintenance you choose to perform.

These factors are interwoven and should be considered together before you plant a hedge. Consider the look you want and the maintenance you can or are willing to provide.

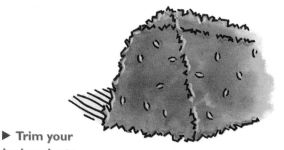

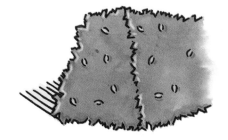

► Trim your hedge plants wider on the bottom so that the lower portion of the hedge is not shaded from the sun.

◄ For ease in pruning and keeping a hedge level, set stakes at each end of the hedge and run a pruning guide along and through the hedge. A pruning guide is a taut strand of twine that marks the desired line of pruning. The length and shape of the hedge may require several guides.

Remember, a formal sheared hedge requires more effort. An informal hedge will require pruning, but it may be as seldom as once a year.

Planting a hedge

Equally important as the style of hedge is how you set the plants. Formal hedges require plants laid out in a single straight row. Mark the centerline of where the mature hedge will be. Dig a trench as deep and twice as wide as the root ball of the plants. Know the mature size of the plants and space them with a 25 percent overlap. Set the plants in place and backfill the trench.

If you are planting an informal hedge, stagger the plants so they are not in a straight line. Use the same method described for a formal hedge to determine spacing.

Hedge maintenance

Taking care of a hedge can be as hard or as easy as you want it to be. It depends a lot on decisions made before you pull out the pruners.

In regard to hedge maintenance, there are the standard issues of care and culture, such as weeding, feeding, and watering. Maintenance is perhaps more important with a hedge than other parts of a garden. Keep hedge plants healthy for the best results. Replacing a single shrub as part of a mixed bed and have the garden still be in balance is a lot easier to do than to lose one plant in a row of many identical shrubs and have to find a replacement that matches.

The keys to successful hedge pruning are knowing the shape you want and using pruning guides to achieve it. The illustration at left shows some formal hedge shapes; the illustration above shows how to use a pruning guide to make this task a little easier.

Hedge Plants

The best shrubs for use as a hedge planting share some characteristics. They are usually dense and compact, forming a solid mass. They are relatively slow-growing, so they don't need frequent pruning. Their foliage is easy to shear. Other desirable characteristics are color, texture, or fragrance that will enhance the area.

The plants listed fit most or all of these criteria. To find the perfect plant for your garden, check some of the websites that allow you to enter a range of criteria and provide you with a list of suitable plants (see resources on page 386). Or visit your local botanical garden and take a firsthand look.

(C = clipped)

Small

Trees and shrubs less than 4 feet tall

EVERGREEN
- Azaleas (some varieties) *Rhododendron* spp.
- Common boxwood *Buxus sempervirens*
- Indian hawthorn *Rhaphiolepis indica*
- Convex holly (C) *Ilex crenata* 'Convexa'
- Korean boxwood *Buxus microphylla koreana* 'Winter Gem'
- English yew (C) *Taxus baccata* 'Repandens'
- Pfitzer juniper (C) *Juniperus x media* 'Pfitzeriana'
- Wall germander *Teucrium chamaedrys*

DECIDUOUS
- Dwarf burning bush *Euonymus alata* 'Compactus'
- Cotoneaster *Cotoneaster* spp.
- Japanese barberry *Berberis thunbergii*
- Japanese quince *Chaenomeles japonica*
- Redleaved barberry *Berberis thunbergii* 'Atropurpurea'
- Shrub roses *Rosa* spp.

Medium

Trees and shrubs 4 to 8 feet tall

EVERGREEN
- American arborvitae (C) *Thuja occidentalis*
- Bay (C) *Laurus nobilis*
- Canadian hemlock (C) *Tsuga canadensis*
- Eugenia *Eugenia* spp.
- Mugo pine *Pinus mugo*
- False cypress (C) *Chamaecyparis pisifera* 'Plumosa'

DECIDUOUS
- American hophornbeam (C) *Ostrya virginiana*
- European beech (C) *Fagus sylvatica*
- European hornbeam (C) *Carpinus betulus*
- Privet *Ligustrum* spp.
- Siberian peashrub *Caragana arborescens*
- Washington hawthorn (C) *Crataegus phaenopyrum*

Large

Trees and shrubs more than 8 feet tall

EVERGREEN
- Douglas fir *Pseudotsuga menziesii*
- Eastern white pine (C) *Pinus strobus*
- Japanese black pine *Pinus thunbergii*
- Japanese pittosporum (C) *Pittosporum tobira*
- Scotch pine *Pinus sylvestris*
- White spruce *Picea glauca*

DECIDUOUS
- English hawthorn (C) *Crataegus laevigata*
- Laurel willow *Salix pentandra*
- Littleleaf linden (C) *Tilia cordata*

English yew

Arborvitae

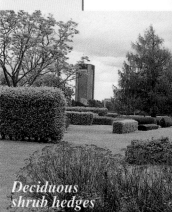

Deciduous shrub hedges

CHAPTER 6

OUTDOOR ROOMS

Organize your outdoor space

TERRACES AND PATIOS

Areas for outdoor enjoyment take on many forms. One of the most popular is the patio or terrace. There are more similarities than differences between the two; proximity to the house is the main distinction. Both features are defined by level areas with a firm surface that is usually paved. As a general rule, a terrace adjoins the house, whereas a patio may or may not be connected to the house.

No matter what you call them, these features, along with decks, are the workhorses of outdoor entertaining. For the sake of simplicity, both terraces and patios will be referred to as patios throughout this chapter.

Siting a patio

The success of a patio depends on its location. Its siting affects how much it is used and influences how well it serves the intended purpose.

If the patio is for outdoor dining, having it close to the house—and kitchen—increases the likelihood of its being used. A remotely located patio makes a great area for outdoor dining, but be realistic about how you respond to "out of sight, out of mind" situations. You may end up not using a remote patio as often as you had planned.

Another factor to consider when siting the patio is microclimate. A spot that is convenient to the kitchen may have too much or too little sun or an unpleasant view. Wind, sound, and privacy should also be considered. You may be able to screen the unattractive views, add shade, or remove limbs to bring sunlight into the area. Or, you may need to find another location for the patio. A master plan will help in dealing with these situations.

▲ **When designing a patio, choose a style and materials that fit the surroundings, as does this curvilinear patio made of tile.**

When building the patio, consider the proximity of large trees that may suffer root damage or damage the patios themselves. Even shallow roots can damage a patio in time. Also consider accessibility to utilities such as electricity for lighting or water for a fountain.

◄ **Add interest to a patio by using containers filled with colorful plants to define different areas.**

▶ **Outdoor dining areas are more likely to be used when they are located adjacent to the house.**

Give the patio some walls

A sense of enclosure adds to the enjoyment of a patio. Whether the walls are solid or planted, make use of them by hanging a bird feeder or wind chimes from limbs or putting a fountain on a wall.

Have materials blend

Look to the immediate surroundings, as well as the rest of the landscape, for clues on materials you can use to build a patio that ties in with the rest of the garden design.

Give the patio a purpose

A detached patio, as shown here, is more inviting if there is a reason to use it. The reason can be as simple as a table set for two.

◀ **A change in level of just one step creates a sense of separation, even if the patio is close to the house.**

▲ **The canopies of nearby trees provide wanted shade. For further enclosure, add an open arbor.**

▲ **Consider the view from where you will be sitting. If the view is attractive, you might frame it.**

TERRACES AND PATIOS *continued*

Patio styles

The design of a patio should take into account the style of the house and the surrounding garden, and the purpose the patio is to serve.

One of the first considerations is the size of the patio. The information on page 145 will come in handy for determining size in relation to the number of people you expect to be using the patio at any given time.

Another consideration is levelness. A patio should provide a firm, level surface for seating and entertaining. That's one of the big advantages of a patio over a lawn, which can be a difficult base for setting up tables and chairs—especially after a rain when it may be spongy or uneven.

Open and airy As a general rule, a patio is open and exposed; it visually spills into the surrounding areas (above center). To avoid feeling exposed, consider adding a pergola or other overhead structure to give the patio a sense of containment.

Private and secluded A patio is a private outdoor room. As the photo above right

shows, you can create a sense of privacy by using the existing walls of the house or garage. You need not completely enclose the area as you would a courtyard. Instead, consider building a screen or fence to enclose part of the patio, leaving the other sides open. Partial enclosure creates a sense of intimacy, making the patio especially suited to outdoor dining.

Close to home Having a patio close to the house has many advantages. If it is

visible from inside the house, it has a tendency to be used more because you are constantly aware of it. A patio can also serve as a transitional area between the house and the garden.

Change of grade Add interest to a patio by having it slightly elevated or sunken (above left). This is especially appropriate if your garden is relatively level. If you plan on setting the patio below the surrounding grade, you will need to add a catch basin (see page 44) that connects to an underground drain line. A raised patio will drain easily if you build the surface with a slight slope.

Underutilized area Sometimes paving a narrow side yard or other small area can turn an otherwise unused spot into a functional patio. This is especially true of areas that receive little sunlight and might otherwise be difficult spots in which to maintain a lawn or other planting.

STEP 1 **Determine your needs.** Make a list of all the ways you want to use the patio. This list might include an area for reading and relaxing, for an intimate dinner for four, or for a casual gathering of 20 friends. It may be all of the above and more.

As you enumerate the various uses for the patio, indicate which of them are most important to you. Many homeowners have an occasional need for the patio to accommodate large groups, but the vast majority of the time it needs to have enough room for only up to four people. One way to have a larger patio that still feels intimate is to use potted plants to frame part of the space. They can be moved when you need the extra room.

STEP 2 **Determine the type and amount of furniture required.** Once you know how many people you need to accommodate, you can select the furniture. Typically this includes tables, chairs, and benches. Note anything else you want in the space, such as a grill or drink cart.

If you already have or know the type of furniture you will use, measure all the pieces so you can plan the patio exactly. If you don't know what furniture you will have, you can use the general guidelines offered below.

STEP 3 **Figure the amount of space you need.** The size of your patio is a personal decision, but there are some guidelines that may help you determine the right size for your needs.

If all you want is space for two people to sit with a small table in between, you can get by with a patio as small as 10 feet by 10 feet. Keep in mind that a patio this small may look out of place if it is attached to the house.

For an attached patio, start with 10 feet by 20 feet as a minimum. That will provide enough room for four chairs and a small dining table.

As you map out the exact dimensions of the patio, plan for about 3 feet by 3 feet per chair. This allows room for the chair and a comfort zone around it.

The average garden bench requires about 6 feet by 3 feet.

Table sizes vary, but a standard bridge table is 3 feet by 3 feet. This may be too small for dining; the recommended space for a dining table for four people is 4 feet by 4 feet.

Sketch the general shape, size, and location of the patio onto grid paper, with each grid equaling 6 inches. Then cut out pieces of paper to scale to represent chairs, tables, and benches. Move them around on the sketch to make sure you've allowed enough space. Be sure to leave room for people to walk around the furniture.

Patio Amenities

Furniture, lighting, and accents such as a fountain or plants contribute to the overall look, usefulness, and enjoyment of a patio.

Furniture The most common and useful amenity for a patio is furniture. It provides a place to sit, dine, or otherwise enjoy the space, and it helps organize the space. When choosing patio furniture, consider the style and how it matches the surroundings, as well as how comfortable and durable it is. Outdoor furniture that has to be protected or that stains easily when exposed to the elements will probably prove to be more trouble than it is worth. Invest in furniture that will stand up over time without a lot of extra care.

Lighting Add lighting to make the patio useful even after the sun goes down. If the patio is attached to the house, you can mount floodlights on the eaves for full illumination. Consider putting the lights on a rheostat so you can control the brightness. If the patio is not adjacent to the house, consider mounting lights on tree limbs, an arbor, wood posts, or decorative lampposts. For more on lighting, see pages 262–267.

Covering A canopy over the patio provides shade and visually contains the area.

Options include extending a lath or other open structure from the house (if the patio is attached to the house), building a freestanding structure, such as a

▲ **Help the patio blend with the surrounding architecture by repeating materials from the house in any structure added to the patio, such as this arbor.**

pergola, or relying on the limbs of an existing shade tree. It is not necessary to provide a rainproof covering. It is more important to filter the sun and create the illusion of a roof. You might choose to have a canopy over part of the patio with the rest left open. This gives you another good option, because there are times when you want all the sun you can get on the patio.

Planting Just because a patio is paved doesn't mean it has to go without plants. There are several ways to add plants

◀ **If your patio doesn't have a good view, create one with flowering shrubs and a simple structure such as this trellised arbor.**

◄ The soothing sound of water on a patio can drown out unwanted noise.

Be sure that the containers match the style of the patio. For example, a whiskey barrel planter may look out of place on a formal brick patio where classic terra-cotta or dressy, painted wood planters such as Versailles tubs provide a more appropriate look.

Another alternative is to have built-in planting areas on the patio. This is best done when you design and build the patio; leave open spaces to act as in-ground containers that you can plant directly into. This method creates more protection from freezing temperatures and plants need less irrigation than if they are grown in containers. It also allows you to grow low groundcovers that help soften large expanses of paving.

If you include a built-in in-ground planter, it is vital that the planting hole drain adequately and the soil does not become too alkaline as a result of adjoining mortar. Here's how to get the best results: Once the patio is built, including the planting holes, excavate a hole at least 3 feet deep, do a percolation test (see page 43), line the hole with heavy plastic, make several large slits in the bottom of the plastic so water can drain, then fill the hole with good soil.

► Cutouts in the paving of a patio allow you to introduce trees and shrubs to the patio planting plan.

Water features Whether elaborate and built-in or simple and freestanding, water features are desirable amenities for a patio. For more ideas on fountains, see pages 174–179.

Ornaments In the same way you would decorate a room inside the house, use yard art to accent and otherwise decorate your patio. If the patio can be seen readily from inside the house, the use of ornament such as wire spheres, metal obelisks, or topiary frames with or without plants can help link the indoors with the outdoors.

Drainage Proper drainage is essential to a successful patio. This is especially true of a sunken terrace, which can quickly turn into a pond if it doesn't drain properly. A patio flush with or above ground can be drained by building it with a slight pitch that drains water off the patio and away from the house. It is important to plan the drainage before you build the patio.

▲ Details including a bench, built-in pedestal for garden ornaments, and a planter complete this patio.

to a patio setting. The easiest and most versatile way is to use containers. Evergreen shrubs in containers can define areas of a patio, provide privacy and shade, or serve as a windbreak. Smaller pots of perennials, annuals, or bulbs can introduce seasonal color to a patio.

One advantage to using containers is that they are portable, which means you can move the plants around to suit your mood and their needs.

Patio Materials

A wide array of materials is available for surfacing a patio. The material you choose should blend with the surroundings and other materials used in the landscape while providing the right surface for the intended use of the patio.

For an outdoor entertainment area (especially for dining), a solid, level surface, such as brick or cast pavers, is best. Flat stones, such as slate, also create an even surface. Fieldstone, due to its naturally uneven surface, will not be perfectly level.

Loose material, such as pea gravel, is not recommended for dining areas because table legs can settle unevenly into the stone. Crushed granite, however, once it is compacted, forms a surface almost as stable and firm as concrete, and water can percolate through it.

Whereas the surfacing material is largely a matter of taste and cost, the foundation upon which the material rests and how the surface is set in place are key structural considerations. The foundation determines slope of the patio and its levelness.

As described on page 150, excavating a level area and putting in a gravel base topped with sand are essential parts of building any patio, whether poured as a slab of concrete or topped with pavers. Once the base is sloped and smooth, the next step is to decide whether to set the pavers in mortar or on sand.

▲ Sometimes the look you want involves mixing materials, as in this brick-bordered paving with a slate center. This approach is useful if your home is brick, but slate is compatible with the garden.

▲ Concrete is popular, easy to work with and affordable. Dress it up with bands of brick, called headers. Enhance it with stains and stamps, as discussed on page 149.

▲ Brick is a traditional patio surface material. Here, aged brick is used to make a new patio look as though it has been there for years. Bricks and pavers allow variety in patterns such as these graceful arcs.

▲ Large fieldstones are used to create a patio that has a natural, woodland feel. Groundcover planted between the stones softens the area further. Ground covers can be used with any type of paver.

Staining and Painting a Patio

Concrete is one of the most popular and common materials used for patios. There are many finishes and colors available to enhance concrete. Most can be found at home improvement centers and are easy to use.

One way to enhance concrete is to create a texture or pattern on the surface. Although the tools, techniques, and level of difficulty vary slightly, they all use the same basic principle: A mold or stamp is pressed into semihardened concrete to create the desired texture.

Stamps and molds are available to give concrete the look of cobblestones, individual pavers, fieldstone, and slate. It may take a few tries to master the technique, so you will need to practice before doing the real thing.

Another option is to color the concrete. The best way to do this is to purchase a powdered dye that is mixed into the concrete while it is wet. The benefit here is that the color is throughout the concrete; as the surface wears, the freshly exposed concrete will be the same color.

The alternative method is to apply a dye or stain to plain concrete. This is the only option if a patio is already in place. Staining requires cleaning and preparing the surface of the concrete, then applying the dye. You can also use acrylic paint to add a decorative pattern to the patio.

▼ **This six-month-old concrete slab was stained to look weathered.**

How to build a sand-based patio

Building a patio is well within the skill level of the average homeowner. The method shown here is for a square patio, but the process can be used to make any rectilinear shape. This patio is designed for pavers not mortared in place; the options on page 151 offer alternative ways to finish the patio.

MATERIALS

String and stakes
Mattock and shovel
Landscape fabric
2×6s
8d galvanized nails
Expansion-joint material
Gravel
Screed
Sand
Pavers
Broom

STEP 1 **Lay out and prepare the bed.** Rough out the shape and size of the patio, then use the triangulation method shown on page 120 to make right angles with strings intersecting on the inside of each corner of the patio.

As you determine the exact size, you will need to plan for the paver you intend to use, making sure that there will be room for all the pavers in the pattern you want, allowing for a tiny space in between pavers caused by the lack of uniformity from one paver to the next.

Once the patio has been laid out, use a mattock and shovel to dig out an area equal to the size of the patio and about 5½ inches deep. If you are removing turf to make room for a patio, use healthy turf to patch other areas

of the lawn or to create a new area of lawn.

STEP 2 **Cut landscape fabric.** Measure and cut out a piece of landscape fabric large enough to cover the patio. This prevents weeds from working their way up through the gravel. This may require several pieces of fabric, depending on the size of your patio and the size of the roll of fabric.

STEP 3

Establish first corner. Lay out a 2×6 perpendicular to the house and cut the lumber so it ends where you want the edge of the patio to be.

Align the board with the string guides and drive a stake on the outside of it to

hold it in place. Nail the stake to the board.

STEP 4 **Build rest of frame.** Continue to make the frame with the 2×6s, overlapping the corners as shown. Before you nail each board, use the triangulation method to make sure that everything is square. Otherwise, the pavers will not fit evenly.Once the frame is built, set stakes against the outside of the 2×6s every few feet to hold it firmly in place.

STEP 5 Add gravel and level it.

First, place a piece of expansion-joint material between the house and patio area. Then pour in enough gravel to provide a depth of about 1 inch throughout. Make a screed with a short section of 1×4 or other scrap lumber. Starting at the house, scrape the gravel until it is level from side to side and gradually slopes toward the opposite end of the patio.

STEP 6 Prepare a sand bed.

Add a layer of builder's sand on top of the gravel. To calculate the sand depth, subtract the thickness of your pavers from 4½ inches. Make a second screed by notching a long 2×6 to the depth of the pavers, then level the sand. If the top of the frame was set at the appropriate slope, the sand will be at the right slope too.

STEP 7 Add pavers.

Arrange them in the desired pattern, fitting them snugly together to ensure good stability. (This is not the time to change patterns, because if you do, the pavers may not fit.) Run string from one end of the patio to the other to form a guide line. This will help keep the pavers in a straight line. As you move around in the area, keep your knees on the sand, rather than on the newly laid pavers, because the pavers won't be stable until the area is completely filled. It's much easier to re-screed small areas of disturbed sand.

STEP 8

Stabilize with more sand.

After all of the pavers are in place, toss handfuls of sand over the entire area. Then, working from one end, use a kitchen broom to gently sweep the sand down into the cracks between the pavers. Spray the entire patio with a mist to help settle the sand. Allow the sand to dry. Then add a second layer of sand, sweep it into place, and wet it down. Repeat this process a week later, as well as any time you feel a paver wobble.

OPTIONS

You can use the same basic method described above for other patio styles.

Stone Substitute stone for the pavers. There are several beautiful varieties available in many different shapes and thicknesses. You can work with the pieces exactly as they come from nature or have the stones cut to your specifications. You also can experiment with different edging materials.

Concrete Fill the entire bed with concrete. Use stamps or stains (see page 149) to add texture or color. Divide the bed into quadrants, and use one material in the upper left and lower right sections, and a different material in the other two quadrants.

DECKS

▲ **With good design and craftsmanship, a deck can be an elegant addition to the home and landscape. Note the attention to detail where the steps blend with the patio.**

Decks are as American as apple pie and have become a standard feature in landscapes from coast to coast. Yet decks have been used with frequency only since the 1950s, when home building boomed and rot-resistant lumber became readily available. Today, decks rival patios for the number one spot for outdoor entertaining and relaxing.

Where to put a deck

When deciding where to put a deck, you don't have to settle for the obvious. Although a deck is an ideal way to create a level outdoor area on a sloping site, you can also build a deck on level ground. In most cases, decks can be built just about anywhere you would build a patio or terrace.

A deck can create an entry area. It can be a small, intimate space adjoining a bedroom or study. Or it can follow the typical model and be joined to the back of the house, with access from either the kitchen or family room.

You can also build a freestanding deck in a remote area of the garden.

Your decision on where to build a deck should

◄ **A low deck can be surrounded by plants so that it seems to hover just above the garden.**

apply the same process of program development and site analysis as any major garden feature. For more on this process, see pages 8–13.

Uses for a deck

By far, most decks are attached to the rear of the house. This makes them true extensions of the home. Ideally, there is access from more than one room as well as the garden.

As an extension of the home, decks take their design cues from it in materials, colors, and overall style.

Decks can be used for just about any purpose—entertaining, cooking, dining, gardening, or relaxing. Knowing how you intend to use the deck is helpful in designing the right structure.

If you plan to use the deck for large gatherings, estimate the number of people and include that information when designing the infrastructure. If you are building the deck yourself, check local building codes, regulations, and zoning restrictions. Height limits, overhead structures, construction parameters, and even where you can build this type of structure may be dictated by these rules.

Wood decks tend to have a softer, more casual effect on the landscape than terraces and patios built more formally of masonry such as bricks and mortar. They may also be much less costly to construct.

One of the strongest points about a deck is that it can make use of an otherwise difficult site. Building a deck over steeply sloping terrain is usually

easier and less expensive than terracing the area. Because decks typically place you above the level of the surrounding land, they can command views of your property and beyond. The steeper the terrain, the higher the deck will be off the ground; planning one calls for professional advice. Seek the counsel you need to be sure your structure is safe and enduring.

If you inherited a patio that is in poor shape, consider building a deck that sits just above the old concrete.

▲ **To help link a deck to the rest of the garden, use steps that are broad and generous at their base, then taper as they rise to the deck.**

Combining a deck and patio

Decks seem an extension of the house, even those that are not literally attached to it. Patios seem more a part of the garden. This is partly due to their height. Decks are usually built just below the floor level of the house, whereas patios are built at ground level (or even below it).

Just as a patio that is adjacent to the house serves as a transition area between the house and garden, a deck plays the same role. Taking the idea of transition one step

further, consider having a deck that is attached to the house, stepping down to a patio. This creates a gradual movement from the completely controlled environment of the home to a wood-surfaced outdoor room next to the house to a stone-surfaced, ground-level room adjacent to or surrounded by the garden. If you are building a combination deck and patio, pay attention to where the two features meet. The union should be stable and safe, and the materials should match or blend.

Depending on how you plan to use your outdoor rooms, a combination deck and patio may turn out to provide one space used primarily as a sitting room and one dedicated to outdoor cooking and dining.

▼ **Attention to detail makes a big difference, as with this bench and railing combination and the wood skirt that hides the deck framing.**

▲ **If your home is built on steep terrain, chances are you have at least one good view. A deck is a good way to take advantage of it.**

Deck Ideas

As with a patio or courtyard, the enjoyment of your deck is influenced by details. Before building, review your program that outlines why you are building the deck and the ways you intend to use it. Consider features you can add to enhance various activities.

Built-in seating Most decks are built with the intention of people gathering on them. You can purchase outdoor furniture and arrange it as discussed on page 145. Decks also offer the option of built-in seating, which can substitute for a railing. Although built-in furniture is less versatile, bench seats come in handy when you have a crowd.

▲ Extend the railing posts of the deck and use slats to fill in the spaces in between for additional privacy.

◀ **Add lighting to the deck to extend your use time. Built-in lighting looks better but costs more.**

▼ **Decking is a good way to cover a cracked concrete patio. Here, the deck is covered with a pergola sporting twig lathe.**

Lighting For security, safety, and nighttime enjoyment, add lighting to the deck. Whether mounted on the house or built into the railing, lighting extends the use time of the deck. If you have steps, lighting them is a must to prevent mishaps.

Canopy Although decks don't absorb light and heat the way paving does, a little shade or shelter is helpful. For dappled shade, consider extending a pergola from the house, or extend deck posts 8 feet above the deck floor to support a lath structure.

Planting Container gardens make decks come alive with color and scents, and even fresh herbs to toss on the grill. For tips on deck planting, see page 159.

Cooking One of the most popular deck activities is cooking. There are simple steps for enhancing your outdoor cooking experience. If you use a gas grill, run a gas line to it instead of using bottled gas. Consider adding a custom-built grilling area with an extra-wide railing to serve as a shelf. Put a waterproof canopy over the grill to protect the area during a storm. Be aware that cooking with charcoal on a deck is illegal in some communities because the burning embers present a fire hazard on a wood surface.

Screening To increase the sense of privacy, consider adding a screen to block unwanted views.

◀ **A gas grill is much safer than charcoal. Before building the deck, run a gas line to where you intend to have the grill.**

Deck Rails and Decking

Deck railings are required first as a safety feature. In fact, most local building codes require a railing for any deck that is built more than 30 inches off the ground. These codes also dictate certain characteristics of the railing, including the minimum height, the minimum and maximum distance between the decking and the lowest horizontal rail, and the distance between vertical rails.

Be familiar with these codes before designing and building any railings. Even if your community doesn't have restrictions, you should still consider these issues. As a basic guideline, the design of a railing should not allow a softball to fit between the decking and the lowest horizontal rail or between vertical rails. The typical height for a deck railing is 30 to 40 inches.

When these basic safety requirements are met, there is no limit to the style of railing. The illustrations at left offer a few examples.

When designing a railing, look at features on the house for ideas. Shutters, window frames, eaves, and roof details should all be considered as starting points for the design of a railing that will match the architecture of the home.

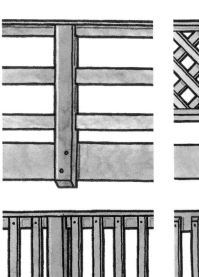

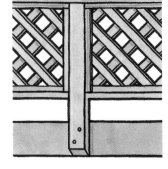

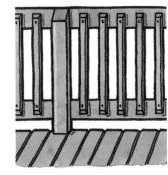

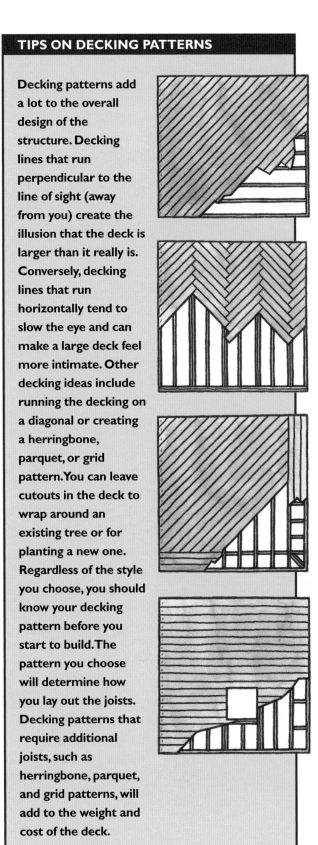

TIPS ON DECKING PATTERNS

Decking patterns add a lot to the overall design of the structure. Decking lines that run perpendicular to the line of sight (away from you) create the illusion that the deck is larger than it really is. Conversely, decking lines that run horizontally tend to slow the eye and can make a large deck feel more intimate. Other decking ideas include running the decking on a diagonal or creating a herringbone, parquet, or grid pattern. You can leave cutouts in the deck to wrap around an existing tree or for planting a new one. Regardless of the style you choose, you should know your decking pattern before you start to build. The pattern you choose will determine how you lay out the joists. Decking patterns that require additional joists, such as herringbone, parquet, and grid patterns, will add to the weight and cost of the deck.

Deck Materials

There are several options for decking material, with four factors that affect your choice: durability, availability, looks, and cost.

Redwood This is a popular, naturally rot-resistant wood. With a clear sealer applied biannually, redwood will last a long time. It is easy to find on the West Coast and at large home improvement centers elsewhere. The reddish hue is not suited to the look of every home. It is the most expensive decking material, so consider using another wood for the framing and redwood for decking.

Cedar This rot-resistant wood is strong and durable. It is more common in the South and on the West Coast. Cedar weathers silvery gray unless you apply a sealer. It costs about 20 percent less than redwood, depending on availability.

Cypress Another rot-resistant wood, cypress is most popular in the Southeast. It is not as strong as cedar, redwood, or pressure-treated wood. Consider using a pressure-treated wood for the frame and cypress for decking. It costs a little less than cedar in the South and a little more everywhere else.

Pressure-treated lumber This is the strongest and most readily available lumber. Most comes with a greenish cast that weathers to a silvery gray, but you can also get it prestained to look like cedar or redwood. It is the most affordable of these materials.

◄ **Redwood is a top-of-the-line decking material and has a characteristic color.**

▲ **Pressure-treated lumber can be stained to look like a more refined wood such as cedar.**

TIPS FOR USING PLASTIC WOOD

Forget what you may have seen or heard about plastic wood. The technology has caught up with consumers' demands for good-looking and durable material.

Plastic lumber is made by recycling plastic materials, such as milk jugs and soda bottles, adding binding and strengthening agents, dyeing the mixture to look like wood, then pressing the molten material into a wood-textured mold. The result closely resembles wood and has remarkable durability.

Advantages to this kind of material include contributing to a healthier environment because it

uses recycled plastics. The advantages for the individual homeowner are that plastic wood doesn't need staining and doesn't rot. All indications are that it will outlast natural wood.

The downside to this material is that it is in limited supply, so it may be hard to find. And no matter what you do, it will never look exactly like wood, so it may be hard to blend it into the landscape. Although available in a range of colors, it does not take stain well (if at all). Follow the support and spacing guidelines to the letter, or the plastic wood will sag, especially on hot days when the sun softens the plastic.

Deck building checklist

✓ Planning

- **Good instructions.** Follow the standard guidelines for spacing beams, posts, and joists. Not only is fudging on spacing unsafe and shortsighted, but you may also have to start over if local codes require approval from a building inspector.
- **Professional advice** Before you build, show the plan to a qualified contractor for approval. This will prevent problems and you might get some ideas for making the deck better.
- **Utilities** If you want electricity, gas, or water on or around the deck, first establish the location of these utilities. Do the preliminary work before building the deck.
- **Sun patterns** Knowing the seasonal patterns of the sun will help you determine the deck's exact position. It also shows where you might need shade structures or if you need to remove sunblocking elements.

✓ Tools

- **Power equipment** Two tools make building a deck more enjoyable: a nail gun and a screw gun. Use a nail gun to attach decking. A screw gun rapidly drives in screws. Both come in corded and cordless versions, and if you have a big job, you might look into rental tools that run on compressed air.
- **Joist hangers** Made of lightweight galvanized metal, joist hangers are nailed or screwed at a predetermined position by using a short piece of a joist as a measuring device. Then all you have to do is slip the joist into place and screw it to the hanger. This method is much easier than trying to hold a joist straight up and down and at the correct height and angle with one hand while nailing or screwing it into place with the other.

✓ Building

- **Footings** Pay special attention to footings. This

area, where the posts meet the ground, is the most vulnerable part of any deck; it is where wood and water are most likely to come into contact. Even if your building codes don't require it, set the posts in a hole with a gravel base to promote drainage away from the wood. Use concrete around the posts, with the top of the concrete tapered so water drains away from the post. Another option is to use a post anchor, or stirrup, a metal sleeve set in concrete that a post rests in or on. For additional protection, apply a tar sealer to any below-ground posts.
- **Screws** If possible, use screws to hold the deck together. Screws make a tighter, more permanent fastening than nails.
- **Predrilling** A good idea to avoid splitting wood is to predrill holes. This is especially true of the framing members.
- **Ledgers and flashing** A ledger is used to support the joist next to the house on an attached deck. Always use lag screws to hold a ledger to the house; nails can pull loose over time. Flashing—a thin piece of galvanized metal shaped like a stair step—keeps water from seeping into the house. The vertical edge of the flashing—placed flush against the house—angles over the top of the ledger and steps down flush against it. Use caulk where the flashing meets the house for additional water sealing.
- **Cupping** This is a bigger concern with pressure-treated lumber than with naturally rot-resistant wood. Cupping occurs when the wood dries out and curls along the natural curvature of the former tree trunk. To avoid this, note any rings on the end of the lumber and place the wood with the outside edge of the "tree" facing up. Using screws to fasten decking also prevents cupping.

Deck Finishes

The appearance and durability of a deck are affected by the finish you apply. The deck materials listed on page 156 don't require a finish, but a sealer, whether clear or colored, will extend the life of the wood.

The choice of a clear sealer or a colored stain is an aesthetic one. A clear sealer will preserve the natural coloration of redwood, cedar, and cypress. Because pressure-treated lumber usually has a greenish tint due to the chemical used in treating it, a clear sealer may not be desirable. These sealers are best applied with a brush but can also be applied with a sprayer. The advantage of a brush is that it tends to make better contact with the wood, filling any pores. A clear sealer

▼ Painting a deck is a good way to tie it in with the architecture. Paint is best used on areas free from heavy foot traffic.

▲ Apply a clear sealer to give the deck a lustrous sheen and protect wood from scuffing and decay. Stain wood the color you want, then brush on the sealer.

protects against wear and tear on the wood and will prevent some scuff marks.

Redwood and cedar are rarely stained, because they have such distinctive colors. Cypress and pressure-treated wood, with their lighter colors, can be stained to match your setting or house. Stain ranges from the palest sand color to the reddish orange of redwood. Stains are also applied with a brush or sprayer. Because stains are more fluid than paint, you can use stain-soaked cloth to rub it on the

wood. This is helpful when staining thin members such as railings.

Paint is best reserved for railings or other areas that won't be subject to a lot of wear. If you paint the decking itself, plan to repaint it at least every other year, depending on the amount of foot traffic.

Before applying a sealer, stain, or paint, be sure to allow the wood to dry out completely. Under normal spring or summer weather conditions, this should take about six weeks. Painting wet wood may result in blistering of the paint as moisture tries to escape.

Cleaning the deck

To slow down decay and keep up appearances, clean the deck annually. Although a high-pressure water spray may be sufficient, it could also remove some stain or paint.

Another method is to mix 1 cup of trisodium phosphate (available at hardware stores), 1 cup of powdered detergent, and 2 cups bleach in 2 gallons of water. Use this mixture and a stiff-bristled brush to scrub the deck—one section at a time—rinsing with a hose after you finish each area. Use plastic sheeting to cover and protect plants that may be damaged by the runoff.

◄ An alternative to painting the entire deck is to paint only vertical elements.

Deck Planting

Though made of wood and raised above the ground, a deck can be a perfect location for plants—on and around it. The advantages of deckscaping include softening the edges, adding colorful accents, organizing space, providing privacy, reducing glare, and adding shade.

Whether the plants are on the deck or planted adjacent to it, the introduction of a little green will help the deck blend into the garden and not appear as an object. If your deck is high off the ground, you might consider planting some small, ornamental trees around the base so that the canopy of the

▲ **Container-grown plants, in combination with built-in planters, help ease the transition from a heavily planted hillside to the deck below.**

plants is at eye level. This softens the edge, can add privacy, and may even cast some shade. When choosing a tree, consider flower color and fall color. If the plant has fragrance, try to place it on the upwind side of the deck.

Whether in containers or built-in structures, plants add color and accent to the deck. They can tie the structure to the garden (right), break up large expanses of open areas, highlight an entryway, or enliven a seating area.

Plants can define different areas of a deck. Use four containers of evergreen shrubs to establish the corners of an outdoor dining area. Line them up side by side to screen an area for sunbathing.

Make use of the walls of the house and train a vine or espalier a tree or shrub to soften the wall. For more on how to do this, see pages 164–165. Take advantage of the view from the deck and create patterns of planting in the garden beyond it.

◄ **This built-in planter creates a deck-level bed. When planning these built-in features, set them out of the way of traffic.**

How to add a deck planter

If the deck is no more than 2 to 3 feet off the ground, you can plant a tree or shrub directly into the ground with the foliage showing above the decking. Design the framing of the deck so a joist runs where you want one side of the opening to be. Position another joist to frame the other side of the opening. Close the frame with two crossbraces cut from a joist. Then add the decking.

If the deck is too high to plant in the soil, make a built-in planter. Follow the method just described, but use wood treated with preservative that is rated for ground contact. Use 2×10 joists to make the frame (even if using another size joist elsewhere in the framing). Cut a piece of ¾-inch plywood the size of the frame and drill several ½-inch drain holes in it. Screw the plywood into place from below to form a bottom for the planter. Line with landscape-grade plastic, poke holes aligned with the drilled holes, and fill with soil.

COURTYARDS

There is a unique charm to a courtyard, partly because it conjures up images of colonial homes in cities such as Charleston, New Orleans, and Savannah. Another appeal is that a courtyard comes closest to being an outdoor room.

Making the most of an existing courtyard

There is much you can do with an existing courtyard. Consider the following design aspects when refurbishing an existing courtyard or when building a new one.

▼ **Because a courtyard is an extension of the house, it is typically furnished in much the same way.**

Enclosure A distinguishing characteristic of a courtyard is having the space feel as though it has four "solid" walls. Solid is more visual than literal. A vine-covered trellis or a hedge may close in a small space (perhaps less than 10 feet square) without making it feel claustrophobic.

An open roof or canopy adds even more sense of enclosure. Whatever structure you use should allow plenty of light into the courtyard so there is no mistaking its feeling of welcome.

A retractable awning is one way to add enclosure. A temporary roof that covers the courtyard completely in winter also extends the time you can use the area and protects the plants within.

Styles The style and look of the courtyard is to some extent predetermined by the walls that define it.

▲ **As you design a courtyard, keep all the views in mind, including the one from above.**

However, these walls can be altered to create the setting you want. See page 162 for ideas.

Scale An aspect of design you do have control over is scale. The absence of a roof makes the space feel bigger than it is. A grouping of tables and chairs that feels comfortable on an open patio may look cramped in a walled courtyard. Scale also comes into play when selecting plants. In terms of both design and horticulture, it works better to have fewer, larger pots than many little pots that dry out quickly and blow over.

Views The main concern for a courtyard is usually the view into it rather than out

◀ **Give your courtyard a single-color theme, such as this "white room." The key is to match the house and to use a color that is not overbearing.**

same structure 15 or 20 feet from the house. The additional costs you will incur are for one wall (the one that will no longer be shared with the rest of the house) and the hallway required to connect the new structure to the existing house. You can then enclose the courtyard using a fence or dense hedge. Then, of course, there is the cost of the courtyard itself.

If you plan to add a courtyard, consider how it is oriented to the sun and how you will enter and exit from the

house and garden. The more entries, the more you are likely to use the space. Be sure the courtyard paving, no matter the material used, drains away from the house. Also consider ways to provide a partial canopy by extending the rafters of the roof over the new structure.

of it. As you design, examine views from any windows (including those overhead) and doors that enter the courtyard. Also, if you have an attractive view from the courtyard, consider cutting a window in a wall of the courtyard to frame it.

Adding a new Courtyard

If your home is already built, plan a courtyard when adding onto the house. This may not add as much cost to the project as you might think. For example, when adding a study, extra bedroom, or even an attached garage, you can add the

▶ **Create a secluded courtyard using lattice walls opposite the walls of an inside corner on the outside of your house.**

▶ **Create a rustic courtyard by enclosing part of the outdoor room with split-log walls.**

Courtyard Details

▲ **Build a decorative lattice against a wall and train shrubs or vines on it. Training a shrub directly on a wall could cause damage.**

◀ **A hanging planter with flowers in complementary colors can break up an expanse of wall.**

Although the walls of an existing courtyard are fixed and the material for them has already been chosen, you can accessorize the walls to suit your taste. Be as creative and flexible as you would with an indoor wall, since you actually have more flexibility outdoors.

Paint the walls or cover them with weatherproof art. One of the advantages of being outdoors is being able to grow plants on a wall, add a hanging fountain, and add large gas or candle sconces for lighting.

Planting

Because a courtyard has limited floor space, using the walls is a good way to add life and color. There are several ways to add green to walls.

Espalier This is the word used to describe training a small tree or shrub against a wall in a specific design. For more on espalier, see page 164.

Trellises Whether a permanent one made of wood or a simple one made from wire, trellises support climbing vines and offer an alternative to espalier for covering a wall with green.

An advantage to a permanent wood trellis is that, if it is designed and built properly, it adds relief to the wall and looks good even when plants aren't on it. A trellis may be an attractive solution if you grow annual or deciduous vines, which will leave the walls bare for part of the year.

The plants will need something to grow in. If planned for from the beginning, you can leave a cutout in the floor of the courtyard and plant the vines or shrubs directly into the soil. Otherwise, you will need to build a raised bed or, depending on the size of the plant, grow it in a container.

You can also use individual containers and decorative brackets to hang plants on the wall (lower left and below). Use a mix of upright and trailing plants.

Microclimate Determine how the climate within your courtyard differs from the rest of the garden so you can choose and tend plants accordingly. The protection of the walls and limited air movement create their own microclimate. Although there is less damage of freezing or damaging wind,

▲ **The soft glow of candlelight may not illuminate the entire courtyard, but it is enough to make you want to stay.**

▼ **Use a garden plaque or frieze to adorn a courtyard wall. This plaque doubles as a planter.**

there may be a higher incidence of fungus due to poor air circulation and lack of sunlight.

Accents

Adding details to the courtyard can give it personality and comfort.

Paint the walls Select a color or colors that match the style and look you want and completely cover the walls with a solid color. Consider painting each wall a different color. Keep in mind that hot colors, such as red and orange, will jump out at you, whereas cooler colors, such as blue, lavender, and light green, tend to recede and make the space feel larger.

If you are an artist or know one, consider using one or more walls as a canvas and paint a mural. Use a sealer over the mural to extend its life.

Fool the eye To make a courtyard feel bigger, consider using tromp l'oeil (the French term for fool the eye). This can be as simple as hanging a mirror on one wall or part of a wall. For more on tromp l'oeil, see page 246.

Ornaments Many sculptures, plaques, and friezes can be used outdoors. Select

▲ **Planting a wall need not be complicated. These simple but elegant metal hangers hold everyday terra-cotta pots.**

those that match your sense of style and the style of the rooms that adjoin the courtyard. Consider framing the art with vines grown on a wire trellis.

Lighting Utilize the walls for lighting. Walls can be used for mounting lights or the walls can be illuminated themselves. Use walls to hang candles or electric fixtures. Whether the wiring is standard or low-voltage, the trick is to hide it. Snaking well-insulated wire behind a trellis is one way to do this.

Another idea is to mount lights on the eaves of the house so they shine down on the walls. This reflected light is often adequate to illuminate the entire courtyard without having lights shine in your eyes.

Fountains Wall fountains are self-contained and usually operate at a low volume. This is an advantage in a courtyard where sound tends to reverberate, making even a tiny splash go a long way toward drowning out unwanted noise.

▲ **If the terrain allows, introduce a change of level to the courtyard. This is one way to ensure that water drains away from the house.**

How to espalier

Espalier is the term used to describe the process of training trees, shrubs, and woody vines against a flat surface, such as a wall. You can also train them to a freestanding fence or trellis.

To espalier, prune to create a main vertical stem, then train the side branches to achieve the desired shape. Depending on the plant, this can take a year or two to establish and requires regular care. Thereafter, an espalier requires only light pruning to hold its shape.

STEP 1 Choose a **location.** Any solid wall will do as long as there is enough light for the plant you want and room to plant (or you can use a container). For more on containers see pages 252–257.

STEP 2 Choose the **plant.** Most plants can be espaliered, but those with naturally spreading branches, such as apple, pear, quince, and camellia, work best. Look for a plant that already has a start on the branching pattern you want. Make sure the plant is suitable for the location.

STEP 3 **Prepare the support.** Run wires between nails set in the wall or posts set in the ground to create three horizontal lines. Wire isn't necessary for vertical branches; they will grow that way naturally. Use heavy-gauge wire that can resist the pull of the branches as they try to grow toward the sun.

STEP 4 **Plant the tree or shrub.** Set the plant about a foot in front of the structure that will support it. Position the plant so that at least two of the strongest branches run in the direction of the wires.

STEP 5 **Train the branches.** Remove all but two shoots on each branch. Attach the remaining shoots to the wires with soft ties.

As the central trunk grows, keep removing side shoots. When the trunk reaches the next wire up, allow two side shoots to develop (remove the rest) and attach them to the wires.

As the side shoots grow, either let them continue as shown in A, or turn the branches upward to create the patterns shown in B and C.

If you really want to be creative, plant several trees and train them in a Belgian fence pattern, as shown in D.

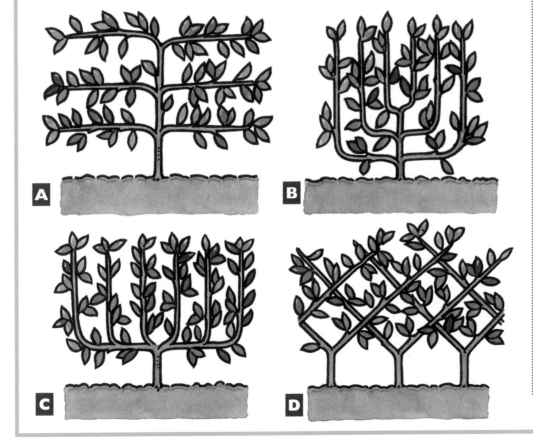

How to make a wire trellis

Creating a pattern with wire and training a vine to it achieves an effect similar to that of an espalier.

STEP 1 Choose a location. Decide where you want to add this feature. It is an effective way to dress up the side of a garage or a wall adjacent to a patio.

If the area receives a lot of sun, you will have more choices in vines. If there is room to plant in soil, maintenance will be less, but you can also grow vines in containers. For more on containers see pages 252–257.

STEP 2 Choose a vine. Note the conditions and choose an annual or perennial vine suited to the site. If it is a blooming vine, choose a color to complement the setting.

STEP 3 Sketch the pattern and set nails in place. Use a yardstick to trace the pattern on the wall. Drive an 8d broad-headed nail or a woodscrew everywhere two lines meet or where guidance is needed around a curve.

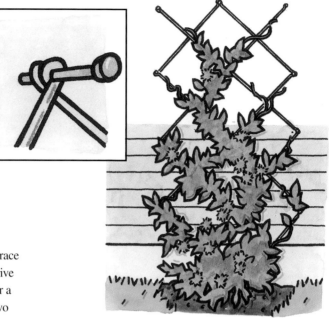

STEP 4 Attach the wire. Following the lines of the pattern, start at the bottom and run a length of coated 8-gauge wire from one nail to the next. Wrap the wire at least once around the nail, then go to the next nail. Repeat until the pattern is completed. If you have to cut the wire, tie the end around the last nail you wrapped; then use diagonal-cutting pliers to trim the ends.

STEP 5 Plant and train the vine. Place the vine in the ground or a container. When it reaches the lowest nail, attach it to the wire with a twist tie. Check it every few days and slowly fill in the pattern.

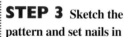

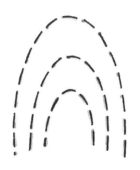

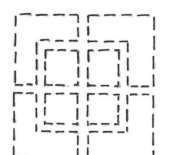

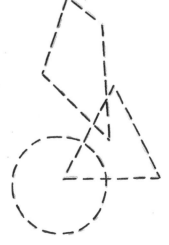

ENTRY GARDENS

The area around the front door has a definite spatial quality. Like a welcome mat to a visitor, the design, scale, planting, and maintenance around the entry help determine whether the arrival is a pleasing one.

One of the first things to consider when designing an entry garden is how well it matches the architecture of the house. An important consideration throughout the garden, this is vital at the entry. For most homes, an entry garden is the most public garden space.

The design of the entry garden sets a mood. A pair of carefully pruned boxwoods in containers flanking the front door speaks of order and formality. A mixed border sets a more relaxed tone.

Because the majority of garden design and activity takes place in the backyard, it is perfectly acceptable to have a formal entry garden to match a traditional house and foundation planting in the front yard and a loose, more informal garden style in the back of the house.

Another consideration is scale. An entry garden offers you the opportunity to create a transition from an open garden or lawn without a ceiling to the more intimate, human scale of the interior of the home. Tricks for doing this include having a walk narrow as it approaches the front door. This tapering of the paving focuses attention on the entry itself. You can still expand the area right around the door so you have ample room to gather as you say your hellos and good-byes.

You could also use a series of transitional spaces, such as an arbor or short flight of stairs. This use of a series of spaces or outdoor rooms gradually moves a visitor down in scale from larger exterior spaces to a smaller interior space.

The planting plan of an entry garden requires careful thought, from choosing

▲ An entry planting should draw you to the front door. This front yard is the sunniest part of the garden, making it ideal for welcoming flower beds.

the right size and position of plants that create the scale you want, to choosing the plants themselves. Visitors waiting to enter your home will be close to the plants you have selected. Take advantage of this captive audience to use a range of colors, textures, and shapes to hold their interest and maybe even surprise them.

Fragrant plants are ideal for entry gardens. They smell good for your guests, and scent the house every time the door is opened.

Consider using plants that are inviting to the touch. Ferns, soft-needled conifers, and some ornamental grasses fill the bill. Avoid thorny or spiky plants such as yucca or cotoneaster, right by an entry.

If your entryway is covered or otherwise has limited access to sunlight, be sure to select plants that will thrive in

▲ The simplicity of this single planter echoing the stark lines of the architecture promotes a feeling of unity.

shade or partial shade. Caladium and impatiens are two examples of plants that can brighten a shady entry.

Another way to add color to the entry is with plants in containers. Container planting allows you to change the color easily from season to season, perhaps starting with an array of bulbs in spring, followed by annuals the rest of the year. Container plants are especially helpful if the entry is shady. You can also plant duplicate containers of sun-loving annuals, keeping one in a sunny part of the garden and the other by the door, and rotating them weekly.

An overhead canopy is helpful in the transition from garden to home, especially if the structure is at about the same height as the ceiling of the room you enter. A canopy also keeps you and your guests dry as they enter the home. And it needn't cast shade, as the plexiglass awning (page 166) proves.

If you have an overhead structure, either at the entry itself or along the pathway to the entry, consider covering it with a vine or other climbing plant. A bower of green can soften a stark structure.

Because the entry garden is visible to all who come to your home, and because guests have time to take in this garden, maintenance is an important concern in planning and design. Be realistic about how much maintenance you are

willing to do and design accordingly. Even if you aren't installing an irrigation system or lighting anywhere else in the garden, consider it for the entry garden. This will help the area look presentable year-round.

Hardscape needs maintenance too. Cracked concrete and loose or missing bricks make a poor (and potentially unsafe) first impression. Add a weekly inspection of the entry as part of your gardening routine.

▼ A vine-covered arbor is an attractive way to mark the entry to a garden.

◄ An entry garden can start before the front door, greeting guests the moment they arrive.

▼ Level changes and the boundary created by the porch railing help define this entry.

167

GARDEN GETAWAYS

▲ **Vibrant color gives this getaway its charm and appeal.**

For some, the entire garden is a respite. From border to border, the garden serves as a haven from the hectic activities dealt with on a daily basis. On the other hand, many gardens have to fill a wide range of uses, from vegetable gardening to a play area for children to a gathering and entertaining area. Even so, you can still carve out a portion of the garden for the specific purpose of having a place to get away from it all.

Creating a secret retreat within a garden is something anyone can do in any garden. It's a matter of knowing what you want, knowing all the options your property has to offer, and applying any of the techniques outlined on the following pages. A quiet place to be alone will undoubtedly become one of your favorite parts of the garden.

Create a room

One way to make a garden getaway inviting is to make it feel like a room. To start, provide an overhead canopy to help contain the area and bring it down to a human scale.

A canopy needn't be a solid roof. An open structure—as in the gazebo (below) or the vine-covered hideaway (left)—allow plenty of light and air to move through the area while still providing shelter.

Next, choose the seating for the number of people you intend to have in the space. Most successful secluded spots have seating for at least two.

▼ **Choose a remote corner of the garden for a rustic, tranquil retreat.**

▲ Although this secret garden is seemingly carved from a woodland setting, it started as an open lawn. The sense of privacy and enclosure was carefully crafted through planting.

A place to go

Whether the getaway mimics a room or is simply a pair of chairs in a secluded part of the lawn, it should create a feeling that it is a place you actually go to. You may not be able to see it in its entirety from the house or major areas of the garden, and you may not be able to hide it completely, but you want to provide some sense of destination.

Locate the secret garden in a remote-feeling part of the property. This doesn't have to be far from the house. If the ideal space is tucked beside your garage, instead of taking the quickest and closest route to get there, have a path that leads around the garage instead. Each step helps you shed the echoes of the outside world and allows time to anticipate the respite. If this sounds unlikely, try it; you might be surprised at how well it works.

▶ **The meandering approach to this seating area creates a feeling of solitude.**

Try planning a winding path that never gives a full view of the secluded area until you reach it. If space is tight, plant large ornamental grasses on either side of the path to create a sense of mystery. Hide the entrance, so you have to brush the grass out of the way to enter.

▼ **Any detached structure on the property can be turned into a private haven or at least can help define the area for one.**

Sense of enclosure

Your meditative retreat should have a sense of enclosure. It will help you focus your thoughts inward. It also gives a feeling of protection. Above all, enclosure creates a sense of privacy.

The whole idea is to get away from the rest of the garden, so screen the garden from view if possible. Planting is the best way to accomplish this. A formal or informal hedge, a loose screen of plants, or even a bed of tall perennials can give you the privacy you want.

If planting a screen is not an option, orientation is another way to gain a sense of privacy. The use of orientation simply means putting your back to the view you don't want to see. For example, in the middle photo below, facing the chairs away from the house and having the

▼ **An open, vine-covered arbor gives a sense of enclosure without restricting views or breezes.**

spiral staircase form a wall of the outdoor room gives this little nook a sense of privacy and detachment even though it is very close to the house.

As these photos show, a secluded area does not have to be large. In fact, the smaller and more intimate, the better. A space as small as 8-feet square is large enough for a couple of chairs and a small table, which is all that is needed for quiet, tranquil place.

Change of level

If your property has many levels, take advantage of them. Going up or down a flight of steps contributes to the sense of destination and literally creates a separation from one area to another. To accentuate a level change, you can add a few steps on sloping ground.

Level changes are also useful in blocking unpleasant views. An elevation of a few feet can be enough to obscure the view of the house or anything else you don't want to see. If the level change isn't quite enough to hide the view you are trying to block, you can plant a row of shrubs on top of a mound or berm (an artificial mound of soil). The same thing can be accomplished by siting your hideaway on the far side of a hill, mound, or berm.

Taking the idea of level changes to the extreme, if your property is flat, you can create a level change by digging a sunken garden or putting your getaway in a tree.

Keep in mind that level changes and some of the other ideas discussed here can be used to enhance your view out of a space as well as control who can see in.

Consider your surroundings

Once you reach your destination and feel secure and private, you need to enjoy what you see. Pay attention to the view you have and other details.

Your favorite spot for relaxing may borrow a view from off-site. Perhaps it is

▲ **A getaway only needs room for two and a pleasant setting.**

◄ **The arc of the staircase and an orientation away from the house makes this space feel removed.**

the skyline of the city, a view up a stream, or a vista of the horizon.

Accents and details

Pay close attention to details, especially in the realm of comfort. Be sure the seating you use fits your body. A good-looking chair that is not suited to your favorite relaxing position won't draw you to use it. This is a place where looks matter to only you, so let comfort predominate over style.

If you do not have any outer views to take advantage of, create your own views within the secret retreat. Add the plants and yard art that you enjoy the most. This is a good place for mirth and personal expression. Keep a large basket of pottery shards or colorful stones and create a mosaic around where you sit, adding to it or changing it with each visit.

Specimen plants or favorite plants are good additions to a private and very personal meditation spot. Because this garden is for you, you should choose the plants that make you feel most comfortable and that you enjoy taking care of. Avoid overdesigning a space that might look good on the cover of a magazine but that feels too formal or stiff for everyday use, or that becomes a maintenance burden.

▶ A change of level is a good way to create a sense of separation—important for a getaway.

◀ The canopy of branches from a nearby tree shelters a getaway that has a view of the garden.

Another consideration is fragrance. Scent is the most evocative of all the senses and can make you feel as comfortable as any chair or majestic view. For more on fragrant shrubs, see pages 277 and 369.

Sweet sounds

You could use all the ideas covered on these pages and have a wonderful getaway only to have your time there marred by distracting sounds, such as a jet flying overhead, honking cars, or a barking dog. A fountain may help to drown out unwelcome noise. By adding a fountain with a variable jet, you can adjust the white noise to the level you desire when you desire it.

In addition to masking unwanted sounds, you can add pleasant ones. Wind chimes are a quick and easy way to introduce pleasantly distracting sound to the getaway. For more on sound in the garden, see pages 240–241.

WATER

A complement to any garden

FOUNTAINS

For centuries, people have used fountains as a means of cooling an area, connecting with nature, and adding the soothing quality of splashing water to their environment. Today, fountains are the most popular water feature for home gardens—for the effects they create and for their ease of installation. For example, you can decide one morning that you want a fountain in your garden and, depending on the type of fountain, you could have it up and running by that evening. Few garden features can rival a fountain for the impact it can provide without a large investment of time and money.

General considerations

There are many types of water features you can add to your garden. Planning will help you decide on the perfect one for you.

If you decide on a fountain, there are many styles from which to choose. You can make an intelligent decision about a fountain once you understand the basics of the two different types: freestanding and built-in. These pages will serve as your guide to them.

▲ Garden ponds can have moving water. A recirculating pump serves as the engine for a waterfall, creating a fountain effect.

◄ If space is limited, consider combining different water features, such as a water garden, fountain, and waterfall.

Freestanding fountains

Freestanding fountains come in a wide range of attractive, versatile, dependable, and readily available styles. The range includes the smallest tabletop fountains; midsize fountains the size of a half whiskey barrel; and large, ornate fountains that are the focal point of the garden. All are portable—some more so than others.

The best feature of a freestanding fountain is its simplicity. Whether it's a kit or a fountain that's ready to fill up and plug in, a freestanding fountain provides quick results and is the most inexpensive type of water feature.

Another advantage to a freestanding fountain is that even if you have only basic skills—if you can paint, attach a hose to a pipe, and plug a cord into a grounded electrical outlet—you can make a fountain from almost any watertight container. For those with a creative bent, building a fountain can be a beautiful and unique project, as you can see from the photographs on page 176.

There are some obvious limitations to size and, therefore, what you can do within a freestanding fountain. Some people consider a freestanding fountain to be a container garden—only with water instead of soil.

Built-in fountains

Built-in fountains are just that: structures that are permanently set into place. You can invest a great deal of time and money to

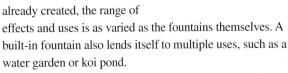
▼ This elevated fountain pumps water through a millstone, creating a gentle, steady sound. The walls also function as seating.

▲ Wall fountains provide the sound of splashing water and add interest to a wall.

create a unique, built-in fountain that is ideally suited to your taste and needs. Or you can pare down your vision and opt for a much simpler and more affordable fountain. As the photographs on this page depict, even a small fountain can have a big impact on your garden and outdoor space.

The versatility of a built-in fountain means that there is a fountain design suited to any size and style of garden. Because you are not bound to what someone else has already created, the range of effects and uses is as varied as the fountains themselves. A built-in fountain also lends itself to multiple uses, such as a water garden or koi pond.

The issues to consider here focus on permanence. If you are going to invest the time and money to build in a fountain, proper planning and thoughtful design are musts. Done well, a built-in fountain can become the focal point of a terrace or the entire garden.

Maintenance

In most cases the maintenance of a fountain is less than for any other type of water feature. Because fountains are self-contained systems with built-in filters, routine periodic maintenance usually is just a matter of cleaning the filter. If fish and plants are part of your system, they will have their own maintenance requirements.

If you live in a cold-winter area with hard and prolonged freezes, there are some additional winterizing requirements. The following pages go into detail about the maintenance needs of all types of fountains.

Freestanding Fountains

The quickest way to add the charm of water to your garden is with a freestanding fountain. Whether you make one from a kit or build it yourself, a freestanding fountain can take as little as a few hours to create.

As with any ornamentation, location and style are prime considerations. Decide which vantage point(s) from the house or garden should have a view of the fountain. Site it where you can see—and hear—it best. An advantage of a freestanding fountain is that it's portable. You can try it in different locations. Even a big old sugar kettle is easy to move if it's empty.

A power source for the pump must be accessible and the outlet must be grounded. You can turn the fountain on and off by unplugging it or installing a switch.

Find the right style for the setting. There are many ready-made vessels from which to choose. Get an idea of styles and prices by visiting garden centers or home stores, or look in garden catalogs.

Making a freestanding fountain is a fun project. A kit can be assembled quickly; some are ready to go with the addition of a small pump. Choose from a range of materials; recycle an old pot or even a bathtub.

The minimum size for a fountain is 2 feet across— wide enough for a shooting stream of water to be caught in the pool without splashing out. Water may be lost to evaporation, but overspill should be avoided.

The intensity of the sound of water splashing is directly proportional to the size of the vessel and the height of the fountain. A small fountain will not muffle undesirable sounds—traffic or neighbors. For that type of sound suppression, you need to make a big splash.

Maintenance is simple and straightforward—clean the filter (part of the pump) and keep the fountain free of debris. If you live in Zone 5 or colder, empty the fountain and remove the pump before the first hard frost in autumn.

▲ **Any watertight vessel will work for the pool of a fountain. It needs only a power source that can be run from underneath.**

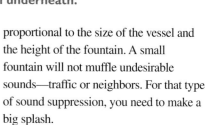

◀ **A deer scare runs on a small pump, which fills a length of bamboo with water and then dumps it noisily to be recirculated.**

◀ **Choose a vessel that reflects the character of the garden. Here, half a whiskey barrel suits the informal landscape.**

How to build a freestanding fountain

MATERIALS

Rubber or latex gloves

Old paintbrushes

24- to 36-inch clay pot with a drainage hole

Pitch, resin, or other material suitable for waterproofing terra-cotta

Submersible pump with a fountain jet (see page 186 for pump sizing)

Putty knife

Tube of silicone sealer

Several bricks

STEP I Seal the container.

Protect your hands with rubber gloves. Using an old paintbrush, waterproof the pot by painting the inside with pitch. A dark color will enhance the reflective quality of the fountain. Create a waterline by leaving the top 2–3 inches of the pot uncoated. Make sure the line is level all the way around the pot—neatness counts. Throw the brush away when you're done. Allow a day or two for the sealer to dry before applying a second coat with another brush. Allow this second coat of sealer to dry completely before continuing.

STEP 2 Wire the pump.

Place the pump in the pot and run the electrical wire through the drainage hole. If the hole isn't large enough, cut the plug off the cord, run the wire through the hole, and reattach the plug using a three-prong plug kit. Leave at least a foot of wire inside the pot to allow you to move the pump. Use a putty knife to apply silicone sealer around the wire. Fill in the entire drainage hole with the silicone sealer. Let dry.

STEP 3 Position the fountain.

This step requires some trial and error; you may get wet. Place the fountain. If the pot is on a solid surface—a deck or concrete—elevate it slightly (use upright cross sections of a 1-inch dowel to raise the fountain, or use commercial "pot feet") to allow for the wire. If the pot is on soil, dig a small trench for the wire. Most pump wires are short; use an extension cord to reach an outlet.

Fill the pot with water. Attach the fountain jet, following the manufacturer's directions. Stack bricks inside the pot so that when you place the pump on them (as close to the center as possible) the jet is just above water level.

▲ Although this project requires only a few hours of your time, allow several days for the pitch and sealer to dry.

Plug in the pump. Adjust the flow of the fountain. Experiment with different spray patterns until you achieve the look you want. Use coins or washers to level the fountain if necessary. You may need to weight the top of the pump with stones to hold it in place.

Once the fountain jet is adjusted, hide the cord and enjoy your new water feature.

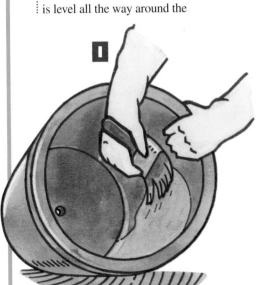

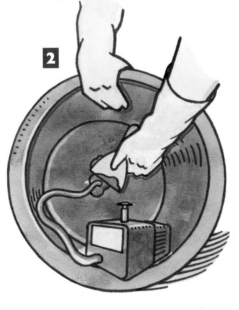

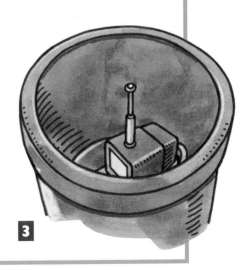

Built-in Fountains

A built-in fountain is usually larger than a freestanding fountain. Because it is often custom-made, a built-in fountain has a wider range of effects and may cost a little more than a freestanding one. A built-in fountain is an important part of the garden and often serves as a focal point.

Style and location

The first step in planning a built-in fountain involves style. The choices are many. A fountain can be large and formal, small and informal, contemporary, or traditional—the choice is yours to make according to your preferences. The design of your home and garden can provide clues to help you choose the shape, style, and materials for your fountain.

▼ A built-in fountain can fit in any space. It should use materials to match the surroundings.

Another consideration is power. Consult an electrician to ensure a safe supply of electricity with cutoff switches at both the house and the fountain. You will need a water source—to fill the fountain initially and to replace water lost to evaporation. In most cases a garden hose will suffice.

Location is another consideration. Built-in fountains usually require a flat area. If you have sloping yard, you can build a level terrace (see pages 50–51).

When considering a site for the fountain, remember that you want to be able to see and hear it. To check this out, have someone sit where you want to view the fountain while you kneel at the proposed fountain site. Run water from a hose into a bucket to simulate the sound of the fountain. The other person should be able to see and hear you. If not, move around until you and the water can be seen and heard.

If you live in an area with strong winds, be aware of the effects wind will have on the spray. Avoid siting the fountain where the water can blow onto paths or walkways.

▲ Use a wall to give height to your fountain.

Fountain basics

Fountains have two main components: a pool and a pump. The pool holds the water, determines the shape, and cannot be easily removed or repaired. When determining the size and shape of a pool, decide whether you want plants or fish. For either, the pool must be at least 18 inches deep. Masonry offers greater design flexibility but costs more than vinyl liners. Precast pools are easy to use and readily available, and are affordable.

Pump size is determined by the volume of the pool and the effects you want. A large pool with an intricate spray pattern requires more pump power than a small, simple one. A filter should be part of the pump package. Most pumps come with a kit that includes several spray patterns. If the kit doesn't have the spray pattern you want, you can buy a separate spray head kit.

How to construct a built-in fountain

MATERIALS

Shovel

4-foot-diameter plastic tub at least 18 inches deep

6 bags of concrete mix

Small adjustable, submersible pump with a fountain jet

Five 20-inch-long sections of 4-inch-diameter PVC pipe

Gravel (enough to fill the tub)

Water

6×6-foot piece of heavy plastic

4-foot-diameter millstone (or a circular or square slab of concrete with a 4-inch hole in the center)

Decorative stone (enough to cover an area 12 inches wide around the millstone)

STEP 1 Prepare the site.

Dig a hole deep enough so the top of the tub will sit 3 inches below soil level with a 2-inch space between the sides of the tub and the surrounding soil. Make certain that the bottom of the hole is level. Prepare 2 bags of concrete mix and spread a 2-inch layer over the bottom of the hole. Allow the concrete to cure for at least 24 hours.

STEP 2 Secure the tub.

Center the tub in the hole with its rim an inch below soil level. Mix the remaining 4 bags of concrete. Shovel the concrete into the space between the tub and the surrounding soil. This provides support for the sides of the tub. Wait 24 hours before continuing to the next step.

STEP 3 Assemble the fountain.

Set the pump in the center of the tub. Extend the fountain jet as far as it will go. Slide one of the pieces of PVC over the pump. Snake the electric cord out of the tub onto the ground. Position the other four PVC sections to form corners of a 2×2-foot square to support the millstone.

Fill the tub with gravel. Then fill it halfway with water. Plug in the pump. Adjust the jet to the desired height; it is difficult to adjust once the millstone is in place. Turn off the pump.

Center the plastic over the tub, cutting a large X in the middle to allow the fountain jet to protrude and to clear the four columns supporting the millstone. The edges of the plastic, lying on the surrounding ground, should be approximately an inch higher than the top of the gravel. This will allow the

▲ This elegant millstone fountain is easy to build and creates the illusion of a spring.

water to splash off the millstone, onto the rocks, then funnel back into the tub to be recirculated.

Get help to center the millstone over the tub and jet. Adjust the jet so it is flush with the top surface of the millstone. Add decorative stone to cover the plastic completely. Turn on the pump and enjoy.

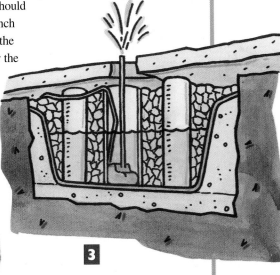

STILL WATER

▲ **Still water has a soothing effect in the garden. Its reflective quality is enhanced by a dark stain on the bottom and sides of the pond. Although lovely unadorned, the pond is anchored by the reflection of a tall plant.**

Pools of reflecting water have long been key components in meditation gardens. They engage the observer in a way that is as compelling as a fountain, although quite different.

When planning for still water, there are some unique considerations that differ from other water features. The most important is location. Still water generally requires a level area.

The impact of a reflecting pool is less effective if the surface of the pool is littered with leaves or other debris, so careful thought must be given to what is overhead and nearby. Avoid locating a reflecting pool beneath trees that drop leaves, flowers, pollen, and other debris year-round. Sometimes, however, this can't be avoided. For the full tranquil and reflective effect in such instances, you may need to do a little extra cleaning at certain times of the year. Or cover the pool during seasons of exceptional litter with a material such as deer netting, screening, or chicken wire. Although it detracts from the pool's reflectivity, you can remove it for a special occasion and when the dropping season has passed.

It is important to be able to fully appreciate a still water feature. Unlike a fountain, which can be enjoyed for its sound alone, still water must be seen to be appreciated. Plan to have seating near the pool so you can relax and enjoy the view.

Most reflecting pools are formal in design and materials. Although style is always a personal choice, the reflective quality is enhanced by clean edges. An informal, rock lined pool will have a different effect than one edged with brick or slate. The impact of still water, as page 181 shows, is not dependent on the size of the project. A small runnel can change the mood of a garden as much as a large pool.

Consider what will be reflected and seen from the primary vantage point, and adjust the pool accordingly. For example, it would be a shame to plan a pool to reflect a distant mountain, only to have the peak of the mountain cut off from the reflection.

The two descriptives of a reflecting pool are shallow and dark. A reflecting pool is rarely deeper than 24 inches; 12 inches is usually sufficient because of the dark finish required for the best reflectivity. If you are using a liner or a precast pool, be sure it is a dark color. Hard plastic pools are more reflective than flexible liners. If you use masonry, apply a dark-colored pool stain to the finished walls. Plan on refinishing the walls every five years or so. To save on maintenance, stain the concrete before pouring.

Adding a pump to your pool allows you to recirculate the water when you're not viewing it and helps prevent algae build-up. It also allows you to have fish in the pool.

◄ **Still water features can be effective, even if they're small. Here, a scooped-out stone basin reflects the sky above.**

How to build a runnel

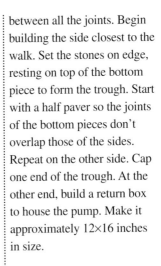

▶ A runnel is a long, narrow, shallow channel filled with either still or moving water.

A runnel can connect water features or stand alone. A runnel can be as long as you wish; the hose length of the recirculating pump is the only limiting factor. Courtyards, terraces, parking courts, or entry walks are all good spaces for a runnel. It is often easier to include a runnel in the hardscape when it's built rather than add it later.

This runnel is a stand-alone feature that can be added to an existing walkway. Have the stone cut to fit the exact dimensions of the runnel, or build it based on the size of the stone. It might be fun to work with random lengths.

MATERIALS

Shovel
String
2 stakes
Fine gravel
Slate or concrete pavers, limestone, or other natural or man-made stone in sizes of your choice
Rubber mallet
Level
Masonry epoxy
Silicone
Submersible pump

STEP 1 Prepare the trench.
Depending on the size of material you've chosen, dig a trench at least 10 inches deep and 12 inches wide adjacent to an existing level walkway. The distance between the edge of the trench and the walk should be equal to the width of the stone or paver. Tie string between two stakes to keep the line straight. Add 2 inches of gravel to the bottom of the trench.

STEP 2 Build the runnel.
Lay stones flat on the gravel to form the bottom of the runnel. Tap the stones into place with a rubber mallet. Ensure that each stone is level. Apply masonry epoxy between all the joints. Begin building the side closest to the walk. Set the stones on edge, resting on top of the bottom piece to form the trough. Start with a half paver so the joints of the bottom pieces don't overlap those of the sides. Repeat on the other side. Cap one end of the trough. At the other end, build a return box to house the pump. Make it approximately 12×16 inches in size.

STEP 3 Finish and seal.
Lay pavers flush with the walk and flush with the side of the runnel closest to the walk to form the edging. Repeat the process on the opposite side and around the return box. Once the pavers are in place, use silicone to seal any joints that will be underwater. Place the pump in the return box and plug it in to a grounded outlet. You may want to attach a return line to the pump. Placed at the far end of the runnel, it will move the water the entire length of the feature.

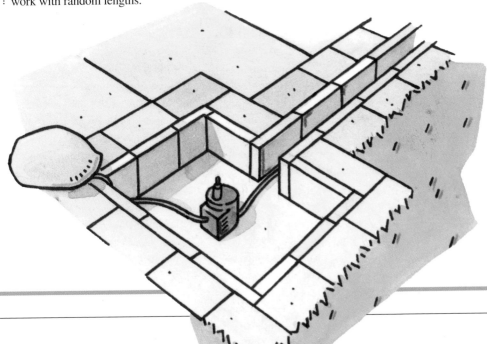

Birdbaths

Not all water features are for the sole enjoyment of humans. Water is the single most attractive element to lure birds into the garden; almost any water feature will do. For more information on attracting wildlife, see page 183.

For more information on attracting wildlife, see page 183.

▼ A birdbath doubles as a sculpture in the garden, so select a style that is in harmony with your landscape.

◄ If you want a birdbath in the garden, be certain that nearby flowers are no more than 6 inches above the water.

▼ You will attract more birds if you provide a flat surface, such as a stone, where they can perch.

Style and location

Birdbaths often serve as sculptural elements in the garden. Carefully consider the style and placement of the birdbath. Choose a birdbath that will fit in with the overall scheme of your garden, especially if you will be placing it on a pedestal, hanging it from a tree, or putting it in any other highly visible spot. A birdbath is made to be seen; otherwise, you could use an old dishpan and the birds would be just as happy.

When deciding where to place the birdbath, consider your interests as well as the birds'. If you want to see the birds as they frolic and bathe in the water, be sure the birdbath is visible from your favorite window or outdoor seating area.

For their part, birds need to be able to see or hear the water to know it is there.

Birdbath tips

There is more to attracting birds than just purchasing a birdbath and setting it in the garden. Nothing attracts birds to the garden—and your birdbath—as readily as the sound of splashing water. Even something as simple as a steady drip will let them know that water is there. Otherwise, birds are solely reliant on sight and may fly past without ever knowing your birdbath is there. Many garden catalogs and garden centers sell devices that attach to a garden hose on one end while the other clips onto the edge of the birdbath and provides a steady (and audible) supply of water. You can also make one yourself by using parts from a drip irrigation system.

Provide a place for the birds to perch. Although most birds are more than content to rest on the edge of the bowl, a stone or flat object that rises out of the water will attract finicky birds. They use it to stand on as they bathe, which is easier to do from the middle of the bowl than from the edge. The stone also adds visual interest to the feature when no birds are around.

Remember that birds need water in winter too. In cold-winter areas, use a heating element in the bowl to keep the water from freezing. A water heater is unobtrusive in winter, and you can easily remove it when warm weather returns. Heating elements are readily available from garden centers, garden suppliers, and magazines and catalogs that target bird enthusiasts.

The type and quantity of wildlife will vary depending upon whether your garden is suburban, urban, or rural. Geographic location plays a big role too.

- **Determine what you want to attract.** For the most part, wildlife is viewed as an asset. However, animals such as deer, rabbits, raccoons, and possums are not always welcome. Birds and butterflies, the most common visitors, cause the fewest problems.

Attracting birds

Like any living creature, birds need water, food, and shelter. Their requirement for water is discussed on page 182.

- **Determine which birds to attract.** Different birds may frequent your yard at various times of the year. Decide which ones you want to attract. Learn their food and habitat preferences. Your county extension service and the local chapter of the Audubon Society are good resources.
- **Choose the food.** Birds will go to their favorite and most accessible food first. Bird feeders come in many styles suitable for different types of food.
- **Match the feeder to the food.** Thistle, which attracts bluebirds, is a small seed that spills out of an ordinary bird feeder. A specific feeder is required to contain it. Hummingbird feeders are purposefully bold in color and should be used as decorative accents.
- **Plant for the birds.** Growing foods birds like is a good way to provide a perennial food source, contribute to the garden design, and, in most cases, discourage the squirrels that compete with birds for birdseed. Plants that provide berries or fruit, such as firethorn, holly, Kousa dogwood, and barberries contribute to the overall garden scheme as well.
- **Plan for shelter.** Your local county extension service and the Audubon Society can provide information on birds' nesting habits and housing preferences.
- **Provide shelter.** Evergreens or densely branched deciduous trees and shrubs are vital for winter

shelter. Many birds avoid a feeder or birdbath unless they have a clear view of the surroundings so they can detect any predators. The most popular bird feeders are located near shrubs, trees, or ornamental grasses, where birds can shelter while waiting their turn at the feeding station.

Attracting butterflies

One reason for the popularity of butterfly gardens is that these gardens are big, bright, and colorful—virtues that extend beyond the silent winged creatures.

- **Know the butterflies.** Your local county extension service has information on butterflies native to or passing through your area and what their needs are.
- **Determine the siting.** Locate your butterfly garden in a sunny, protected area. Butterflies can't compete with strong wind, so plant a screen to protect them in the garden.
- **Provide warmth and water.** Set a few stones in a sunny location for butterflies to rest on. Sink a shallow bowl and fill it with water; butterflies prefer water located at ground level.

▲ Flowery evidence of an overhead tree floating in this birdbath indicates that shelter for birds is nearby.

PONDS

BUILD A POND IN A POT

To build a pond in a pot, follow the directions on page 177 for building a freestanding fountain, with one exception. Avoid terra-cotta—the sealant required is toxic to plants and fish. Use a fiberglass or plastic pot (available in finishes that resemble terra-cotta), or line a wood or metal container with plastic. A pond in a pot needs a pump that recirculates the water. However, if you want it to double as a fountain, add a head and raise the pump to the desired height by setting it on bricks.

Whether you choose to call them ponds or water gardens, their distinguishing features are a combination of plant and animal life. In effect, each is an ecosystem and should be treated as a garden bed.

Style and location

It is helpful to review the process for a built-in fountain to determine what type of pond you want and the best location for it. Keep in mind that most fountains can be converted into water gardens.

Loose, informal ponds or water gardens look more natural. Formal ponds, in geometric shapes or lined in brick, may look out of place in natural settings. On the other hand, the addition of plants to a formal pond or fountain can create a striking effect.

The key considerations for siting a pond are level ground and good accessibility. A pond can be any size you want. Locate the pond where you can enjoy it from a favorite window or outdoor area and where you can keep an eye on it daily.

Pond upkeep

Tending a pond is easy once it is established. Some plants need to be pruned and divided occasionally. If you live in an area with below-freezing winter temperatures, move tender plants indoors in autumn.

The key to a healthy pond is filtration. There are two ways to filter a pond: Buy a pump and filter designed for the capacity of your pond, or build a self-cleaning ecosystem with plants and animal life. There are pros and cons to each, and dozens of books on the topic are available.

For more information on pond plant maintenance, see page 192.

▲ Water plants add interest to formal or natural ponds.

▲ Lining the sides of a pond with a short wall of stones adds to the natural look and makes it harder for cats and raccoons to get at your fish.

Keep the pond in sight

Putting a pond near your house makes it visible, enjoyable year-round, easy to check for maintenance, and accessible to sources of water and electricity.

Use the pump

Most ponds require a pump to move the water. Recirculate the water over a waterfall or through a fountain jet to add the sound of splashing water and aerate it for the fish and plants.

Plant the edge

Border your pond with moisture-loving plants to create a transition to the rest of the garden. If necessary, you can grow bog plants in individual containers without drainage holes.

Building a Pond

Once you have decided where to put the pond and have dug the hole, assembling the pond and adding plants is relatively easy.

Materials needed

The pond below is made with a 15×15-foot flexible liner. It is on a level site, has an informal shape, and is rimmed with stone. The process described here applies to any shape you can make with a flexible liner. In addition to the liner, you will need an underwater light and a submersible recirculating pump and filter that doubles as a fountain. You'll also need sand, mortar mix, and enough stone and mortar to rim the pond.

Choose a pump and filter that can recirculate half the volume of the pond every hour. To determine volume, multiply the actual or approximate length of the pond by its width and depth in feet. This gives you cubic feet. Multiply cubic feet by 7.5 to convert to gallons. Half that amount is the number of gallons of water that must be pumped per hour. Most pumps are rated based on gallons per hour, so match your number with the rating listed on the pump package or the specifications given in a catalog. If your pond volume is a little more than a pump's capacity, choose the next larger pump.

Lighting the pond

Dramatic effects are created when light moves through water. The light is bounced around the garden, and it allows you to see colorful fish and night-blooming water lilies. Submersible lights, which cost about the same as a small pump, are available in water garden supply catalogs, and are simple to

▲ **Whether a pond is formal or natural in design, adding water plants makes it come to life with exceptional leaves and flowers.**

install. You can also use low-voltage lighting to illuminate the pond from the side or overhead. For more on lighting, see pages 262–267.

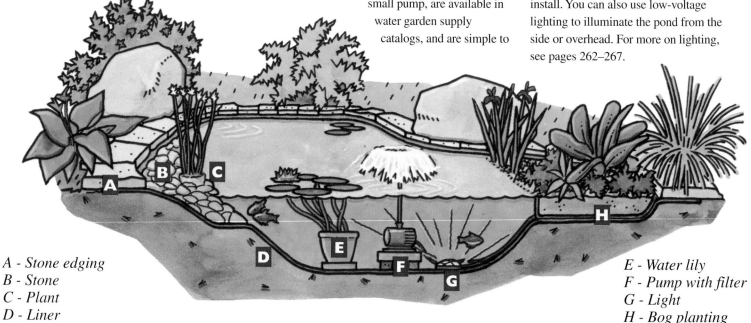

A - Stone edging
B - Stone
C - Plant
D - Liner

E - Water lily
F - Pump with filter
G - Light
H - Bog planting

How to build a pond

MATERIALS

Garden hose

Garden spade and shovel

Level

Builder's sand, dampened (or an old rug or piece of carpet)

Pond liner

Recirculating pump with fountain attachment

Low-voltage underwater lights

Flat stones or pavers

Mortar

STEP 1 **Lay out the shape of the pond.** Place a garden hose where you want the edge of the pond. Strive for strong, simple lines. Dig along the hose or use spray paint or lime to mark the shape. Dig a shelf 12 inches wide and 18 inches deep inside the edge to act as a ledge for plants that like shallow water. Dig the rest of the pond 30 inches deep. Ensure the shelf and floor are level. Remove any rocks or roots.

STEP 2 **Line the bottom, sides, and shelves of the pond.** Put down a 2-inch layer of damp builder's sand or old carpet as a cushion for the liner to prevent punctures. Drape the liner over the sand and slowly fill the pond with water. Stand barefoot in the pond, smoothing the liner as it molds to shape. Place the pump and lights and run the electric cords out past the edge of the liner and onto the ground.

STEP 3 **Edge the pond.** Let the liner settle for several days. Cover the edge of the pond with flat stones or pavers. Set the stones loosely, cantilevering them at least an inch over the lip of the pond. The stones give a clean edge to the pond and protect the liner from deteriorating from prolonged exposure to the sun's UV rays. When you're satisfied with the placement of the stones, set them in ½ inch of mortar.

STEP 4 **Trim the excess liner.** Cut off any liner that shows outside the stones. Remove any debris from the pool. Pump the water out of the pool and wipe the liner clean with a sponge or towel.

Refill the pool with fresh water. If the water is chlorinated, adjust the water before adding fish or plants: Allow the pond to sit 10 days before planting and a month before adding fish, or purchase a water treatment kit that does the job much faster.

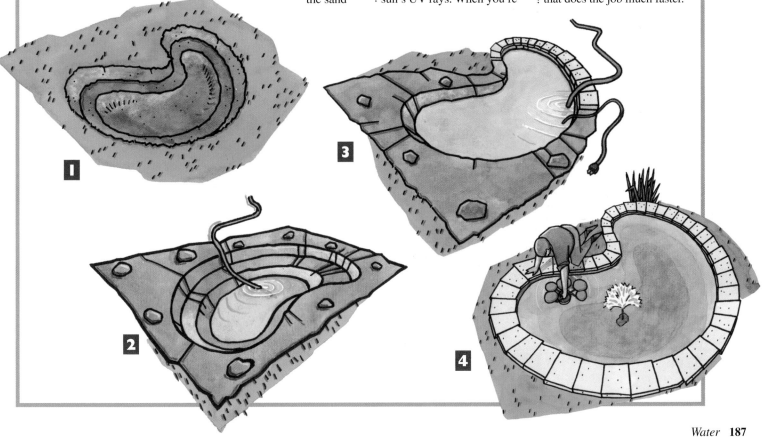

Splashing Water

Water is a delight to hear as well as see. Splashing water can drown out undesirable sounds such as traffic, noisy children, or a ringing telephone.

At the same time, splashing water has a meditative quality that can soothe frazzled nerves. It also attracts birds to the garden. And splashing water reminds you that the water feature is there and that it is working.

There are two ways to add the sound of water to the garden: fountains and waterfalls. Both are easy to install yourself and in most cases can be incorporated into existing water features.

Fountains

A pump that is designed or adapted to accommodate a fountain head is the easiest way to add the sound of splashing water. Fountains come in a wide array of styles. The fountain jet—the piece that attaches to the pump—controls the volume, height, and shape of the spray and determines specific effects, such as a gentle hissing, a steady stream, or random splashing.

Normally the pump and head can be adjusted to achieve the desired sound. For the best results, and to get the most sound, use a strong, steady stream of water that shoots as high into the air as possible while still being caught within the confines of the vessel you are using. Adjust the jet so that no more than a few drops splash out every few minutes. Otherwise, you will have to refill the vessel frequently.

◀ Ponds lend themselves readily to waterfalls. Here, water flows over the falls into a pond. It is then recirculated and pumped back to the top of the falls.

Pay attention to the effect that wind has on water, so you don't have to keep refilling the fountain. A thin jet of water, which creates a pleasant and unique sound, is easily buffeted by wind. One way to limit water loss is to use the fountain only on special occasions.

Waterfalls

For ponds and pools, waterfalls add a soothing sound and can look as though they are part of a natural system. Because most ponds require a large pump to recirculate the water, you may already have all the equipment you need.

Adding a waterfall can be as simple as attaching a hose to the outflow of the pump and positioning the hose so that the water falls over rocks and into the pool before being recirculated. An extra benefit of a waterfall is that it aerates the water. The added oxygen benefits all the plants or animal life living in your pond. Tricks such as an echo chamber (page 189) will maximize the sound of your waterfall.

▲ Thin streams of water create a soft splashing sound. This type of fountain works best in a protected area so the wind doesn't disturb the water.

▲ **Get the most sound from your waterfall by creating an echo chamber.**

How to build an echo chamber

If you are going to have water, you may as well be able to hear it. The concept of an echo chamber is simple: Instead of having water drop straight into a pond and in front of a solid wall, a hollow chamber amplifies the sound of the water falling over the rocks.

STEP 1 **Create the chamber.** Cantilever a large, flat stone several inches over the edge of the pond and at least 6 inches above the surface of the water. You may want to experiment with sound reverberation by stacking a flat stone vertically at the back of the chamber. Or you may prefer to let soil and plants absorb the sound.

STEP 2 **Build the waterfall.** Stack a pile of rocks at least 2 feet high on the cantilevered stone. As you place the rocks, tilt them slightly toward the water. This creates a channel for the water.

STEP 3 **Adjust the water.** Run a hose at approximately the same volume of water as your pump will, and move the rocks around until you achieve the desired sound effect. Take the waterfall apart, then rebuild it to accommodate the tubing. Run the tubing from the return portion of the pump between the rocks, stacking rocks so the flow of water is not pinched off.

Turn on the pump and make any final adjustments of the rocks to get exactly the sound you desire.

Crossing Water

For the full enjoyment of water in the garden, you need to be close to it. Standing near a pond or pool and looking at it is one thing; standing over it or walking across it is quite another. Bridges and stepping-stones in water allow you to get close to your water feature, and they make it easier to use a water feature to divide different areas of the garden.

▲ When choosing a style of bridge for your garden, keep the surrounding architecture in mind. Some prefabricated bridges come with elaborate detailing not suited for every garden or gardener.

▼ Build your bridge with a destination in mind. Check your local building codes regarding railings.

Bridges

A bridge provides connection, contact, or transition. Most often a bridge is used to span a narrow stream, providing a connection from one side to the other. Even if a bridge is not the fastest or only way to get from one area to another, few ways are more appealing.

When planning your bridge, determine the length of the span. For ease of building, low cost, and avoiding hassle, the shorter the span, the better.

Another consideration is the footing at each end of the bridge. If you are planning to span a pond, avoid any damage to the pond when digging the footing. You will need to wear socks or go barefoot whenever you actually stand in the pond to place the footing to minimize the risk of damage to the liner.

When determining exactly where a bridge will go, consider the entire experience. Think about how you will get to the foot of the bridge and where you will be (or go) once you cross the bridge. You can tie the span in with an existing path or make it a frivolous detour.

The style of your bridge is a matter of taste and cost. Kits are available; you can even purchase them already put together from many garden centers. Many bridges are ornate and have a Victorian quality that may look good in the catalog or store but may be too fussy for in your garden. If you intend on building a bridge yourself, be certain you comply with your local building codes. Call your county building department to get more information.

Most bridges will be safer, and the user will feel more secure, if a railing is attached. In some cases, a rail is required by law. Check local building codes.

Stepping-stones

An alternative to a bridge is to place stepping-stones just above the surface

of the water. This increases the excitement of crossing the water—there is no railing, and you are at water level—but the risk is minimal. You can add stepping-stones to any water feature whether large or small (below).

Two keys to success and safety are to have stepping-stones firmly attached to a solid base and to use stepping-stones only when they are dry. When selecting stepping-stones for the bridge, choose rocks with a rough surface. Products are available to apply to stone and masonry to keep them from being slippery.

◄ A stepping-stone bridge presents an irresistible invitation to cross it and discover what lies beyond.

How to build a stepping-stone bridge

Building a stepping-stone bridge through a shallow pond is easy, especially if you do it when you build the pond. Otherwise, you will have to drain the pond—as in this example—and move any water plants or fish elsewhere during construction.

MATERIALS

Stepping-stones or nonskid pavers, 2 inches thick and at least 18 inches wide
Stakes and string
Line level
Carpet scraps
Concrete blocks (8×8×16)
Mortar

STEP 1 Decide where the bridge will go. For safety as well as aesthetics, the stones must sit on a level surface. Avoid any irregularities in the bottom of the pond.

STEP 2 Determine the spacing. Lay out the stones on dry land (driveway or lawn works best), positioning them so you can walk across them comfortably in the pond. Once you're satisfied with the layout, sketch the configuration on paper, marking all dimensions.

STEP 3 Establish the top level of the stones. Drive a stake on either side of the pond to form an imaginary line that passes above the area where the steps will cross the pond. Run a level string between the stakes. Measure down from the string to the point where the water's surface will be and write down this distance.

STEP 4 Build the piers. In the empty pond, lay down a scrap of carpet where each stepping-stone will be to protect the pond liner. Using the sketch as a guide, lay two concrete blocks on their sides, next to each other, on top of each piece of carpet. Stack the blocks and stones until the top will be just above the surface of the water, allowing for ½ inch of mortar between each

level of blocks and stones. You may have to try different stones to get the right height.

STEP 5 Disassemble the piers and mix several batches of mortar. Do one pier at a time so you can keep track of the proper block placement and general layout. Reassemble the pier, using ½ inch of mortar between each block all the way up to the stepping-stone.

Allow the mortar to set for three days. Cover the steps with a tarp if rain is predicted. Once the mortar has dried, refill the pond. Now you can walk on water.

Stepping-stone
Mortar
Concrete block
Carpet scrap
Liner
Sand

Planting in Water

▲ Use water plants in and around a pond or water garden to soften the hard scape.

Many species of aquatic plants are readily available for the pond or fountain. These plants add more than charm and beauty. Water plants serve practical functions and help keep the pond a healthy ecosystem.

Design the planting

Plan the plantings in your pond the same as you would any garden bed. Consider the design and the maintenance required. Take into account the ease of accessing each plant. Plan on having to wade into the pool or pond periodically to adjust or tend various plants. If you have a vinyl-lined pond, do this barefoot or wearing socks (see page 190) to avoid damaging the liner.

Sketch out a plan before making any purchases. As you design, determine the primary point from which the pond will be viewed. Use lower-growing plants toward the front, graduating to taller plants toward the rear. If the pond will be viewed from all sides, place taller plants in the middle, then step them down in size as you near the edge of the pond.

As you choose plants, be aware of how they grow and the functions they perform. There are several basic types of water plants. The first and most important are called oxygenators. As the name implies, these plants add oxygen to the water through photosynthesis. They provide shade and compete with algae for light and food, thereby helping keep the water clear. Most oxygenators are grasses that prefer the bottom of the pond, shooting their foliage high above the surface of the water. They also provide hiding and nesting places for fish.

Floating aquatics are another type of water plant. These plants literally float on the water and get their nourishment through their dangling roots. They also help keep down the algae population by blocking light. Water lettuce and water hyacinth are two examples.

TIPS FOR ADDING UNDERWATER LIFE

▲ Koi are the biggest and boldest of all pond fish and come in many different colors.

Colorful fish and other water creatures bring new dimensions to your water garden—movement and life. They also help in the overall health of the pond by eating insects and algae. As a bonus, waste from water animals such as fish, snails, turtles, and frogs serves as fertilizer for the plants. But pond creatures do more than work. They are fascinating to watch, and most do not harm the plants.

- **Check the water.** Before you add fish or other creatures to the pond, be sure the water is not toxic. Water-testing kits are available at most garden centers and pond equipment suppliers.

- **Treat the water.** Let city or tap water sit in the pond for a month before adding fish. This allows chemicals, especially chlorine, to dissipate. Or treat the water with a neutralizing formula, available at garden centers.

- **Selecting water animals.** Plan on one 8-inch or two 4-inch fish and two snails for every square yard of pool surface. Koi, catfish, and other predators need about 25 square feet of surface area per fish and do best in pools at least 3 feet deep. These larger fish may gobble up goldfish, guppies, and mollies, so don't mix them.

- **Releasing fish into the pond.** Leave the fish in their container and float it for 30 minutes in your pond. Then slowly pour them into the water.

▲ **When choosing water plants, use a mix of heights and textures, as you would with any garden bed.**

▲ **Water gardens offer the opportunity to grow striking and unusual plants, such as this horsetail.**

Water lilies and lotus are two of the most commonly known water plants. Hardy water lilies will overwinter in the water to Zone 4 and lotus will overwinter to Zone 5. Tropical water lilies are rarely hardy in areas colder than Zone 9; in colder regions, dig the tubers in autumn and overwinter them indoors. Or treat tropicals as annuals, so that each plant lasts only one growing season.

Create a transition from the pond to the rest of the garden by planting marginal aquatic or marsh plants. Moisture-loving plants such as iris, arrowhead, ornamental grasses, and some lilies are ideal. If your pond is self-contained, grow these plants outside the pond by sinking them in a bucket without drainage holes.

Make plans for one water lily and about six oxygenating plants for each square yard of pool surface. A sampling of water plants is found on pages 194 and 195.

Planting in water

Give each water plant its own container. This makes it easier to move plants to achieve the desired effect. Plastic containers work best; they are lightweight, durable, and don't release toxins that could harm plants or fish. Using individual containers also allows you to move each plant to its proper depth. Some plants like the top of their container a foot underwater. Other plants need to have the soil line just above the surface of the water.

For the greatest ease and success, your pond should accommodate plants at different depths with shelves or concrete blocks, bricks, or anything else that is sturdy and has a level surface. If your pond has a flexible liner, put down a towel or carpet scrap under the blocks to avoid tearing the liner.

Most plants prefer heavy, sandy soil. Grow water lilies and lotus in large tubs to allow plenty of room for their vigorous seasonal growth.

Many water plants are fast growers, especially in warm climates. Plan on dividing water plants every other year. To feed water plants, use fertilizer tablets that you push into the soil.

◄ **Allow for varied plant depths. A shelf 6 to 8 inches below water level is best for edge or marginal plants. Blocks 12 to 16 inches thick in a 24-inch-deep pond allow other pond plants to be at the proper depth.**

Recommended Water Plants

Choosing a water plant is just like choosing a garden plant. Besides color, shape, and size, you need to know the growing conditions it requires, its rate of growth and mature size, its ongoing maintenance needs, and its life span. You also need to know the role the plant will play as it becomes part of the ecosystem.

You can get information about the best water garden plants for your area from your local water garden society, where water garden enthusiasts meet to share their experiences. Locate it through a botanical garden or the local extension service. Water garden societies often offer plant sales and swaps too.

Water lily

LAEVIGATE IRIS

Iris laevigata

Perennial; edge/marginal plant
Hardiness Zones 4–9
24–42" tall
Blue flowers; late spring–early summer
Sun to partial shade

The blooms of laevigate iris add a bright exclamation of color at the edge of the water garden. The plants multiply well and need to be divided every three years or so.

FLOATING FERN

Ceratopteris pteridioides

Perennial; floater plant
Hardiness Zones 9–11
3–4" wide; floats flat on water
Sun to light shade

Also known as water fern, the velvety pea green leaves turn dark red or purple as cool weather approaches. Floating fern survives the winter by means of submerged fragments. Can be aggressive.

PARROT'S FEATHER

Myriophyllum aquaticum

Perennial; oxygenator plant
Hardiness Zones 10–11
9" tall (above water)
Part sun

This feathery plant may be evergreen or deciduous. It has a wide, spreading growth habit underwater. The blue-green leaves may turn red in cool climates if it grows above water.

PICKEREL WEED

Pontederia cordata

Perennial; edge/marginal plant
Hardiness Zones 3–10
3' tall
Sun

Striking lance- or ovate-shaped leaves with lovely spires of purple or white flowers in summer. Native to eastern North America, pickerel weed adds a touch of much-needed blue to the water garden landscape.

WATER HYACINTH

Eichhornia crassipes

Perennial; floater plant
Hardiness Zones 9–11
5–6" tall
Sun to light shade

Easy to grow. The flower resembles a garden hyacinth, held above the leaves on a strong stem. Can be very invasive. Control by lifting out excess plants; don't dispose of them in sewers or streams.

HORSETAIL

Equisetum spp.

Perennial; marginal/edge plant
Hardiness Zones 3–11
18–48" tall
Sun to light shade

Also known as scouring rush, horsetail is invasive. Plant in pots at the pond edge with the crown of the plant 6" below the water surface. Dwarf horsetail is 8" tall; plant it with its crown 1" below water.

SWAMP LILY

Saururus cernuus

Perennial; marginal/edge plant
Hardiness Zones 5–10
12–30" tall
White flowers in summer
Sun to light shade

A deciduous plant that forms dense clumps of rich green leaves at the edge of ponds and bogs. Its flowers resemble gooseneck loosestrife.

AMERICAN LOTUS

Nelumbo lutea

Perennial; water plant
Hardiness Zones 6–11
2-3' tall
Pink/white flowers in summer
Sun

This much-desired plant requires a large space; the leaves can reach 6' across. Some varieties have leaves splotched red in the center. Seedpod is very showy.

WATER LILY

Nymphaea spp.

Perennial; water plant
Hardiness Zones 3–11
18" tall; 4–12' spread
Sun or part shade

Evergreen and ever-blooming in frost-free areas, dies back in winter in other zones. Flowers open in morning and close by late afternoon, resting on the leaves. Some are fragrant.

WATER POPPY

Hydrocleys nymphoides

Perennial; floater plant
Hardiness Zones 10–11
3–4' tall
Yellow flowers in summer
Sun

This delightful oval-leaved plant can grow free-floating or rooted in a pot, or in soil at the edge of the pond in shallow water. Easy to raise as an annual in colder areas.

WATER SNOWFLAKE

Nymphoides indica

Perennial; floater plant
Hardiness Zones 7–11
3–6" tall; 20–30" spread
Star-shape white flowers in summer
Sun

Easy to grow as an annual in colder areas. A yellow-flowered species, *N. peltata (*yellow floating heart), is hardy to Zone 6. Both species have attractive mottled leaves.

SWIMMING POOLS

▲ **An important part of enjoying a swimming pool is having a private place to lounge or entertain at poolside.**

Swimming pools used to be an indulgence reserved for the elite. Today, a wide range of styles and materials makes them affordable. Pools offer a place to play, exercise, relax, and entertain that is achievable for more people than ever before.

Enter a pool-building project slowly. Proper planning for the use of the pool, its shape and size, as well as safety and maintenance issues should be examined thoroughly before meeting with a contractor. And remember, a swimming pool will probably be the dominant element in the garden.

The purpose of pools

Knowing how you intend to use the pool will guide your other decisions. For example, if you want a pool for floating and relaxing, it can be much smaller and shallower than one designed for diving. If you prefer to play water volleyball, you'll need a large shallow area and no deep end. For exercise and swimming laps, you'll want a pool at least 50 feet long—but it need only be 5 feet wide and deep.

Other considerations are poolside entertaining and sunbathing. They affect where to locate the pool and how the area around it is designed. Your program analysis should guide you through all of these decisions (see Chapter 1).

Safety

Use common sense to prevent mishaps. If you have children or pets, a fence is a must. Check local building and zoning ordinances for safety requirements regarding pools. Most cities require a fence with a self-closing and self-latching gate around the entire perimeter of a pool. It must be a minimum distance from the edge of the pool. Should a fence be required, or should you choose to add one, the same principles in selecting a fence apply as elsewhere in the garden. For more on fences, see pages 116–123.

If you have children, another safety concern is the ability to supervise the pool from inside your home. In addition, the surface around the pool should be a nonskid material to minimize slipping. Be sure to check how adding a pool will affect your insurance.

Cost

Pool costs vary greatly, depending upon the site, the size and shape of the pool, and the materials you use. In most cases, the pool itself represents only about two-thirds of the total cost; the rest is spent on decking, fencing, plantings, and other amenities. The cost of most pools can be recovered when a home is sold, provided the pool cost does not exceed 10 percent of the home value.

Another cost issue is maintenance. Check into local pool services to see what it would cost for carefree maintenance. Tending the pool yourself is not difficult, but it does require regular attention.

◀ **Poolside plantings blend the pool with the surrounding landscape.**

Have a poolside retreat

Add to the enjoyment of a swimming pool by having a private place from which to enjoy it. Walls and fences used to create this kind of space may be required by law, so check local ordinances.

Edge the pool

Provide a border or decking around the entire edge of the pool for safety and to make cleaning the pool easier. Plan on making it at least 3 feet wide.

Plan ahead for fun

Amenities such as a slide or a fountain add to the enjoyment of a pool. These details are much easier and more affordable if planned for from the outset of the project.

Pool Considerations

Pool types and materials

Pools are divided into two basic categories: aboveground and in-ground. In-ground pools are more common, but aboveground pools have advantages too.

An aboveground pool costs substantially less than one built in the ground, mainly because excavation is not necessary. Such a pool is ideal in northern climates where freezing and thawing can pop a pool out of the ground. The disadvantages of an aboveground pool are that it lasts only about 10 years, the water warms up more quickly, and the pool is more visible in the landscape.

An in-ground pool offers many positive features. It can be constructed of concrete or fiberglass. Some have vinyl liners. A concrete pool is built by excavating a hole that is the shape of the pool, building a frame, molding the frame with concrete, and adding a smooth plaster finish. It is more durable than vinyl or fiberglass, lasting many decades if built and maintained properly. It lends itself to a wide range of settings and finishes.

An in-ground pool costs considerably more than an aboveground pool. If something goes wrong, repairs are rarely a do-it-yourself job. And if you change your mind about the pool, there's not a lot to be done short of filling it in.

Pool location

Pools are so large there is sometimes no choice where to place a swimming pool. If you are fortunate enough to have a choice, there are questions you should answer:

– Is the ground firm enough to bear the weight of the pool? Does your soil drain well enough to keep the pool from popping out of the ground?

– Will building the pool threaten your home's foundation or other structures?

– Are any underground utility lines or large tree roots in the way?

– How much sunlight does the area receive at various times of the day, and does that suit your intended use?

– How close is the desired pool location to existing water and power sources? Pool costs increase the farther a pool is from utilities.

– What are the wind patterns where you want the pool? Will prevailing winds blow debris into the pool? Can you add a windscreen?

– Is the pool far enough away from overhanging tree limbs that you won't have to constantly clean the pool?

– Can you see the pool from your house or other desired vantage point?

Pool size and shape

There are few rules about size and shape other than the guidelines at left for a pool with a diving board. If you are using a liner or want an aboveground pool, you may be limited to simple shapes such as squares and rectangles. Concrete pools can be many shapes as shown by the sampler of shapes on page 199.

When it comes to size, the main considerations are cost and maintenance. The bigger the pool, the greater the cost, not only for the pool itself but for the equipment to operate it. Maintenance will also increase proportionately with size.

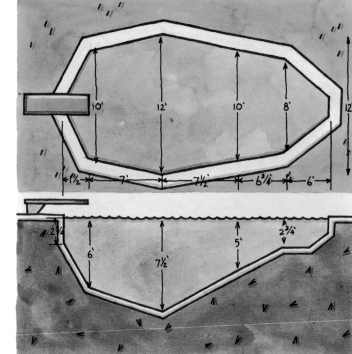

▶ **This diagram shows the minimum dimensions for a pool with a diving board.**

Pool Shapes

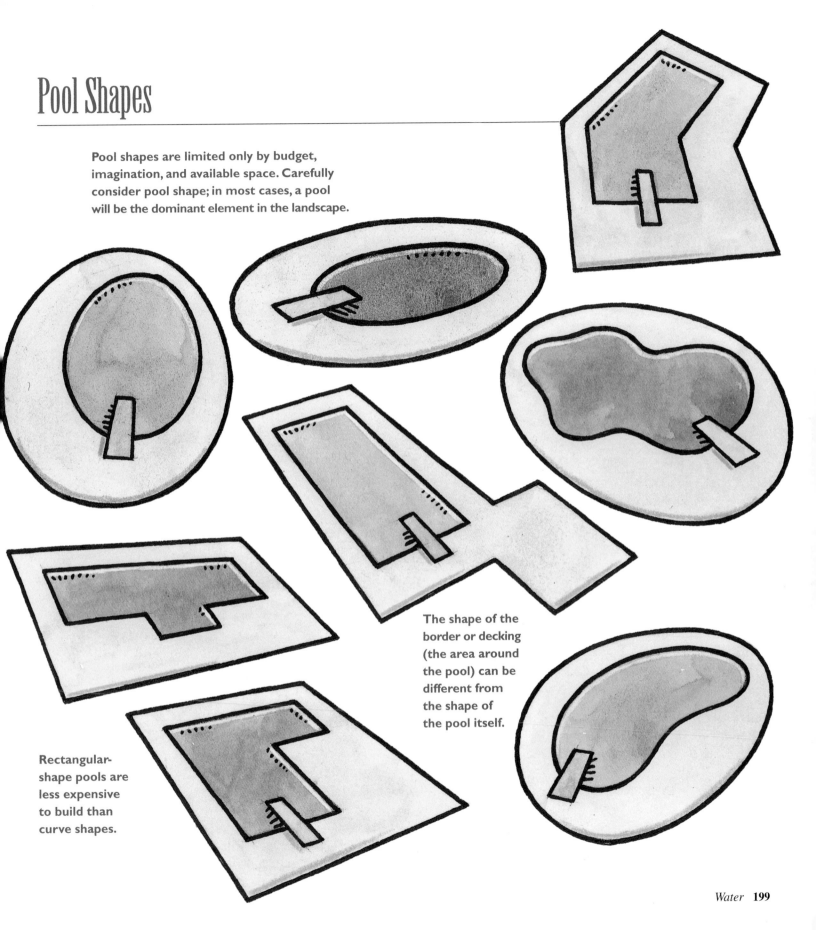

Pool shapes are limited only by budget, imagination, and available space. Carefully consider pool shape; in most cases, a pool will be the dominant element in the landscape.

The shape of the border or decking (the area around the pool) can be different from the shape of the pool itself.

Rectangular-shape pools are less expensive to build than curve shapes.

Pool Decking, Coping, and Staining

Pool decking is the solid surface surrounding a pool and is usually made of stone, wood, or masonry. Pool coping is the point where the decking meets the edge of the pool. Staining refers to the finish of the pool and, in some cases, the decking itself. All these components are important to the look, enjoyment, and safety of your pool.

Decking

Pool decking serves as a safe and stable surface for getting in and out of the pool. It offers a place for poolside entertaining, and it helps keep out insects and debris.

Decking should be at least 3 feet wide around the pool. Because most activity occurs at the shallow end, make the decking wider there. If you know the type of poolside entertaining you will do, use the guidelines on page 145 to estimate the space required.

Decking materials vary, but your choice should blend with the overall design. The decking should have a nonskid surface. Most pool-related accidents occur outside the pool. Concrete is the most common, affordable, and safe material. Slate and marble look good but cost a lot and are slippery when wet. You

▲ **What appear to be koi swimming in the pool are actually trompe l'oeil figures painted on the bottom.**

can also use modular tiles, brick, or stone with a coarse surface. All these materials heat up in the sun, so consider a concrete base with a cooling surface that is available from most pool construction companies. Wood decking is a good choice if the pool is above ground or on a slope.

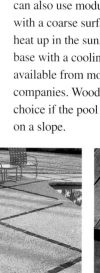

◀ **Stamped concrete decking provides the rich look of brick with a rough surface for better traction.**

▲ **Pool decking should be a solid, nonskid surface.**

▲ **If using wood decking, be certain the area beneath drains away from the pool.**

Coping

Coping is to a pool what molding is to a room. It adds character and accentuates lines. The coping should complement the material of the pool, the decking, and elements of the landscape. For example, if you have a brick home and use concrete for the pool and decking, brick coping will pull everything together visually. This is true of any material you extend from the edge of the pool to the waterline.

Coping should have a smooth or rolled edge to avoid scrapes when getting in or out of the pool. Both the coping and the decking should drain away from the pool so puddles don't form. This is safer and keeps storm runoff from overflowing the pool during a heavy rain. Many copings include a scum trap to capture debris before it can fall into the pool.

Staining

Staining is optional and purely aesthetic. It can also be pure fun. A simple dark stain helps the pool blend with its surroundings. It also absorbs light well, allowing the pool to warm up more quickly in spring and stay warmer in autumn. (The water temperature difference in summer is negligible.) A dark pool also cuts down on reflective glare, allowing the surface of the water to reflect the surroundings.

Stains are typically applied when the pool is plastered. If your pool is already in place and you want to stain it, you can do it yourself the next time you need to replaster or repair the pool.

◀ **Stone coping with a smooth edge can be used for a natural look.**

▲ **A navy or black stained pool has the greatest reflective quality.**

▲ **When planting around the edge of a pool, consider pool and plant care.**

▲ **Coping can extend from decking to the waterline.**

TIPS ON POOL MAINTENANCE

A great many labor-saving devices, such as automatic pool skimmers or a pool service, can make a pool more fun. The following tips should help too:

- Regular skimming of the pool reduces strain on the filter and pump.
- Be sure your pump is properly sized for your pool. Too big is a waste of money. Too small means a dirty pool.
- Regular filter maintenance prolongs the life of the pump and reduces the need for water treatments.
- Place pumps and filters 2 feet above ground.
- Pool covers keep a pool clean and safe during the off-season.
- The pH level of your pool is usually adjusted by adding acid and should be checked at least once a week.
- A pool vacuum is essential to reach debris that settles to the pool bottom.
- Some sanitizing alternatives to chlorine, such as copper electrodes, may be less environmentally friendly.
- Add chlorine after swimming, not before.
- A heavy rain can seriously alter the quality of the water so that it requires extra chlorine.
- Some systems monitor chlorine continuously and add it on an as-needed basis.
- In cold climates, pools can sometimes be adequately winterized without draining. For example, floating a sealed barrel in an aboveground pool can protect the walls from expansion.

SPAS

Over the years, spas and hot tubs have waxed and waned in popularity, but few can argue their effectiveness in providing relaxation. But buying a spa and dropping it in the yard may cause more headaches than it massages away. Proper planning always pays off.

A spa can take the place of a pool if all you want is to relax in water. It won't dominate the landscape and it costs less than a pool. Because a spa's water is heated, there is generally a longer season of use. If you have children, you can easily cover a spa for safety.

▲ A combined pool and spa can share a pump and filter required to keep them both clean.

Placing the spa

The key in placing a spa is to put it where you will use it most. This may be on a deck or patio right outside your bedroom. It could be adjacent to your pool. The spa might be nestled in a corner of a deck or terrace, or it may even become the centerpiece of an outdoor room. Keep in mind that if a spa will be adjacent to a swimming pool or built as part of a terrace or courtyard, you will save money on material and labor if you plan and build both features at the same time.

When determining where you will use a spa most, consider privacy, exposure to sun or shade, wind exposure, access to a power supply, and the ability to get in and out of the spa easily and safely. For more on creating privacy, see chapter five. For

◄ Place a spa where it will be used and maintained most often.

more on how to determine sun and wind exposure, see the discussion on site analysis on pages 14–19.

Spa types

With a general location in mind, it is time to deal with specifics. First of all, how many people do you want in the spa at one time? There are one-person, two-person, four-person, and larger spas. A realistic evaluation of how the spa will be used should guide your decision.

The next important consideration is the type of spa or hot tub you want. Spas and hot tubs can be built-in or freestanding; they can be custom-made of concrete and plaster or prefabricated of fiberglass or vinyl. There are benefits and drawbacks to each type and each material, primarily in terms of cost, comfort, and durability.

Many times a spa is custom-built from concrete and lined with tile. These are set into the ground to mimic a natural hot spring. A custom-built spa will cost more but may be worth the extra effort and money in the durability and style it offers. Generally, it is less body-conforming than a fiberglass model.

Freestanding spas are the most common and affordable. They have the advantage of being easily moved or removed. Freestanding spas, whether made of fiberglass or vinyl, come in a wide array of colors and shapes. The best way to know if a spa suits you (and other users) is to give a test run. Sit in the spa and change positions. As you do this,

For most people, privacy is a major factor in determining how much they enjoy their spa. A sense of seclusion can add to the overall experience of relaxing.

● **Check the site.** Set a chair at the approximate place and height where you want to position the spa. Take a look around and note what you see. More importantly, notice from where you can be seen.

● **Correct the view.** Turning 180 degrees can often improve the view. Controlling the view may be a little trickier. The use of screens (see pages 126–127), arbors (see pages 210–215), and fences (see pages 116–123) can deter potential prying eyes.

◄ **Details such as these towel hooks embedded in a stone wall add fun and function to a spa area.**

replacing, and you shouldn't have to tear apart your spa support to replace a fuse.

Tips for spa use and maintenance

● Be sure the spa has an effective and accessible on-off switch.
● Never use glassware in or near a spa. If broken glass gets in it, drain the spa.
● Be sure you have lighting around the spa if you plan on using it at night.
● Be aware that drinking alcohol while in a hot tub can be dangerous.
● Avoid staying in a hot tub for more than 20 minutes.
● Keep electrical devices at least 5 feet from the spa.
● Have a timer that shuts off the heat and jets should you fall asleep in the spa.
● Invest in a cover to keep your spa safe, warm, and clean.

check for more than comfort. Note where jets hit your body and how accessible the controls are.

With the right spa, you need the right setting. Unless the spa is set flush with its surroundings, steps are a must. In some cases, an entire deck is built around the spa for easy access. A small change in elevation can create a sense of privacy.

Be sure the inner workings of the spa are accessible. Filters, pumps, heaters, and other components will eventually need

◄ **A spa can take the place of a pool as the dominant water feature in the garden.**

CHAPTER 8

GARDEN STRUCTURES

Add shelter, shade, storage, and utility

GAZEBOS

azebos are unique among garden structures. Whereas many other features become part of—or enhance—an outdoor room, a gazebo *is* an outdoor room. It has walls, a floor, and a ceiling. As such, its impact in the garden setting is, in most cases, rivaled only by that of the house itself. Building a gazebo from scratch is a fairly significant project in terms of time, expense, and expertise. Often a contractor is hired to build a gazebo. Or a homeowner can build one from a kit.

It's important to select the right type of gazebo. For the greatest success, consider the intended use for the structure, the style, its location within the garden, the materials you will use to build it, and the details you will add. Details help a gazebo fulfill its purpose, and they add character so the gazebo is in keeping with the overall landscape.

The first step in planning the perfect gazebo is knowing how you intend to use it. There is no right or wrong way—it is a matter of personal choice. You may want the room to be a getaway or a retreat. It could include sleeping accommodations for warm, sultry nights. You may want a place to entertain, whether casually or formally. Or you may want to have a gazebo for its looks alone. Make a list of all the activities you want to do in the gazebo as well as other functions you want the gazebo to fulfill, including being a focal point. Let this list guide you through the decisionmaking process.

Gazebo styles

When choosing materials and a style for your gazebo, incorporate features and details from the architecture of the house or other existing and visible structures, to tie the gazebo to the rest of the garden. A review of some common styles will help get you started.

Modern A contemporary gazebo, like the one shown on page 207, stands out and makes a bold statement. This style is best suited to complement a contemporary house.

Traditional The traditional gazebo (left) fits more garden styles, especially when you consider finishes. The natural stain on this structure allows it to blend into the landscape; the same structure painted white would stand out more.

Rustic A rustic gazebo could be made of rough-hewn logs and even be lashed together with rope. This style lends itself better than the others to a woodland setting.

◀ If you live in an area with biting insects, consider installing screens on your gazebo so you can enjoy it more often.

Create a view

A gazebo can be a focal point all its own. Keep in mind that you will also want a pleasant view (or a way to block an unpleasant one) when looking out from the gazebo.

Add lighting

The evening is one of the best times to be in the garden, so consider illumination in or around the gazebo. It's easier to put wiring in place when you build than to add it later on.

Match your style

Pay attention to the design and details of your house and other nearby structures. They will help you decide on the design of your gazebo so that all structures have a unified theme.

Siting the gazebo

Deciding where to build your gazebo is strongly linked to how you plan to use it. Review your site analysis while going over the following suggestions.

Put it close to the house. If you plan to use the gazebo for entertaining—particularly dining—you might want it near the house. It will be more convenient in terms of cooking and serving, and it becomes an extension of the house. You might think about building the gazebo near other major structures such as a swimming pool or terrace. These areas are typically used a lot; having the shelter of the gazebo nearby enhances the experience of the existing structure and promotes the use of the gazebo.

Make it a destination. Instead of siting the gazebo where it's visible from the house, hide it. Make it a surprise you find when you round a corner of the garden path. Or tuck it away so discreetly that only those intimate with the garden will know it is there—ideal for creating a getaway or retreat. If you want it to be a retreat, site the gazebo as far from the parking area, play areas, or the street as possible. If you don't have such a place, consider creating a private nook. For tips on how to do this, see pages 168–171.

Use it as a focal point. You might want a gazebo purely for its aesthetics. It can take on a sculptural quality that makes it the dominant part of the garden. Keep scale in mind. If you have a small garden, design a small gazebo. A large one, no matter how attractive it is, would look out of place.

You can also use a part of the gazebo as the focal point, such as the roof peeking out from above a hedge, to draw visitors into the garden and help create a sense of intrigue.

If you want the gazebo to serve as a focal point, consider all the views from which you want to see it. In most cases there is more than one vantage point.

Consider the views. You need to consider what the views will be like once you are in the gazebo. Start by looking at your site analysis for particularly good views from your property. Note any views you want to avoid.

Keep in mind that the walls and ceiling of the structure can be used to frame views. If your gazebo will be a foot or two off the ground, stand on a footstool at the height of the finished level of the gazebo to check out the view. Alternatively, you could sink the floor of the gazebo a couple of feet if that's what it takes to achieve the best view.

Catch a breeze or a ray. Know the prevailing wind direction in the seasons you plan to use the gazebo. Orient the gazebo to take advantage of cooling breezes in summer or block chilly winds in early spring or fall. If you plan to have afternoon tea or morning coffee in the gazebo, site it to take advantage of the angle of the sun during those times. You may wish to orient the structure to frame the sunrise or sunset. Site the gazebo so that you will take advantage of it and enjoy it.

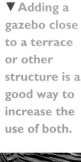

▼ Adding a gazebo close to a terrace or other structure is a good way to increase the use of both.

▲ If you have an attractive view from your garden, a gazebo is a good way to get the most from it.

Gazebo details

Details can make the experience of being in the gazebo more enjoyable. They can also make the gazebo look better and tie in to the rest of the garden.

Lighting This works in two ways. If the outside or inside of the gazebo is lit at night, the gazebo becomes a sculptural feature, drawing the eye to it from other parts of the garden and adding depth to the garden. Lighting also extends the use of the gazebo by making it functional at night. When adding lighting to a gazebo, include a master switch from the house. In the gazebo, put the lights on a dimmer switch so you can adjust the lighting to match the mood as well as the ambient light. Before installing any lights that would illuminate the outside of the gazebo, stand in it at night to be sure the lights are not glaring in your face.

Cooling and heating A roof blocks the sun and makes the gazebo cooler, but it may also thwart breezes. A good way to keep the gazebo pleasant on even the hottest and muggiest days is to install a ceiling fan. If the design of the roof does not lend itself to one, or if it can't be adapted easily, consider an oscillating fan. The sound of a fan creates a pleasant white noise.

When it is comfortable enough to be outdoors with a light jacket or sweater, a source of heat will make your gazebo a cozy retreat. Tiki lamps, a built-in fireplace, or a fire pit just outside the gazebo can add charm and warmth. When siting a fire pit, be aware of prevailing winds; otherwise, the smoke may run you out of the gazebo. Or consider an electric or kerosene space heater. Whenever you add heat to a wood structure, make certain you have a fire extinguisher on hand.

Seating Provide ample seating for the number of people you intend to have in the gazebo. The seating arrangement guide on page 145 may be helpful in planning the floor size of the gazebo. The seating can be one continuous bench around the inside edge, or it can be a set of Adirondack chairs. Another possibility is a futon or a hammock for napping and overnight enjoyment.

Sound Adding sound blocks out unwanted noise and focuses attention inward. The sound can be soft music from a portable stereo or a built-in, weatherproof one; the splashing of a nearby fountain; birds drawn to a nearby feeder and birdbath; the whir of a fan; or the crackle of a fire.

Utilities Wire the gazebo for basic utilities even if you are unsure about how you will ultimately use the gazebo. Power is essential for a fan, lighting, a stereo, or a pump for a fountain. Consider having a nearby water source—especially helpful if you plan to use the gazebo for dining and if you need to douse the fire pit before calling it a night. Also consider a phone line, or an intercom if the gazebo is too far from the house for good reception from a home-based cordless phone. You can always turn off the ringer if you don't want to be interrupted.

▲ **A traditional gazebo, whether custom-made or built from a kit, offers an inviting respite from a sunny garden.**

ARBORS

An arbor is one of the most romantic structures in the garden. It is intimate in scale and limitless in style. There are many arbor kits on the market, but the average homeowner can easily custom-build one with basic tools and carpentry skills.

You need to ask yourself a few questions before you start building. What do you want the arbor to accomplish? What style should you use? What materials? What finish should you use? These questions will be answered in the pages ahead. As always, the best starting points for ideas on location, style, and use are your site analysis and master plan (see page 14).

▼ A dark stain enables an arbor to blend into the garden so that the bright flowers can take center stage.

Using arbors

An arbor is versatile. Knowing how you will use it will help you decide where to place it as well as what style to choose.

Entry An arbor is ideal for marking an entry or indicating an opening along a fence line or hedge. It takes the guesswork out of a visitor's experience, making a more comfortable first impression.

Using an arbor as an entry also creates a transition from one place to another—from the sidewalk to the garden or from one part of the garden to another. Most people recognize arbors as passageways and are naturally drawn toward them. A subtle psychological effect occurs when one passes through an opening. You can enhance this experience by taking into account the views you would see as you pass through the arbor from either direction.

Double duty An arbor may draw the eye as a passageway does, but it is also a destination. The arbor can serve double duty if it is equipped with a bench or a swing.

Focal point Because an arbor frames a view with its basic shape, it makes a good focal point. The view can be part of

▲ This arbor is a destination that doesn't disappoint, treating the visitor to a shaded bench.

the garden on the other side of the arbor, a distant view, or something within the arbor itself. An arbor placed against a solid fence or wall provides an ideal place to hang a frieze or plaque.

◄ An arbor marks the entry to a garden. This structure is literally the threshold, serving as a transition from street to house.

Arbor styles

The choice of style is based on personal preference and clues you get from the garden or your master plan. The key is to make the arbor part of a comprehensive plan. If the arbor is the first structure you will build, subsequent structures, such as fences and deck railings, should mirror the details used on the arbor. If you paint the arbor white or a bright color, it will attract attention, so it should be able to hold up to scrutiny and fit in with the rest of the garden. If you plan to cover the arbor with climbing plants—especially evergreens—style is less important, because the arbor will be hidden. A review of common arbor styles may be useful.

Formal Most arbors fit into this category. They are ornate and are often painted white. They have a permanent, ordered sense about them that projects an attitude throughout the garden. Such arbors evoke images of formal estates, both in America and in England. This is worth noting, because the garden styles that gave rise to the prominence of arbors may or may not be appropriate for your garden.

If you like the look of an arbor but are unsure whether it is appropriate for your garden, choose a formal style and finish it with a dark stain or paint that plays down its prominence but still has impact when you are up close.

Informal An informal arbor is more playful and evokes a sense of fun instead of order. Because it can come in a wide range of materials, colors, and fanciful styles, this type of arbor is more versatile. With styles ranging from contemporary chic to Medieval romance, you can match the arbor to almost any style of architecture or garden, although it may look out of place in a formal garden or against a formal fence or house.

You can make an informal arbor of almost any material. Unlike a formal design, the style and details of an informal arbor do not necessarily need to be echoed in other structures. By virtue of its informality, you are communicating that there is a different type of order in your garden.

Rustic Usually made of tree limbs or split logs, this style of arbor is ideal as a transition from a wooded path into a casual garden. Any arbor lends itself as a support for growing vines, but a rustic arbor seems to beg for them. You may be hesitant to let vines cover a structure that cost you time and money. A rustic arbor gives the appearance of having been in place for a long time. If this style appeals to you, try to use materials you find on your property. Materials from off-site can detract from the impression of its being part of the garden.

▲ This open, formal metal arbor will eventually be covered with climbing roses. Metal is the best material for training vines because it won't rot.

> **Set posts in gravel**
>
> Set arbor posts 2 to 3 feet deep, then fill the holes with gravel to make the structure sturdy. You'll be able to move the arbor at a later date without causing any damage to surrounding lawns or plantings.

ARBORS *continued*

Arbor materials

Just as the style of an arbor can set a mood in the garden, the same is true for the materials you use to build it. Although there are certain limitations to each material, primarily finished lumber, metal, and rough wood, it is up to you to mix and match materials and styles. For example, you could develop a traditional design but build the arbor out of old tree limbs.

Finished wood Most arbors are made of finished lumber. Wood is readily available, easy to work with, affordable, and comes in uniform sizes. Because most arbors are traditional or formal in design, the uniformity of the wood lends itself to this type of project. Finished lumber can also be treated to resist rotting, making it especially suitable for outdoor projects. It can be painted,

▲ You can build a simple yet elegant variation of this entry arbor by following the plans shown on page 213.

▲ Deadwood—tree limbs from the nearby woods—was used to construct this high-roofed arbor.

stained, or allowed to weather naturally—each treatment resulting in a different effect. Finished lumber is also popular because most how-to instructions are based on this material— all you need are basic woodworking tools and skills.

Metal A beautiful material for an arbor, metal is the most enduring but the most costly. This is especially true if you want a custom-designed or custom-built arbor. However, there are many prefabricated metal arbors and arbor kits available in garden centers, home improvement centers, and mail-order catalogs that are more affordable.

Metal arbors have two distinct advantages over wood: They can withstand the pull of a woody vine, such as wisteria, and they are relatively impervious to the effects of moisture trapped by vines. To prevent rust, ensure the arbor has a triple coating of primer under a double coat of paint.

Rustic This style and its materials are not suited to every garden. Using uniform sizes of wood—whether bought or found—makes a rustic arbor easier to build. Even if you use naturally rot-resistant wood, such as cedar, expect the material to last only half as long as finished lumber. Join pieces with standard hardware. Using material found on-site helps make the arbor look as if it belongs.

How to build an arbor

MATERIALS

Four 8-foot 1×4 beams
Jigsaw (optional)
Four 12-foot 4×4 posts
Drill
Sixteen 36-inch 1×2s
3-inch galvanized
   deck screws
Saw
Eight 8-foot 1×2s
1⅝-inch galvanized deck
   screws
6-inch lag screws
Shovel
Gravel
Level
Stakes
13 precut deck spindles
Four 1-foot braces cut
   from the 4×4s
Concrete

STEP 1 Prepare front and back pieces.

(Optional: Make decorative cuts at the ends of each beam using a jigsaw.) Cut all four posts to 11 feet in length, saving the cutoff pieces for the braces. Lay two parallel posts 5 feet apart—center to center—on a flat surface. Place one beam flat on the posts, with its top flush with the post tops, then predrill holes through the beam into the front face of each post. Flip the posts over and predrill the second beam. Repeat with the other two posts and beams.

STEP 2 Set posts in place and add beams.

Dig a 30-inch-deep hole for each post, spaced 2 feet apart (center to center) on the sides and 5 feet apart (center to center) at front and back. Add 6 inches of gravel to each hole. Using stakes and braces, plumb and stabilize the posts in position. Then add more stability by attaching the two pairs of beams to the posts with lag screws.

STEP 3 Attach the sides.

Space eight 36-inch pieces of 1×2s in a ladderlike pattern. Fasten with deck screws. Cut the 8-foot 1×2s to the desired length and attach them vertically to the ladder 1×2s with four deck screws along each vertical 1×2.

STEP 4 Add top slats.

Angle-cut the braces and attach them with lag screws. Then evenly space the deck spindles across the top and screw them to the beams. Recheck posts for plumb and set in holes with concrete.

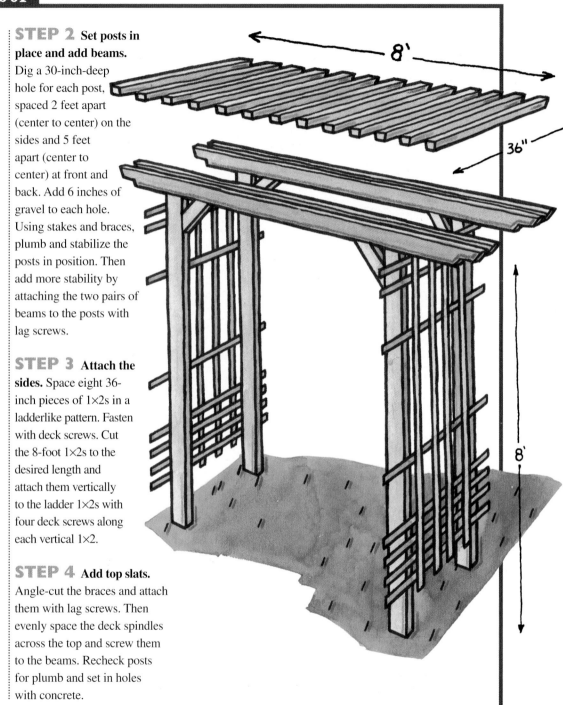

▲White is the most common color for finishing an arbor. It makes the structure stand out, even when covered with vines.

ARBORS *continued*

Arbor finishes

Adding a finish to the arbor benefits the wood significantly in two ways. It makes a big difference in the overall look of the arbor and it prolongs the life of the structure.

Paint Most painted wood arbors are made of pressure-treated lumber. Always make certain the wood is dry before painting. Unless pressure-treated wood is labeled as cured, let the structure stand exposed to the sun and air for at least six weeks after building before you paint. Otherwise, the paint may bubble as the moisture in the wood tries to escape. Rot-resistant wood, such as cedar and redwood, usually comes cured or dried and often is not painted.

There are three methods for painting an arbor; each works equally well. Use a brush or sprayer to paint the structure when it is in place. Or paint part or all of the arbor while building it, and apply touch-up paint once it is in place.

Stain This finish is used most often on rot-resistant wood. Stain is much thinner than paint and tends to run more; most people find it easier to apply with a rag than a brush. Moisten the rag with stain and rub it on the wood. You can stain pressure-treated lumber—usually pine—to look as if it is actually cedar or redwood.

You may prefer to use a clear sealer instead of a stain. A sealer prevents moisture from seeping into the wood while allowing the wood to weather to its natural color.

Vines Vines growing over and around them give an arbor a finished look. When choosing a vine, you need to know how the vine attaches itself and what help, if any, you need to give it (see page 126).

Unless you are planting an aggressive woody vine, such as wisteria, the plant won't threaten the structure. The thin strips of lattice found in many arbors are susceptible to rot, however, and vines trap moisture and prevent the sun and air from drying out the lattice.

Consider using annual vines. They provide coverage during the growing season and allow the wood to dry in winter.

▲ If using a rot-resistant wood, such as cedar, you can allow it to age naturally. Left unsealed, this arbor will eventually turn gray.

How to build a pergola

A pergola is like an arbor, only wider and less ornate. It creates shade in the garden.

MATERIALS

Four 10-foot 4×4 posts
Drill
Shovel
Gravel
Jigsaw (optional)
Two 8-foot 2×6 beams
2 stepladders
Four ¼×6-inch carriage bolts
Eight 8-foot 2×4 rafters
3-inch deck screws
Four 2-foot 2×6 corner braces
Twenty-four 8-foot 1×2s
2½-inch spacer
6d galvanized nails
Concrete

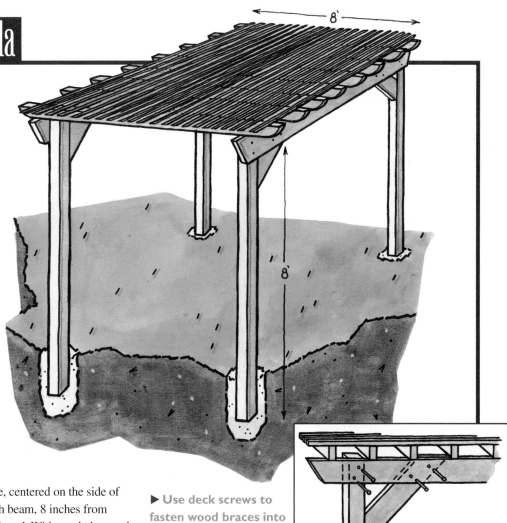

STEP 1 **Set the posts.** At the top of each post, mark a point at the center of the post 2¾ inches from the top. Drill a ¼-inch hole through each post. Dig a 2-foot-deep hole in each corner of a 7-foot square. Using the method shown on page 121, plumb and brace a post in each hole. (Do not add concrete yet.) Ensure the predrilled holes in the posts are aimed correctly.

STEP 2 **Attach the beams.** (Optional: Make decorative cuts on the ends of the beams.) Drill a ¼-inch hole, centered on the side of each beam, 8 inches from each end. With one helper and two stepladders, use carriage bolts to attach each of the beams flush with the tops of the posts. Fasten wood braces into place with lag bolts.

STEP 3 **Add the rafters.** Space the rafters evenly across the beams. Mark where they will go. First attach the two end rafters into the beam with angled deck screws, then fill in with the other rafters.

▶ **Use deck screws to fasten wood braces into place for additional support of the finished pergola.**

STEP 4 **Lay on the 1×2s.** Start at one end and lay a 1×2 perpendicular to and flush with the ends of the rafters. Nail it into every other rafter. Using a 2½-inch spacer, lay the next lath and attach it. Repeat for remaining laths. Recheck the posts and structure for plumb and level, then fill holes with concrete.

GARAGES

Whether attached to the house or freestanding, a garage is an extension of the house and usually the second most dominant structure on the property. As a result, the garage should blend with the architecture of the house and help set the tone for the garden style.

When building a new home, you can make your garage harmonious with your house through proper design and planning. If you inherited a detached garage that doesn't match the house, that is more of a challenge. Drive around your favorite neighborhoods with a camera and record how others have handled this situation. Use the tips and ideas offered here.

▼ A cupola and weather vane atop this garage create the sense of a carriage house.

Windows and doors

As a result of small lot size and trends in home design, most garages either face the street or are at the end of a straight driveway. The strong line of the driveway draws the eye right to the garage, placing tremendous emphasis on a structure that is primarily utilitarian. Avoid having the structure look like a plain garage, even if it is. Adding entry doors and windows can make the garage look more like a wing of the house. They also allow more light into the garage and provide access without opening the large door.

If adding a door or windows is too expensive or is not an option for other reasons, there are less involved and more affordable ways to dress up a garage. The tip box on page 217 offers several ideas.

Of all the features of a garage, the door draws the most attention. One way to downplay its prominence is to paint

▶ Using trim and door colors that match the house helps this garage blend into its surroundings.

the door the same color as the rest of the garage and not add a trim around it. The effect is to make the garage appear as a single plane.

Another option is to screen the structure from view with hedges or other tall plantings. Or you can turn the garage into a multipurpose structure. Consider designing it so that—when entertaining—you can open the door, pull the cars out, and use the structure as a pavilion. Paving can enhance this use. To make a garage seem more inviting, let the paved area in front of it function as a terrace. For more on this idea, see page 108.

▼ An extended overhang allows the garage to double as a covered patio.

TIPS TO DRESS UP A GARAGE

- **Trim color** Match the trim of the garage and the door color to the trim color of the house to tie the two together. If the design or location of the garage makes it difficult to match the style of the house, minimize the impact of the garage by not painting the trim.
- **Lighting** Garage lighting serves several purposes; the most obvious are security and safety. Motion detectors make lighting even more effective. Light fixtures can unite a garage and house. Using light fixtures for the garage door similar to those at the front door of the house helps to harmonize the two structures.

- **Plants** Dress up an otherwise dull structure with plantings. Add window boxes (or paint windows on the garage and hang window boxes under them). Flank the doorways with container gardens. Grow vines up and over the entrance; let them run wild or train them to a specific shape. Screen the garage from the yard with tall narrow plants such as bamboo.
- **Theatrical illusion** Adding a window or door takes extra money, and often a garage doesn't lend itself to such treatment. Fake it with trompe l'oeil, which means "fool the eye." Hang a window frame with mirrors in it on the garage. Paint the garage door to look like siding, or paint it to look as though it contains windows and window boxes.

OUTDOOR FIREPLACES

There are many ways to add ambience to the garden, but few things rival fire for impact. Fire adds light, heat, and motion. It can also add sound, smell, and interaction. Using an outdoor fireplace extends the seasonal use of a patio, terrace, or gazebo, sometimes adding as much as a month to either end of the normal outdoor season. A fireplace can also double as an outdoor oven or a grill.

Before you invest time or money in this feature, check local codes that regulate outdoor fires. There may be restrictions on the type of wood burned. Some cities require a chimney, and some localities ban any type of outdoor fireplace.

Using fire outdoors

As with everything else in the garden, the first step is to decide what you want to accomplish with a fireplace. This will direct all future choices.

If the primary purpose for the fireplace is to provide heat so you can extend your outdoor pleasure, a wood-burning fireplace is the best choice. A fire pit does not reflect heat, and gas does not give off enough heat to make a difference. If you want a fireplace purely for ambience, you have a broader range of choices. A fire pit is the least expensive approach if you want to see the dancing flames, smell the occasional trace of smoke, and hear the crackling and popping of burning wood.

▲ A fireplace just outside the house next to a terrace allows you to enjoy the fire whether you are inside or out.

◀ A cover for the fire pit keeps water out when it rains. Drainage holes at the bottom ensure that any rain water that does get in can escape.

Another choice is a freestanding prefabricated fireplace. Most are light enough to be moved around. A permanent masonry structure takes more of an investment of time and money.

If you want to use the fireplace for heat or to cook food, it should be custom-built. Racks can hold a grill or hooks from which you can hang pots, making it easy to cook directly over the fire. You could also build a chamber to one side of the fireplace to serve as an oven.

Siting an outdoor fireplace

One of the most important decisions you will need to make is where to put the fireplace. The biggest factor influencing that decision is wind. Most locations have some wind—inevitably blowing in the wrong direction—but you can minimize the problem by studying prevailing winds on your property. Your site analysis (see pages 14–19) should have most of the information you need. Be aware that fences, hedges, and structures that you or your neighbors added since you did the site analysis may have altered the way the wind moves across your property.

▼ A chimney helps channel the smoke up and away from the seating area. Some local ordinances require a chimney. Check before building.

To extend your outdoor season, put the fireplace near an area that is already frequently used, such as a pool, gazebo, or terrace. You may want to make the fireplace a destination in itself. If so, plan to have space for at least a few chairs for yourself, family, and guests to sit and gaze into the burning embers.

No matter where you decide to site the fireplace, look up to see if any overhanging tree limbs pose a fire hazard. Chimney caps, which capture floating embers and release only smoke (below left), may help. Even with a cap, be aware of the amount of heat given off by the fireplace and how it will affect nearby structures or plantings. The instructions that come with prefabricated fireplaces tell you how close they can be to structures.

There are a few other practicalities to consider. First is the availability of wood. Keep the wood stack or bin covered so the wood stays dry in all weather. The second consideration is the ease of cleaning. If you are using the fireplace for cooking, you need to be able to clean it easily and often. A greasy or dirty fireplace can attract rodents. Finally, there is the issue of safety. Site the fireplace near a source of water that can be used to put out the fire completely at the end of the evening or to control any errant flames. If a water source is not feasible, you should have a fire extinguisher on hand.

Where there's fire...

Study and know the prevailing winds in your garden. Site a fireplace to minimize the amount of time you will have to spend dodging smoke.

◀ To make a simple fire pit, dig a hole 2 feet wide and 1 foot deep. Form a circle of bricks around the hole.

GARDEN SHEDS

A garden shed allows you to store all your equipment and supplies in one location and provides a small workplace. A garden shed is essential especially for gardeners without a garage or basement, and it can be an attractive addition to the yard.

Garden sheds can be almost any size or style. They can range from detailed and intricate (below left) to a simple conversion of an old pantry (below right).

▼ **Storing tools in an orderly manner makes gardening easier and prolongs the life of the tools.**

Determine your needs

Decide the purpose you want the shed to serve. If you want it to hold all your tools, make a list of every tool you own and note whether it is best for the tool—and most convenient for you—stored on a shelf, hung on the wall, or set on the floor. Include all power equipment, such as mowers, trimmers, tillers, and blowers, that requires a lot of space.

Next, ask yourself if you want to do any work inside the shed. Is it where you will repot plants? Do you want a table and vise for sharpening tools? Will you be doing plant propagation or soil mixing? Will you be building anything?

Convert your answers into dimensions: Add up the square footage of floor space and estimate the amount of wall and shelf space required. This gives you a starting point for estimating the size of the structure. Sketch a floor plan to see what kind of footprint the structure will require. Start thinking about the location of the shed, which may limit its shape. Sketch the wall plans to show how much wall space you'll need for tools and shelf space.

▼ **Convert an unused pantry into an indoor garden shed. Add sturdy hangers on the wall for tools.**

▶ This attractive potting shed provides only minimal protection from the sun, wind, or rain.

Choose a style

The choice of styles for a garden shed is almost limitless. Be creative; convert a utility shed, old gazebo, or other structure into a garden shed.

A quick and easy way to get the structure you need is to purchase a prefabricated shed or utility building and dress it up. Cut a window or two into the wall of the shed, paint it to blend in with the rest of the garden, and add a window box. Applying lath on the surface can be a quick and inexpensive way to add charm.

Select a location

There are several practical issues involved in deciding where to put the shed. It should be convenient to gardening activities that involve use of the tools and other equipment that is stored in the shed. It should be near utilities. Whether or not the utilities are actually connected to the shed, it is handy to have a hose nearby for rinsing off tools. It is also useful to have a light—on or in the shed—for security and safety so you can see when returning tools to the shed at dusk after an enthusiastic day in the

▲ Peruse garage sales for a cabinet or cupboard to store small items.

garden. If the shed is unattractive, you may want to tuck it out of sight.

If you are going to store pesticides, bags of synthetic fertilizer, herbicides, or other chemicals in the shed, it should be well-ventilated and have a secure lock.

TIPS FOR PLANNING THE PERFECT SHED

- **Use the walls.** Using the walls optimizes the space and allows you to see your tools at a glance. A wide range of devices is available for hanging tools on the walls—from specialty tool clips to a standard perforated board with metal hangers. You can also use coat or funky hat racks that can often be found at garage sales.

- **Add power and water.** Electricity allows you to have lights in the shed to find or put away tools at dusk and work in the shed on a dark day. It also allows you to have outlets for a fan (or heater in cool weather), electrical devices to sharpen or repair your tools, or power tools. A sink—at least a spigot for a hose—is handy for cleanup, mixing solutions, and drawing water for fresh-cut flowers.

- **Install a phone line.** A phone can keep you in touch with the rest of the world while you engage in your favorite pastime.

- **Secure a lockable area.** It may not be necessary for the entire shed to be locked, but there should be at least one area that can be secured. Use it to store dangerous (or expensive) tools as well as any chemicals.

- **Ensure adequate ventilation.** Check with the local extension service for regulations about chemical storage. Ventilation is a safety essential, especially in an area where chemicals are stored. Even if you don't plan to store chemicals, good air circulation makes the shed comfortable.

- **Decorate the outside.** If the shed is visible from a public area, invest in a coat of paint and dress it up with some flowers, a mural, or a garden plaque. Or make a decoration of old garden tools mounted on the wall above the door.

POTTING BENCHES

TIPS ON POTTING BENCHES

- **Choose the height.** Adjust the bench to a comfortable height. You can use cinder blocks or bricks to elevate the bench, or cut the legs to lower it.
- **Have multiple levels.** Install shelves at different heights for convenience.
- **Have compost handy.** Locate the potting bench near a primary sources of "black gold."
- **Place it near storage.** Site the bench near (or in) the potting shed so it is close to tools and fertilizers.
- **Stay in the shade.** A bench that's in the shade of a tree keeps you cooler and protects new transplants from the sun. If there are no trees, use an inexpensive polyurethane canopy.
- **Place it on flooring.** Set the bench on a sheet of plywood or masonry board large enough to extend at least 2 feet out from the front of the bench to prevent a soggy or muddy area underfoot.
- **Use utilities.** Even if you have to run a hose to the area, having water will make your work easier. Electricity allows for a fan, radio, or even a laptop computer.
- **Tuck it away.** Choose a location where you won't mind abandoning a work-in-progress for a few days.

A potting bench is a utilitarian structure with a form that follows function. To that end, you can take an inexpensive banquet table, elevate it on cinder blocks to the desired height, and be in business. But if you have spent much time potting plants, you know how useful a *well-designed* potting bench can be.

Page 223 has a design for a basic potting bench. Follow the directions, or use your imagination and the tips in the box at right to customize a bench for your needs. Imagine an ideal potting bench. It could be adjusted to the right height for comfort—for you and others in your household who might use it. It could be built to hold everything you need close at hand. Perhaps you want built-in bins for different types of potting soil and compost, and space for a plastic tub to premoisten soil.

The location of your bench is almost as important as the bench itself. Think cool, comfortable, and logical. You'll save time and energy if you locate the bench near the compost bin and potting shed where tools, fertilizer, and other materials are stored. You may choose to design a garden shed large enough for a potting bench. If the shed has a floor, soil spilled when potting up plants can be swept up when you are finished.

▼ Make certain your bench is at a comfortable height for you and has plenty of working room.

How to build a potting bench

This bench is solid and heavy; build it where it will stay.

MATERIALS

Five 8-foot 2×6s
Six 2-foot 2×6s
3-inch wood screws
Two 3-foot 4×4s
Two 4-foot 4×4s
Table saw
Twenty-five 27-inch 1×4s
One 4×8-foot sheet of ¾-inch
   plywood, ripped into two 8-
   foot pieces—one 27 inches
   wide and one 8½ inches wide
One 11¼-inch 2×4

STEP 1 Build the frame. On the floor, make two boxes using two 8-foot 2×6s and two 2-foot 2×6s for each. Secure with two screws per joint. For the top frame, evenly space the two 2-foot 2×6s as braces. The 1×4s of the bottom shelf will brace the bottom frame later.

STEP 2 Attach the legs. Use 3-foot 4×4s for front legs and 4-foot 4×4s for back legs. Prop one box 6 inches off the floor; attach to the 4×4 legs with screws, as shown. Have a helper hold the second box flush with the top of the front legs and screw into place.

STEP 3 Add the bottom shelf. Use a table saw to cut down two of the floor pieces to a width of 2¾ inches. (You'll use one of these at each end.) Then screw down the 1×4s, working from one end to the other.

STEP 4 Attach the work surface. Notch the back corners of the plywood to fit around the legs. Cut an opening for scraping soil into a bin on the shelf below. Lay the plywood on the top frame and screw into place.

STEP 5 Add the shelf and backsplash. Attach an 8-foot 2×6 to the front of the posts at the back side of the bench. Toenail the short 2×4 to the plywood to brace the shelf support. Screw the 8-foot-long, 8½-inch-wide plywood shelf to the tops of the 2×6, posts, and short 2×4.

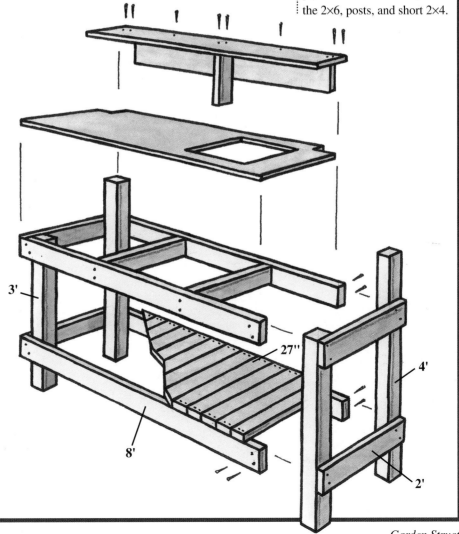

COMPOSTERS

With the help of earthworms and microorganisms, you can turn leaves, kitchen scraps, small branches, and other plant debris into rich compost—the most effective soil amendment there is. Best of all, it's free. Composting is one of the easiest of all gardening chores. Doing it properly means having the right size composter in the right place and feeding it the right stuff.

Choose a location

Consider these parameters when deciding where to put your composter. It needs to be where it is not visually obtrusive and not upwind. Site it in a convenient spot; you don't want to travel far in the winter with kitchen debris. It's helpful if the composter is close to where you will be using the compost, such as the vegetable

▲ Fill a drum-type composter completely and turn the contents daily. It helps to have two—when one is filled, start filling the second.

garden or potting bench. If you are using a composter that requires daily attention, put it where you can see it. That way you will be more likely to turn it as often as recommended.

Determine volume

The ideal size for a compost bin is 3 feet high, 3 feet wide, and 3 feet deep. One compost bin may not be enough for your needs, so you should know how much debris you generate. Track the amount of

◀ A triple-bin composter allows you to aerate material as you move it successively between bins. By the time it's in the third bin, it's ready to use.

biodegradable kitchen waste (vegetable matter—no meat, bones, or cooking oil) and yard waste you generate in a month during the growing season. To do this, get the largest plastic trash can you can find and put all your waste into it. When it fills, dump it where the compost will be. Keep track of how many times you empty the trash can in a month, and use that figure as a guide for determining the number of compost bins you need. As a rule, have room to store two months' worth of debris per bin. With three bins, by the time the second one is full, the first one will be delivering compost and the third one will be ready to fill.

How to build a compost bin

TYPE A Wire-framed bin This is the simplest type of compost bin you can make. Dig four 2-foot-deep holes for four 6-foot 2×4s so they form a square 36 inches on each side. Set the posts in place with concrete.

Decide which side will be the gate. Using wire staples, attach turkey or chicken wire on the other three sides; hammer the staples in firmly. Attach the hinge side of the wire mesh to the post using oversized staples that can go at least 1½ inches into the post; allow slack for the wire mesh to swing freely. Attach a row of four similar staples to the 4×4, which will be the latch side of the gate; press the mesh against the post and slide a dowel or metal rod through the staples to hold the gate shut.

TYPE B Slatted bin Set the posts as you did for the wire frame composter. Use pressure-treated 2×6s to box in three sides, leaving a gap of at least ½ inch between boards to allow for air circulation.

To make a channel for the gate, use six 3-inch wood screws to attach a vertical 2×6 flush with the outside edge and top of each front post. The 2×6 will extend about 2 inches beyond the front edge of the post. Along the inside face of each front post, use six 3-inch wood screws to attach a 2×2 so that it is flush with the top of the post and spaced so it leaves a 2-inch gap between the front edge of the 2×2 and the back edge of the 2×6.

Measure the inside distance between the front posts, subtract ½ inch, and cut enough 2×6s to close the front opening when the 2×6s are slipped into the channel.

TYPE C Tiered This type is built like the slatted version described at left. The only difference is that the bins share a common wall. You can make a series of bins side by side so that when turning the heap, you dump the contents of one bin into the bin beside it.

To speed up the composting, set a 4-inch-diameter piece of PVC pipe with holes drilled into it in the middle of the pile. The pipe helps add moisture and air. A 4-foot square heavy plywood floor makes collecting the compost easier.

C

A

B

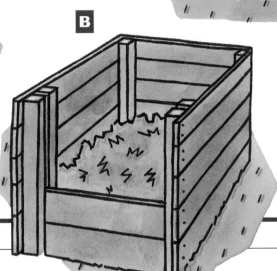

CHAPTER 9

ACCENTS

Delight in the details and personalize your garden

COVER-UPS

Despite the best planning and design, a few unsightly items always seem to stand out in the landscape and beg to be covered up. Many of these distracting features are utilitarian, such as air-conditioners, utility meters, trash cans, and utility poles. Before deciding that you have to live with them, explore the following pages for tips and ideas on camouflage.

Even before you commit pencil to paper, check with the utility provider and explain what you intend to do. Some restrictions or rules may apply.

Meters

There is nothing attractive about utility meters—for power, gas, or water. Their design is utilitarian; accessibility and ease of reading are the main reasons why they look the way they do and why they are placed where they are. But there are ways to make them appear less obtrusive.

Your local utility provider may have

▲ When masking your meter, be sure that it remains accessible and readable.

solutions you have not considered. If you proceed without consulting it, you may face a fine and have to remove your cover-up if the meter reader cannot easily access the box.

One approach is to build a box or cupboard around a meter, using materials, colors, and a design that match the garden style. Be sure that the meter can be read and serviced easily inside the box. Let the meter readers know where the meter is. Be aware that wasps may be attracted to the enclosure.

A simple solution—if allowed by the utility company—is to paint all metal components of the meter to match the color of the house or other structure where the meter is mounted.

The glass still shows, but the rest of the meter blends into its surroundings.

If painting is not an option, build a freestanding trellis or hang a piece of framed lattice in front of the meter so it can be read between the slats of the lattice up close but is barely noticeable from a distance.

Another solution is to set a narrow screen (or one on each side) perpendicular to the wall on which the meter is mounted blocking the meter from view unless it is faced straight on.

Air-conditioners

Find out if the air-conditioning unit (or other utility) has to be where it is. Often the answer is yes. If there is a choice, learn what the options are and be prepared to act on them if you replace the unit.

Assuming that the unit has to stay where it is, there are two issues to contend with: appearance and noise. Central air-conditioning units are usually

▲ Training a vine on an open trellis is a simple way to conceal an unsightly utility meter.

large metal boxes set against a house. You can paint them to match the house or use a dark color so they appear to recede into the background. Although you don't need permission to do this, it may alter the warranty or service agreement, so check with the manufacturer first.

Screening is the best option for dealing with appearance. A structure for screening can be as simple as a trellis (below). Be aware that air-conditioners emit hot air, which can dessicate—scorch or dry out—nearby plants. Use evergreens so the screening will be effective year-round. Most evergreens resist dessication better than deciduous plants.

The second concern is noise. It is not uncommon for an air-conditioning unit to be located 5 feet from a deck or other frequently used outside area of the property. Ironically, it is summer when these areas are used the most—the same time the air-conditioner runs the most. A dense planting of evergreens can absorb some of the noise.

Another alternative—one that addresses both sight and sound—is to build a solid wall in front of the unit or on two sides of it (below). For the most effective sound control, use solid panels that extend twice the height of the unit to direct sound up and away from the garden. Where screening is more of an issue than sound control, panels that are just slightly taller than the air-conditioner are adequate. To further hide the unit, and beautify your yard, plant shrubs and flowers around the wall.

If you build this kind of frame, check with the local power company and the manufacturer of the unit to make sure it will not affect the efficiency of the air-conditioner. As a general rule, leave at least 2 feet between the base of the unit and the frame so the unit can be serviced easily and the flow of air is not restricted.

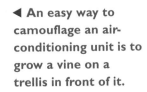

◄ An easy way to camouflage an air-conditioning unit is to grow a vine on a trellis in front of it.

◄ A simple wood frame around an air-conditioner screens it. Taller frames channel the noise up and away from the garden. For further sound buffering, line the inside of the frame with pieces of plastic foam.

Trash cans

Despite the amount of trash a typical family generates in a day, siting trash cans is often an afterthought. Because most people deal with trash frequently, convenience is an important part of the formula for success. If you have to walk across the yard to dispose of the trash, you may end up setting the bags outside the door.

Assuming that the site for the trash is logical and convenient, the next two concerns are sight and smell. Trash may be cleverly stored in such a way that no one sees or smells it. An area created specifically for a pair of trash containers presents an orderly appearance. Using dark-colored trash containers helps them seem to disappear into the background.

◄ **Build a lattice box for trash cans to keep them tidy and out of sight. The lattice allows air to circulate, which reduces odor. It can also keep out large animals, such as dogs and raccoons.**

If you have room, an ideal solution is to create a larger version of the air-conditioner screen shown on page 229. This becomes a small outdoor "room" where your garbage is kept until it is hauled off. The room doesn't have to be big enough to walk into; it needs only to be tall enough to easily roll or slide trash containers in and out. An advantage to this method is that it completely encloses the garbage area—which is extremely useful if raccoons or dogs are prevalent.

Closing in the trash raises the issue of odor. Fully enclosed trash (if it includes food refuse of any sort) results in a blast of nasty-smelling air when you open the door. The odor can be diminished by keeping the storage area ventilated. Siting the storage area upwind of the house makes odors less noticeable. Refer to your site analysis for the prevailing winds.

▶ **Lattice is an inexpensive, all-purpose screening material. Use it plain, as in this garden, or train vines on it for an even better disguise.**

◄ Plant tall evergreens to screen power lines, telephone poles, and utility boxes.

Utility poles and power lines

Utility structures can have a major impact on a garden, limiting what you can and can't do at the ground level. For example, you may want a tree to serve as a focal point and block the view of a neighbor's garage, but you can't plant a tree directly under a power line. Times are changing. Many utility companies are moving toward underground lines and yours may be able to bury your lines. If that is not an option, ask about moving the lines to another part of the property. You might find it worth the cost.

If the power lines and poles must remain where they are, you have three choices: direct attention away from them, screen them, or mask them.

Directing attention away from them is the best solution, at least from the utility company's point of view. The principles and elements of design discussed on pages 20–25 offer ideas about catching and holding attention in the garden.

If trying to distract the eye doesn't solve the problem, the next step is to screen the poles from sight. Because power lines and poles are tall, the screen should be tall as well. A row of fast-growing pines may do the trick. Keep in mind that anything planted close enough to the power lines and poles to screen them may fall under the provenance of

the utility company, which can prune or remove them to keep the lines clear. Always check before planting.

The last option is to mask the poles (there is nothing you can do to mask the lines themselves). You can paint a metal pole or grow vines on a metal or wood pole. It is imperative that you get permission before painting or planting.

◄ If you can get permission from the utility provider, train a clinging vine, such as ivy, to the pole to keep it from being so stark.

EDGING

▲ **Low hedges of holly and barberry create an interwoven pattern known as a knot garden. This type of planting makes an ideal edging. For more on knot gardens, see page 236.**

Edging plays several important roles in the garden. Most well-designed gardens consist of a series of shapes and forms, each representing an area set aside for a different purpose. Edging accentuates each garden area and maintains the shape and form of the overall design.

Edging creates a clean, crisp line between beds and other areas. It is most apparent between a lawn and the adjoining garden, evident in the photograph on page 233. Edging can define a flower border, shrub bed, or the transition from a terrace to the surrounding garden. It emphasizes the lines of beds and it leads the eye.

From a practical standpoint, edging keeps turfgrass from spreading into surrounding garden areas. At the same time, it prevents soil or mulch from the garden from spilling onto the lawn. It does the same for pathways made of loose material, such as gravel or mulch; it maintains clearly delineated pathways while keeping the path materials in place.

Use somewhat taller edging, such as low hedges (left) or low fencing (below) to direct traffic and keep people on paths. Edging also serves to keep people out of areas where you don't want them to go.

Another practical aspect of edging is that if it is flat and wide enough, it can serve as a strip for the wheels of the lawn mower to roll upon. This mowing strip eliminates the need for manicuring the edges with a string trimmer and it prevents you from mowing over tender plants in beds at the edge of a lawn.

◀ **Building up the height of the edging keeps both the lawn and bed in place.**

▶ **This low fence, called a bedboard, makes a clean edge and a friendly-looking barrier.**

Think sturdy

Be sure your edging is set firmly in place. Otherwise, mowers, garden carts, children, or your own garden clogs can unsettle it and you will be resetting materials in place constantly.

Choose a style that fits

The mix of brick walk and edging shown here is in keeping with the informal lines of the garden bed. For more formal beds and edging, use uniform materials, such as steel, wood, brick, or other prefabricated masonry.

Pick edging color carefully

The color of the edging has a big impact. Use a color that either complements or clearly contrasts with the surrounding foliage and flowers. You can link the edging to the bed by using plants of similar color.

Edging Materials

There is a wide range of materials suitable for edging. The one you choose will be based on function, style, and cost.

Form fits function. If the edge is a divider between the lawn and garden bed, it can be as simple as a trenched edge or a V-shaped ditch. If the edging acts as a mowing strip, use flat, wide material such as brick or flat stones. If its function is to keep a heavily mulched bed in place, use a material that extends at least 2 inches above ground (and 4 inches below). If the edging is purely aesthetic, your imagination can run free.

Style considerations include other materials in the garden. Edging can be a strong unifying factor or, if it introduces a new material to the garden scheme, a distraction.

Costs depend on materials chosen. Stones and uniform limbs found on-site are free; fancy tiles can be very expensive. When deciding how cost will affect your decision, keep in mind that you can use a fancy edging in areas that will be seen up close and most often, and switch to a more affordable material elsewhere. Also consider the cost (whether in time or money) of putting the edging in place. Page 235 gives you a better understanding of what is involved in edging installation.

▲ **BRICK** Elegant and long-lasting, brick comes in a multitude of styles, including this saw-toothed edging. Brick is a good idea when a uniform look is desired.

▲ **PLASTIC** Most affordable and easy to install due to its flexibility, plastic edging comes in many grades. The least expensive looks it, so invest in the best.

▲ **CONCRETE** You can purchase preformed sections of concrete edging that are ready to be set in place, or you can make a simple form and create a custom edge.

▲ **WOOD** Affordable and easy to work with if there aren't a lot of curves, wood adds an informal, organic look. Count on wood edging to last about 10 years.

▲ **STONE** One of the more versatile edging materials, stone can be carefully set in mortar for a refined look or placed more casually for a looser appearance.

▲ **WATTLE** This technique involves weaving saplings of pliable wood, such as willow or dogwood, into a low fence. Wattle works well for holding back mulch.

The method of installation you use for edging depends on the type of edging you choose. No matter what type of edging or method of installation, it is important to set the edging material firmly in place. Edging that gets knocked loose looks unkempt, detracts from a clean edge, and won't serve its purpose of providing a barrier.

METHOD A

Stone, brick, or pavers on sand. The drawing below shows stone but you can also use this method for brick or precast pavers.

The upright portion of the edging is what keeps mulch in its bed and provides a barrier to the grass. The horizontal piece doubles as a mowing strip.

To install this type of edging, dig a trench about 2 inches deeper than where the bottom of the vertical piece of stone will be when the top of the stone is positioned at the desired height. The width of the trench should be the total of the width of the horizontal paver and the thickness of the vertical piece plus 2 inches.

Spread 2 inches of sand in the trench, then position the vertical piece, using a rubber mallet to tap it into place against the soil. Fill the trench the rest of the way with sand, leaving room to place the horizontal paver so it is flush with the surrounding soil. Sweep loose sand into the cracks and lightly sprinkle with water to settle the sand.

METHOD B

Mortared brick or stone edging and mowing strip. The method is identical for brick or stone. Dig a trench 4 inches deeper than where the bottom of the vertical brick will be when the top of the brick is at the desired level. Spread a 2-inch layer of sand in the trench. Add 2 inches of concrete mix, position the vertical piece, then add concrete until a brick set down on top of the wet concrete is flush with the surrounding soil.

METHOD C

Wood edging. You can use regular pressure-treated 1×4s or prefabricated wood edging. The prefabricated edging has notches on the back side of each piece, that allow you to shape the edging into curves more readily.

To install, dig a trench about an inch deeper than where the bottom of the board will rest when the top of the board is where you want it.

Spread an inch of sand in the trench. Add the boards, bending them so they conform to the desired shape. Hold the boards in place with 12-inch-long 2×2 stakes set flush with the back side of the edging. Drive the stakes into the soil so the top of each stake is at least an inch below the top of the edging. Attach the edging to the stake with 2½-inch galvanized screws.

KNOT GARDENS AND LABYRINTHS

Most people think of accents as something they add to the garden. In the case of a knot garden or a labyrinth, the garden itself becomes an accent. Although there are both subtle and distinct differences between a knot garden and a labyrinth, they are both fine examples of the garden floor as a palette upon which you paint a picture with plants.

Knot gardens

The two images on this page are knot gardens. A knot garden is an intricately patterned bed that is planted with "strands" of plants that appear to weave in and out of each other as if in a knot. This type of garden has been popular since the Middle Ages. There are two basic styles: closed knots and open knots.

A closed knot typically uses at least two types of plants of different colors,

▲ **This closed knot garden pairs crimson barberry with green boxwood to create the appearance of a woven tapestry. Colored stones or bedding plants can be used to fill the spaces between shrubs.**

which are arranged to look as though they are actually intertwined. The photo above is a closed knot garden.

An open knot garden (left) uses one type of plant. Although it forms a definite pattern, it lacks the color and textural variation of a closed knot. Instead it forms a single geometric pattern. This type is easier for the first-time knot gardener and can be designed for easy conversion to a closed knot at a later date.

Plan and plant a knot garden

Laying out and maintaining a knot garden can be a lot of fun and greatly rewarding, but it takes time. The pattern you choose can be simple or ornate, with corresponding levels of difficulty. Use plants that grow slowly, hold their form, and thrive in your area. Regular maintenance is crucial to developing and retaining the effect of plants being interwoven.

◄ **This open knot garden uses holly to draw a simple geometric pattern with plants.**

▲ **Alternating bands of brick and stone form the borders for a simple dirt path in this traditional seven-circuit labyrinth.**

▶ **An arrow points to the entrance of this turf and brick labyrinth.**

◀ **An evergreen groundcover, such as lilyturf, forms the boundaries of the path, which is a combination of gravel and large stones.**

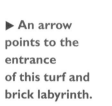

▶ **One of the easiest ways to make a labyrinth is to lay stones on existing grass in the desired pattern.**

Labyrinths

If a knot garden is about intensity and control, a labyrinth is about relaxing within boundaries. Not to be confused with a maze, a labyrinth has no dead ends or tricky turns. In a labyrinth there is only one path, no matter the number of switchbacks, and it leads only to the center. The same path that leads to the center guides you back out. The idea is that the journey to the center is peaceful and relaxing—the mind can wander because there is only one way for the body to go.

True labyrinths (shown in the photographs on this page) are created by marking a series of concentric circles on the ground. The number of circles around the center defines the labyrinth, such as a 3-, 5-, 7-, 9-, or 11-circuit labyrinth. Once the circles are defined, the path is delineated. A simple way to create a labyrinth that doesn't involve complex geometry is shown on pages 238 and 239.

Variations on a theme

Labyrinths have been used for thousands of years. Those shown on this page are Cretan labyrinths, the simplest kind to make. Many modern-day versions are patterned after an 800-year-old installation at Chartres Cathedral in France. Many communities have installed labyrinths in public areas, such as parks, churches, and airports. Labyrinth societies can be a resource for adding one of the features to your own garden. As shown here, the choice of materials used to delineate the paths is as broad as your imagination—grass, stones, bricks, groundcover plants, sand, straw, and even upside-down bottles.

How to create a labyrinth

Design the labyrinth on paper to figure out the widths of the path and the edges that define it. Translating the drawing on paper to the outside space is when the fun begins. The whole family can get involved.

To create this three-circuit labyrinth, you need a level area at least 20×20 feet. A three-circuit labyrinth is the simplest labyrinth, and requires the least amount of space. Unlike a maze, a labyrinth has low borders—no tall shrubs that hide the path. It is not a maze in which you get lost; instead it is a single path that you follow to the center and back out again.

The labyrinth is equated with the convolutions of the brain. The action of moving through the labyrinth is said to produce a sense of well-being and balance because all of the turns are balanced on the inward and outward journey.

MATERIALS
Pencil
Paper
9 stakes
Roll of twine, flexible garden
    hose, or heavy rope.
Sand
Bright color (not green) spray
    paint (optional)

GETTING STARTED
Practice on paper. A labyrinth is easy to draw and understand, but practicing it on paper a few times before you lay it out in the garden will help. You'll get an idea of the size that will fit your space. Use the drawings below to guide you.

Prepare the ground. You can create a labyrinth on existing turfgrass and mark the lines with stones, bricks, or other objects. An alternative is to clear the site completely, so that you have bare ground to work with. Then you can make the lines out of stone and create a gravel path. Or make the path of straw or another mulch. There are many options.

One the easiest labyrinths to make is a mown pattern. Using this method, you lay out the pattern in tall grass with string, or spray paint it, then use a lawn mower to delineate the paths of the

labyrinth. Make sure the mower can negotiate the tightest curve of the path.

STEP 1 Mark the starting points.
Place stakes at the four corners of a 6×6-foot square (A, B, C, and D). If you are finicky, you can use the triangulation method on page 120 to get everything square. Then place four more stakes, each one in the middle of one of the four sides of the square. Connect these latter four stakes with twine to form a cross (E to G and H to F).

STEP 2 Draw the first curve.
Using a flexible material, such as rope or garden hoses, connect points B and E. Lay the rope on the ground in a 3-foot-wide arc between B and E.

STEP 3 Make the first ring.
Connect points F and A as in step 2. The arc of this ring should be 3 feet from the

previous one. Smooth the rope to form anb even curve.

STEP 4 Add the second ring.
Connect points C and H as before.

STEP 5 Make the last ring.
Connect points C and G.

STEP 6 Outline the path.
Using stone or any other material, trace the pattern you've created. As you do this, adjust the stones so the curves are even. If you are not making the labyrinth on lawn, fill the path with the material of your choice. For a mown labyrinth, mow the paths and leave about a 6-inch-wide unmown area between the paths to serve as the divider. If the labyrinth is walked a lot, there is no need to mow further; the foot traffic will keep the grass down.

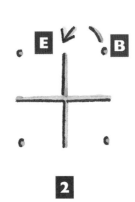

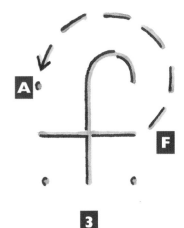

LABYRINTH ALTERNATIVES

There are other two-dimensional patterns you can create to have fun with the groundplane of the garden.

For example, you can make a simple spiral of painted stones (right). Or make a series of mosaics from decorative concrete blocks filled with a variety of materials (page 250).

You can even use stones and groundcovers to create a faux knot garden. Draw a pattern on the bare ground with sand. Fill some spaces with plants and some with gravel, colored glass, or other items. Bottling or other glass factories often have glass granules that are textured like shattered windshield glass.

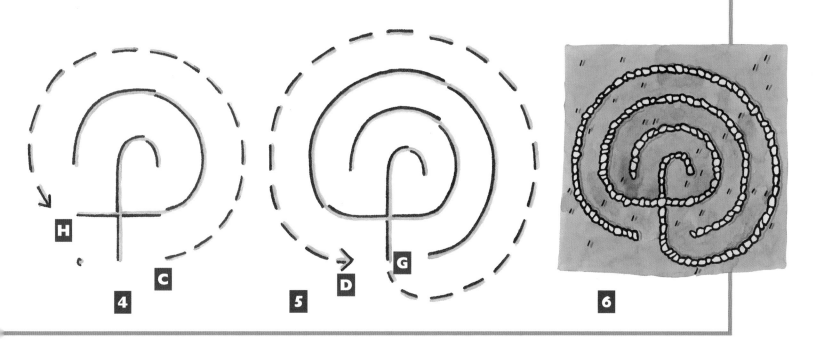

H

C

4

D

G

5

6

SOUND IN THE GARDEN

A garden should be designed to tickle all of your senses. Sight and smell are predominant factors when planning the garden. Touch and taste are often considered as well. Perhaps the most underutilized and least planned sensory aspect of a garden is sound. Sound has a way of making the garden come alive. There are many ways you can introduce sound into the garden.

The reasons for adding sound are many. Natural or man-made sounds can drown out unwelcome noise, such as traffic. If music adds to your gardening pleasure, include outdoor speakers. Sound is also an easy way to become more engaged with nature.

Sources of sound

Water Moving water is one of the most versatile and pleasing sounds in the garden. It provides a natural, organic murmur and, if you choose the right type of water feature, it can be adjusted from a gentle trickle or hissing spray to a hearty splash. With the ready availability of self-contained, freestanding, portable fountains, just about any location can offer the bubble and splash of water, provided that there are nearby sources of power and water.

▲ A clump of ornamental grass left over the winter creates a rustling sound as wind passes through the dry stalks.

To get the most from a fountain or other sources of watery sound, locate it near a deck, terrace, or any other place where you can enjoy the music it makes. For more on choices of water features, see pages 174–189.

Foliage The rustling of leaves moved by the wind can be soothing. To incorporate these sounds into your garden, plant fountain grass, maiden grass, or pampas grass. Even at their most lush during the height of summer, tall grasses make themselves known when a breeze rustles through them. But autumn is the season when they really sing, as the leaves and flower stalks dry. To enjoy this grassy music as long as possible, wait to cut the grasses back until they begin growth the next spring. Refer to your site analysis (see page 14) so that you locate the grasses in an area that take advantage of prevailing winds during the seasons you most want to listen to the sound.

◄ A splashing fountain placed to the rear of the garden draws you in and adds depth to the space.

Wind chimes The tinkling or mellow ringing of wind chimes is one of the most popular ways to add sound to a garden. Wind chimes respond to the breeze, and their random music has a calming, meditative value. When purchasing wind chimes, give them a good ring before you buy. Wind chimes come in a wide range of tones, from a high-pitched tinkle to deeper carillon sounds. Avoid buying a set of chimes based on looks alone—you want a sound you can enjoy. Place several different tones in various areas of the garden prone to breezes. Hang them securely to withstand strong wind gusts.

Music Several companies manufacture high-quality stereo speakers that are weatherproof, allowing you to pipe music into your garden. Some speakers are designed to look like rocks so they blend into the garden.

Birds As with the sources of sound that rely on wind, you may not have much control over when you get to hear the sound of singing birds, but there are steps you can take to attract birds. For more on this, see page 183.

Gravel The crunching of gravel underfoot as you move along a garden path is another way to add sound to the garden. It announces your arrival and may scare away unwanted animals. On the other hand, it can be disruptive and may scare away birds.

▼ **Wind chimes come in a myriad of styles and tones—from delicate tinkles to harmonic chimes.**

▲ Crunching gravel has a distinctive and familiar sound. It can sound a warning that someone is coming.

▲ Generally, the larger the chimes, the deeper their tone.

SEATING

Whatever the size or style of your garden, you need a place to sit. Working and walking about in a garden are ways to enjoy it, but nothing compares with sitting down, relaxing, and simply being in the garden.

Although you can plop yourself down on the ground just about anywhere or drag a lawn chair to your favorite spot, permanent seating designed for maximum comfort will add immensely to your garden pleasure.

You can use a range of objects as seats, and you can put the seating anywhere you like, but carefully consider your options to ensure satisfaction.

▼ **Solid and weathered, these heavy chairs have a permanent home beneath a shade tree.**

The right seating

From formal entertaining to quiet meditation, the kind of activity you want to accomodate with seating should be reflected in its style and placement.

Relaxation Sometimes seating is used for the sole purpose of kicking back and enjoying the garden. If that is what you are looking for, there are a few things to consider. First, select a location ideally suited to your kind of relaxation. Then, place the chairs or benches where they will enhance the experience. The seating area may be near a gurgling fountain or situated so that you have the best view in the garden. Or it may be tucked far away from the phone and television. Even if you can't get too far from the house, you can orient the seating so that you can pretend you are far away. For more tips on creating a garden getaway, see pages 168–171.

Another advantage of creating a spot that is designed and planned specifically for relaxation is that the furniture can stay in one place; it doesn't need to be moved every time you want to relax. That way, you can use heavy chairs or

▲ **Put your garden furniture to use from a design standpoint, letting it add a colorful punch.**

benches and even plant around them. This kind of setting also allows you to have built-in furniture.

When planning to place furniture in a permanent location, be sure to select a spot that is off paths and walkways. That

◄ **Even chairs that aren't used a lot add scale and personality to the garden.**

makes moving around the garden easier. Use the furniture to define areas or create focal points, such as at the end of a path. Having the seating against a wall, fence, or planting bed makes the space feel more intimate.

Entertaining An outdoor seating area with tables, benches, and chairs allows you and your guests to gather in the garden. It may be more convenient to use seating that is lighter in weight than you would use for permanently installed seating because it is easier to arrange.

For more information on how to determine the amount of space required when setting up an area for outdoor entertaining, review the guidelines on page 145.

Aesthetics Many gardens have tables and chairs that serve little purpose other than eye appeal. This use of seating takes on the same effect as sculpture.

The choice of furniture makes a difference in the aesthetic. You can allow

▲ Choose a chair that fits your body, and place it where you like the view.

wood to weather to a natural gray, paint ornate iron with a simple, elegant black or white, or paint all or part of a wooden chair in bold colors.

Whether or not you intend to actually use the chairs, where and how you place them in the garden helps to establish a sense of scale for the area.

▲ You can customize even simple garden furniture by adding cushions or making decorative cuts with a jigsaw.

▼ Place a bench by an arbor or a pergola for cooling shade and the added fragrance of climbing roses.

Seating considerations

Although cost, availability, durability, and ease of movement are all considerations in choosing your outdoor furniture, the two primary considerations are looks and comfort. Avoid cutting corners on either.

Seating style The type of seating you choose can either dress up or dress down the garden. There is a wide range of ready-made furniture and easy-to-assemble kits from which to choose.

Rustic furniture made from cut limbs sets a casual, earthy mood. Wrought-iron chairs evoke a formal, traditional mood. A folding chair projects a feeling of mobility and usefulness. You will find furniture in many styles and price ranges.

No matter which style you start with, remember that you can always customize your furniture by painting it. You can even change it from season to season with a coat of paint to match your garden as it evolves.

Comfort Assuming that the seating fits the setting and looks good, comfort is the next most important consideration when selecting furniture. No matter what the view or the look of the chair, if it isn't comfortable to sit in, you won't want to sit.

Sit in a chair or on a bench before buying it. When you are at the store, give yourself a few minutes to settle in to get a feeling of what it will be like. Nestle down and imagine yourself in the garden. Remember that you can add cushions for both comfort and looks. Test them on the seating too.

Take into account the soundness of the footing. Consider using the same kind of coasters used to protect carpet from chair legs to keep garden furniture stable and level if it will be set on grass.

Make your own seat

If you can't find exactly what you want in terms of comfort, size, or style, make your own garden furniture. It's fun and easy.

The bench shown at the right is one example. Most home and garden centers have free plans showing how to build simple furniture, requiring only basic skills and tools. You could also customize a kit or a prefabricated bench or chair.

▲ Create an outdoor dining room by placing a table and chairs beneath the spread of a shade tree.

▲ Simple twig furniture suits this informal setting along a garden path. Invite guests to sit and enjoy the garden in a wide part of a pathway.

▲ In addition to having chairs in the garden, place cushions on a low wall for extra seating.

◄ Be sure to provide a footing that is both stable and wide enough for the chair legs.

MATERIALS

One 8-foot 6×6
Saw
Two 8-foot 2×8s
Eight 7½-inch carriage bolts
Drill with ½-inch wood bit
3-inch deck screws
Two 8-foot 2×2s
Twelve 8-foot 2×4s
8d finishing nails
Nail set
Plastic wood

STEP 1 Make the legs. Cut the 6×6 into four 2-foot lengths.

STEP 2 Build the front and back of the frame. Cut each 2×8 into one 6-foot and one 2-foot piece. Measure 12 inches from each end of the 6-foot pieces and mark a line from top to bottom. Mark two points on the line—one 2 inches from the top and the other 2 inches from the bottom. Use a ½-inch drill to bore holes through the wood at those points.

Lay two legs on a flat surface. Position one of the 6-foot lengths so it extends above the top of the leg the height of a 2×2. Mark on the leg the location of the center of each hole. Move the board and drill ½-inch holes through each leg as marked. Center the board over the legs so the holes align and fasten with carriage bolts. Repeat with the other 6-foot board and bench legs.

STEP 3 Add the sides to the frame. Prop up the front and back pieces—or have someone hold them—and attach the 2-foot lengths of the cut 2×8s inside the ends of the longer front and back pieces to form the frame sides. Attach with two screws at each corner. Set the screws only partway in.

STEP 4 Add the seat supports. Along the inside of the front and back frame and on each side of each leg, hold a 2×4 on edge flush with the top of the frame. Mark where the bottom of the 2×4 hits the inside of the frame. Cut short 2×4s to fit between the end of the frame and each leg and cut longer 2×4s to fit between the legs. Align the tops of these 2×4s with the marks you made and attach each one to the frame pieces with screws every 6 inches.

STEP 5 Add the seating. If the distance from the inside front of the frame to the inside back of the frame is 2 feet, you are still on course. Cut thirty-eight 2-foot 2×4s and eight 2-foot 2×2s. Place them all in position on top of the seat supports so they fit between the front and back of the frame and flush with its top. Now pay particular attention to the 2×2s. Because the posts are 5½ inches wide—compared to a total width of 6 inches when four 2×2s are placed side by side—ideally you will want to be able to lay the 2×2s on top of the posts so the outer two overlap the sides of the post top about ¼ inch each. Move the seat pieces around until you arrive at a satisfactory layout. Then drive one nail through the frame into each end of the 2×2s and two nails into the 2×4s. Finally, set the screws in end pieces.

STEP 6 Finish the bench. Use a nail set to recess the nails. Fill holes with plastic wood. Sand. Stain or paint as desired.

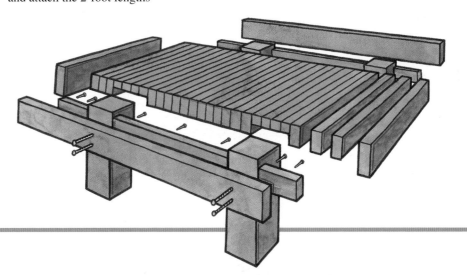

FOOLING THE EYE

All gardeners should be familiar with the French phrase trompe l'oeil, which translates as "fool (or deceive) the eye." The original method for trompe l'oeil was painting a false perspective or view onto a wall. In the garden, applying trompe l'oeil allows you to get more from your garden than you really have.

This technique creates the illusion of a garden space being bigger than it really is. This is especially useful if you have a small garden. Mirrors and false perspectives do for an outdoor room the same thing they do for a room indoors—they create a sense of depth when there isn't any. In the photograph below, a small courtyard appears twice as big as it is because of the illusion of an adjoining garden room. This technique is also helpful to disguise a blank wall of a house or garage. If there is a window in the garage, you can replace the window with a mirror to have a view into a garden instead of a view into the garage.

Another reason to fool the eye is for the sheer fun of it. There is an element of surprise when a person goes to look through what appears to be an opening in a fence or wall, only to see his own face reflected. Or in the case of the photograph at left, the false perspective created by a two-dimensional wood trellis makes one believe that there is a passageway through to another trellis.

▲ From one angle, the framed mirror looks like a window into a separate garden. From this angle, it shows off a sculpture.

Tips for fooling the eye

There are several ways to go about fooling the eye. The easiest and most playful way is with mirrors. You can also use false perspectives or illusionary murals to achieve a similar effect. You need to be a fairly competent artist or be willing to hire one. Regardless of the method you choose, there are several things you can do to enhance the effectiveness of trompe l'oeil.

Placement The positioning of a mirror or false perspective is important to how well it creates a sense of illusion. Ideally, the primary vantage point from which such a mirror is viewed should be other than straight on. When visitors see their reflection right away, the element of surprise is lost. In some cases, a mirror can be placed in such a way that viewers never see their reflection and may never know that they have been tricked. A false perspective or mural, on the other hand, is typically viewed straight on.

◄ From this angle, the mirror-backed arbor looks like a passage into another garden area.

Another aspect of placement involves what, if anything, you intend to have in front of the mirror. Placing a sculpture or plant is a lot like hanging a picture in a house; it doesn't have to actually be level as long as it looks level. Likewise, the positioning of objects in front of a garden mirror depends on the vantage point from which they will be viewed. As a general rule, start with the object centered in front of the mirror but not right up against it. Allow at least 2 feet between the object and the mirror.

Keep in mind that you can also use mirrors to show off an entire object without trying to create the illusion of additional space. The top photo on page 246 is a case in point. Although you may initially think there is a room beyond the wall, the purpose of the framed mirror is to allow a visitor to see both sides of the sculpture in one glance.

Hide the edges Whether it is a mirror or lattice perspective, avoid having visible edges. A hidden edge makes it less obvious that some trickery is taking place. Plants are the best way to hide edges, and vines are the best plants for the job. One exception to hiding the edge is when you are using a mirror in place of a windowpane.

Safety and maintenance

You need to consider the possibility of doing too good a job of fooling the eye. This is most important where you've created the illusion of a path leading into another part of the garden. You don't want someone to walk into a full-length mirror. This poses a dilemma, because anything you do to prevent such an accident is likely to detract from the mirror's effectiveness. Perhaps the best advice is to accompany first-timers as they explore the garden. People aren't the only ones likely to be fooled. Birds often accidentally fly into a window that reflects light and acts like the mirror. A well-done mural or false perspective could present the same problem.

Another tip for success with trompe l'oeil is to make it sturdy. If you use a thin mirror, warping is likely, which eliminates the desired effect. Lattice that is not cut, treated, or fastened properly may warp, altering the effect of the perspective.

Keep the mirrors sparkling. Avoid surrounding them with messy plants that will force you to clean often.

▼ What appears to be a vine-covered stone wall is a trompe l'oeil. The vines and even the stones are painted on concrete.

▲ Mirrors add interest to a wall, create a sense of depth, and bounce light back into the garden.

YARD ART

▲ **Practical and beautiful, a birdbath has stand-alone value as a piece of art.**

Ornaments are part of the bones of the garden because they do not change from season to season. They can add color and interest to an otherwise drab, dormant winter landscape, or a touch of whimsy at the height of summer. Above all, it is a fun way to express yourself. The best thing about garden ornaments—or yard art—is they transform *a* garden into *your* garden.

Why add ornaments?

Any ornamental addition you make to the garden may serve many roles.

Fun At the top of the list is the sheer fun of yard art. Whimsy and humor have a place in the garden; ornamentation is a good way to express a more playful side.

Surprise Ornaments offer a chance to give visitors something they weren't expecting, such as grass growing atop columns, as shown on page 249.

Ambience You can help create one mood by using an ornament that is formal and quite another mood by using one that is frivolous or funky.

◀ **The sculptural value of this row of birdhouses is enhanced by the fact that birds actually live there.**

Artistic value Some yard art is artistically important. The placement of such art in the garden is an ideal way to show off the art while adding strength to the character of the garden.

Practical purposes Ornaments can perform dual duty, as do the birdhouses and birdbath shown at left. They look good and they attract wildlife to the garden.

Design roles Use ornamentation to provide a focal point in a design, much as you would a specimen plant. It can help balance a design by serving as a focal point or visually balancing a planting bed. For example, a tall piece of sculpture can balance a tree in another part of the garden. The color of the art can also pick up colors in surrounding beds and helps unify the garden, as with the white cat sculpture on page 249.

Personality The pieces you choose and how you use them say a lot about your personality. Ornamenting the garden is also a chance to break the mold. Remember, in most cases the ornaments are not permanent and can be moved (or removed) to follow the evolution of both the garden and gardener.

◀ **You can mix and match yard art to create a garden tableau.**

▶ These whimsical columns planted with grass command attention in the garden.

▲ The subtly painted metal cat complements the color of the surrounding flowers.

Choosing and placing sculpture

What you choose to ornament your garden with and where you put the ornamentation are interrelated. They hinge on why you are adding the ornament in the first place.

If the purpose is to serve a definite design function or some other practical end, the location is largely decided for you. If it is for pure aesthetics or fun, you have much more latitude.

Regardless of the why and where of a piece of yard art, there are several criteria to use when selecting a potential ornament for your garden. Be sure that it

is something you can live with. Mark Twain said, "His problem is he fell in love with a dimple and married the whole girl." Be sure you really want an item of yard art before investing the time, money, and trouble of getting it into the garden.

Durability is another factor. If the object of your choice is wood, it will probably decay over time. You can retard the decay by protecting the piece with clear sealer. If it is made of metal, keeping it painted will slow the rust.

The final consideration is setting the ornament firmly in place. Be sure that wind, deer, or a bump of a wheelbarrow won't dislodge it.

◀ Ornaments need not be elaborate. A stone sphere makes a strong statement.

▶ Regal and sophisticated, this sundial is aesthetic as well as practical.

▲ An endless array of birdfeeders and birdbaths allows you to choose a combination that suits your taste.

How to make stepping-stones

MATERIALS

(For each paver)
Four 2-foot 2×4s
2-inch wood screws
OR
One 24×24-inch piece
of foam-core board,
2 inches thick
Large, textured leaf
Thin, serrated knife
AND
3×3 piece of ½-inch
plywood
Concrete mix

STEP 1 **Make a mold.** This can be as easy as screwing four 2×4s together to form a box form, or making a custom frame the shape of caladium leaf (right).

To make a mold for a leaf-shape (or other intricate) paver, use a 2-inch-thick piece of foam board for each paver. For variety, make four different molds using four different leaves. Trace the outline of a leaf onto the piece of foam. The leaf outline should be at least 6 inches from the outer edge of the foam. Use a bread knife or other thin, serrated blade to cut out the leaf. Smooth the cut edge with your hands.

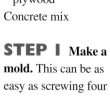

◄ **An easy way to make ground-level yard art is to use decorative masonry stone such as the ones at left, with hollow centers. Use ground glass, colored stone, pieces of broken pottery, beads, or anything else that pleases you to fill the spaces and create the desired effect. It's best to draw a scale plan on paper first.**

▲ Use the directions provided below to make these unusual leaf-shape pavers.

STEP 2 **Add texture.** Set the mold on a piece of plywood. If you are doing a square mold, you can add texture by setting the frame on top of a crumpled piece of plastic drop cloth.

STEP 3 **Mix and pour the concrete.** Place the concrete mix in a bucket and stir in water. Aim for a well-blended sturdy consistency that is neither soupy or dry. If you want color, add dye to the mixture. For the more delicate leaf mold, fill the mold with concrete by hand. Tamp the concrete with a dowel to remove any air pockets.

Gently press the leaf face into the concrete. Wait about 30 minutes before peeling off the leaf. You may have to experiment with concrete texture and cure time to get this just right.

STEP 4 **Unmold the pavers.** If the paver doesn't slide out, unscrew the wood mold to release it. For the foam mold, you may have to break away the foam and make new molds for more pavers. (But first try cutting around the concrete.) You can accentuate the leaf paver by painting the lines created by the veins.

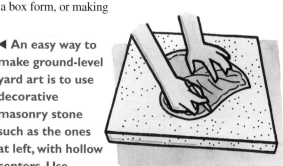

1

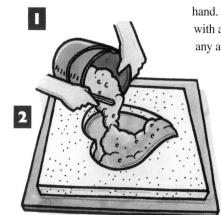

2

3

How to age concrete

You can treat new concrete pieces to appear much older than they really are.

STEP 1 Prepare the piece you want to age.
To be sure the concrete will take a finish, you may need to use coarse sandpaper to rough up the surface and create pore spaces.

STEP 2 Mix the treatment.
Although chemical treatments designed to give a weathered look to concrete are available at garden centers and craft stores, you can try a homemade method first. Mix buttermilk or yogurt in a 50/50 combination. This creates an environment for lichens and algae.

STEP 3 Apply the treatment.
Use a paintbrush to coat the entire ornament. For at least a week, keep the treated object out of direct sunlight and away from rain to allow the mixture to slowly dry, and to prevent rain from washing off the material. Manufacturers of chemical treatments may recommend placing the object in the sun (but protecting it from rain).

STEP 4 Touch up.
If you don't see the desired results in a few weeks, or if the staining is uneven, reapply the finish. The microclimate where the object is located plays a part in how fast aging occurs.

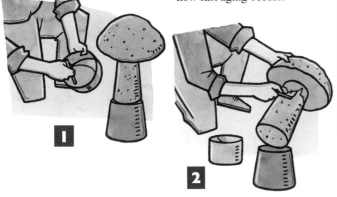

TIPS FOR SOURCES OF YARD ART

Yard art can be found in likely and unlikely places.

- **Garden centers** The most traditional source of garden ornaments, garden centers offer a chance to see exactly what you're getting. If you have a good relationship with the owners, they may allow you to take something home on a trial basis.

- **Catalogs** You can buy just about anything via mail order these days, and garden ornaments are no exception. The Internet is a good source too. Keep in mind that the heavier or bulkier the item, the more it will cost to ship.

- **Garage and estate sales** One man's junk is another man's treasure. Moving sales are a good source of yard art, because many people leave most of their garden behind when they move. If you're at a moving sale and see something you are interested in, ask about it, even though it's not for sale. Chances are the owner may part with it.

- **The shore and woods** Driftwood, boulders, and gnarled limbs become sculpture in the right setting.

- **Window-shop** Look around the neighborhood and elsewhere. If you see something you like, ask where it came from. The owner may be delighted to tell you.

CONTAINERS

▲ Use container plants to frame a space and add color where plants normally wouldn't grow.

◀ Have fun with containers. Make and decorate a tire planter (see page 257 for instructions).

Containers provide one of the most versatile ways to garden. When placed in the middle of a garden bed, a large container filled with a pleasing blend of plants makes a strong statement. Like all aspects of garden design, the best results come from a plan that includes knowing your options. Here are a few.

The many uses of container gardening

There are a lot of reasons for planting in containers. Once you explore some ideas, take time to map out where you want to use containers, the type of effect you want, the container you want, and the plants you will use.

Accent The combination of a well-chosen container and the plants in it can draw attention to an area and serve as an accent. This is especially true in hardscape areas.

Portability With a container you can have a sun-loving plant in full shade (if only for a day or two) by growing it where it does best most of the time, then moving it where you want it for special occasions. You can rotate duplicate containers throughout the seasons as they each reach their peak.

Where nothing else will grow Often containers are the only way to add green to an area. Decks, terraces, and entryways are good examples.

Style An aged container (see page 251 for tips on aging concrete) lends an established look even to a new garden. A pair of large matching urns planted identically can flank an entry to the home or part of a garden to project a formal and ordered look. Or you can get playful and use a tire planter (below left).

Types of containers

Just about anything can be used as a container for planting, as long as it will hold soil and can drain. Some materials are better than others, and they all serve different design purposes.

Terra-cotta The most popular type of container, terra-cotta, or clay pots, comes in thousands of different shapes and sizes. One reason this material is so well-suited to container gardening is that it "breathes," allowing air and water to pass through its walls. A drawback to terra-cotta is that it is prone to freezing and cracking and pots dry out rapidly after watering. Salt residues may cause a white buildup on the outside of pots.

Concrete Another popular material, cast concrete is more durable than terra-cotta but also heavier and more expensive.

Synthetic Plastic and fiberglass are other choices to consider. Plastic pots have been around a long time and they are lightweight, sturdy, and durable. They just

▲ Layering plants in one container adds vertical height and visual interest as well.

look synthetic. Fiberglass (or fiberglass/resin mixtures) pots are lightweight and durable, though not as strong as plastic. Some of the newer ones have an uncanny resemblance to concrete or terra-cotta.

Wood Wood is a good choice when adding built-in planters to a deck or putting them in conjunction with seating. It often looks out of place in other areas. Wood will decay over time. You can slow decay by using a liner.

Metal Cast iron, cast aluminum, copper, tin, and stainless steel can be used to make containers. Although expensive, they are frequently used as accents.

Customized An old shoe, an antique washing machine, or anything else you can think of has probably been used as a planter at one time or another. Consider

▲ **Flanking identical planters creates a formal and ordered look.**

▼ **Planting a sheared hedge in containers allows you to rearrange the hedge at will.**

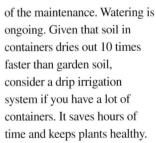

adding a few playful planters to your garden for an element of surprise.

Maintenance considerations

A big part of success in garden design is knowing what long-term commitments are being made. Container plants are like pets. They rely solely on you for food, water, and light. Starting off with a good soil (see page 36) and putting plants in the right location for light takes care of a lot of the maintenance. Watering is ongoing. Given that soil in containers dries out 10 times faster than garden soil, consider a drip irrigation system if you have a lot of containers. It saves hours of time and keeps plants healthy.

▲ **Combine containers, yard art, and plants for a fanciful look.**

▲ **Contrast the colors of the containers with the flowers planted in them.**

Three Planting Designs for Containers

Each container you plant offers the chance for a small but distinct garden. Use containers to test combinations before giving them a permanent home in the garden.

Edibles If you're an urban gardener or simply have limited space, think how convenient it would be to have fresh produce such as tomatoes growing on your balcony or front porch. Dwarf varieties of many vegetables and fruits make this possible.

Herbs No matter what size your garden is, it is handy to have your favorite herbs within reach. Grow all the seasonings for an Italian dinner or Mexican salsa in a large pot. Keep rampant growers, such as mint, in separate pots to hold them in check.

Cut flowers Fill a few containers with your favorite flowers for arranging and set the pot just outside the door for a handy source of cut flowers.

Tropicalismo This term refers to big, bold, colorful plants that evoke images of the tropics. One container at the entrance to your home can have a big impact on visitors. The container can also be easily moved for winter.

Fragrance Whether planting a lone gardenia or a mass of flowering tobacco, use containers of fragrant plants—one type per pot—to perfume the garden. Move them around to take advantage of prevailing winds to waft the scent in the desired direction.

Year-round An evergreen with a few ornamental grasses as anchors, and supplemental plantings through the seasons, can take one container through an entire year.

Foliage A container filled with richly textured foliage plants can be as appealing as bright flowers.

WATER GARDEN

TRAILING COLOR

VERTICAL ACCENT

How to plant a container

MATERIALS

Container with drainage hole
Soilless planting mix or
  potting soil
Moisture retention product
Slow-release fertilizer

STEP 1 Plan the pot.

Know what you want the finished, planted container to look like. This is important to help avoid overcrowding and to select the right plants and pot for the job.

STEP 2 Mix the soil.

The soil you use for container gardening is different from what is recommended for a garden bed. For one thing, it should be lighter in weight so you can move the pots around easily. Even if you want the plant to stay in one place, use a mix that absorbs and holds water, has a lot of pore space so there is plenty of oxygen for the roots, drains well, and is free of weeds and disease.

Though you can make your own mix, the commercially available mixes, which are already sterilized and lightweight, do a good job and are much easier than mixing your own soil.

However, if you plan to fill a lot of pots and cost is a factor, you can make your own mix by using equal parts of rich garden loam, sphagnum peat moss, and perlite. Baking soil in an oven at 400 degrees for an hour will sterilize it.

You might also consider mixing a moisture retention product into the soil. Containers dry out quickly, but these products can cut the need for watering by more than half. Find them at your local greenhouse or garden center.

STEP 3 Prepare and add the soil.

Before you fill the container with soil, mix in a balanced (10-10-10) slow-release fertilizer at the rate recommended on the label. It gets plants off to a good start and is easier to add now than after the pot is planted.

Fill the pot about two-thirds of the way with soil. Gravel or pot shards are not needed in the bottom of the pot; they only add weight.

If weight is a concern and your pot is large enough, invert an inexpensive plastic pot in the middle of the container, then pour soil around it. This reduces the amount of soil needed. There should be at least 8 inches from the top of the inverted pot to the top of the soil.

STEP 4 Plant.

Have all of your plants on hand. While they are still in their pots, arrange them in the container in the configuration you want, keeping in mind the rate at which the plants will grow and how large they will be at maturity.

Remember the configuration, or sketch it out, then remove the plants and unpot them. Use your hand to rough up their root balls and splay the roots out a bit. Return the plants to the pot and gently pack soil around the roots.

STEP 5 Water.

Using a water wand or other gentle sprinkler, water the container until water flows from the drain hole at the bottom. Fill any depressions where soil settled and gently press plants that floated up into place.

Decorating Containers

A big part of the design impact of container gardening is the container itself. Although you may find exactly what you want already finished and ready to plant, you'll miss the fun, savings, and opportunity for personal expression to be found in transforming an ordinary pot into an extraordinary one with a little of your handiwork.

Painting and coloring

One quick and easy way to decorate a container is to paint it. Make sure the pot is suited to being painted. In most cases, plastic and other synthetic containers do not accept paint; it simply runs off. Concrete, terra-cotta, wood, cast aluminum, and iron take paint well.

Once you know you can paint your pot, you can plan, design, and come up with a color scheme to match what you'll plant in it. Sometimes, as in the photo below left, you can simply highlight patterns already on the pot.

Another approach is to visit a do-it-yourself pottery shop where you can select a vessel, then add a glaze, and have the shop fire the pot for you.

Mosaic

You can cover an entire pot with a pattern using various materials, or decorate the rim, or just do one side of a pot to turn an ordinary container into something unique. Sketch a design, then use mastic (a readily available adhesive) to attach pieces of broken plates, glass, and other objects to the outside of a pot. Allow the adhesive to dry overnight, then use unsanded grout to fill the spaces between the pieces. Wipe off any excess and let dry.

Playful additions

You can add an element of surprise to the container garden. Whimsical objects such as shown in the photo at right add interest to containers that will be viewed up close.

▲ Do-it-yourself pottery shops allow you to create a look and a glaze that are your very own.

▲ Use paint to highlight the relief of a terra-cotta pot, or create a new pattern.

▲ Use novel accents such as artificial reptiles or fallen leaves to enliven a container planting.

How to make a tire planter

Planters made from an old tire are fun and funky and a good way to recycle.

STEP 1 Get an old tire.

To make this work of art, use a tire still attached to a rim. Standard automobile tires work best. Truck and tractor tires can be used, but they are harder to handle. Golf cart tires work too. Avoid radial tires; they are stiffer and more difficult to turn inside out.

STEP 2 Cut the pattern.

Use a strong, sharp knife (finely serrated blades work best) to cut an even, scalloped pattern on one side of the tire along the sidewall. It helps to trace the pattern on the tire with chalk before you cut.

STEP 3 Turn the tire inside out.

Flip the tire so the cut side is down, then slide your hands into the opening, place a foot firmly on the rim, and with one hand pulling and the other pushing, turn the tire inside out, as shown in 3 and 3A. Depending on the tire, this can turn into a bit of a wrestling match.

STEP 4 Trim and adjust the top edge.

Once the tire is inverted, point the top edge up and use a large pair of tin snips to trim the edges to your liking.

STEP 5 Decorate and plant.

Put the tire exactly where you want it (you won't want to move it once it is planted), and paint the tire with latex paint in any color or colors you choose. Then fill it with soil and plants.

MAILBOXES

We all have one, we use it every day, and in most cases, we take it for granted. Odd that for something that provides such a strong link to the rest of world, a mailbox is typically stuck out in the yard like an afterthought.

On these pages are images and ideas to get you to consider dressing up your mailbox, whether you do it literally or by creating a pleasing setting for mail delivery.

The U.S. Postal Service has no guidelines that govern what you can and can't plant around your mailbox. It is the local postmaster who determines whether

▲ The red flag that alerts the carrier to pick up outgoing mail is cleverly included in this design as the chimney.

the mailbox and the approach to the mailbox are "clear of obstructions so as to allow safe access for delivery."

On the other hand, the Postal Service does have some guidelines about the box itself and the post upon which it sits. To be on the safe side, check with your local post office before building or buying a new mailbox to be sure it conforms to regulations.

Design considerations

The Postal Service guidelines dictate the height and size of the box. Beyond that, you can have the typical austere mailbox

shown below or an innovative one as shown to the left. Because you see the box every day you are home (and so do your neighbors), choose a design in keeping with the rest of your garden. Painting the post and box the same color as the house, trim, or nearby fence will tie it into the landscape.

▲ U.S. Postal Service guidelines for mailboxes allow this Uncle Sam design.

▼ The simplicity of this mailbox blends well with the rustic look of the house and garden.

How to dress up a mailbox

METHOD 1 Create a **planting island.** If you are happy with the mailbox itself but it sits in the middle of nowhere, incorporate it as part of a planting bed, even making the mailbox the focal point. Be sure there is clear access to the mailbox and that the path is stable and nonslippery.

METHOD 2 **Train a vine to it.** Check with your postmaster before training a vine on your mailbox. Be sure to keep the mailbox opening clear of the vine at all times, and be sure the address is clearly visible.

METHOD 3 **Make it disappear.** Make the mailbox blend in so well that you barely notice it. Incorporate it into a fence or wall or paint it the same color as a dense evergreen hedge.

METHOD 4 **Turn it into a work of art.** Art is subjective. Who is to say that your mailbox isn't already sculpture? Within the confines of U.S. Postal Service regulations, turn your mailbox into a work of art. The options are limitless.

▲ Add netting around a mailbox post for clematis to climb.

▲ A sturdily built rustic mailbox is suitable for this site and discourages vandals.

▶ Painting a mailbox personalizes it for your home and garden.

▲ This homeowner welded used auto parts together for a touch of whimsy.

HOUSE LOCATORS

◄ At first glance the numbers look like a carved stone sculpture. Painting the numbers slightly darker will make them more visible.

▼ Place your house number near your mailbox to make it easy for the postman to locate.

Just as with mailboxes, many homes have a house number announcing that, "Yes, indeed, this is where I live." The numbers making that announcement can be as plain as numerals painted on a curb, decals stuck on the mailbox, or the same black metal numbers tacked over the garage that everyone else on the block has.

Although there is nothing wrong with any of the above-mentioned locators, they may represent a missed opportunity to set the tone for your guests and to demonstrate how much pride and care you have taken in designing your entire landscape, even down to the choice of house numbers.

There are two basic considerations when you are selecting your house number: visibility and style.

Visibility

The most important function of a house number or house locator is that it be readily seen from many vantage points, including a car traveling at moderate speed, night or day. Although this may sound like a tall order, the examples shown on these pages do just that, and none of them is obtrusive.

▲ The front door is a logical place to look for a house number. Use contrasting colors to make it stand out.

◄ This cast-metal plaque matches the stately-looking stone pillars.

107 SANTEE TRAIL

▲ **Combination house numbers/mailboxes are readily available and are often used to unify a neighborhood.**

▼ **Simplicity is the key to this elegant faux-marble inset.**

104

15

◄ **If you have a fence post in a visible location, let it double as a house locator.**

650
MOUNT JOY

The keys to having the numbers be visible include the size of the numbers, where you place them, and the style of the numbers.

To determine what you think is the right size, first decide if your house number will be on your house or placed streetside. Then drive around a few neighborhoods. Every time you see a house number that you can easily read (whether on the house or streetside), stop and measure it, if you feel comfortable doing that. A numeral that seems too big when holding it in your hand in the store may be just right above your garage.

Style

The style of your house number affects visibility and character. Fancy, ornate scrolling can be difficult to read. Plain, simple numbers work better. If possible, use contrasting colors, such as black on anything light colored. Black wrought-iron numbers on a dark brown trim will all but disappear. It is even better to use light-colored numbers on a dark background, because of how the eye perceives color. It's the same principle that the highway departments use—many signs are dark green with white lettering.

With these practical considerations taken into account, you can choose the right numbers, place them in the right location, and set them against the right background to clearly mark your property.

400

◄ **This handmade tile provides a personal touch from the homeowner.**

▲ **Placing your house numbers near an outdoor light ensures that nighttime guests can find your home.**

LIGHTING

You can keep on enjoying the garden after the sun goes down. In fact, in some cases, nighttime can be the ideal time to be in the garden. It is cooler and you are less tempted to "work" in the garden, so you can see it in a whole new light. Pun intended.

Reasons for lighting

Night lighting is used for a wide range of visual effects and other purposes. On the practical side, night lighting makes movement through the garden safe and easy. It is essential for entry areas, parking courts, pools, steps, drives, and other areas where people move about.

When planning lighting for these types of practical uses, be aware that in addition to the specific function you need the lighting to serve, you can also use the opportunity to visually enhance the property.

The patterns and forms created by lighting should be given the same attention as the design of the garden itself. Keep in mind that the fixtures may be visible during daylight, although they blend well with the landscape and can be used for ornamentation. For more on fixtures see pages 264–265.

Types of lighting

There are three basic types of lighting: downlighting, uplighting, and sidelighting.

Downlighting looks most like natural light. As the name implies, the light shines down upon an object or area. It is the most effective way to shed light on a path, drive, or entry.

For uplighting, a fixture is placed at the base of an object or plant and the light is directed upward. This results in dramatic forms and can also be used to create shadows against a wall.

Sidelighting is also used to show off an object or plant. When fixtures flank the object, they almost completely illuminate it.

To achieve moonlighting, place fixtures high up in a tree and have them pointed downward. Four or five feet beneath the higher fixtures are less bright lights facing up to illuminate foliage and obscure the source of the downlight.

The drawings on page 263 show examples of different lighting types. You can mix and match to achieve the desired effect.

◄ **Night lighting accents shapes in the garden and directs visitors to your front door.**

Lighting Patterns

▶ **Silhouette lighting**—Used to silhouette a plant by lighting the background.

▶ **Uplighting**—Used to highlight plants and objects. Shows off form.

◀ **Security lighting**—Practical lighting used to illuminate areas of access and eliminate hiding places.

◀ **Downlighting**—Can be used to spotlight a single object from overhead and fill an area with light.

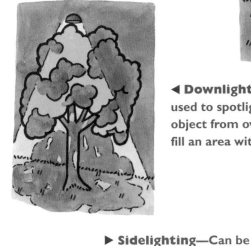

▶ **Step lighting**—Primarily a safety feature, it can also create dramatic effects.

▶ **Sidelighting**—Can be adjusted to totally illuminate an object or accentuate its form.

◀ **Shadow lighting**—Lights placed to cast an object's shadow against a wall.

◀ **Walk lighting**—A form of downlighting used to focus light on walks and paths.

▶ **Moonlighting**—A combination of uplighting and downlighting that mimics moonlight.

▶ **Wash lighting**—Used to cast a broad swath of light over a flower bed or other area.

Voltage and Fixtures

Selecting the right lighting fixture is essential to getting the desired effect. It should have appropriate brightness and pattern of light, and it should blend with the garden design.

Standard- vs. low-voltage lighting

Before choosing fixtures, decide what kind of night-lighting system is best suited for your garden. Night lighting is broken down into two major categories: standard voltage and low voltage.

Standard-voltage lighting uses 120-volt currency. Because that amount of current can shock you, this type of wiring is best left to professionals. Standard-voltage lighting has several advantages. For one, it is the best type of lighting for a streetlight and for fully illuminating an area such as a parking court or an entryway.

Low-voltage lighting also has many advantages. The biggest plus is that it is easy to install. Whether you purchase the components separately or buy a complete kit, this type of lighting can be installed by the homeowner in a day. Step-by-step directions on how to install low-voltage lighting can be found on pages 266–267.

In addition to the ease of installation, low-voltage lighting is usually less expensive than standard voltage lighting. There is no need for an electrician as long as you have a grounded outlet located

▲ **This custom-made light fixture, which uses standard voltage, illuminates an entry path and is attractive.**

on the outside of your house near where you want the lighting to be placed.

With low-voltage lighting, there is virtually no risk of injury due to electrical shock. This is a comfort when you (or your children or pets) are digging in the garden and can't recall exactly where all the lines are located.

Fixtures

Whether using standard- or low-voltage lighting, you will find a wide range of ready-to-use, prefabricated fixtures. If you don't find exactly what you are looking for, or find

◄ **Night lighting can be as simple as wrapping a string of low-voltage lights around a tree.**

▲ **Make an attractive accent light by placing a large shell over a low-voltage fixture.**

the prices too high, you can customize a fixture or build one from scratch to suit your needs.

The most common light fixtures for the home garden are usually made of black plastic and typically have a pagoda or mushroom shape. These lights work fine and the dark color helps them recede into the background during daylight hours. There are alternatives. The Internet has "virtual showrooms" that allow you to peruse various styles. In many cases, you can get pricing. Even if you want to purchase locally versus mail-order, you can identify the types of fixtures you want from your home.

Prices vary, based largely on the two factors: style and material. The more ornate the fixture, the more it costs. The

materials from which a fixture is made have an even greater impact on cost. Copper, bronze, and other cast-metal fixtures are usually the most expensive, but they often look the best. Metal is also more durable than plastic or wood and will protect the fixture and wiring longer.

As you choose the fixture, consider how it will age. A wood fixture will weather unless it is stained or painted, so consider how it will look in its surroundings in several years. Likewise, a metal fixture may start out shiny, but it too will weather. In the case of the copper fixture shown at right, the patina on the metal has turned the fixture a soft green, making it attractive in its own right while helping it blend into the landscape.

Regardless of the type of electrical lighting you use, consider having the system controlled by a rheostat or dimmer switch. This allows maximum control over the mood you create.

One last thought: Consider natural fixtures. Tiki torches, candles, and firepits all add light to the garden without electricity. There are obvious limitations, but there are also aesthetic advantages.

▼ **Copper fixtures will weather to a green patina unless treated.**

◄ **The dark color of this handsome yet simple fixture blends with the surrounding bed.**

How to install low-voltage lighting

Before purchasing electrical fixtures or hardware, develop a plan of action. Use a copy of your base map or master plan and identify all areas you want to illuminate, whether for safety, looks, or practicality. A comprehensive plan will show what your needs are. For areas that need only a modicum of lighting, low-voltage fixtures work fine.

Areas needing a lot of light do best with standard 120-volt fixtures which should be installed by a licensed electrician. The following instructions are for low-voltage lighting only.

You may already have a grounded outlet right where you want it. If not, weigh the pros and cons of adding one instead of having to run longer lengths of lighting cable to get lights where you want them.

MATERIALS

We recommend using a low-voltage lighting kit, which will contain all you need for a simple system. For a more complex system, you may need several kits or accessory packs.

STEP 1 Make a shopping list. Use the needs list developed from the lighting assessment plan and determine how many of what type of fixture you need. Then figure out the total amount of wiring you will need. With this information, you can determine what your transformer needs are. Most transformers can handle a load of 100 to 300 watts. Each transformer will indicate the total number of lights you can run off it and the total length of cable it can handle. In short, a transformer that can handle eight fixtures near the house may be able to feed only four fixtures at the far end of the garden. Some people prefer a transformer that comes with a photoelectric eye so they can set the system to come on automatically at dusk, no matter how much the hours of daylight change. If you have a plain transformer, consider getting a timer when you purchase the hardware. Cable, transformer, timer, and the fixtures themselves are all you'll need. When shopping, explore potential savings by purchasing kits. In some cases, an entire kit with fixtures, transformer, and cable is the same price as a transformer alone.

STEP 2 Lay out the fixtures. Using your lighting plan as a guide, walk your property and set fixtures exactly where you want them. Make sure the desired method of securing each fixture works where you have placed it. For example, if you want evenly spaced lights along a walk, be sure there isn't a pipe or huge rock right below where you want to position a light.

STEP 3 Trench for the power line. The two main reasons for burying the line are to hide it and to avoid cutting it or catching the fixtures with a tool or your own foot. If all the lighting is going in a flower bed that you keep mulched, ignore this step and skip ahead to step 4.

Use a wide screwdriver to dig a very narrow trench about 4 inches deep and just wide enough to press the line into it. It's a good idea to connect the fixtures with straight lines. This means less digging and less wire, and you can easily map out where everything is buried for future reference.

STEP 4 Lay out the light cable. Starting at the power source, unroll the cable along the trenches, leaving a loop of about 1 foot of cable everywhere there is a fixture.

STEP 5 Connect the fixtures. Fixtures vary slightly in how the cable is attached to them. All fixtures come with instructions, and the methods are simple. Usually it is a matter of doubling the loop of wire you left at each fixture and sliding it through a clamp, then into the base of the fixture. Contact is made by twisting the clamp.

STEP 6 Set fixtures in place. Set fixtures partway into the ground or wherever they will go until you are sure everything works and is placed where you want it.

STEP 7 Connect the cable to the transformer. As with the individual fixtures, this method varies a little, but it is simple and instructions are provided with the cable. Once the cable is connected, plug in the transformer and turn on the lights.

STEP 8 Make final adjustments. With everything wired, have a helper move lights as you study the effects you get from different vantage points in the garden. Once satisfied, set fixtures permanently and fill in the trenches.

PLANTING

Bringing a design to life

TREES

Their size and the prominent roles they play set trees apart from the other plants in the garden. From smaller ornamental trees in the 20-foot range to shade trees and evergreens that soar to 80 feet and higher, trees set the scene for the landscape. They establish boundaries in the garden and define space; they frame portions of a garden, the whole garden, or an entire neighborhood.

Large trees evoke a sense of history and permanence. You need only envision favorite homes, streets, or neighborhoods to realize the predominance of trees. In many practical ways, trees are assets to the garden.

Shade and canopy Depending on their location, large trees can shade all or parts of the garden. Deciduous trees cast their shade only when in leaf; evergreens—broad-leaved or needled—provide shade year-round. Before adding a new shade tree to the landscape, be aware of the direction and angle of the sun so the shade falls on the desired area.

The spreading branches of broad-leaved trees, such as oaks and maples, provide a canopy for shade-tolerant shrubs, bulbs, and perennials as well as shade when the sun is directly overhead.

Framing Use trees to frame views of the landscape from a specific point—often a picture window, patio, or deck.

Privacy Evergreens—large and small—are ideal for blocking views into the garden. Deciduous trees work in summer but leave the garden exposed in winter.

Color Besides their myriad shades of green, trees add color with flowers, fruit, and fall foliage. The flowers of most trees are insignificant; showier are small trees such as dogwood, redbud, and cherry. Some trees, such as holly, have colorful fruit that spices up a winter landscape. As leaves change to autumn hues, the garden comes alive with color. The chart on page 271 lists trees with good fall color.

Leaf mold Rake up all the leaves that fall in autumn, and make a pile. In time it will disintegrate into leaf mold, which is as beneficial to the garden as compost.

▲ Plant small trees, such as these native flowering dogwoods (*Cornus florida*) in groups of three or more for a foreground of spring color.

▲ A showy tree, such as this Weeping Higan cherry (*Prunus subhirtella* 'Pendula'), makes an excellent specimen. Set apart, its form takes center stage.

Tree Shapes

Be aware of what the mature shape of a tree will be before you purchase or plant it. When a tree is young, it is difficult to tell what it will look like in 5 or 10 years; the change can be dramatic. When buying a tree, consider the reason for the tree (shade or spring color, protection from wind, temperature moderation of the house, or privacy screening), the eventual height of the tree, and a shape that suits the purpose. Plan the spacing of trees with these points in mind. Crowding them when they are young may give an instant effect, but it will necessitate removing some of the trees as they grow.

If you want to sit in the shade of a tree, select an open, spreading, or vase shape. For screening or to frame a view, columnar and oval-shaped trees are best; they can be grown side by side, creating a solid wall of foliage.

Although weeping trees take up a lot of space, they introduce a special character to the garden. The sounds and movements created as a breeze blows through them are incomparable. Plant round and pyramidal trees in groups to create a background for the garden. Whether they are deciduous or evergreen, their distinctive geometric shapes make them ideal as individual specimen plants.

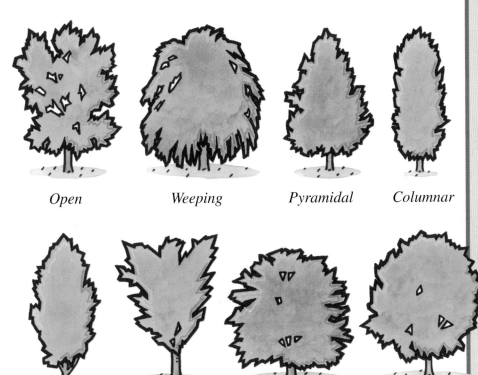

Open *Weeping* *Pyramidal* *Columnar*

Oval *Vase* *Spreading* *Round*

OUTSTANDING TREES FOR FALL COLOR

In many areas, the gardening season ends with a fiery display of fall foliage ranging from yellow and gold to orange, red, and burgundy. You can plan an array of fall foliage color as you would spring flower color. For dazzling fall color, the soil moisture, day and nighttime temperatures, and amount of sunlight must be just right. Plan for ideal colors and optimal conditions; enjoy whatever happens.

Yellow and Gold
Pawpaw (*Asimina triloba*)
Shagbark hickory (*Carya ovata*)
American chestnut (*Castanea dentata*)
Hackberry (*Celtis occidentalis*)
American beech (*Fagus grandifolia*)
Ginkgo (*Gingko biloba*)
Quaking aspen (*Populus tremuloides*)
Golden weeping willow (*Salix alba* 'Tristis')
Littleleaf linden (*Tilia cordata*) var. *vitellina*
Thornless honeylocust (*Gleditsia triacanthos inermis*)

Orange
Sugar maple (*Acer saccharum*)
American hornbeam (*Carpinus caroliniana*)
Franklin tree (*Franklinia alatamaha*)
Ohio buckeye (*Aesculus glabra*)
Pin cherry (*Prunus pensylvanica*)

Red
Amur maple (*Acer tataricum ginnala*)
Red maple (*Acer rubrum*)
Sweet gum (*Liquidambar styraciflua*)
Scarlet oak (*Quercus coccinea*)
Northern red oak (*Quercus rubra*)

Burgundy
Flowering dogwood (*Cornus florida*)
Sourwood (*Oxydendrum arboreum*)
Japanese stewartia (*Stewartia pseudocamellia*)
Sheepberry (*Viburnum lentago*)

How to plant a tree

STEP 1 Dig the hole.
Use a wheelbarrow, garden cart, or pickup truck to move the tree exactly where you want to plant it.

Dig the hole. The latest research suggests that you dig a hole just to the depth of the root ball and twice as wide, whether the plant is in a container or balled and burlapped as shown in the illustration above.

If you suspect poor soil drainage, do a percolation test before planting. See page 43 for directions.

STEP 2 Plant and level.
Lift the tree by the root ball, not by the trunk. If the root ball is large, make a ramp using a 2×12 to help slide the tree into place. If the tree is in a container, lay it on its side and gently slide the tree out. Take care to keep the root ball intact. Gently turn the tree until it is facing the direction you want. If you will be viewing it from various angles, it may take a few tries to get it right.

If the tree is wrapped in burlap, cut off and remove as much of the burlap and string as possible. (Fabric under the ball can remain.) Remove anything else—wire or a plastic basket—from around the root ball.

Lay a shovel or board across the hole. If necessary, add soil beneath the root ball so that the top of the root ball is flush with the shovel.

STEP 3 Fill the hole, then water. Use the original soil to backfill the hole. Do not amend it unless it is extremely rocky or sandy. If amendments are necessary, replace one-third of the backfill soil with compost or humus before backfilling and mix well. Fill the hole halfway with water, then tamp the soil. Add more soil to the level of the surrounding ground, then water again. Add a 3-inch layer of mulch; keep it several inches from the trunk. Making a water dam around the tree is no longer recommended unless you are planting on a slope.

Staking and Wrapping

Until recently, gardeners were advised to stake and wrap any tree they planted. Today, these practices are suggested only in a few cases. For those instances, it is important to stake and wrap them properly so the tree isn't staked too tautly, the wire is removed when it should be, and the wrapping does not constrict the tree growth.

Staking

If a tree is 5 feet or less in height you should not stake it. A small tree is unlikely to have branches and foliage large enough to catch the wind and blow over. In fact, gentle movement promotes a healthier root system and better trunk taper. Trees taller than 5 feet usually do need staking.

To stake a tree, drive two 24-inch stakes a foot into the ground on opposite sides of the tree just beyond the root ball. Cut two sections of garden hose, each about 12 inches long. Run a medium-gauge wire from one stake up and around the trunk (about 3 feet off the ground) and back to the stake. Add 2 feet to that length; cut the wire. Repeat the process at the other stake. Remove the wires and tie, nail, or staple one end of one of the wires to one of the stakes. Slide the free end of the wire through the hose and wrap the hose around the trunk of the tree. Make sure that only the hose is touching the bark. Attach the other end of the wire to the stake. Repeat with the other wire and stake. Be sure that the wires are not too tight to allow some movement of the tree.

Wrapping

Wrapping overlaps and covers the trunk of a young tree with crepe paper (available at most nurseries). In nature, the trunk is sheltered from direct sun by the canopy of surrounding trees. In your backyard, it may be exposed to the full intensity of the sun. Wrapping protects the bark from cracking during a freeze that follows a thaw and from physical damage caused by rabbits. Wrap the tree in late fall and remove the wrapping in the spring to avoid damage from insects and disease.

TIPS FOR BUYING A TREE

A tree is an important, long-term investment in the landscape. As discussed on page 15, there is a financial return on the investment; the presence of trees raises property values. Trees are also important to the garden from a design and function standpoint. When choosing a tree, use the following guidelines.

- Know the correct botanical name, including the cultivar name (if there is one), for the plant you want. There are dozens of different dogwood trees and just as many oak trees, so you need to be specific. A common name often is not enough.
- Check that the tree is tagged with the correct plant name. If there isn't a tag, ask the nursery employee to make sure that it is the right tree.
- Ask if the tree was grown locally. Just because it is in a local nursery or garden center does not guarantee that it is suitable for your climate. A tree that is native to the area is often the best choice.

- If the tree is container-grown, pick it up to see if any roots are protruding from the drain holes in the bottom of the container. If the roots are visible, the tree is pot-bound, may be stressed, and will likely get off to a slow start.
- If the tree is balled and burlapped, squeeze the root ball to feel whether the soil is loose. Loose soil is a sign of rough handling, which may have damaged the roots.
- Check the tree from top to bottom for physical damage. Nicks on the trunk or broken limbs indicate rough treatment of the plant. A gash in the outer bark will leave a scar as the tree grows.
- Have the nursery employee move the tree you want into an open area. Walk around it and be sure it has the form you want from all desired angles.
- Ask for advice on planting, care, and maintenance. Follow that advice.
- Request a money-back guarantee in case the tree performs poorly or dies within a year.

SHRUBS

▲ **Massing shrubs to form a solid bank of green in front of a house helps tie the house to the surrounding landscape.**

The difference between trees and shrubs is not so much about size (shrubs are usually less than 20 feet tall; trees are taller) as about trunks. Generally, a tree has a single trunk and a shrub has multiple trunks. The range of shrub size varies greatly—from low-growing junipers and cotoneasters that stay below 18 inches tall to lilacs or Russian olives that can easily reach 15 feet or more.

Even more than trees, groundcovers, or flowers, shrubs are the true workhorses of the garden; they can be used for many different purposes. Because shrubs come in such a wide range of sizes, colors, and textures, it is easy to find one to suit your needs.

Shrub types

There are several ways to categorize shrubs. The two basic types are evergreen and deciduous. Within these two groups are small, medium, and large shrubs, as well as flowering and fruiting shrubs. With literally hundreds on the market, it is usually best to determine what you want to use a shrub for, then find the right one to fit your needs. Start with the list of shrubs on pages 368–371.

Evergreen shrubs (with year-round foliage) are useful as hedges, screens, and foundation plantings. A number of evergreens, such as hollies and firethorn, keep their fruit through the winter, adding color and attracting birds to the garden.

Deciduous shrubs can be used in the same ways as evergreen shrubs, but in winter most have no color, only the form created by the branches. Some, such as viburnums, bear dramatic colored fruit. Most deciduous shrubs make up for lack of winter color with their blooms. Use flowering shrubs to create sweeping masses of color.

▲ **The form and colors of some deciduous shrubs, such as this red-osier dogwood (*Cornus stolonifera*), add interest to the winter garden.**

◄ **Design a bed with your favorite shrubs in the same manner as you would a flower garden.**

▲ Include evergreen shrubs in your designs. Their range of foliage, color, and texture makes them as versatile as blooming plants.

Using shrubs

As with any aspect of your garden design and planting plan, the first step is to decide what you want to accomplish. Then choose the right plants to do the job.

Massing An effective way to use shrubs is to mass them in large sweeps. The step-by-step illustrations on pages 278 and 279 show you how to lay out a large shrub bed.

In your design, create waves or groups of each kind of shrub instead of a collection of individual shrubs. This helps to unify the garden and creates a sense of rhythm in the planting.

Hedge Shrubs are *the* plants to use as hedges. With their low branching structure and multiple trunks and stems, they present a solid block of foliage that goes from the ground to the top of the hedge. In addition, many shrubs thrive with frequent shearing—essential for a formal hedge. For more information, see page 334.

Screen Use large evergreen shrubs and densely branched deciduous shrubs to create a living screen to block wind or undesirable views. Choose shrubs that have an upright growth habit and space them a little closer than recommended. This allows them to grow together into one solid mass of foliage.

Defining space Whether planted in a mass, or as a hedge or a screen, shrubs help define areas of the garden the same way a fence or wall does. Planting shrubs on an open lawn can give the illusion of the walls of an outdoor room.

Foundation planting The practice of planting close to and along the front of the house has its pros and cons (see pages 290–293). Evergreen shrubs are essential to any foundation planting. With their year-round foliage,

▶ Plant shrubs in sweeping masses to draw bold lines across the garden.

they provide a consistency that deciduous plants cannot.

Groundcover Planting low-growing shrubs in front of a bed (left) solidly covers the ground in the same way as ornamental grasses or more traditional groundcovers.

Accent There are interesting-looking shrubs from which to choose, such as the red-osier dogwood shown on page 274 or the corkscrew willow with its curly stems. Consider using one of them as a specimen plant.

The colorful blooms of many shrubs are another reason to use them as accent plants. Be aware that it is easy to overuse flowering shrubs and end up with a cacophony of color instead of a symphony.

Background Sometimes the best use of a shrub is to let it take the back seat. A solid mass of evergreen foliage highlights the beauty of the plants in front of the shrubs.

How to plant a shrub

Planting shrubs in the proper manner is as important as choosing and placing them. Once they are off to a good start, most shrubs require only minimal maintenance.

STEP 1 Prepare the planting area.
Take all the shrubs to the general area where they will be planted. While they are still in their containers, move them around to get the configuration you want. As you do this, keep in mind that the planted shrubs will not be quite as tall as they were in their pots.

With the plants placed where you want them, use a trowel to mark around the base of each plant. Dig a planting hole that is as deep as the root ball of the shrub and at least twice as wide. Perform a percolation test to make sure the hole drains properly (see page 43).

To remove the plant from its container, lay the container on its side and roll it gently. Pressing down on the side of the container will help separate it from the root ball. Holding the base of the shrub with one hand, tip the container and slide the root ball out.

STEP 2 Place the shrub in the hole and position it.
Examine the root ball of the shrub to see if it is pot-bound, which is evidenced by long yellow roots growing around the root ball. If it is, unravel the roots and splay them out. Whether or not the shrub is pot-bound, gently pry open the base of the root ball with your hands to loosen the soil. This will stimulate root growth. Clip off any broken roots.

Set the plant in the center of the hole. Step back and view the shrub from all sides. Adjust it so it looks good from all desired angles.

Add soil beneath the root ball as needed to raise it so the top of the root ball is even with or slightly above the surrounding soil.

STEP 3 Backfill and water.
Using the soil dug from the hole, backfill around the root ball until the hole is half filled. Water with a slow-flowing hose and let it drain away. This settles the soil and promotes good root-to-soil contact.

Fill the hole with soil. Water again. Repeat as necessary, until the hole is filled. Spread a 3- to 4-inch layer of mulch around the base of the shrub, keeping the mulch several inches from the base of the plant.

How to place a fragrant shrub

STEP 1 Identify the prevailing winds. Knowing the wind direction is the most important aspect of properly placing a fragrant plant. If you have already done a site analysis, you have the information you need. If not, now is a good time to do one (see page 14). Find out how prevailing winds change from season to season from your local county extension service or weather person. A good way to verify the directions typical winds will carry fragrance is to place a can of smoldering charcoal at the plant site, sit where you want to enjoy the fragrance, and notice if you smell smoke. Do this several times over several days or weeks to get an accurate measure. It will give you a sense of what you can expect from the shrubs.

STEP 2 Find out when the shrub is fragrant. Most shrubs have a season or two during which they are scented. The fragrant season should coincide with the prevailing winds. Locate fragrant plants in different parts of the garden to get sweet scents throughout the season.

STEP 3 Place the plant. Position the plant upwind of where you want to enjoy the fragrance. If the fragrance is subtle, locate the plant close to this area.

Scents can be intense. If a shrub has a strong fragrance, use only one plant and keep it at a distance. Like perfume, a hint of scent is more appealing than an overpowering wave.

Some plants, such as four-o-clocks and flowering tobacco, are fragrant only at night, while others, such as 'Carol Mackie' daphne, have a more intense scent at night.

STEP 4 Channel the scent. Use walls and hedges to direct the wind to carry the fragrance to the locations you want it. A single fragrant shrub or a grouping just upwind from a patio probably won't require any special channeling of the scent.

▲ A single gardenia (*Gardenia agusta*) can fill an entire garden with its sweet scent.

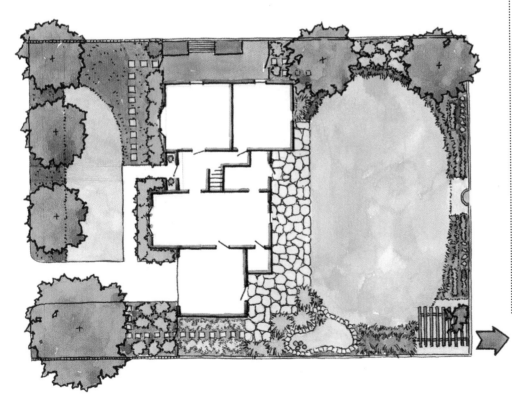

N

How to plan and plant a shrub bed

The process for laying out a shrub bed is similar to planning and planting any type of garden bed. The biggest difference between planting a shrub bed and a flower bed is the weight of the plants and the size of the holes you need to dig. These practicalities make starting with a good plan on paper even more important.

Although you can expect to adjust a design slightly once the plants are on site, the more time you spend with the design on paper, the more money you will save by purchasing the correct number of the right plants, and the more time, energy, and sweat you will save when it is time to dig.

► **Whether planting large masses of a single plant or mixing plants, plan a shrub bed the same as you would any other bed.**

STEP 1

Begin the design.
On a sheet of graph paper, sketch the shape of the bed. When designing, use circles that reflect the mature size of the shrubs. Decide the angle(s) from which you will view the bed.

Before deciding what to plant at the back of the bed, take a hard look at the existing background. If the house or wall forms a backdrop, it may influence what you will add.

On paper, draw a row of the tallest shrubs along the back of the bed. They will define the back border.

STEP 2 Add a second tier of shrubs to the design.

In front of the back row, arrange the next line of shrubs. They should be no more than one-half to two-thirds the height of the background shrubs. Avoid planting in

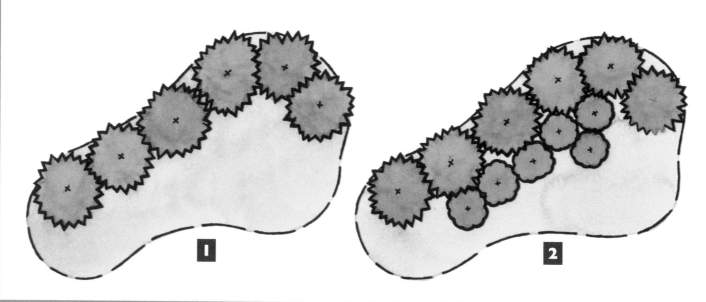

straight lines or rows. Instead, stagger the plants for a more natural-looking design.

Take note of the bloom times, flower color, fall color, and the foliage color of these and any other shrubs added to the bed. Even nonflowering shrubs with no distinctive fruiting or fall foliage contribute to a well-designed bed of varying textures and shades of green.

STEP 3 Fill in the design with low-growing shrubs.
Cluster three or more types of shorter shrubs in front of the second tier until the entire bed shape is filled. Although shorter than the previous levels, these shrubs can vary in height. Create sweeping masses with a group of smaller plants, which has more impact than a sprinkling of one or two plants of different shrubs.

STEP 4 Purchase and place the plants.
Mark the center of each plant on the plan with a dot or an ×. Make a list of the number of each type of plant required. Go to the nursery or garden center and handpick each plant; seek out the best and most similar forms. You will see that two shrubs of the same species can differ in appearance. The tree-buying tips on page 273 apply to shrubs as well.

Lay out the shape of the bed with a hose or rope. Mark the outline of the bed with sand, lime, or spray paint. Using the plan, place each shrub (still in its container) in its corresponding place in the bed. Make any necessary adjustments to achieve a good arrangement. Turn the plants so the best side faces you.

STEP 5 Plant the shrubs.
You can plant individual shrubs as described on page 276, but it is better to prepare the entire bed before planting. Dig the bed, add generous amounts of compost or well-rotted manure, and mix in some slow-release fertilizer. Till or dig these amendments into the soil. Each time you plant two or three shrubs, step back and decide if you want to adjust the placement of the next group of plants before they go into the ground.

4

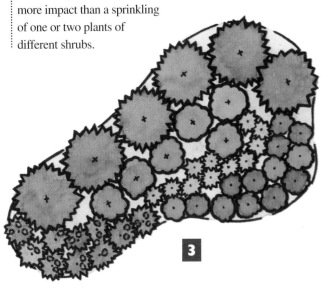

3

5

SPECIMEN PLANTS

A specimen plant is a single plant chosen for specific attributes and placed so that all its assets can be seen from the desired viewpoints. Most specimen plants are trees or shrubs; they are larger than most flowering plants and are visible all year long.

Choosing a specimen plant

When choosing a plant to grow as a specimen, consider all its aspects, especially shape, size, texture, and color.

Shape It is most important that you like the shape of the plant. Keep in mind that it will be viewed all year—without leaves in the case of deciduous trees in winter.

Size The reason for having a specimen plant is that it serves as an ideal example of the given species. For this reason, you want to see the entire plant from any vantage point you choose. Keeping that in mind, you wouldn't place a large tree right next to a patio if the patio is the primary vantage point for viewing the tree. Instead, use a small tree so you can appreciate the entire form. Plant large trees in the distance.

Texture Many good candidates for specimen plants are deciduous—for at

▲ Placing a white-flowered dogwood against a dark backdrop will make the tree's form and color stand out.

least part of the year they do not have leaves. As a result, their form, branching structure, and bark texture need to hold your interest. Trees such as birch, crape myrtle, stewartia, and paperbark maple have striking trunks that make these plants worthy of attention even in the middle of winter.

Color A specimen plant does not have to be showy. Rich green- or bronze- colored foliage is subtle and muted, yet it can still make a strong design statement. You can be bold and splashy with color; consider variegated and multicolor-leaved plants. Color can be seasonal; note how the plant will look in all seasons as it goes through the process of fruiting and flowering. Fall leaf color and bark color are other considerations when choosing a specimen tree.

▲ The dramatic form of the trunk and branches coupled with stunning fall foliage make a Japanese maple (*Acer palmatum*) an ideal specimen tree.

Plant placement

Once you have decided on the plant you want, you need to find the spot that will best showcase it.

Views from within The view you get from a window may reveal a good location for a specimen plant.

Views from outdoor rooms Most leisure time in the garden is spent on patios, decks, and other outdoor rooms. The area around these living spaces is ideal for a specimen plant.

As you enter Where the drive meets the street, along the drive or walk, or right by the front door, a specimen plant near an entry route is an attractive choice.

Maintenance

Because of its prominent location, a specimen plant needs to be kept in optimal condition. Losing such a plant creates a void unlike that of losing one of a dozen shrubs in a shrub border.

If the right plant is chosen for the conditions and you get it off to a good start, you may have only minimal annual maintenance. On the other hand, if you have selected a plant a bit out of its hardiness zone, it may require more maintenance than the ordinary feeding and pruning, such as winter protection.

▲ Color interest goes beyond flowers. For many plants, the fruit is just as showy or showier.

How to site a specimen plant

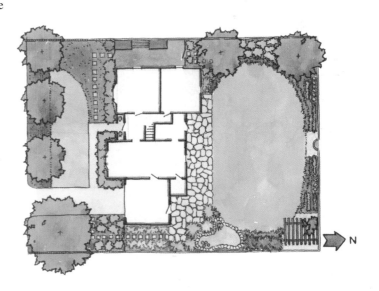

METHOD 1 **Use the house as a backdrop.** If you place a specimen plant in the front of the house, you treat guests to a nice view as they enter. And you can take advantage of the house as a background to show the plant at its best.

METHOD 2 **Plant it close to seating areas.** Site it close to where you spend the most time outdoors. Position it so it can be seen in its entirety from your favorite lounge chair.

METHOD 3 **Consider the view from within.** Whether from the dining room, kitchen, or den, or while you're lying in bed, identify the views to the outside that matter the most to you. Let a specimen plant be a focal point of that view.

METHOD 4 **Place larger plants farther away.** Planting a large tree in a far corner of the yard enables you to see the whole plant from the house.

ROSES

▲ Growing roses on a pergola or arbor gives them all the light they need and provides good air circulation, which cuts down on disease.

Some call roses the queen of all flowers because of their elegance and stately quality. Others perceive them to be as demanding as royalty. For the most part, their reputation for being hard to grow is undeserved. Choose the right rose, get it off to a good start, learn how to take care of it, and it will reward you with years of bloom.

Types of roses

Hybrid tea For many, this group of roses epitomizes the elegance and grace of the flower. They have the classic long stem topped by a single perfect flower—pointed in bud and chalice-shaped when open. The plants are not very cold-hardy and have a rangy habit, but they are held in high regard for their flowers.

▼ With a color palette limited to shades of pink, this large bed of different roses retains its unity.

Floribunda This relatively modern group of roses was bred for hardiness. These roses are lower-growing, more compact, and bushier than hybrid teas. Floribundas bear clusters of flowers. They require less care than hybrid teas and fit well in a mixed border.

Grandiflora A cross between hybrid teas and floribundas, grandifloras are large shrubs that are less hardy than floribundas but not as tender as hybrid teas. Flowers may be borne singly or in clusters. Use them as a screen or hedge.

Old Garden roses This class includes many heirloom or heritage roses. Species roses can also be included in this group. Generally, this group has large, fragrant, many-petaled blooms. Many flower only once in the season and do not rebloom, as modern roses do. Their bushy form makes them ideal for a mixed border.

Climbing/rambling roses Despite the name, these roses do not have the same mechanisms to climb that vines do. Their canes are long—to 20 feet or more. Support them on an arbor, trellis, pillar, pergola, or fence. If left unsupported, they make an unusual groundcover.

Miniatures These compact shrubs grow up to 18 inches tall. They may be small, but they bloom more profusely and are hardier than most roses.

▶ Knowing how each rose grows allows you to take advantage of all stages of their blooming.

Miniatures are good choices for containers and low beds.

English roses Because old garden roses have grown in popularity, hybridizers started working on new varieties that would have all the charm of the old roses—large, fragrant, double to quartered flowers that open wide and rebloom throughout the growing season. David Austin of England has been breeding these "new oldies;" many of his cultivars are available. Shrubby and rather voluptuous, they fit into a cottage garden or a mixed border.

Where to plant roses

Treat a rose as you would any other garden plant that likes full sun and rich, well-drained soil. Decide why you want to grow it (for cut flowers or to add to the overall beauty of the garden), what its cultural requirements are (good air circulation prevents fungal diseases), and whether your garden suits them; then choose the right plant.

All but the climbers and miniatures need to be cut back at the beginning of the growing season so plant them in easily accessible locations.

Too frequently, roses are set aside in their own bed and more attention goes into the quality of each bloom than how well the plants fit into the landscape. Grow roses so they both complement the garden and produce beautiful blooms.

Flank an entry walk with a swath of miniature roses or fill a container by the front door with them. Use climbers to cover an arbor or entry porch or to frame the back door.

Floribunda, grandiflora, and Old Garden roses are effective as an informal hedge or a screen. Some roses, such as *Rosa rugosa*, are especially thorny and will create a barrier impenetrable to animals—and people.

For a very formal look, train a climber or rambler into an espalier. For information on espaliering plants, see page 164.

How to plant a bare-root rose

Before planting, soak the root ball of the rose in tepid water for a few hours or overnight.

STEP 1 Prepare a planting hole. Dig a hole 2 feet deep and as wide as the root span. Loosen the soil at the bottom of the hole with a garden fork. Amend the soil from the hole with well-rotted manure or compost and a tablespoon of Epsom salts (to promote strong canes). Fill the hole with water to check drainage; if it has not drained in an hour, find a new location.

STEP 2 Mound the soil. Use the amended soil to form a cone at the bottom of the hole. It will help hold the roots in the proper position.

STEP 3 Place the rose. Splay out the roots around the cone of soil. Trim off any overly long or broken roots.

STEP 4 Plant at the correct depth. Adjust the depth of the rose so the swollen graft union is 2 inches below ground level. In frost-free areas, keep the union at soil level. Partially fill the hole with soil; add water. Then fill the hole to ground level with soil and add more water. Mulch well. Water the equivalent of 1 to 2 inches each week.

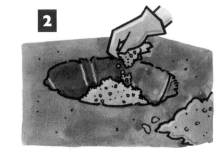

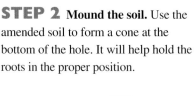

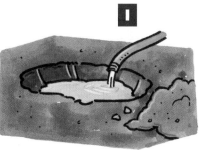

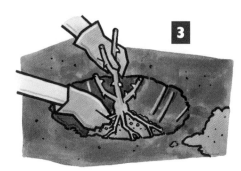

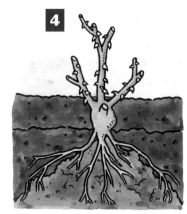

FLOWERS

Imagine a garden without flowers—very dull. In addition to their beauty, color, and fragrance, flowers attract various creatures—big and small, friend and pest.

The way perennials and bulbs come and go reminds us of the passing seasons. Because of their relatively short bloom time, a good selection of plants can provide three different looks from a single bed within a growing season. Annuals, on the other hand, add continuity. With little effort—some deadheading or shearing back—they bloom from spring to frost.

When buying plants, keep your garden plan in mind. A flat of flowers that catches your eye at the garden center may end up stuck in the ground haphazardly if there are too many plants and too little space. There is nothing wrong with impulse buying; trying out new plants is a fun part of gardening. But limit the impulse to one or two plants to avoid a hodgepodge. Or relegate the new purchases to a test bed—a simple 4×4 square bed will do—so you can try out new plants without involving the overall landscape design.

Using flowers

Flowering plants are versatile. Use them lavishly as the dominant element or sparingly as accents. Most gardens fall somewhere in between, with a solid framework of shrubs and groundcovers, using flowers to highlight different areas.

When designing a flower bed, take a good look at the background. A contrasting background makes flowers stand out more than one that matches them. A uniform background is better than a busy or cluttered one that competes with the flowers for attention.

◀ **Loose, informally designed flower beds can have a mixture of annuals, perennials, and shrubs.**

▲ **Although plants from bulbs are effective in small groups or as single plants, a large bed such as these tulips makes a big impact in spring.**

Flowers are ideal for filling small spaces such as narrow or curbside gardens. For more information about this kind of flower bed, see pages 296–299.

Use flowers to create colorful accents. Plant a small cluster of flowers in an open area of a shrub bed or grow them in containers. The flowers have a greater impact when you plant them in groups of three, five, or seven rather than singly.

Types of flowers

Flowers are herbaceous (not woody) plants that fall into one of four categories: annuals, biennials, bulbs, and perennials.

Annuals grow from seed each year, bloom, set seed, and then die. With luck, the seeds germinate and a new plant grows the following year. Annuals are sold as seeds and as transplants.

Biennials germinate and grow one year, flower the second year, and then die. Many biennials, such as foxgloves and hollyhocks, germinate in the fall, so it appears that they bloom every year. Other biennials, such as some of the silvery sages, are appreciated more for their foliage the first year than the flowers that come the second year.

Bulbs are different from other flowers because the flowers appear above ground for only a short time. Photosynthesis replenishes the food stored in the bulb, so that it can live on—without leaves—for the rest of the year. Mark where the bulbs are—especially any fall bloomers—so you don't accidentally dig them up when planting in spring.

How to plant bulbs

Regardless of which method you use, follow the recommended planting depth. Most bulbs are planted with the pointed end up. If in doubt, plant them sideways.

METHOD 1 **Plant a bed.** Using graph paper, design the configuration of bulbs you want. When you space bulbs, measure from the center of one bulb to the center of the next. Prepare a bed as described on page 288 and place the bulbs according to the design. Use an auger or bulb planter to dig the planting holes to the proper depth.

METHOD 2 **Plant individually.** This method is a little more random than the previous method and works well in a cultivated area or in the lawn. Use a narrow trowel with a ruler etched on the back of the blade. Thrust it into the ground to the proper depth, pull it toward you, and drop the bulb in the space behind. Push the soil back to cover the bulb.

METHOD 3 **Layering.** Lay a tarp along the edge of the planting area. Dig the area to the depth of the deepest bulb and put the excavated soil on the tarp. Place the deepest bulbs where you want them, add soil to the recommended level of the next deepest bulb, and repeat until all the bulbs have been planted.

METHOD 4 **Naturalize.** Grab a handful of bulbs, toss them in the air, and plant them where they fall. This works well where the garden meets the woods. For more on naturalizing, see page 300.

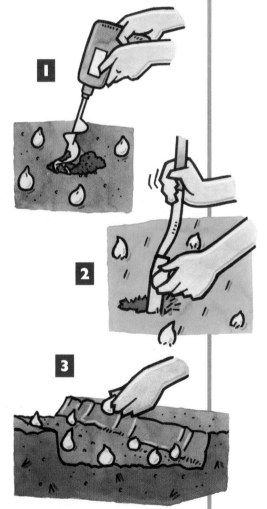

Perennials

A perennial is an herbaceous or semi-woody plant that returns year after year. Until recently, the average homeowner had only a vague notion of perennials. Today, they are as popular and commonplace as annuals.

Reasons for using perennials

The options that perennials add explains their ever-increasing popularity. Most garden centers and nurseries have a large selection from which to choose. Many mail-order nurseries specialize in

▲ Instead of using a variety of plants to edge a bed, make a swath of one type of perennial for a stunning border.

perennials; there are literally thousands of them available.

To help you make a selection, the garden section of your local library or bookstore has dozens of books that show the range of perennials. See pages 350–353 for a list of reliable perennials to try.

As the name indicates, perennials persist. At the very least, they last more than two seasons; at their best, perennials are permanent fixtures in the garden. Most will last for many years, after which the stems may become too thick and woody, resulting in an undesirable look. Or they may simply stop producing flowers as profusely. Both are signs that

it is time to divide the plants.

Perennials are great time-savers. Unlike annuals, which need to be planted each year, perennials are planted once and that's it. Each spring or fall you will have to cut back the spent foliage from the previous season's growth, but that takes less time and effort than planting new annuals each spring.

Annuals have been favored by gardeners because they bloom all season long, whereas perennials have a fairly limited bloom time. With proper planning, you can have different perennials in bloom from spring through frost. In addition to some long-blooming perennials, gardeners are now looking at perennials for the color and texture of their leaves, which are prominent before and after the flowers bloom.

Get the most from the bloom season by deadheading (removing the spent flowers) once they finish blooming. In some plants, deadheading promotes a

▲ The loose and open forms of many perennials make them well-suited for softening the edge between woodland and garden.

◀ To fully appreciate the ever-changing colors of a perennial bed, design and plant it so there is a path that places you close to the flowers.

second flush of flowers. For tips on deadheading, see page 339.

Designing with perennials

Because perennials have a relatively limited blooming time, careful planning is needed so a perennial bed is attractive throughout the growing season. Take into account the foliage—color and texture—as well as the form and shape of the plants.

One way to design a bed is to draw the outline of the bed and use circles to indicate all of the plants. Make each circle's size relative to the mature size of the plant, not the size of the plant when you purchase it. Make one copy of the plan for each month of the growing season. Color each plant; note which months the leaves of each plant emerge, when it starts blooming, when it stops blooming, and what is left after it blooms. As you do this for each plant for each month, expect to make some adjustments to avoid having all the bloom occur at one end of a bed in one month and the other end of the bed the next.

No matter how well-planned a perennial garden is, there may be the occasional bare spots as one perennial begins to fade and another is just starting to show color. Mix some annuals in with the perennials. It is often preferable to buy plants rather than sow from seed when you need a stopgap. If the holes in the garden are planned, the selection of annuals from seed is greater than from transplants.

Another option is to fill the gaps with good-looking edible plants, such as Swiss chard, kale, beets, or any herbs. Or plant a bean, pea, or miniature pumpkin teepee; it's edible and ornamental. Make sure the plant you use is suited to the cultural conditions of the space you need to fill. Most edibles prefer well-drained soil in full sun.

How to plant a perennial

No matter which method you choose, amend the soil with compost, leaf mold, or well-rotted manure before planting.

BARE-ROOT PERENNIALS Many mail-order sources ship plants bare root (free of soil, wrapped in damp newspaper). Don't postpone planting. Inspect the plants for any damage or drying. Dig a hole 8 to12 inches deep and as wide as the plant foliage. Form a cone of soil in the hole. Spread the roots over the cone so the crown (where the stem meets the roots) is level with the surrounding soil. Fill the hole with soil. Water well.

CONTAINER-GROWN PERENNIALS
Place the plants where you want them in the bed. Avoid planting them too close together. Dig a hole as deep as the container and one and a half times as wide. Gently remove each plant from its container; don't pull by the stem. Loosen the roots; if potbound, split the bottom with a knife. Put the plant in the hole, back-fill with soil, press the soil firmly around the roots, and water well.

TAPROOTED PERENNIALS Some perennials have a long taproot. If such a plant is grown in a container, plant as described above. If you receive it bare root, be careful to keep the root structure intact. Prepare the soil to a depth one and a half times the length of the taproot. Work a trowel back and forth to create an opening wide enough and deep enough for the taproot. Slide the plant in place and press soil around the root. Water well.

How to plant a flower bed

When creating a flower bed, invest the time and energy to do it right. It will pay off in the long run in the form of vigorous, healthy plants year after year. Adding organic matter feeds the soil, improves its texture, holds water, and introduces micro-organisms.

A well-planned design is essential; take height, color, and succession of bloom into account. Rough out a straight-edged bed with string and stakes; use a hose or rope for a curved border. If there is existing vegetation—shrubs or perennials—that you decide to keep, incorporate it into the design.

STEP 1 **Remove existing vegetation.**
Dig up perennials, shrubs, and weeds by their roots. Relocate them, give them away, or add them to the compost pile.

If the area is covered in turf, transplant the grass if possible. Use a square-nosed shovel to scoop up the sod. You can use the sod to patch bare spots in existing lawn or create a new area of lawn. If the sod is poor quality, toss it on the compost pile, soil end up (not Bermudagrass; it spreads readily by runners and can invade the pile). If you are not in a hurry to plant, cover the area with black plastic (see page 70). Within six weeks, the lack of sunlight and moisture will kill the grass. You can use a non-selective herbicide to speed the process.

STEP 2 **Amend the soil.** Add compost, well-rotted manure, or leaf mold and dig it in to a depth of least 12 to 18 inches. Perform a percolation test to make sure that the area drains properly (see page 43). Add gravel to improve drainage.

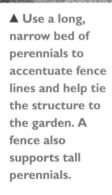

▲ Use a long, narrow bed of perennials to accentuate fence lines and help tie the structure to the garden. A fence also supports tall perennials.

◀ A sunny front yard is ideal for planting a perennial bed.

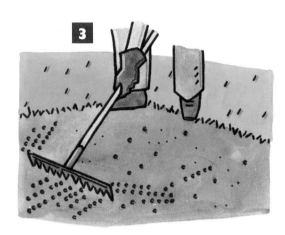

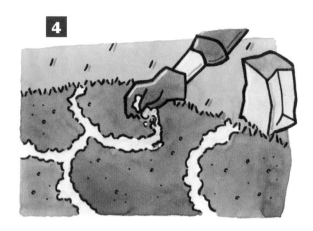

STEP 3 Smooth the soil.

Rototill or deeply fork the bed several times to loosen the soil, mix the amendments, and create a finer-textured soil. Use a bow rake to smooth the area and create a crown on the bed so the middle of the bed is higher and gently slopes down to the edges. This will improve the drainage as the soil firms over time.

STEP 4 Lay out the exact design of the bed.

Translate the design you have created on paper to the bed. Most flower beds are planted in drifts or groups of one type of plant. Outline the areas for the various groupings. Using a colored pencil, draw a shape around each grouping of plants on your plan. For example, in one part of the bed you might have five Powis Castle artemisia in front of three daisies that are beside seven rose campions. You'll have three shapes, but you will have incorporated a total of 15 plants. Repeat this procedure for the entire plan.

Use flour, lime, or sand to sketch these basic outlines onto the prepared soil. Make adjustments if necessary and move lines around. Even for the most experienced gardeners, the design always looks a little different when you actually start to place it in the garden. The use of sand, lime, or flour allows you to erase any mistakes and otherwise make adjustments easily. If you are using a lot of different plants, place a stake or marker of some sort in the center of each of the outlines to make it easier to identify what goes where when it comes time to plant.

STEP 5 Plant the flowers.

Starting at the back of the bed (or the middle if it is an island bed), begin filling in the various areas. Use a broad board to stand or kneel on (or include stepping-stones in the design) so you do not compact the well-tilled soil with your weight.

Do one section at a time. Keep the plants in their containers and set them where you want them. Then use a trowel to dig a hole the size and depth of the container and put the plants in the ground.

Mulch between the plants and water the bed daily for two weeks. Continue to water regularly the first growing season, especially in very hot weather.

FOUNDATION PLANTING

In the Old South, houses were raised and the unsightly area underneath used by sleeping dogs and chickens was camouflaged by plantings. The tradition of using a foundation planting became prevalent during the Victorian era when homes were set on tall foundations. Large shrubs around the base of the foundation connected the large homes to the surrounding garden. A contemporary example is shown in the photographs below.

▲ Covering a gentle slope with plants keeps the house from appearing to loom over the garden.

◀ **From the front, a foundation planting masks the area between house and ground.**

This band of green also hid the foundation, which was often less ornate than the house. Although that style of architecture is no longer the norm, the practice of planting a row of shrubs around the house is still common—even though many homes are now built on slabs of concrete so the point where the house meets the foundation is just above ground level. Although it is rarely a necessity, there are still reasons to consider planting around the base of the house.

Anchoring the house to the landscape

Using foundation plantings to tie the house to the land was a must for the tall homes of the Victorian era. Though houses have changed, that principle still applies today. Even if a house sits only inches above the surrounding soil, a planting around the base of the house serves as a transition from the large structure to the garden surrounding it.

◀ **Staggering heights from low to tall make this foundation planting effective from the side as well.**

As you do this, you need to understand how terrain affects design. If the lot is fairly level, the foundation planting may need to be extended farther out horizontally to connect the house and garden. If the house is on a slope or slight rise, planting the slope from the walk or lawn to the house keeps the house from looking like it is popping out of the ground.

Hiding utilities

A practical reason for adding a foundation planting is to hide any exposed utilities such as water or gas meters (electric meters are rarely placed that low to the ground).

Other utilitarian features that may need a cover-up include vents, small basement windows, and the wells that surround these windows.

As you plan a design that addresses these concerns, don't overlook the fact that these features have a purpose. Be sure your design allows their functions to be performed.

Complementing the architecture

A foundation planting can be used to accentuate any prominent features in the architecture of the house. Likewise, it can downplay any feature you may not particularly like. Take time to look at the architecture and colors of your house, making notes of the features that stand out. Not all features lend themselves to being mirrored or complemented in the landscape, but many of them will.

In the stone house shown in the photograph below, the even row of shuttered windows is echoed in the row of plants in front of the house.

In the photograph at right, the pastel color of the house is complemented by pastel-colored flowers in the foundation bed and in the window boxes.

▼ If your home is built on a slab or has strong architectural character, pull the foundation planting a little farther away from the house.

▲ A casual garden path made of mulch blends well along this meadow setting. This type of path needs high edging to keep the mulch in place.

Framing the house

A foundation planting need not always be low-growing. Trees and large shrubs can be used to frame an entry or balance a low and a tall side of the house. The illustrations on pages 292–293 help communicate these ideas.

Creating privacy

A planting in front of the entry to the house can screen the entry from public view as well as complement the architecture and tie the house and garden together.

▲ Use a foundation planting to blend a raised landing with the surrounding landscape. Evergreens serve the purpose year-round.

Soften the edges

Considerations when designing

Use photographs. One of the best ways to design a foundation planting is to use an enlarged photograph of what you have to design and the features you really want.

To do this, take a snapshot of the house head-on. Enlarge the print to the size of a sheet of paper. Lay a piece of tracing paper over the photograph and use a pencil to play with rough shapes and ideas until you get the look you want. You can even use different layers of tracing paper, with the major plants (such as the corner plantings or those by the front door) on the first sheet and overlays with different versions of the filler plants until you come up with the desired look.

Taking this idea a step further, you can scan the photograph into your computer, then use one of a variety of landscape design programs to position photographs of plants. This is a good way to test a look before you start buying and digging. These programs are available at most computer software stores and are sold through gardening magazines.

Keep your balance. Balance is an important part of designing a foundation planting. As shown in the drawings below, plants can offset a structure that is not symmetrical.

One way to do this is to look at your house from across the street. Visualize the house resting on a fulcrum beneath the front door. Note which way the house "tilts" and how you can use plants to weigh down the end that is "light".

You can also use a foundation planting to soften a corner or other sharp vertical lines that need to be softened (below

right). For more ideas on corner gardens, see pages 294 and 295

Match the rest of the garden. As you plan your foundation planting, consider the style of the planting design. Repeat plants used elsewhere in the garden, especially areas that can be seen from the front of the house. The concept of repetition also applies to groupings of plants and pruning techniques.

Choose the right plants. When selecting plants, take into account the function you want them to serve, the garden setting, and the maintenance they require. Think about the mature size of a plant. It is easy to find examples of overgrown shrubs blocking a window or crowding an entry (page 293, below right).

Another size-related issue is giving the plants room to spread. Use the guidelines

Create a balance

Leave room to grow

shown in the illustrations above as a way to determine how close to the house you should plant a shrub or tree.

Avoid separation. A single row or hedge of shrubs lined up along the base of a house separates the structure from the garden instead of tying the two together, acting as an extension of the house. If you already have this type of planting or want it, consider the hedge as part of the house and plan a foundation planting to go in front of the hedge.

Add variety. Mix up the plants in a foundation planting. Using all one color, size, or texture is to a foundation planting what a blank wall is to the front of a home—in a word, boring.

Alternate shapes, foliage color, texture, and seasonal blooms. Use groundcovers at the front of the foundation planting to make a smooth transition from bed to lawn. Consider them the last layer of a multitiered design.

Use seasonal changes. Take advantage of seasonal changes so that in every season something of interest is taking place in the foundation planting— blooms, fruit, or fall foliage. Whatever you plant will be there year-round. If you base your plan on a glorious explosion of color that lasts only a few weeks, you still have to deal with the rest of the year.

Lead people to the entry. Most guests enter the home through the front door, which is often the focal point of a foundation planting. Build on this emphasis and make sure the design you use helps lead people to the main entry.

One way to accomplish this is through the placement of plants that frame the

entry. Another way is to taper plantings, with the tallest one at the edge of the house and the shorter ones by the entry.

Plan on maintenance. The plants you choose and the design you use must mesh with your commitment of time and resources to take care of the planting.

For example, you can design a series of espaliered roses and pruned boxwood with seasonal beds in front, but someone will have to tend them every week.

Although there is no such thing as a no-maintenance garden, by choosing the right plants that mature at the right size, you can eliminate a lot of the maintenance. You can also use plants such as azalea, barberry, and juniper that grow so slowly they need pruning only every three or four years to keep them in check.

Choose plants the right size

CORNER GARDENS

Most gardens have areas that form a corner. Whether the corner is inward-facing or outward-facing, it needs to be dealt with. Some issues, such as softening corners, are addressed on page 292. Of course, your home and garden face the challenge of corners in places other than the front of the house. There are two types of corners: those that face outward and those that face inward.

Outward-facing corners

The challenge is dealing with the hard, vertical edges at the corners of a house. You can plant something in front of them or use a wire trellis and grow a vine up the corner.

A planting that wraps around a corner forms a bridge between the foundation planting and the rest of the garden. Plants against the house should grow to one-half to two-thirds the height of the house. Step down in size from there. If you want a plant taller than the roofline of the house, avoid putting it where the plant touches the eaves or roof of the house.

If a path goes around the planting, make sure you use plants that can take being stepped on occasionally. Curve the lines of any beds that wrap around a corner. This helps to soften the line of the house.

▲ A collision of corners is made more appealing by softening all the angles with plants. Here, a groundcover edging of lilyturf ties the beds together.

Inward-facing corners

There are several advantages of an inward-facing corner. It is halfway to being a courtyard. Consider closing in the other two walls with a hedge or a built structure. For tips on courtyards, see page 160–163.

The enclosure of the two walls forming the corner creates a backdrop; it is like having a stage. As you design, use the ideas on page 295, and review pages 162 and 163 on using the walls of a courtyard. Many of the ideas apply here.

Other advantages to an inward-facing corner are the privacy created by the walls and the fact that, depending on the orientation, the walls may protect plants from freezing.

Shade is the biggest challenge posed by an inward-facing corner. Be aware of the sun and shade patterns and choose plants that will thrive under your conditions.

▲ Corners aren't always created by walls. Here, an inward-facing corner bed draws the eye to the center of the corner, then to the woods beyond.

How to plan a corner garden

The process for planning a corner, outlined below, assumes that the corner is formed by a wood fence or the walls of a house, garage, or other structure. You can follow the same process and achieve the same results if the corner is created by two living walls, such as a hedge or other screen.

STEP 1 **Establish the shape of the bed and frame a focal point.** Draw an arced or curved line between the two walls to show the size and shape of the bed.

Add a focal point toward the rear and center of the angle created by the walls. The focal point can be a piece of sculpture, a gazing ball, a birdbath, or a specimen plant.

Frame the focal point by adding a few plants on either side. These will be the largest plants used in the design. Here, a small tree or tree-form shrub is used on one side, balanced by a pair of large shrubs on the other side. To balance the two, be sure the color, form, or texture of the two smaller shrubs is strong enough to equal the visual weight of the larger plant.

Make sure that the plants are far enough away from the house so they will clear the house when mature.

STEP 2 **Add medium-size plants.** Place two or three different kinds of shrubs or ornamental grasses between the plants already on the plan. This starts to connect the plants.

The size of the plants can vary, but be sure they are all smaller than the plants that will be behind them.

Select plants that have a range of color and texture, but keep them similar in form. This helps to organize the bed.

STEP 3 **Fill in the bed and train a vine on the wall.** Choose four or five kinds of low-growing shrubs, grasses, or perennials. Group them in five or six odd-numbered clusters (threes, fives, or sevens).

Repeat at least one cluster of one kind of plant. For example, have a group of seven salvia on the left side of the bed and repeat that with a group of eleven salvia on the right side or the center of the bed. Repetition helps to unify the planting plan, making it read as one bed.

If you have a wall that receives enough light, consider building a wire trellis on the wall and training a vine up it. For more information, see page 165.

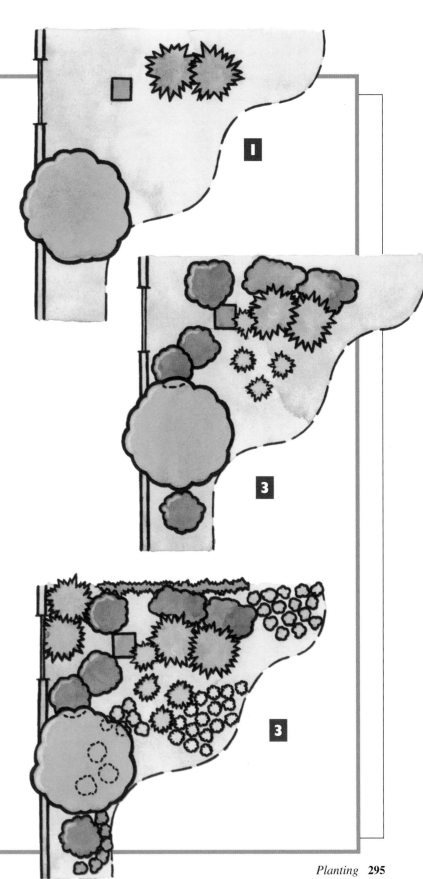

NARROW SPACE GARDENS

Throughout the garden you may have narrow strips of space you don't know what to do with. Instead of viewing these as problems, see them as opportunities to create bold bands of color.

In addition to this aesthetic role, narrow spaces can be used for practical purposes, such as growing herbs, vegetables, and flowers.

Types of narrow gardens

In gardenspeak, "narrow" refers to gardens that are 3 feet wide or less. They are usually found between a fixed structure, such as a house, garage, or wall, and a paved area, such as a walk or drive. Each type of narrow garden has its own considerations.

Between a house and pavement
Although the soil in these strips is usually bad and there are other tough cultural conditions to overcome, you need to plant it with something or it will be invaded by weeds in no time. A quick and easy solution is to plant it with turfgrass, a sturdy groundcover, or a tough shrub.

Between a wall or fence and pavement
This type of narrow garden often has more light available, and it is protected from winds by the walls. Also, the soil is likely to be better.

Site conditions

Narrow strips, especially when abutting a house, present tough conditions for plants. Soil is the first concern. It may be

▲ With good bed preparation and plant selection, even the toughest growing conditions can be overcome.

fill dirt and devoid of nutrients. It may have been subjected to runoff from the drive, which brings with it oil and metals. You may even find construction debris mixed in. And you can expect it to be alkaline due to the proximity of cement.

Other cultural considerations are the potential for heat and glare caused by reflected light. Or the site may be in deep shade from the adjacent house and roof overhang.

The area may receive too much water runoff when it rains.

To prepare a narrow garden, completely excavate the bed and replace it with rich garden soil. Address any drainage problems by building a high edging that keeps runoff from getting into the bed.

▲ Even with paving flush against the house, you can grow plants in containers and raised beds to create a narrow band of color.

▶ Plant the often overlooked space between the street and a privacy fence or wall with a colorful welcome mat.

How to plan a narrow garden

METHOD 1 SINGLE COMPOSITION BED

Illustration 1 is the plan view of a bed; 1a is a perspective drawing of the same bed. A single composition bed is balanced but does not repeat a theme. It tends to be more informal, taking on the look of a cottage garden or other loose, informal style.

METHOD 2 REPEATED THEME BED

Illustration 2 is a plan view of the bed; illustration 2a is the

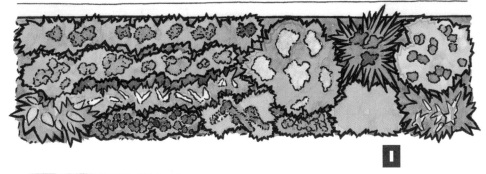

perspective drawing. An advantage of repeating a planting theme is that you can design a 3- to 4-foot stretch of garden and then repeat it as many times as necessary to fill the space you have.

With a plan on paper, purchase the plants you need. Set out the plants on the bed according to the plan and make any desired design adjustments before planting. Many nurseries will allow you to return or swap plants that didn't work the way you wanted.

CURBSIDE PLANTINGS

Many homeowners are faced with the challenge of dealing with a narrow planting strip between the street and sidewalk or between the sidewalk and their property.

The space between the street and sidewalk—property often owned by the local municipality that the homeowner is responsible for maintaining—has an impact on the setting of your home and front garden.

Know the rules

The first step in planting a curbside bed is to find out if you have the right to do so. Because it is most likely owned by the city, there may be restrictions on what you can and can't do. Check with the city to find out what guidelines exist and follow them.

Many communities encourage citizens to plant these strips and give annual awards to recognize those who have done a good job. Other communities welcome the idea but have height restrictions in place, which are primarily for safety. Even if your community doesn't require it, avoid using plants that are taller than 2 feet; they could block a motorist's view.

Be aware that the city owns the property and retains the right to tear out the planting to do any street or utility repairs or improvements.

▲ **When planting along a drive or street, whenever possible leave a buffer of mulched ground for the errant car tire.**

Cultural considerations

The biggest challenge in curbside planting is the harsh conditions the narrow strip faces. Expect the soil to be heavily compacted, poorly drained, and of poor nutritional quality. Plan on completely removing the soil and replacing it with good soil. Before you dig, check with all utility companies to find if power or water lines are in the way. Also watch out for any debris that may be buried there.

◄ **Plant flowers between a fence and drive so the garden begins before the gate.**

▼ **Take advantage of the full sun to grow sun-lovers such as roses.**

Another important cultural consideration in northern climates is the presence of salt. A fair amount of road salt ends up in curbside beds. Plants used in these strips should be salt-tolerant.

Drought tolerance is a consideration in curbside plantings, because the area may be difficult to irrigate. Even if you can get a sprinkler to it easily, a narrow bed exposed to the heat and glare of the surrounding pavement will dry out more rapidly than other beds. A curbside bed is a good candidate for the addition of water-retaining edging (see page 235).

Design ideas

When designing a curbside bed, make a list of plants that do well under your conditions. The list at right is a start.

The design process is the same for any narrow garden. The two bed designs shown on page 297 could be adapted to curbside plantings.

Because this bed will be visually linked to the street and neighborhood as well as to your own yard, use plants that relate to both. Note any prevalent plants visible in surrounding yards, including yours, and include at least one of each in the bed. And be aware of maintenance. Even friendly neighbors might complain if you allow a "neighborhood" bed to go unattended.

▲ In northern regions, curbside strips may be subject to salt residue from snow and ice control. Choose plants accordingly.

NATURALIZING

The term "naturalizing" may conjure up different images for different people. Here, it is used to describe garden areas that, for the most part, take care of themselves once established. They can be large or small plantings, in public view or tucked away in the most remote area of the garden.

The scale of a naturalizing project is less important than knowing where and how to go about doing it. If this idea appeals to you, in addition to the information on these pages, review the tips on naturalizing listed on page 303.

Where to naturalize

Applications of this technique vary, depending upon the size of your property and the type of landscape you have.

For example, you could turn your entire front yard into a wildflower meadow (see pages 302 and 303). This is a good alternative to a lawn that demands far less maintenance than a lawn or traditional flower beds. It is exciting to look at because it evolves through the seasons and it attracts wildlife.

Another approach is to convert the back edge of your property into a large area that you allow to go wild. This doesn't mean you can't be selective about what gets to stay and what doesn't. By selectively removing weedy trees or other plants you don't want, you can be a partner with nature to help direct the establishment of a plant community.

If a portion of your property is wooded, you can introduce ferns, bulbs, and wildflowers that are native to the area. You'll soon have a woodland garden that requires zero maintenance in return for a lush and colorful forest floor.

Plants suited for naturalizing

Native plants—those that are indigenous to your community—are the easiest to naturalize. Some of them may be well-known and sold commercially. Many will be newcomers to your gardening palette.

◀ Using meadow flowers as a substitute for lawn reduces maintenance and adds interest.

▲ Established in a few seasons, a mature meadow creates a full and lush carpet of flowers as an entry garden.

If you venture beyond the plants native to your area, there are several groups of plants to consider. They all share the same characteristic—their tendency to colonize. Check with your local county extension service before establishing a naturalized area with non-native plants to be sure that what you intend to use is not invasive and won't take over the garden (or the entire neighborhood).

Self-seeding annuals are good plants for naturalizing. The same is true of perennials that will multiply without requiring you to dig them up and divide them. Daylilies are one example.

Many bulbs, such as daffodils and crocus, will colonize. You can start with 50 bulbs and in a few years have hundreds of plants.

How to xeriscape

The term "xeriscape" is derived from the Latin word *xeri,* which means dry. But the principles of xeriscape go beyond drought tolerance. Xeriscaping saves energy; reduces the time, money, and other resources required for maintenance; and creates a healthier ecosystem—all without sacrificing beauty.

The concept represents a holistic approach to gardening and is based on the seven commonsense principles outlined below.

STEP 1 **Develop a plan.** As with any good garden, the first step in xeriscaping is to have a well-thought-out plan and design. As part of the plan, factor in each of the remaining six principles of xeriscaping.

▼ Once it has a foothold, a naturalizing plant, such as this blue phlox, will fill large areas.

STEP 2 **Create a healthy soil.** This is key to any garden. Conduct soil tests (see page 37) and percolation tests (see page 43) and amend the soil with humus so it can retain as much moisture as possible.

STEP 3 **Reduce the lawn area.** Lawns require more resources than any other use of the landscape. The more you reduce the lawn area, the less you will have to water and fertilize.

STEP 4 **Choose attractive plants that will thrive naturally.** Purists argue that you should use only native plants. The important thing is to choose plants adapted to your conditions. These will be comfortable with the amount of rainfall you get and the average high and low temperatures, and they will be resistant to pests and diseases prevalent in your area.

▲ Drought-tolerant gardens can be lush and colorful, as proven by this xeriscape garden.

STEP 5 **Develop an appropriate maintenance plan.** If you follow all of these steps, the plants will largely take care of themselves. The result is less fertilizing, spraying, watering, and pruning. Regardless, know what the plants' maintenance needs are and stick to a program. Healthy plants are better able to withstand occasional drought and can better thwart pests and diseases.

STEP 6 **Use mulch.** Cover any unplanted areas with a layer of mulch. This keeps down weeds, holds soil moisture, and adds nutrients to the soil.

STEP 7 **Water wisely.** Set up an irrigation plan in zones rated as no watering (plants survive on normal rainfall), low water (plants need watering during droughts), moderate watering (plants need an inch of water every 10 days without rain), and high watering (plants need an inch of water a week). Strive to have most of the garden in the no- or low-watering categories.

How to plant a meadow

Reading and following the tips on page 303 is the first step to a successful meadow. It will help you know what to expect from this kind of garden and guide you through the process of determining what kind of seed to plant as well as how much and when to sow. With that information, use the following steps to establish the meadow.

STEP 1 Get rid of the existing vegetation. For the best results, eradicate everything that is currently growing where you want your

▼ Site the meadow so that you can appreciate it from both indoors and out. You'll see many birds and butterflies enjoy it.

meadow to be. The safest and easiest way to do this is to cut everything back, dig up any woody plants, then cover the area with black plastic and hold it down with bricks. Let this sit for six to eight weeks. Use this time to do your homework in finding the right seed mix for your meadow and in ordering the seed. For sources, see the box on page 303.

STEP 2 Till the soil.
Remove the plastic and use a large rototiller to prepare the area for planting. You can till right over the dead vegetation. If your soil is poor, help the meadow get off to a good start

by covering the area with a few inches of compost and tilling it into the soil.

Another method is to till the soil, then allow the newly turned soil to germinate any exposed weed seeds. Cover with plastic again. Plant seed through the dead foliage.

STEP 3 Smooth the soil.
Use a bow rake to smooth the

soil. It is important that the area be as free of debris as possible. This promotes good contact between seed and soil. Remove any lumps of dead grass or other plants that were churned up by the tiller, and break up large clods of soil.

STEP 4 Sow the seed.
There are several ways to approach this. The method

you use depends partially on the type of seed you are sowing and the area you need to cover. You can hand-broadcast most seed, although it is difficult to be uniform. You can rent, borrow, or purchase a whirligig spreader for a nominal cost. These give a good, even distribution of seed that disperses in a wide, circular pattern.

STEP 5 Make good seed-to-soil contact.

Most wildflower and meadow grass seeds are used to the hardship of nature and therefore may not germinate as quickly as commercially bred flower seeds. To improve the germination rate, be sure the seed is in contact with the soil. You can rent a roller, partially fill it with water, and press the seed into the soil. Or broadcast a thin layer of soil over the area once the seed is sown. Or you can use a combination of the two.

STEP 6 Water.

When establishing a meadow, add at least an inch of water weekly for the first two months. After that, no watering is needed.

STEP 7 Annual maintenance.

Remove any weeds that find their way into the area. Burn or mow the meadow to a height of 4 inches in late fall or early spring. Local ordinances may prohibit burning, and you may want to rent a heavy-duty mower for the job.

EDIBLE GARDENS

▲ There is nothing like the taste of homegrown produce. With a little planning, you can have good taste on the table—and in the design of your edible garden.

Vegetable and herb gardens have a long and proud heritage in America, and for good reason. Most regions of the country have a climate and soil that make it easy to grow a bumper crop of fresh food each year. Even though the convenience of the supermarket makes it easy to get almost any edible plant we want, anyone who has tasted a homegrown tomato or carrot knows the value of growing your own.

Additional benefits to having edibles in the garden include the health advantage of eating fresh, organically grown produce. Having fresh herbs and vegetables only steps away from the kitchen will promote your experimentation in cooking. Vegetables are relatively easy to grow and a good way to involve the entire family in gardening, including the children. Sharing your harvest with friends, neighbors, and family will make you a welcome sight throughout the gardening season.

Types of edible gardens

Vegetable garden The standard vegetable garden is frequently planted in straight rows. It is often planned to provide for a family, with leftovers for canning and freezing. Function is more of a consideration than form; in most cases, optimum yield outweighs appearance.

Kitchen garden This is the more typical type of edible garden today. It is of a size and mix of plants that is designed to supplement the pantry. It can include flowers, fruit, and vegetables.

Herb garden An herb garden is relatively small. Historically, this type of garden was often ornate and formal, although it can be adapted to any style.

Speciality garden These are edible gardens with a specific use in mind. For example, a salsa garden might include tomatoes, onions, peppers, and cilantro.

Mixed edibles and ornamentals This idea, discussed on page 305, incorporates edibles—fruit, flowers, and/or vegetables—throughout the landscape.

◀ A simple bed of row crops is made more appealing by bands of colors created by different foliage.

Mixing Ornamentals & Edibles

Having a separate vegetable-only garden is a relatively new phenomenon, brought on, no doubt, by the modernization of agriculture that rendered the need for a full-scale vegetable garden obsolete. The traditional kitchen garden was always a combination of edibles and ornamentals—fruit, vegetables, and cut flowers for the household. The idea holds up well today.

The two main reasons to consider this approach are the aesthetic value edibles can add to the garden and the fact that many families need only a handful of vegetable plants.

Many of the vegetables grown today are beautiful in their own right, especially the heirloom plants that have found their way back into the mainstream.

For example, a wide range of eggplants boast fruit that ranges from a shiny black to pearl white. Kale comes in

▲ **The strategic placement of a few colorful flowers accents this formal edible garden.**

an astounding array of colors. If you want something tall, try tricolor corn which has pink, cream, and green foliage and bears edible ears. Fava beans produce true black-and-white flowers. Fun edibles include 'Ruby' chard, which is at its best when the sun shines through the leaves, making them look like stained glass. The 'Silver Fir' tomato has silvery foliage and delicious fruit.

From a practical point of view, a person is more likely to tend and use these edibles if they are located outside the kitchen door or patio instead of being tucked into a faraway

◀ **Tuck a few herbs with edible flowers, such as these thymes, calendulas, and chamomile, in sunny, well-drained spots.**

▲ **An annual vine climbing up an arbor tempers the utilitarian feeling of this edible garden.**

corner of the garden. To avoid having to deal with the holes they leave behind once harvested, use only part of the plant at once. For example, lettuce makes an attractive border and can last all season if you pick the leaves one salad at a time.

Don't overlook flowers—they can do a lot more than garnish a plate. Edible flowers add spice, flavor, and color to foods as well as stimulate conversation. Be sure that the flowers you choose are classified as edible.

Herb Gardens

Herbs are diverse plants. They have obvious appeal for their flavors and oils. But many also have striking textures and shapes.

Herbs are ideal candidates for incorporating into the landscape as ornamentals. They can be used to make low-growing shrub borders or as accent plants in a shrub bed.

Extremely low-growing herbs, such as some of the thymes, can be used as a groundcover, with the bonus of giving off their scent when brushed against or stepped upon.

Herb garden designs

For centuries, herbs have been used to create formal gardens. They were (and still are) the principal plant used for ornate knot gardens (see page 236), which represent the ultimate in making edibles ornamental.

Even today, it is common to see herb gardens laid out in geometric forms such as the one shown below.

Most well-known for their foliage, many herbs also have rich, colorful blooms. Sage, lavender, and chives all flower in shades of lavender. Thymes range in color from white to pink to magenta. Chamomile flowers resemble daisies. Before getting too far into the planting design of your garden, spend a little time looking at books on herbs and learning more about the array of colors, textures, and flavors they bring to the garden.

Growing herbs

Herbs have simple but stringent cultural needs. They demand a lot of light and excellent drainage in order to survive. Once those requirements are met, you can count on the plants thriving.

In fact, when planted in the ideal location, some herbs, such as mint, thrive too well and rank as some of the most

▲ Adding herbs to the garden saves money and promotes experimentation in your cooking. Nothing beats the fresh flavor of herbs.

aggressive spreaders in the garden. If you want to grow mint, pennyroyal, lemon balm, or other rampant spreaders, grow them in containers. If you want them as part of a garden design, sink the containers into the ground so that an inch or two of the rim is above the soil line.

▼ If space allows, design an herb garden so that each bed has a theme, such as Italian herbs, pickling spices, or tea herbs.

Vegetable Gardens

As the photographs on this page depict, there are many different approaches to having a vegetable garden. Before you buy seed and a hoe, ask yourself a few questions about why you want this type of garden. Read the tip box on page 308.

One question is whether you care if the vegetable garden has aesthetic value. If the purpose of the garden is purely utilitarian, and you have a sunny area where you can put it, there is no need to invest in dressing up the garden. This is purely a personal choice, but it is one that needs to be made before you start designing and planting that garden.

An example of a purely utilitarian vegetable garden is shown in the photograph second from the top. Although it is neat and tidy, it is also simple and functional and has limited aesthetic appeal.

On the other hand, even if you have a large area and it is removed from the rest of the garden, your sense of style and aesthetics may prompt you to have a utilitarian garden that also looks good. You may not get any more or any better-tasting produce from a more handsome garden, but you might reap personal satisfaction in having a garden that looks as good and orderly as the one at top right.

Moving closer to the ornamental garden, the one in

▶ **This edible garden blends good looks and function. Note the generous path width.**

the bottom right photograph is handsome enough to abut the rest of the garden, yet it is tightly packed and designed to produce a maximum yield from the space. Note the use of trellises, which can triple the yield of some plants by letting them grow up instead of out.

The garden shown below is more in keeping with the traditional kitchen garden. It is surrounded by what most would consider a flower garden, it is close to an outdoor entertaining area, and it is a mix of edibles and ornamentals. The different shades of green of the lettuce rival the nearby flowers for attention.

▲ **Although utilitarian, this simple vegetable plot is presented in a neat and orderly manner.**

▶ **Plan your edible beds to match your needs. Here, a few lettuce plants provide daily salads.**

▲ **By careful planning and the use of trellises, you may be surprised by how much produce a square foot yields.**

TIPS FOR DESIGNING AN EDIBLE GARDEN

Following are a few simple tips to help you get the most from your edible garden.

- Make a list of your favorite foods and note which ingredients can be grown in the home garden. Of the foods you like most, note which are superior in flavor if homegrown. Decide which taste distinctly different to you. Use this information to develop a list of plants you would most like to grow.

- Using your favorite vegetable garden resource, do a little research on each type of plant you want to grow. To say you like tomatoes is one thing. To decide which of the 150 varieties you have to choose from is another. For each crop, decide the specific varieties you want to grow. Then, based on your anticipated consumption, figure out how many of each variety of plant you need to grow.

- For each variety of each plant, note how much space it requires, then figure the total space required for the garden.

- Identify which of the edibles, if any, can be planted with ornamentals, in containers, or anyplace other than the edible garden.

- Review your site analysis and determine all the areas that lend themselves to edible gardening. Make a list of the spaces you have available and decide the location for the garden. As you do this, consider sunlight, levelness, proximity to the house, and access to a water source.

- Create a border for the garden. This frames the area and, if made of some type of fencing, can keep out pests such as rabbits.

- Within the area, lay out beds that total the amount of linear feet of row space you determined you need. Keep beds to a width of 4 feet or less.

- Have a generous path that goes to all the bed areas. The path should be at least 3 feet wide; 4 to 5 feet is better for maneuvering a wheelbarrow or garden cart. As a path material, gravel is not expensive, is easy to install, and drains well, but it is difficult to push a loaded wheelbarrow through it.

- Use raised beds. They allow you to build the ideal garden soil and control drainage, and the elevated height makes it easier to work the beds.

- Explore the world of heirloom plants. Leave room in the garden each year to have at least one row of vegetables you have never grown before.

- Practice crop rotation. Avoid planting tomatoes, peppers, corn, potatoes, cabbage, broccoli, and other heavy feeders in the same place each year.

- Add lighting to the area to extend the time you can work and harvest in the garden.

- Locate the compost bin (or at least *a* compost bin) adjacent to the garden to save miles of walking.

- Decorate the garden with yard art, fountains, ornamental plants, and anything else that tickles your fancy.

Three edible-garden designs

These three sample designs for edible gardens are meant to be a starting point for your own plans. Specific vegetables are not listed, nor is that important in communicating these design ideas. Use ideas from any or all of the gardens to develop your own garden design. Be sure to read the tip box on page 308 before you design.

TRADITIONAL GARDEN

Borrowing from designs found in Colonial Williamsburg, the layout of this traditional vegetable garden (below left) is highly utilitarian. However, there is an elegance to the garden. The entire garden is surrounded by a picket fence with the entrance through a gated arbor. All beds are edged and flush with the surrounding ground, and the pathway is covered with hay.

FORMAL GARDEN

The design of this garden (right) was taken from a parterre design of an Italian villa. It is a symmetrical design and looks stately. The garden is bordered on all sides by a waist-high evergreen hedge to give a sense of enclosure that doesn't block the sun. The entrance is beneath an arbor, and a bench is located at the opposite end of the garden. Two sculptures are positioned in the wings of the garden. Beds are perfectly even; all of them are raised. The paving is crushed granite.

INFORMAL GARDEN

The shape and forms of this garden (below right) have no historical foundation. Instead they are random and chosen for fun. Though there is the same amount of linear row space in all three of these gardens, the crops are not as readily accessible in this one. This garden is surrounded by a split-rail fence and the beds are mounded earth with stepping-stones placed through the large area of the bed for access. The pathway for this garden is made of mulch to enhance the informal tone.

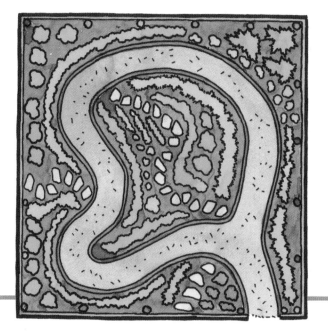

RAISED BEDS

A garden with raised beds says something about the gardener who uses it: The person is serious about growing. It also says that the gardener is either experienced or getting and heeding good advice. There are few steps that can be taken to make gardening easier than raised beds.

The value of raised beds

Soil One of the best reasons for using a raised bed is that it allows you to garden regardless of the soil you have in the rest of the garden. You can set a raised bed on hardpan clay or pure sand and have a successful garden.

Raised beds require you to fill them with soil. When you do that, you can blend a soil ideally suited for what you want to grow in the beds. Because the soil is rich and well-blended, it is extremely easy to work, which means that transplanting, amending the soil, and pulling weeds are easier than in typical garden soil. Your plants will thrive.

Drainage Because you are mixing the soil yourself, it will be well-drained, which means that water will move freely through the bed. Because the bed is sitting on top of the ground, water will drain through the bed and away from it, so drainage will not be a problem.

Weeds Though still susceptible to airborne weed seeds, a raised bed—because of its walls and separation from surrounding soil —serves as a deterrent to some spreading grasses, weeds, and invasive plants such as bamboo, ground ivy, and vetch.

Solar gain Being elevated, a raised bed will warm up more quickly than the surrounding soil in spring and allow you to get a jump on the season. If a late frost is expected after you plant, it is easy to drape a blanket or tarp over the bed to protect seedlings.

▲ A ledge atop a raised bed allows room for you and your tools while gardening.

In fact, some raised beds can double as a cold frame, adding weeks to the gardening season.

Comfort Sitting down on the job is unheard of in most aspects of gardening, but with a raised bed, you can literally do just that. You can design a raised bed with a shelf along the top edge wide enough to perch on. You can even have your tools or seeds right there with you.

Style Raised beds are a good way to bring order to a garden, and they are much easier to keep neat and tidy than in-ground beds. You can put a raised bed anywhere you would put an in-ground bed.

Types of raised beds

There are three main types of raised beds. They share most of the same advantages. The style you use is dependent on cost and design.

◄ Raised beds can be used to add order to a garden, with clearly marked bed lines that keep plants in place.

Framed beds This is by far the most common type of raised bed. These beds have sides made of wood, stone, cinder block, or even pavers. Beds with a frame offer several advantages. For one, you can make them fit any setting, from long and narrow to perfectly square. As a rule, beds more than 5 feet wide pose the challenge of how one reaches the center of the bed. For that reason, 4 to 5 feet is the typical width for a bed that can be accessed from all sides. If you can get to the bed from only one side, try not to exceed 3 feet wide. Though 12 inches is tall enough to do the job, beds 18 inches and higher are more comfortable, and the additional depth of the soil is beneficial to some plants.

You can build a bed high enough to fit your sense of comfort. Custom-built beds offer the flexibility of making the top edge of the bed double as a seat.

The most common material used for making this kind of bed is wood, such as 2×12s or other precut lumber. Railroad ties were once a common material for raised beds, but supplies ran low about the same time that concern about the chemicals used to treat the railroad ties ran high, and they fell out of favor. Some of the same concerns exist today about treated lumber. The Environmental Protection Agency stands behind its position that there is no risk of poisoning due to the leaching of arsenic in the treated lumber, but to play it safe, line the inside of a raised bed made from treated lumber with a layer of thick plastic before filling it with soil.

Interlocking plastic wood is also a popular framing material for raised beds. The best way to have an 18-inch deep bed is to use stone or masonry units, such as cinder block. The finished look of concrete block is not as refined as lumber or stone, but blocks are easy to use and affordable.

See pages 312–313 for instructions on how to build a raised bed from lumber.

Mounded beds In a mounded bed (right), the shape of the bed is marked onto the ground and the soil is tilled or loosened. Then the same kind of soil you would use in a framed bed is mounded to a depth of about 18 inches. This is a fast and easy way to have a raised bed, but it will spread and flatten over time and is more susceptible to weeds.

Container beds A large vessel, such as a feed bin, with holes drilled in the bottom, can be used in the same way you would use a framed bed. The drawback is that these containers may be expensive, hard to find, and bulky to move.

▼ A raised bed does not have to have a frame. You can mound soil about 18 inches high, and still reap the same benefits as a built bed.

◄ At its simplest, a raised bed can be made from standard sizes of pressure-treated lumber.

How to build a raised bed

Building a raised bed is a simple process that yields astounding results.

MATERIALS

Square-nose shovel
Stakes and string
Hand sledge
Turning fork
Two pressure-treated 8-foot 2×12s
Two pressure-treated 4-foot 2×12s
Eight 4-inch metal corner braces
1-inch deck screws
2-inch deck screws
Drill
Level
Bow rake
4 scrap pieces of wood

STEP 1 Lay out the raised bed shape. Use stakes and string to mark off the size and location of your project. Use the triangulation technique on page 120 to ensure that your angles are right. As you do this, consider the angle of the sun and how it will meet the needs of the plants you intend to grow in the bed. This is the time for good planning; it's a lot of work to move a bed once you've completed it.

STEP 2 Loosen the soil inside the area of the bed. This is done to help promote good drainage. If the soil is compacted clay, you might consider excavating 6 inches of it to make sure the bed drains properly.

  If the bed will sit in an area of existing turf, remove the sod in the bed to reduce the risk of any weeds or grasses working their way into the bed. Scrape off the sod with a square-nose shovel and use it elsewhere in the yard.

STEP 3 Build the frame. Lay one of the pressure-treated 8-foot 2×12 boards on edge along the prepared area. Next set one of the 4-foot boards so that the two meet perpendicular to

each other. Center two of the metal corner braces on the inside corner of the frame and screw them in place. To help hold the boards in place while you do this, tack a scrap piece of wood across the corner of the boards, as shown in Illustration 3. Keep this brace in place until you have filled the bed with soil.

Repeat this process with the other boards until all four are fastened together to form a rectangular box.

STEP 4 **Brace and level the bed.** With the frame in place, use a carpenter's level to see if the top edge of the frame is level. If it's not, lift the frame at the point where you need to make the adjustment and either add or remove soil. Re-check for level.

Inside the box at the corners and at the center of each of the 8-foot boards, drive a stake into the ground, then screw the stake to the board. This prevents the frame from moving and keeps the longer boards from bowing from the lateral pressure caused by the soil you add.

STEP 5 **Fill with soil and smooth.** Using the best soil mix (see page 340) for the plants, fill the bed to just below the rim. Use a rake to smooth out the soil.

ORDER IN THE GARDEN

◀ A glazed hand-painted ceramic label adds a festive touch to a container planting. Such labels are difficult to write on.

▼ Metal tags such as this copper label can be written on with an indelible marker.

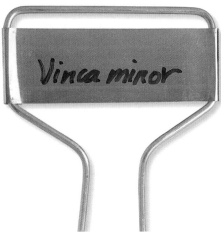

With the wide range of plants on the market, it is no longer unusual for a garden to have dozens of different plants. Plant markers can help you create order in the garden.

▲ Craft fairs and garden boutiques are good sources for unusual plant labels.

Purpose

Markers help you keep up with what you have. A lot of plants look alike, and you may have several varieties of the same species. Knowing which plant is which will help you track the performance of each one.

If you grow bulbs or perennials that you cut back each year, markers can remind you exactly where you have something planted. This is helpful if you want to know where you have space to add a new plant to a bed before the existing plants emerge. Markers also will

prevent you from inadvertently digging up a plant whose foliage has died back.

Appearance

Labels that come with the plants vary from grower to grower. Using them to mark the plants would create a distracting assortment of styles. There are hundreds

◀ If you grow the standard herbs, you may find decorative prelabeled metal markers such as this one useful.

of different styles of markers, from the simple and subtle popsicle stick to elaborate and showy custom-made tiles. Some are prelabeled.

If you want to label each one yourself, consider copper and zinc labels on which you can write with a permanent pen to create a lasting record.

Durability and cost

The range of styles of markers available parallels the range of cost and durability. As a rule, the less expensive markers are less durable.

Inexpensive markers can be made from popsicle sticks, miniblind slats, and juice can tops hung on bent clothes hangers. Several companies make seed packet holders that are inexpensive and are good for one season.

If you are willing to spend more, a look through any garden supply catalog will offer you dozens of choices in a wide range of costs.

▲ An engraved label is permanent; weather will not fade it, and birds and squirrels will not disturb it.

▶ Hanging tags made of sturdy plastic or metal are useful to mark trees and shrubs. Attach them to a lower limb.

TIPS FOR KEEPING RECORDS

Your own experience is one of the most valuable tools in gardening. The best way to keep track of all the nuances that impact your gardening experience is to keep records.

By noting what and where you plant and the conditions under which plants grew, you can begin to understand your own garden in a way that no book or outside expert can rival.

The best way to keep these records is to keep a journal. It need not be fancy or expensive; you'll find a wide selection from which to choose. It can be as simple as a spiral-bound notebook in which you jot down the progress of each of the plants or beds in the garden.

In between a preprinted book or the plain pages of a notebook, there is another option: Make your own journal.

Make journal—keeping a regular part of your gardening day. Over time, you will find that it is your most valued resource.

MAINTENANCE

Keeping the garden healthy

TOOLS

The right tool can turn a gardening chore into a pleasure. When it comes to maintenance, the adage "the right tool for the right job" applies. It is a matter of knowing what type of tool to use, what to look for when purchasing the tool, how to use the tool, and how to take care of it.

The first step is knowing which tool to use for the job. Descriptions of various tools and their typical uses are covered on the following pages. Use this information as a guide, but experiment with tools until you find the right ones for your needs. A spade may be designed primarily for digging into the soil, but it also makes a good tool for removing sod. Borrow tools from fellow gardeners, paying special note to the tools they don't want to lend. Those are usually their most valued.

Become familiar with how a tool is made and what makes a well-made tool. The materials used (stainless steel, aluminum, hardened steel) make a difference in how long a tool holds an edge, how strong it is, and how rust-resistant it is. The same is true for handles. Wood, fiberglass, and metal are the most typical choices. Each has virtues and limitations.

Knowing the right way to use a tool affects how hard you work, how long the tool lasts, and how satisfied you are with the work you do. Doctors have confirmed what many gardeners already know—using a tool improperly can cause injury.

The last consideration is maintenance of the tools. Once you have invested money in a good tool, it makes sense to invest a little time and effort to keep it in good working order. In addition to keeping tools sharp, it is equally important to keep them clean and free of dirt, and the metal parts well-oiled.

Be creative—don't limit yourself to the typical tools. In time, you may discover that a kitchen knife, a crowbar, or even your gloved hand becomes one of your favorites.

Hand tools

Gardening, at its best, is an up-close activity, so hand tools are extremely useful. Although most garden tools are hand tools, here the term refers to short-handled tools. Trowels, forks, weeders, and claw diggers are

▲ Small hand tools, such as this fork, trowel, and claw, allow you to do up-close, precise gardening.

◀ For digging large holes, a round-point spading shovel is the best tool. Select one with a thick top boot tread for greater comfort.

THE BASIC TOOL LIST

The following tools are essential for typical gardening chores. The more you garden, the more you rely on these tools and the more likely you are to add a few "essentials" of your own.

- An array of hand tools
- Round-point shovel
- Garden spade
- Hoe
- Bow rake
- Flexible rake
- Pitchfork
- Garden fork
- Cultivator
- Wheelbarrow
- An array of cutting tools

Round-nosed shovel

Spade

extensions of the hand and provide the best control. It is much easier to dig a precise hole for a prized perennial or the exact shape of a stepping-stone with a trowel than it is with a long-handled shovel.

Forged-steel tools are the strongest. The shank (the part that becomes the handle) and the business end are one piece. Cast-aluminum tools are also one piece; they are lighter but not as strong as steel.

Many hand tools are made with the shank and blade as two different pieces. These may be strong, but they tend to break more frequently than tools made in one piece.

Comfort is a major factor in deciding which tool to buy. It should fit your hand (test it wearing your gloves if you usually wear gloves while gardening), and the heft should be to your liking. Plastic handles are lighter than wood but are more slippery to grip.

As with any tool, the key to longevity is keeping it clean. Rinse off any dirt when you are through using it. Then wipe all metal parts with an oily cloth. Motor oils or spray lubricants work fine.

Round-nosed shovel

The most common long-handled garden tool—and the tool of choice for digging in the garden—is a round-nosed shovel. It has a concave blade and a tapered or pointed tip with a slight edge that makes it useful for digging. Digging shovels also have a thick top edge called the boot tread. This is the part you press your foot against as you work the shovel blade into the soil. The wider the boot tread the better; a thin tread can hurt your foot if you have to push down hard.

The handles of most long-handled tools are wood, but they may be metal or synthetic material (usually fiberglass). Due to the stress placed on the handle of a digging shovel, the weight of the blade, and the load it carries, wood is the material of choice.

Most round-nosed shovel handles are long. However, they also come with D-shape handles, as shown on the spade (right). If you prefer this style and have a hard time finding what you want, purchase a D handle, then cut your regular handle to the desired length and attach the D handle. Remember, it's all about comfort.

As you dig, avoid relying on your foot to do all the work. Grip the handle tightly and bear down on it as well. Rocking the handle back and forth as you press down helps the blade find the easiest path downward. When you are ready to lift a shovelful of soil, let your legs do as much of the work as possible to avoid straining your back.

▲ **A spade is ideal for digging holes that require a neat, clean edge. It's also good for removing sod.**

Spade

A spade (left) looks a lot like a shovel and can be used for some of the same kind of work. The primary difference is that a spade has a flat blade.

This tool is used for cutting straight down into the soil. Because it has a square nose, it is not a good choice for digging in hard or rocky soil. But in good soils, only a spade will leave clean edges.

A spade is also useful for edging a lawn or flower bed. All you have to do is line up the blade and dig down a few inches to cut through the roots of any plants encroaching on the edge you want to establish.

Depending upon the heft and sharpness of the blade, it is a good tool for transplanting shrubs, because it can cut through roots. It is also ideal for cutting beneath and removing entire sections of sod to be used elsewhere.

Almost all spades come with the D-shaped handle shown here. Unlike the case with longer-handled round-nosed shovels, a spade with a fiberglass or metal handle is practical; you don't have to put nearly the amount of stress on the handle and aren't scooping as much soil. High-end spades are forged from one piece of stainless steel. The price may seem high, but the tool will not rust and can last forever.

Handy tool cleaner

Fill a bucket with sand and mix in a quart of motor oil. Keep the bucket in the toolshed. Before putting a tool away, insert it in the bucket, then wipe off the oily sand with a rag.

Hoe

A hoe is an extremely versatile tool. It can be used to furrow a row for planting, skim just beneath the soil surface to uproot weeds, or mix amendments into the soil.

When you think of a hoe, you probably conjure up an image similar to the American pattern hoe (left). There is a wide variety of hoe types, generally differentiated by the size and shape of their blade. An onion hoe is similar to the one shown here only it has a longer, narrower blade. A swan-neck hoe has a curved neck that positions the blade flat on the ground so you do not need to bend when hoeing. A scuffle hoe has an open metal hoop that swings on the end of the handle, allowing you to scrape back and forth to sever weeds from their roots.

Hoe

Bow rake

Flexible rake

Bow rake

A bow rake (right), also called a bowhead rake, is used to remove clods of soil and small rocks from a bed. The solid metal tines can actually help break up the clods as you chop down on them.

The 12 to 14 short steel tines are attached to two curved metal tangs. This design makes the rake more flexible and allows it to ride close to the ground. Once you have removed most of the clods and stones from a bed, you can flip the rake over and use the back side to smooth the bed. Flathead rakes are similar, but have a single tang extending from the center of the tines. These do an even better job of creating a smooth soil surface. When choosing rakes, the lighter the handle the better.

Lawn rake

Also called a leaf rake, a lawn rake is a broad fan of flexible tines bent at their tip to grab leaves, clippings, and other debris.

Another variation is the distance from the end of the tine to where the tine attaches to its support. This varies the amount of flex in the tines and controls the stiffness. You need a stiff set of tines when raking grass clippings on a thick lawn, and bouncy, flexible tines when raking leaves off the top of a bed of groundcover.

Another change is the materials used to make this rake. Metal is a durable material and used to be the most common. Today's plastic versions are lighter, allowing for a much broader span without being too heavy. Plastic rakes are quieter, which makes a difference if you are raking a paved area. Lawn rakes are also available in bamboo, although they do not last as long as the metal or plastic versions.

There are even adjustable rakes that allow you to determine the span of the raking area. All you do is slide a metal clasp to range from a 12-inch to a 24-inch-wide rake. This is especially handy when you are raking a garden path, as well as between plants.

Because little torque is placed on the handle, comfort and weight are the two main considerations when buying a flexible rake.

Garden fork

Cultivator

Pitchfork

breaks down and becomes more soil-like, you'll need to switch to a spade.

If the material you are working is heavy, a D handle gives you a grip with more leverage than a long-handled version. A D-handle attachment is available that slips over the regular handle and clamps into place where it feels most comfortable, allowing you to have two handles on one tool.

Garden fork

Also called a digging fork, this tool can perform many jobs. It can be used to mix compost, peat moss, and other amendments into the soil. It can break up tough, uncultivated soil or clods of soil in prepared beds. Use it to turn the compost pile and to mix soil in a bucket or wheelbarrow.

One advantage to a garden fork is that, as you dig, it creates small channels that aerate the soil. Use the garden fork to work the soil around roots or to pry out buried rocks and other debris. A pair of garden forks, used like salad tongs, makes short work of dividing fibrous-rooted perennials.

Buy forks with forged steel tines or high-carbon tempered steel tines; these are the strongest and sturdiest.

Cultivator

Although a cultivator resembles a hoe, it is more like a hand tool attached to a

long handle. Like the hoe, the cultivator is available in various forms. It is ideal for work that requires precision, such as weeding beneath rows or cultivating small island beds. Because the head of the tool is small, it has the advantage of being relatively light.

Wheelbarrow

Technically speaking, a wheelbarrow is not a tool. Yet it is one of the most useful items in the garden shed. Whether hauling soil or leaves, serving as a mixing bin to create your favorite soil, or acting as a holding area for soil that will be backfilled around a transplanted shrub, it is a workhorse.

A wheelbarrow with a pneumatic (inflatable) tire has an easy, smooth ride. For loads of more than 500 pounds, use a two-wheeled garden cart instead.

Pitchfork

If you need to move a large amount of loose garden debris, such as pine, straw, hay, or compost, a pitchfork is the tool of choice. Whether you opt for the long-handled version (above) or one with a D handle, the long, sharp widely spaced tines pierce deep into the pile and allow you to grab large amounts of material. This is also a good tool for turning compost when it is still very loose and open. As compost

Wheelbarrow

Cutting Tools

Sooner or later every gardener has to take a blade to a plant. Whether shearing, pruning, or sawing, cutting causes more stress for the average gardener than any other aspect of maintenance. Pages 332–337 cover the how-tos of pruning, but first you need to have the right tools for the job. Cutting tools can be divided into three categories: shearing, pruning, and sawing. The photo (right) shows the more common pruning tools. It is worth the time to get to know them.

Shearing is cutting foliage and small stems of a small tree or shrub, to give the plant a uniform shape. Hedges are commonly sheared to maintain the desired form. Topiary and some groundcovers also can be sheared. Shearing tools have long blades that work with scissor action for a smooth, even cut. Their long handles allow the blades to open wide and cut a lot of foliage in one swipe. Another shearing tool is an electric trimmer or hedge clipper. Whether powered by electricity or a battery pack, these tools have blades that move back and forth in opposite directions. Because they cut fast and easily, it is helpful to run a string as a guide to avoid shearing the wrong shape.

Pruners are used to cut limbs ¼ inch to 2 inches thick. They range from single-handed models to long-handled loppers. Their cutting action is either

▲ Choosing the right tool for the job makes pruning easier. Shown here (clockwise from the top) are a pole pruner (for tall limbs), electric pruners (for hedge trimming), hand shears (for shaping hedges or trimming grasses), an anvil lopper (used to cut limbs up to an inch in diameter), a bow saw (for cutting larger limbs), hand pruners (for pruning suckers, roses, perennials, and vines), a folding saw (good for cutting limbs in tight spaces), bypass loppers (for clean cuts on limbs up to an inch in diameter), and a pruning saw (for small limbs).

bypass (two steel blades that bypass each other) or anvil (the sharp top blade cuts through a stem by pressing it against the flat bottom blade). Some models have ratchet or compound action that allows you to cut limbs the size of a broom handle with little effort.

The last group of cutting tools is saws. Use straight-edged saws for cutting large limbs. There are two types of saws—one

with a single row of teeth for a fine cut, and another with a double row of teeth, which cut on both the push and pull strokes. This dual action is efficient, because no effort is wasted. Both the folding model and the bow saw work this way, cutting through limbs a foot or more in diameter.

For high limbs, use a combination pole saw and pruner—which has a curved blade that you drag back and forth over the limb—or a long-handled lopper, which you can operate from the ground. For big jobs (or many small jobs), consider a chainsaw, available in electric and gas versions. Expect better performance from a gas-powered chainsaw. Before buying, check the noise rating and find the most quiet model.

Portable tool holder

Remove the ends of a coffee can. Attach the can to an old shovel handle, about halfway up. Insert the handle in the ground and slide long-handled, upended, tools through the can to keep them handy.

Tool Care

When gardeners are finished with their chores, they tend to toss their tools into a shed. However, if you take a few minutes to prepare the tools for their next use, your gardening tasks will be easier and your tools will last longer. When it comes to tool care, the three guidelines are keep it clean, keep it free from rust, and keep it sharp.

Cleaning tools

Before storing tools, remove any visible dirt from the entire tool, including the handle. If a strong blast from a hose doesn't do it, try a stiff-bristled brush (steel or synthetic) to loosen the dirt. For the toughest dirt, use a scouring pad. An emery cloth works well on metal. An old toothbrush lets you get into tight corners.

Keep a sharp edge

Once the tool is clean, you can see if any edges are dull on tools with a cutting or digging action. If so, use the methods shown here to sharpen the blade and make your gardening chores easier.

Protecting tools

Once the tools are free from dirt and their edges have been sharpened, protect them from the elements. Keep a can of linseed oil in the shed for wood-handled tools. Dab some on an old towel and swipe the length of the handle a few times. This prevents moisture from getting into the wood, which could cause decay. While rubbing in the oil, check for nicks or burs in the handle that could result in a splinter. Sand them smooth. Dry all the metal parts with a towel. Lightly moisten a rag with a petroleum-based lubricant or common motor oil and wipe the metal to prevent the formation of rust.

Labeling your tools or dipping the handles in colored liquid plastic identifies them as yours, so when someone borrows them you are more likely to get them back.

◀ **You'll be surprised at how much easier all gardening chores are when the tools are sharp.**

How to sharpen tools

A whetstone or a 10-inch file are the best sharpening tools.

METHOD 1

Large-bladed tools—
Whetstone: Maintain the same angle of bevel. Make repeated strokes along the front of the shovel blade the full length of the whetstone to smooth out nicks.
File: Hold the file at a 20- to 30-degree angle to the edge of the blade. Using a steady motion and applying firm pressure, stroke the length of the file across the front of the blade.

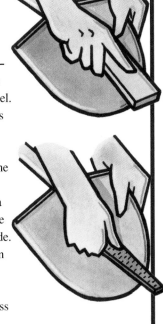

METHOD 2

Small-bladed tools—
Whetstone: Moisten the whetstone and stroke it across the existing angle of the blade. If sharpening loppers, as shown here, sharpen only the upper of the two bypass blades.
File: Apply medium pressure and stroke the length of the file. As you do this, maintain the original angle of the blade.

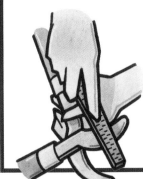

WATERING

Watering can be an enjoyable or a frustrating gardening activity. The experience depends on your awareness of when and how to water effectively and knowing the tools you have at your disposal.

When and how much to water

Water infrequently and deeply. Most plants need 1 to 2 inches of water each week. The amount you actually apply depends on the rainfall in a given week and the type of soil in the top foot of soil, where 90 percent of plant roots are located.

A rain gauge tracks the rainfall and the results can be easily logged in a journal or in the space provided on pages 388 and 389. To determine how much you need to water that week, subtract the rainfall from the 1 to 2 inches required.

Dense clay soil requires about 2 inches of water to slowly percolate to a depth of 12 inches. Rich garden loam typically requires 1½ inches of water to soak the top foot of soil. Sandy soil needs only about 1 inch of water, but because of its sharp drainage it needs to be watered at least twice as often as other soils.

In addition to rainfall and soil type, the choice of plants and the use of mulch affect the amount of water your garden requires. Drought-tolerant plants and other water-conserving measures are discussed in the section on xeriscaping (page 301).

Once you know how much water you need to provide each week, the next step is to deliver the water in measurable increments. How you go about this depends on the method of irrigation you use. The calibration method shown on page 75 is a simple way to measure most home irrigation systems. Drip irrigation and soaker hoses typically come with charts to help you calibrate your individual system.

Timing is as important as the amount of water you provide. Plan on delivering all the water your garden needs in a week in a single watering instead of two or three shorter ones. This promotes deeper roots, which in turn help plants tolerate drought (see page 75).

Water in the morning to reduce the amount of water lost to evaporation. Allow enough time for water to evaporate from the leaves before nightfall to avoid fungal diseases. If your sprinkler throws water up in the air, avoid watering on windy days.

Methods of watering

The most common way to water the garden is with a hose and sprinkler. Refer to pages 326–327 for more information.

Soaker hoses and drip irrigation are effective tools for watering most of the garden—except the lawn. They are addressed in detail on pages 328–329. In-ground irrigation systems are very effective and easy to use but are costly to install and maintain. Hand-watering is relaxing—except for dragging hoses—but it is also time consuming.

▲ Although not the most efficient way to water, a sprinkler ring is soothing and aesthetic. Children love running through it in summer.

Mulching saves water

A thick layer of mulch around the base of a tree can reduce the amount of watering required by up to 40 percent and reduces soil moisture loss around the plant during periods of drought.

Choose the right hose

A heavy-duty rubber hose lasts many years, and rarely kinks. A less expensive plastic hose costs more in the long run, because it has to be replaced often.

Time your watering

For best results, water in the early morning. Breezes are usually light then; the loss of water from evaporation is less, and foliage dries before nightfall.

Hoses

Hoses are the workhorses of home garden watering systems. As you shop around for a hose, you will find a wide range in price. Length of hose, the material it's made of, the thickness of the hose wall, the diameter of the hose, and the fittings all should be a part of your decision.

Hose lengths vary from 25 feet to 150 feet. A 50-foot hose is versatile enough to reach most areas of the garden and is not so long that dragging it and coiling it are difficult.

Most hoses are made of an inner layer of polyvinyl surrounded by additional layers of cording. The type of material and design dictates flexibility. Some hoses have multiple channels, so water flows even when the hose is kinked. The outer layers add to the strength of the hose and also affect flexibility. Rubber—the most flexible hose material—is the best choice. Vinyl is the cheapest and most brittle. Most hoses are a combination of the two.

Hose diameter controls the flow of water, as the illustrations at right show. Keep in mind that a thick hose weighs more and is harder to handle than a thin hose.

Fittings affect hose quality. Look for heavy-duty plastic or metal, and opt for the stronger octagonal shape instead of round. Snap-on couplers reduce the strain on fittings. They make moving hoses and switching attachments a lot easier.

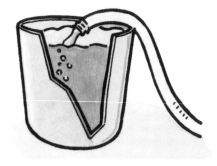

▲ A ¾-inch-diameter hose puts out the most water. It is ideal for large garden areas.

▲ A ½-inch-diameter hose is the most versatile. You get plenty of water flow, and the hose is not as cumbersome or heavy as a ¾-inch model.

▲ With a ⅜-inch-diameter hose, you will notice the reduced volume of flow. This hose is best used for small gardens.

TIPS FOR A SIMPLE IRRIGATION SYSTEM

▲ Timers are the quickest way to make watering a regular, controlled chore.

- **Timers** — An inexpensive timer allows you to turn a hose and sprinkler into an automated irrigation system. This battery- or spring-powered feature screws directly onto a spigot. The hose attaches to the timer. Control options range from minutes to run, gallons to apply, hour of day, and day of week. The cost varies with the features, but even the most high-tech ones are reasonably priced.

- **Couplers** — These gadgets are used to snap hoses on and off spigots and put attachments on and off hoses. They operate with spring releases and don't leak. Couplers also allow you to control water flow and have multiple fixtures run off one spigot or hose.

- **Reels** — A hose reel drains water from the hose as you wind it up. It protects the hose from physical damage. It protects it from UV rays that can degrade hose materials. It allows you to move the hose around easily and keeps the garden neat.

Sprinklers

Sprinklers are one way to water large areas of lawn or garden. Different sprinklers serve different purposes. Take time to learn how each type works. Regardless of sprinkler type, do two things once you get it home: determine exactly where to position it and, if it has adjustable settings, set it up for the irrigation pattern you want.

Purchase as many sprinklers as needed to water all parts of the garden, then set up each one. You can use a marker to indicate where each sprinkler goes and have a corresponding label on the sprinkler if it is not going to stay put. Then all you have to do is put the sprinklers in place.

With location and patterns determined, calibrate each sprinkler so you know how to apply water in ¼-inch increments. If you use the quick couplers, timers, and hose reel as described in the box on page 326, setting up and operating your system will be a breeze.

▲ ROTATING—This fixture is an effective way to cover a round area but cannot be adjusted to other configurations. Each of the two heads can be adjusted to regulate the volume of water.

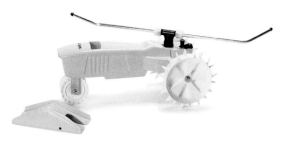

▲ TRAVELING—This sprinkler "walks" along the length of a hose while the spinning head applies water up to 40 feet on either side of the hose. It is ideal for large areas of lawn and for long, linear planting beds.

▲ STANDING—This stationary fixture can be adjusted to create a water pattern in almost any shape—circle, square, and rectangle. It works well on lawns and odd-shaped beds.

▶ IMPACT— This is the best fixture to water shrubs and large flower beds. The single jet of water can be adjusted to water a circle or a pie-shaped wedge of the circle. Varying stem lengths add to its versatility.

▶ POP-UP— In-ground irrigation systems use this type of fixture. It is flush with or below ground level when not in use and rises high enough to throw an adjustable fan of water.

▲ OSCILLATING—A common sight, this fixture uses dozens of nozzles on a horizontal arm to create a square or rectangular spray pattern.

Drip Irrigation

Drip irrigation is the most efficient way to water because there is no waste. The slow application of water—at ground level—allows the soil to absorb the water fully. Water is not lost to evaporation, misdirected by the wind, or blocked by other plants or structures. Drip irrigation places less strain on water lines, because it usually requires a low volume of water. Because this system is strictly on top of the ground, it's used in gardens and in isolated planting areas, rather than in lawns where it would pose a hazard as well as interfere with the aesthetics.

The mechanics of the system are simple. Lay out flexible lines to pass near the base of every plant you want to water. Run secondary lines from the main lines to the actual point where the water will be delivered. Attach emitters to apply water in a steady drip to cover from a 16- to 24-inch-diameter circle. The only other parts are the control valve and filter, which attach to a spigot or timer.

In the early days of drip irrigation, emitters often clogged. The success of this method of irrigation has led to technology that has all but eliminated this problem while making the assembly easier and the price lower.

Maintenance is limited to occasional cleaning of the filters as the manufacturer's recommendations direct and seasonal checks to make sure that all emitters are working at the desired rate. The lines are often covered with mulch to hide them and help hold moisture in the soil. Keeping the area around the emitter clear makes application more efficient and reduces the risk of clogging.

▼ **Drip irrigation earns its name from the method of water delivery—a slow, steady dripping at the base of the plant.**

How to install drip irrigation

The irrigation pattern depends on the type of system. The layout of the lines differs only slightly from one kit to another. Some systems have one size of tubing with emitters on the tube. Other systems have secondary lines connected to the main line. In the system illustrated here, emitters are attached to the secondary lines. Each system has a slightly different type of emitter.

Knowing the coverage of the emitter is essential in laying out the system. Each emitter covers between 16 and 24 inches of space. Large plants may require more than one emitter, whereas just one emitter may be sufficient for annual bedding plants.

Use twine, rope, or a hose to configure the lines needed to reach all the emitters. This gives you the total length of line you need. You are now ready to purchase the right length of line and number of emitters for your system.

Place a marker every place you need an emitter.

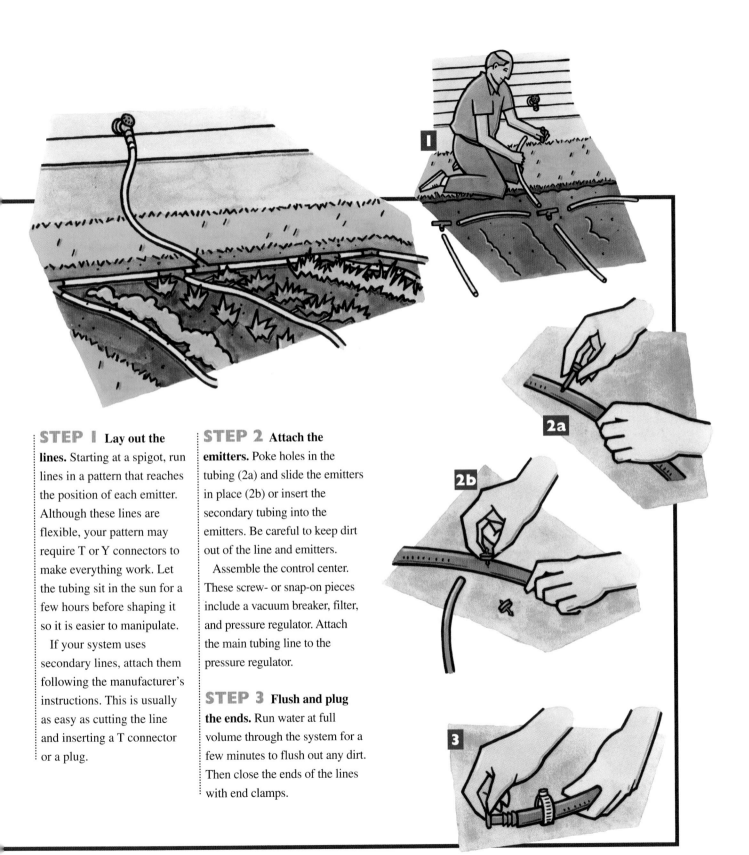

STEP 1 Lay out the lines. Starting at a spigot, run lines in a pattern that reaches the position of each emitter. Although these lines are flexible, your pattern may require T or Y connectors to make everything work. Let the tubing sit in the sun for a few hours before shaping it so it is easier to manipulate.

If your system uses secondary lines, attach them following the manufacturer's instructions. This is usually as easy as cutting the line and inserting a T connector or a plug.

STEP 2 Attach the emitters. Poke holes in the tubing (2a) and slide the emitters in place (2b) or insert the secondary tubing into the emitters. Be careful to keep dirt out of the line and emitters.

Assemble the control center. These screw- or snap-on pieces include a vacuum breaker, filter, and pressure regulator. Attach the main tubing line to the pressure regulator.

STEP 3 Flush and plug the ends. Run water at full volume through the system for a few minutes to flush out any dirt. Then close the ends of the lines with end clamps.

WEEDING

Weeds are the bane of the garden. These uninvited guests sap vital nutrients and water from the invited residents of the garden. Weeds can physically choke (and kill) or block light from desirable plants. Not only do they take up a lot of time and energy, they can completely throw off a carefully designed planting plan. Worst of all, weeds thrive in the nutrient-rich soil of your garden, and it can be difficult and challenging to keep them out.

Dealing with weeds is a three-step process. First, determine what is a weed. Second, try to prevent weeds from getting a toehold in the garden. Finally, get rid of the weeds that make it into the garden in the safest manner.

Identification

The first step in dealing with weeds is to decide what you consider a weed. The simplest definition of a weed is any plant you did not sow or put in the ground and you don't want in the garden. You get to decide what is a weed and what is not. Some gardeners intentionally allow weeds to colonize because they like them—a lawn full of dandelions in bloom, for example. There are a lot of other plants—vines, groundcovers, and even some perennials—that may be considered weeds by a botanist or horticulturist but are welcome in your garden.

This discretionary designation can be a bit risky. You may be fooled by the charm of a plant and not realize that once it gets started in your garden you may find it next to impossible to eradicate. It may take over the garden. Loosestrife and kudzu are two examples of plants that were once encouraged and are now banned in many areas.

Before you can determine whether to treat a plant as a weed, identify it accurately. Three excellent sources for identification are fellow gardeners (neighbors, friends, garden clubs), trained experts (county extension service agents, botanical gardens staff), and printed resources.

When identifying a plant, especially if taking it to an expert, note as many stages of growth as possible. Include when it appears; its size, shape, and color (the entire plant as well as leaves and flowers); and when it flowers or sets seed. Note the conditions in which it thrives. If you can't show living samples, take clear photos—overall and close up.

Prevention

Once you have discovered a weed—outside the garden—you want to keep it from taking root among your plants. Although it may sound simple, the best way to prevent weeds is to have a healthy garden. Healthy plants with strong roots and leaves, and lawns free of bare spots, leave less opportunity for

▶ Dandelions have a characteristic yellow flower, a playful puffball seed head, and one of the most aggressive and ornery root systems in the plant kingdom.

◀A good mulch—such as cocoa hulls— over a layer of landscape fabric is a powerful two-step weed prevention program.

WEEDING TIPS

There are several kinds of weeds. Each has its particular life cycle.

- **Summer annuals** – Most annual weeds are summer annuals. They sprout in the spring, grow in the summer, release their seeds in fall, and lie dormant throughout the winter.
- **Winter annuals** – A winter annual disperses its seed in spring, is dormant during the summer, sprouts in the fall, and grows during the winter.
- **Biennials** – These grow from seed one year but don't bloom until the next. After flowering they set seed and die. To control annual and biennial weeds, hoe them into the soil as soon as they emerge.
- **Perennials** – Perennial weeds come back via their root system or by seed. Though difficult, the best way is to remove the plant, roots and all, and avoid letting it set seed.

weeds to get started. Full coverage in garden beds eliminates sunny, open spots, so sun-seeking weed seeds that may be in the soil can't germinate.

Mulching prevents weeds. Most weeds have a far better chance of germinating and growing in moist, nutrient-rich soil than they do in a mulched bed, where seeds on the soil are hidden from the sun. Landscape fabric or newspaper beneath the mulch add an impenetrable layer; even if weeds do germinate in the mulch, they are unable to get their roots into the soil.

Control

The reality of gardening is that no matter what you define as weeds and no matter how diligent you are in preventing them from growing in your garden, weeds are aggressive survivors. Sooner or later you will have to deal with them. Follow the basics—know their growth habits and attack them early.

The best way to control weeds is to remove them as soon as you see them. It is much easier to remove a seedling than

a fully ensconced weed with a strong root system. With early detection and treatment, you can usually control the situation by pulling or hoeing the young weeds, thus avoiding the use of chemical herbicides. Hoe when the soil is dry; small, mangled pieces of the weeds may regenerate in moist, rich soil.

Any weed can be described as belonging to one of two groups—annual or perennial (there are also cool-season and warm-season weeds). It's important to know which group a weed fits into so you can time your control method for maximum effectiveness. Annual weeds are usually carried into the garden by the wind or birds, in the pots of other plants, or even on crevices in the soles of your shoes. They live for one growing season and die. Many drop seeds that overwinter and sprout the following year. Perennial weeds may seem to die at the end of the season, but they come back year after year from their roots.

If weeds become established, the first plan of attack is digging or pulling. Be sure to get the entire plant, including

the root. Breaking off a weed at its base may actually promote a healthier, heartier weed.

If the invasion is beyond pulling, try pouring boiling water on the weeds. This is effective in a small area and between bricks or pavers. Herbicides are the next choice; the operative words are "careful" and "selective." Select the appropriate chemical; read all label warnings and carefully follow instructions. Choose the least toxic herbicide. Be selective in the application. Spot spray or apply with a brush if possible.

PRUNING

Whether you are removing a single tree limb or rejuvenating an entire shrub, pruning your plants is as normal and healthy as cutting your hair. As with a haircut, even if you don't do a good job of cutting, plants, like hair, will eventually grow back.

You can reduce the risk of bad pruning by understanding the reasons for pruning, the basic techniques, proper timing, and the right tools to use (see page 322 for more on pruning tools). No matter what the plant, the reasons for pruning typically fall into one of the two following categories.

Plant health Damaged and diseased limbs will hold back the development of a plant. Removing them reduces the points of entry for disease and prevents its spread. Weak or damaged limbs are also a threat to people and property. They break readily and can drop anywhere.

Rogue branches jutting into or over a walkway, for example, are dangerous to passersby.

Appearance The natural shape of most woody plants is enhanced by regular, selective pruning. Some people prune to create a desired form such as a formal hedge. Others cut trees and shrubs into living sculptures or train them as topiary.

Pruning promotes flowering or fruiting. As trees and shrubs grow older, they put more energy into their roots and foliage. When you prune, you stimulate the plant to flower and set fruit again.

Hiring an arborist

Shrubs are smaller, more accessible, and easier to prune than many trees. Their multiple branching and faster growth

▲ Removing water sprouts or suckers from the bases of trees promotes central trunk formation and creates a grovelike effect (left).

make shrubs more forgiving of bad pruning. As testimony to the intricacies of the art and science of pruning trees, an entire profession has developed around tree care, primarily pruning. Although arborists know much more about trees than just pruning, they are the best resource when deciding if, when, and how to prune a tree.

An arborist will determine the proper shape for a tree and do regular pruning so the tree attains that shape. Look for an arborist certified by the American Arboricultural Society. Your local county extension service may have an arborist on staff who offers consultations.

Once a tree is well-formed, the need for pruning reduces dramatically. To develop a good basic branching structure, remove suckers, or water sprouts—the small offshoots that come up from the base of the tree (left).

An important aspect of pruning is creating a balanced crown of foliage, with an infrastructure of limbs and branches called a scaffold. You can readily determine the basic form of deciduous trees in winter when the foliage is gone and the distribution of branches is more visible. Ideally, tree branches attach to the main trunk at 45- to 60-degree angles. Winter is also a good time to note any damaged limbs.

How to prune a tree limb

STEP 1 Identify the limbs to be cut. Whether pruning to remove a damaged or diseased limb, to shape a tree for looks, or to open up the canopy to allow more light, trace each limb to see how removing it will affect the overall appearance of the tree. Before you begin the pruning project, look at what needs to be cut. Be realistic about your comfort level when working in a tree. If you need to be on a ladder with a chainsaw to remove a limb, it is time to call an arborist.

STEP 2 Make sure your tools are sharp. Sawing through limbs with a bow saw or handsaw is easy if your tools are sharp. Replace saw blades every few years.

STEP 3 Make the undercut. Use a handsaw or bow saw and make a cut halfway through the bottom of the limb about 12 inches from the trunk. This prevents the limb from tearing a strip of bark off the trunk of the tree when it is cut free.

STEP 4 Remove the limb. Make the top cut all the way through the limb just beyond the undercut, and remove the limb entirely. Be extremely careful as you finish your cut; the limb may spring away from the trunk, posing a risk to you or anyone around the tree. Don't worry if the cut is rough.

STEP 5 Make the final cut. Clear the limb from the tree so you have a safe work area. Identify the branch collar (the swelling where the limb protrudes from the trunk) and make the final cut just beyond it. Use a fine-toothed saw and cut with strong, even strokes for the smoothest job possible. Avoid leaving a stub protruding from the trunk (5A). It is unattractive, can be dangerous, and will eventually start to rot, which can spread to the healthy tissue of the trunk. Make sure the cut is not angled with the wound facing up (5B); it may catch water, slow down healing, and promote decay. Instead, model your cut after the one shown in illustration 5C.

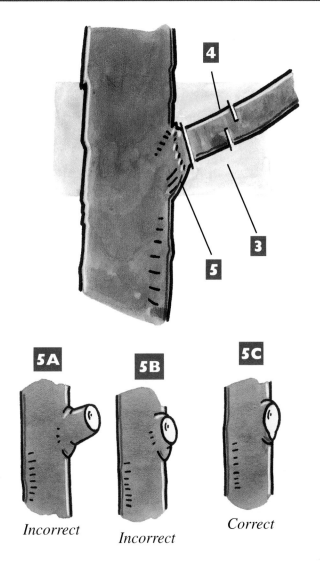

Incorrect Incorrect Correct

Do not paint or seal the wound. This used to be a common practice, but research has proven that covering the wound can trap disease inside the tree. Leaving the cut exposed to the air will retard decay while the healing callus tissue gradually grows over the area.

How to shape a shrub

Sometimes even the best-looking shrub needs direction.

METHOD 1 **Open the canopy.** Mature shrubs may need thinning from time to time. To do this, reach into the center of the shrub and identify the main or central stem. Cut it back to the point where other limbs are beginning to branch off it. Remove no more than one-third of the vertical stems at a time.

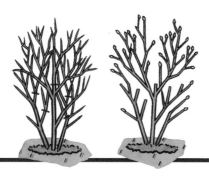

METHOD 2 **Shape the canopy.** Use this method when you have the basic branching structure you desire but want to shape the foliage. Imagine a line running through the top of the shrub about one-third to halfway from the top of the canopy. Run a string as a guide. Use hand pruners to clip branches one at a time for clean cuts.

PRUNING *continued*

Pruning shrubs

Pruning is as necessary a part of shrub maintenance as watering or fertilizing. Pruning need not be any more perplexing than those simple tasks.

Shrub pruning falls into three categories—shaping, shearing, and rejuvenating. Some additional reasons for pruning shrubs are included in the general discussion on pruning found on page 332. Most will require using all types of pruning at one time or another.

The best time to prune shrubs structurally is when they are not actively growing. For most plants, dormancy comes during the cold winter months. Give the plant a touch-up shaping the following spring.

For more information on the proper time to prune, see the chart on pages 336 and 337. Familiarize yourself with the pruning schedule for the plants you have so you don't inadvertently remove flower buds.

Shaping and shearing

Like any healthy plants, shrubs want to grow. Pruning may be necessary to keep shrubs the right size or the right shape.

To reduce the amount of pruning necessary, select plants that mature at the desired height you need. Many shrubs share similar characteristics of color, texture, flowers, and fruit but have different mature sizes.

Rarely will a shrub stop growing, so even the best planned and placed shrubs need pruning from time to time. Proper pruning won't keep the plants from growing, but it will encourage them to grow into the shape you want.

In addition to outgrowing its space, a shrub may display excessive twigginess and long, drooping branches with dense foliage. Such a shrub is unattractive and does not bloom well, and the dense foliage holds moisture that invites fungal and other diseases.

Shaping a shrub can be done in one of two ways—thinning or heading back.

Thinning completely removes a branch or branches at or near ground level. It does not alter the overall shape of the shrub; it merely reduces the canopy of foliage, and allows light and air to get into the interior of the shrub. The result is more foliage growing from the center of the plant. When thinning, remove no more than one-third of the total number of stems in one year. Heading back removes branches at a natural junction where other limbs are branching off. This method reduces the overall size of the shrub while still maintaining its natural shape and form.

For a formal, trimmed appearance, shearing is the method of pruning required. This is the process of removing primarily foliage. Hedge clippers or pruning shears are used for this task, which is usually reserved for hedges. Shearing a shrub prevents it from taking its natural form.

Rejuvenating

Shrubs on a regular pruning schedule probably will not need rejuvenating more than once every five years. If plants have been neglected, rejuvenating can still get them back on track. Rejuvenation promotes new, healthy growth and it gives plants the shape you want.

Start by learning what the plant should look like. Visit a garden center or local botanical garden, or check out garden sites on the Internet or gardening sections of reference books at your local library to see examples of a healthy specimen.

Most rejuvenation involves the thinning technique previously described and shown below. The goal is to remove any dead or damaged branches and then to selectively remove branches until you have the shape you want. Plan on spreading this process over a couple of seasons.

A more radical approach to rejuvenation is to cut back the entire plant. Redtwig dogwood, butterfly bush, and forsythia can withstand being cut back completely. Prune the branches to the ground in winter and the shrub will come back full and strong.

To make your rejuvenation efforts more effective, apply a slow-release fertilizer to the base of the plant, then surround the base with mulch. This provides nutrients and retains necessary soil moisture as the pruning stimulates new growth.

How to rejuvenate a shrub

Even a healthy shrub eventually needs thinning. Although the primary motivation may be to make the plant look better, thinning also frees up energy for the plant to produce fruit, foliage, and flowers. Moreover, a thinned shrub has better air circulation, which helps prevent some fungal diseases.

Timing is key. As a general rule, prune shrubs when they are dormant. Some spring-flowering shrubs, such as azaleas and rhododendrons, should be pruned after they bloom in spring. For a pruning schedule, see the chart on pages 336 and 337.

STEP 1 **Choose the stems to remove.** Identify the thickest and oldest stems. If the stems are all about the same size, remove some throughout the plant so the remaining ones are evenly spaced. Avoid pruning just one side of the plant.

STEP 2 **Make thinning cuts.** Use a pair of long-handled loppers (the long handles make it easy to reach inside a tangle of stems) and cut the stems one at a time. Step back periodically to be sure you aren't making the shrub lopsided. Remove no more than one third of the stems at a time.

STEP 3 **Cut tall stems.** If any rogue stems shoot up noticeably higher than the rest, cut them to a foot or more below the surrounding stems just above a pair of buds.

STEP 4 **Clean the base.** Remove any debris that has built up around the base of the shrub; it could harbor insects and disease.

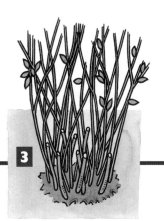
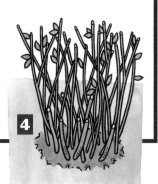

Pruning Schedule

	SPRING	SUMMER
Cold-winter climates	• Check trees and shrubs for winter-kill and broken branches. Remove any deadwood or injured limbs. • Prune Hybrid Tea and Grandiflora roses to 12 inches aboveground. Cut at a 45-degree angle ¼ inch above an out-facing bud. • If shrubs are overgrown, begin a three-year renovation on them. Cut back one-third of the branches to ground level each spring. • Consult a licensed arborist to trim large shade trees. • Cut butterfly bush and other half-hardy shrubs to ground level.	• Prune vines, such as wisteria and climbing roses, after they have bloomed, to train them. • Prune spring-blooming trees and shrubs after they have finished blooming to shape or rejuvenate the plants. • When pruning for shape, avoid unnatural shapes such as lollipops and cubes. Prune shrubs within their normal growth habit. • Prune away any injured or broken limbs of trees and shrubs as soon as possible so that insects and disease don't have a chance to get into the plant tissue and weaken the plant. • Prune excessive growth from evergreens in early summer.
Mild-winter climates	• Begin rejuvenative pruning on deciduous shrubs, removing only one-third of the old wood at any one time. • Prune perennial vines (except spring-blooming clematis). This allows you to train them and keep them within bounds, and it stimulates new growth. • Prune spring-blooming clematis after they finish blooming. • Cut climbing roses to create horizontal stems, which are the most prolific bloomers. • Prune evergreen hedges to shape.	• Look for signs of borers or tent caterpillars. Prune out any infested branches. • For the best bloom, cut back wisteria, leaving seven nodes on each side branch. • Prune summer- and fall-blooming clematis after they finish flowering. • Cut back spring-blooming trees and shrubs to maintain shape and form. • Be alert for summer storm damage and take action as soon as possible.

FALL

- Prune only if absolutely necessary to remove injured limbs or broken branches. Remember that pruning encourages new growth, and tender shoots that sprout in the fall will be killed by heavy frost.

- Once the ground is frozen and the plants have gone dormant, prune any overly long canes of Floribunda, Grandiflora, or Hybrid Tea roses to about 4 feet. Mulch the plants with about 12 inches of compost or shredded leaves, making a cone around the base of the canes. If winds are likely to be strong in winter, loosely tie the canes together and contain the leaves with a burlap cylinder.

- Protect boxwoods with burlap around the sides and over them. This keeps heavy snow from breaking branches. Loosely wrap other susceptible plants, such as pyracantha, to protect them from strong winds.

- Prune any injured limbs or broken branches as necessary.

- In late fall, cut back Hybrid Tea, Floribunda, and Grandiflora roses to give them a rest.

- Cut back grapes after harvest, leaving two nodes past each training wire.

- Prune deciduous trees to remove crossed branches and water sprouts. Keep in mind that fruit and nut trees—citrus, apples, pear, plum, cherry, hazelnut, pecan, and others—require an open center to receive enough sunlight.

WINTER

- Prune fruit trees and grapevines.

- Cut the limbs from your Christmas tree and place them over dwarf conifers as protection from winter damage.

- Prune most shade trees for shape while they are dormant. Remove any water sprouts (arrow-straight, vertical shoots that arise perpendicular to the branch).

- Cut old berry canes to the ground.

- In late winter, make selective prunings of trees and shrubs, such as star magnolia, forsythia, early azaleas, Japanese quince, crabapple, cherry, dogwood, and apple, to force into bloom indoors.

- Prune any injured limbs or broken branches on trees and shrubs.

- Prune to shape deciduous hedges.

- Begin rejuvenative pruning on evergreen shrubs, removing only one-third of the old branches at any one time.

- Clean and sharpen pruning tools. Store tools in a dry place.

- Consider painting the handles of tools a bright color so you can find them easily outdoors.

- Prune to shape evergreen hedges.

CLEANUP

Throughout the year, pay regular attention to garden neatness. Keeping the garden clean actually reduces the amount of maintenance you have to do at any one time. The benefits of keeping a garden neat and clean go a lot further than the obvious aesthetics. It keeps down weeds, diseases, and pests.

Fall raking

Raking accomplishes several things. It removes leaves and other debris that can block light from lawns, groundcovers, or shrubs. It captures material for the compost pile, and it improves the garden's overall appearance.

When raking the lawn, do more than clean up the freshly fallen leaves. Press the tines of the rake firmly to break up and aerate thatch and other debris trapped between blades of lawn grass. Tough raking speeds up the decay of these materials and results in healthier turf.

When raking, start at the center of the lawn. Rake in an ever-widening circle toward the edge of the lawn. Once at the edge, rake the leaves into the surrounding beds to serve as mulch or compost.

If you need to remove leaves from an area, it is easier on your muscles to rake manageable piles, then bag it, rather than rake everything into a big pile and bag it all at once.

Before adding leaves to a compost bin, shred them to speed up their decay. Do this with a leaf shredder (left), or run over the leaves several times with a lawn mower.

Putting the garden to bed

Removing debris promotes healthier plants. Dead limbs of any size can cause physical damage or block light to a plant. Piles of debris harbor a wide range of pests and insects, and foster diseases.

As you begin fall cleanup, work from the top down. First use a pole pruner or a long stick to remove dead limbs that have become stuck in trees. Prune out any diseased or damaged limbs, which will

◀ Gather all the leaves you can before winter sets in. Leaves left to rot on top of grass block light, breed fungus, and are better used as mulch or compost.

▲ Add healthy garden debris—not diseased or infested plant material—to the compost pile. Make a second pile for larger woody material.

▲ When raking large numbers of leaves, rake them into small piles, then bag the piles instead of raking all the leaves into one big pile.

How to deadhead

Deadheading removes spent (dead) blossoms from the end (head) of flower stems. There are two reasons for deadheading. It makes the flowers and bed look neater, and removing the heads before they set seed stimulates some plants to produce another round of flowers. Depending upon the plant, when you deadhead, and how much time is left in the growing season, you may get a second flush of blooms.

METHOD 1 Flowers with individual stems. There is no quick way to deadhead these flowers; cut one flower at a time. Grasp the stem just below where a spent flower is attached, then twist or pinch it off completely.

For thicker, woodier stems, or to save your fingers, use pruning shears or kitchen scissors to cut back the flower stalk completely. Avoid leaving visible headless stems.

METHOD 2 Low-growing flowers. Some flowering groundcovers benefit from deadheading. Splay your fingers and slide one hand, palm up, into a mass of stems. Slowly lift the hand, letting the stems slide by so you end up with a handful of spent blossoms. Use grass shears and good control to shear off the flower heads. Toss them in a bucket to avoid having the bed covered with dead flower heads; add the debris to the compost pile.

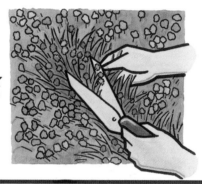

be much more apparent with the foliage gone. Refer to page 333 for techniques on limb removal.

Once you have cleaned all the debris out of the trees, it's time to deal with the leaves on the roof and in the gutters. The wind will probably deposit them in the yard sooner or later, but once most of the leaves have fallen, remove all the leaves and limbs trapped in gutters or other areas of the roof.

Approach the cleanup of shrubs in the same manner as you did the trees. Shake them to knock loose any debris, or use a rake to remove the debris from the base.

Finally, clean up the ground-level garden. Remove any twigs, stems of frosted perennials or annuals, and the remains of harvested vegetable plants. Rake or use a blower to remove fallen leaves from areas of groundcover, or work them down below the foliage so no light is blocked. Be sure to remove all debris from the lawn before snow falls.

The debris you have gathered will make good compost. Rent a chipper or shredder to grind debris into mulch, then add it to the base of trees and shrubs or the compost pile. Avoid adding weeds that have gone to seed to the compost pile.

▶ **Cut back perennials so that only an inch or two of stem remains, then cover with mulch.**

FEEDING THE SOIL

For many, fertilizer brings to mind images of bags of plant food. But bagged fertilizer is not the only source of plant nutrition. The way to provide nutrition to plants is to feed the soil, which, in turn, nourishes the plants.

Living soil

Soil is a living entity, not just a medium in which plants grow. Healthy soil is filled with nutrients, microorganisms, worms, minerals, and tiny pockets of air.

Microbes and worms feed on the organic matter and minerals in soil, breaking them down into individual elements and releasing nutrients into the soil. Rain, sun, freezing and thawing, and wind also break down soil. In turn, the nutrients mix with water in the soil to form a soil solution—a balance of individual elements suspended in water. Only when a nutrient is in soil solution is it available for plants to draw in through their roots. The chart on page 341 covers the basic components and essential individual nutrients necessary for good plant nutrition.

Soil structure (the texture or porosity of the soil) is extremely important. Oxygen is required for chemical processes and to sustain microorganisms. Densely packed soil with little air space is not as healthy as soil with plenty of air pockets.

Fertilizers

Although compost, mulches, manure, and other organic matter contain many of the nutrients a plant needs for healthy growth, there still may be deficiencies. The amount of supplemental feeding necessary depends on the condition of the soil and the needs of the plant. Fertilizers are supplements to healthy, living soil, not a solution to plant nutrition.

The most common fertilizers are granular; spread them directly on the lawn or the soil for easy application. Some waster-soluble granular fertilizers, such as ammonium nitrate or ammonium sulfate, are quickly available to plants, but their effects last only about four weeks. They can also leach quickly below the root zone. Slow-release fertilizers supply nutrients for longer periods, some for the entire summer. These include sulfur- and polymer-coated urea.

▲ A healthy soil is loaded with a variety of organic matter and minerals that slowly break down to provide nutrients for plants.

▶ Screen compost before adding it to the soil to remove any large uncomposted material, stones, or debris. The result is known as gardener's 'black gold'.

Reading a label

A fertilizer label (below) lists three numbers, such as 15–30–15, indicating the relative amounts of the three primary nutrients N–P–K—nitrogen (N), phosphorus (P), and potassium (K)—in the package. Select fertilizers by the ratio of the nutrients to each other. For example, a 15–30–15 fertilizer has a 1:2:1 ratio of NPK. In other words, it is one part nitrogen, 2 parts phosphorus, and 1 part potassium. Flowering plants do well with such a ratio. On the other hand, a typical lawn fertilizer has a ratio of 10–1–1 or 4–2–1. Fertilizers with a 1–1–1 ratio are all-purpose materials.

ALL-PURPOSE WATER-SOLUBLE FERTILIZER

15-30-15

GUARANTEED ANALYSIS

Total Nitrogen (N)......15%	Nitrogen from Ammonium Phosphates and Urea; Phosphoric Acid from Ammonium Phosphates; Potash from Muriate of Potash; Boron from Boric Acid; Copper from Copper Sulfate; Chelated Iron from Iron EDTA; Manganese from Manganese EDTA; Molybdenum from Sodium Molybdate; Zinc from Zinc Sulfate.
6.8% Ammoniacal Nitrogen	
8.2% Urea Nitrogen	
Available Phosphoric Acid (P_2O_5)......30%	
Soluble Potash (K_2O)......15%	
Boron (B)......0.02%	
Copper (Cu)......0.07%	
Iron (Fe)......0.15%	
0.15% Chelated Iron	
Manganese (Mn)......0.05%	Chlorine (Max Avail.): 12.5%
0.05% Chelated Manganese	
Molybdenum (Mo)......0.0005%	
Zinc......0.06%	

SUGGESTED FEEDING INSTRUCTIONS

TYPE OF PLANT	AMOUNT OF PLANT FOOD SOLUTION	HOW OFTEN
LAWNS	1 gallon/25 square feet	Every 4 weeks
DECIDUOUS TREES (Ornamental and fruit that drop leaves in fall)	1 gallon/10 square feet soak soil	3 times a year
EVERGREENS Broadleaf and needle-leaved types	1 gallon/10 square feet	Every 2 weeks
ROSES Large bushes – (greater than 2 ft. diameter)	1 gallon/bush	Every 2 weeks
BUSHES, medium to small (less than 2 ft. diameter)	½ to 1 gallon/bush	Every 2 weeks
DECIDUOUS SHRUBS (Ornamental and fruit that drop leaves in winter)	1 gallon/10 square feet	Every 2 weeks
ALL FLOWERING PLANTS	1 gallon/10 square feet (annuals, perennials)	Every 7-14 days
ALL VEGETABLES	1 gallon/10 square feet	Every 7-14 days
TOMATOES	1 gallon/plant	Every 7-14 days
BERRIES and other small fruits	1 gallon/10 square feet	Every 2-4 weeks

DON'T WASTE PLANT FOOD.
Small, newly planted plants need just enough plant food to wet their root areas.

ESSENTIAL PLANT NUTRIENTS

NITROGEN (N)
Nitrogen, essential for many plant functions, is one of the elemental components of chlorophyll. Nitrogen fuels vegetative growth—foliage, stems, and branches. Plants can deplete soil of nitrogen. It leaches from the soil faster than other elements.

PHOSPHORUS (P)
A stimulant for root growth and seed and flower formation, phosphorus is most available to plants when the soil pH is between 5.5 and 7.

POTASSIUM (K)
Potassium promotes root and bud growth and ripening of fruit. It enhances disease resistance as well as tolerance to drought, heat, and freezing.

CALCIUM (Ca)
As in humans, calcium builds strong "bones"— cell walls—in plants.

IRON (Fe)
Iron is a general-purpose nutrient that plays an active role in the creation of chlorophyll and in photosynthesis. Iron is most available to plants when the soil pH is below 7. At that level, iron is not bound to other elements in the soil and can be absorbed by plants.

MAGNESIUM (Mg)
Another component of chlorophyll, magnesium assists plants in a variety of growth and repair processes.

SULFUR (S)
Sulfur helps to build proteins—essential to plant growth and the maturation of fruit and seeds.

MICRONUTRIENTS
The six essential micronutrients—zinc, boron, chloride, copper, molybdenum, and manganese—are required in tiny amounts for other nutrients to perform basic plant functions. Too much of any micronutrient, however, can be toxic.

PESTS AND DISEASES

Despite planning and good gardening practices, sooner or later some garden pests and problems will reveal themselves, be they insect, mammal, or disease. They come with the territory—they are part of the ecosystems and habitats you create in your garden. Many animals, insects, and fungi are actually beneficial and help keep the overall balance of good versus bad in check. Problems arise when the balance swings in favor of the undesirable pests. Weather, the death of beneficial insects due to pesticides, and pollution contribute to this imbalance. While all manner of pests can be a nuisance, there is no need to fear or be intimidated by them.

The best way to deal with pests is to identify the problem early on and to know the best means for controlling or preventing the problem. Pages 344–345 discuss specific steps on how to establish a responsible pest management program. Before doing battle with these garden invaders, you should at least know the basic categories of pests.

Insects

Bugs abound in the garden. They help pollinate plants, add color and movement, and the beneficial ones actually kill a lot of the harmful ones. That's the good news.

Anyone who has discovered an infestation of caterpillars or Japanese beetles knows the bad news. Insects can strip plants of foliage and flowers in short order.

The key to insect control is similar to any pest control: Detect the problem before the insects can start breeding and colonizing, making them harder to eradicate. For some insects, the life cycle is a matter of days.

Should you have an infestation too big to control by hand removal, try these organic controls.

Bt (*Bacillus thuringiensis*) A bacteria that paralyzes the digestive system of insects when it is ingested.

Diatomaceous earth Mined from the site of ancient oceans, the remains of tiny creatures (diatoms) lacerate the soft underside of insects.

Insecticidal soaps A solution of household soap or a commercial mixture that coats the exoskeleton and suffocates

▲ Aphids, common garden pests, can be controlled with a strong blast of water or with insecticidal soap.

▲ Use chicken wire to protect plants and produce from pests such as raccoons, squirrels, and rabbits.

EXTENSION AGENTS – Professionally trained county extension agents understand many aspects of the local gardening community and share that information freely. Of all their duties, the proper identification and control of pests is most important. You can often mail them a sample of the problem. The best method, though, is to bring them a fresh, living sample of the problem or symptom. Information from your garden journal will help in proper identification. Be sure to contact the extension before you arrive with your sample.

UNIVERSITIES – If you are lucky enough to have a local university or community college with a horticulture department, experts there may be a good source for local pest identification.

BOTANICAL GARDENS – You may not be able to walk in and have someone identify your problem, but getting to know the staff at a local botanical garden is a good way to get on the right track.

GARDEN CENTERS – Some garden centers have staff or other resources to help you identify pests and to offer help on selecting and using the right control.

GARDEN CLUBS – Members of these groups are devotees of local gardening challenges. Consider supporting a club or joining it to gain knowledge.

BOOKS AND THE INTERNET – Even if you have one or more of the above-mentioned sources at your disposal, consider asking those sources to recommend a good book or website for identification of pests in your area. If you are going to rely on a book, look for one that has color images. They are much more helpful than words alone.

aphids, mites, mealybugs, and thrips.

Neem An organic oil derived from the Indian neem tree. It controls some beetles and moths.

Pyrethrin A powder or spray derived from painted daisies that controls beetles, flies, gnats, and other pests.

Dormant oil A heavy oil sprayed in winter to smother insect eggs and larvae.

Sun oil A lighter-grade horticultural oil that can be applied safely any time of the year.

No matter which control you use, it should be certified for the problem you have. Follow all label instructions.

Animals

Deer, squirrels, rabbits, moles, and voles wreak havoc in the garden. A 10-foot-tall fence is the only effective control for deer. Thwart rabbits and squirrels with mesh screens around the base and roots of individual plants. Control moles and other tunneling animals with traps.

Diseases

Most garden diseases are fungal and can be controlled by good gardening

◄ Powdery mildew is an unsightly fungus, and over time it will seriously weaken a plant.

practices. Choose disease-resistant plants, provide good air circulation, use mulch to prevent soil-borne organisms from splashing on leaves, and avoid overwatering, which creates the damp environment that some fungi love. Remove, burn, or discard diseased plants; do not put them on the compost pile.

If you suspect a disease, get positive identification before attempting control. Some diseases have effective controls; others, like viruses, do not.

Responsible Pest Control

oday's gardeners are less likely to spray the garden indiscriminately. Instead they consider what is needed to control a particular problem. Environmentally safe pest management should become part of every gardener's overall healthy garden program.

Integrated pest management, or IPM, is not new to the gardening world. It is based on a range of practices, all grounded in common sense. It doesn't preclude the use of chemical controls. Instead it leads to the careful use of chemicals as the final option of a multistep process.

Know your tolerance threshold

You decide when and if you need to take action against a pest. However, too much tolerance can lead to major problems—not only for you, but for your neighbors as well.

It may come down to a matter of economics. An infestation of an annual bed toward the end of the season may not warrant action. A borer wreaking havoc in your favorite tree may be unacceptable and a call for immediate action.

◄ Not all bugs are bad. Lacewing larvae eat aphids, spider mites, thrips, and leafhoppers.

▼ A mix of one part Ivory soap to 10 parts water is a safe way to control many insects.

▲ One or two Japanese beetles may be tolerable. To control these pests, pick them off early in the day, when they are sluggish.

Be aware of potential problems

"Sources of Information" on page 343 can lead you to people who can help you become familiar with the prevalent insects, diseases, and animal pests in your area, what they feed on, what their habits are, and when they typically appear.

This kind of advance knowledge is a tremendous asset in the prevention and control of pests. It is equally helpful to become aware of how a disease, insect, or pest may affect a plant. Often the damage is only cosmetic, short-lived, and not worth a fight. Knowing the difference will save time and money.

◄ Spiderwebs are harmless and beautiful. Leave them undisturbed to catch insects.

Keep an eye on the garden

Stroll through the garden in search of pests once a week during the growing season. You will learn about how the garden is growing in general, and you will have the benefit of early detection. Insect infestations and diseases, as well as moles and voles, are much easier to control in the early stages.

The identification of pest problems can be as easy as seeing the source of the problem. Other times, all you see is the results of the pest. Even then, don't jump to conclusions about what the problem is.

Perhaps the problem is not an insect or a disease. Nutrient deficiencies and too much or too little light or water can result in symptoms that look like insect damage and disease. If you see insects, be sure you know what kind they are before trying to control them. Beneficial insects keep down populations of harmful ones.

Prevention and control

The best method of control is prevention. Sometimes simple environmental changes can prevent pest problems. For example, increasing air circulation and avoiding standing water or soggy soil reduce fungal diseases and insect infestations. Cleaning garden debris removes the habitats for insects, diseases, and rodents. If you or your neighborhood has an infestation of insects that favor a given plant, consider eliminating that plant from your garden for a season or two.

If you have clearly identified a pest or disease and have taken steps to prevent its recurrence, you can now choose the best way to control it.

For minor infestations or damage, handpicking or removing the affected plant part is the easiest. For heavier infestations, insecticides or fungicides– either organic or synthetic–may need to be used. Be sure to select the right product for the job and read and follow label directions carefully.

Insecticidal soaps can be used for soft-bodied insects. Introducing beneficial insects, such as ladybugs and praying mantis, is a biological method of pest control.

Follow-up

Avoid thinking everything is taken care of because you have applied a control. It may take multiple applications of the control. And you may get a new set of problems when the ecosystem balance shifts as one insect is removed from the mix, allowing another to thrive. Regular pest-monitoring walks in the garden should be sufficient to keep you abreast of how well your controls are working or whether another method is required.

▲ Traps, such as this one for Japanese beetles, lure the targeted insect with pheromones and capture them in a disposable bag.

CHAPTER 12

RECOMMENDED PLANTS

The beauty of the garden

CHOOSING PLANTS

A stroll through the local home and garden center or nursery can be both inspiring and overwhelming—there are so many plants to choose from. Most mail-order seed and nursery catalogs have color photographs that make every plant seem enticing, with accompanying text that extols each plant's virtues. How do you decide which one to buy?

Having a list makes it easier, whether you are buying plants at a nursery or a home and garden center, by mail, or on the Internet. Although the temptations are still there, if you approach shopping with a definite plan and a list of plants (including substitutes) that will fill it, you are less likely to stroll the aisles or wander through colorful pages buying on a whim.

Use the plans

If you are starting from scratch, begin with the basics. If you haven't already read the chapter on planning (pages 6–33), do so to learn how to develop a plan for your yard.

After evaluating your space and deciding what you want to accomplish in each area, you will have whittled down the possible plants for each particular area. The choices diminish automatically as you go through the site conditions: your hardiness zone; the amount of sun the site receives each day; the type and amount of shade; microclimate; orientation to the sun (north-, south-,

◄ **A combination of trees, bulbs, perennials, and lawn makes an appealing garden.**

east-, or west-facing); soil type (sandy, clay, or loam); drainage; air movement; and accessibility (to water, electricity, and people). It is much easier—and the results are more successful—to work with existing conditions than try to change them to suit a particular plant or group of plants. For example, if you live in USDA Hardiness Zone 7 and the site is south-facing, receives full sun, and has sandy soil, you can eliminate shade-loving plants—especially those that prefer wet soil—from your list. Plants that are hardy only to Zone 8 or higher would not be compatible with the site unless you grow them as annuals.

Although you could try to change the site to suit your original plan, you would need a significant amount of time and money. You'd start by bringing in lots of organic matter—compost, leaf mold, or well-rotted manure—and peat moss to amend the soil and increase its moisture retention. Then you'd plant fast-growing deciduous or evergreen trees to provide the needed shade. Frequent watering would be paramount to maintain the required level of moisture. That course of action would involve a lot more effort than planting sun-loving, drought-tolerant plants.

Today more gardeners are working with nature and their existing ecosystems so they can enjoy the fruits of their labors sooner and use resources wisely. The added benefits are less labor expended and less money spent. The choice is yours.

Many plant shopping venues are available today, including Internet sites and large home and garden center chains. Each one has advantages and disadvantages. No matter where you purchase your plants, examine each one carefully. Keep these criteria in mind while looking at the plant, and buy only those plants that you are sure about.

- Check for critters, especially under the leaves. Signs of unseen pests include holes in leaves, skeletonized leaves, a sticky substance on or below leaves, powdery appearance (gray or black), insect droppings, or weblike matter.
- Look at the leaf color. It should be a healthy green (or whatever the plant color is), with no spots or brown edges or centers.
- Feel the soil—it shouldn't be dried out or feel compacted.
- Look at the bottom of the container. Roots should not protrude from the drainage hole.
- Check the overall appearance of the plant—nothing should droop or appear wilted.
- Avoid plants with broken branches.

Nurseries

- Plants offered will likely grow in your area.
- The range of plants is greater than it may appear at first glance. The nursery may carry only one or two of any particular plant but have a large number of different plants in stock.
- Generally if the plant dies within the first year, it will be replaced free of charge.
- Will often special-order plants for you.
- May be slightly more expensive.
- Plants are generally well cared for. Watering, feeding, and repotting is done by professionals.
- Containerized plants available that don't need to be put into the ground immediately.

Home and garden centers

- Plants offered may be outside your hardiness range. Read plant tags carefully.
- Limited range of plant choices, but more plants of each type are available.
- Some offer plant warranties—check with the manager.
- Prices are lower.
- Employees may know nothing about plants or their care.
- Find out when plants are delivered. Plan to shop that day or the next, when there is the most choice.
- Plants may be stressed from lack of water.

Mail-order catalogs

- Hundreds of plant catalogs—from general interest to specific plant types—give you a wide variety of plants, sizes, and prices.
- Some guarantee their plants. Read the catalog closely.
- Plants are often sent bare-root early in the season and must be planted immediately.
- You can shop at your leisure, perusing catalogs during the winter for spring and summer plantings.
- Limited availability on some popular plants.
- The company may substitute a similar plant if your choice is out of stock.
- If you are willing to wait a few years for the garden to fill in, you can save money by buying smaller (younger) plants.

Internet

- Convenience of ordering online.
- There are many sites; find the most reputable.
- Many mail-order companies have websites. Ordering through a website allows you to know instantly whether the plant you want is in stock.
- Comparison shopping is quick and easy.
- Most sites offer complete information about the plant— planting, care, growing, and maintenance.
- A help line gives you quick answers to your questions.

Perennials

Perennials have become the workhorses of many gardens, replacing annuals in popularity. Their virtues are many, but their main advantage is they come back year after year.

Once established, perennials can remain in place for years. Some will require routine dividing, which results in more plants for the garden.

Although the flowers may not last all season, the foliage usually does.

Look for different textured plants (and variety in leaf color) to provide interest once the flowers fade.

California poppy

YARROW

Achillea ageratum 'Moonshine'
Perennial
Zones 4–10
24 inches tall
Blooms all summer
Flat clusters of 3- to 4-inch sulfur yellow flowers
Full sun
Average to sandy soil; drought-tolerant
Notes: Attractive silvery gray leaves. Will not thrive in heavy, moist soil. Grows well in dry, sunny areas. Excellent cut or dried.

LADY'S MANTLE

Alchemilla mollis
Perennial
Zones 3–9
6–18 inches tall
Blooms late spring to early summer
Chartreuse flowers
Full sun to partial shade
Moist, humusy, well-drained soil
Notes: Attractive gray-green leaves hold dewdrops in early morning. Loose flower heads good for cutting. 'Thriller' is 18 inches tall with numerous fluffy flowers.

ARKANSAS AMSONIA

Amsonia hubrectii
Perennial
Zones 5–9
3 feet tall
Blooms late spring
Panicles of sky blue flowers
Full sun to partial shade
Moist, well-drained soil
Notes: A clump-forming perennial with multiseason interest. Flowers are lovely in late spring among the willowy leaves. In autumn the leaves turn golden.

PURPLE PARSNIP

Angelica gigas
Biennial that reseeds readily
Zones 4–9
3–6 feet tall
Blooms late summer, early fall
Dark purple umbels
Sun, full shade, partial shade
Moist, loamy soil
Notes: A relative newcomer to the garden scene. It is much more dramatic than other parsnips, with tall red flower stems topped by large purple umbels. Bees love it.

GOLDEN MARGUERITE

Anthemis tinctoria
Perennial
Zones 3–9
2–3 feet tall
Blooms summer
Daisylike yellow blooms
Full sun
Average to poor soil; drought-tolerant
Notes: Attractive, chrysanthemum-scented, fernlike foliage. Cut faded flower stems to promote continual bloom. Long stems make good cut flowers.

COLUMBINE

Aquilegia canadensis
Perennial
Zones 3–10
24–30 inches tall
Blooms late spring to early summer
White to red, bicolored flowers
Full sun to partial shade
Moist, well-drained soil
Notes: Decorative ferny leaves. Wildflower native to Canada and Eastern United States. Self-sows. Remove any leaf-miner damage.

JACK-IN-THE-PULPIT

Arisaema triphyllum
Perennial
Zones 4–8
1–2 feet tall
Blooms late spring
Spathe may be purple- or bronze-striped
Partial to full shade
Moist, humusy, well-drained, rich soil
Notes: Native to the woodlands of eastern North America, this arum relative is grown for its large three-part leaves and the unique flower form of spathe and spadix.

SEA THRIFT

Armeria maritima
Perennial
Zones 3–9
8 inches tall
Blooms late spring, summer
Pink to lavender-pink clusters of flowers
Full sun
Poor to average, well-drained soil
Notes: Excellent for rock gardens and front of border. Takes salt spray and wind but not prolonged heat. Grows wild along coastal cliffs of the Pacific.

BUTTERFLY WEED

Asclepias tuberosa
Perennial
Zones 4–9
2–3 feet tall
Blooms midsummer
Orange, red, or gold flowers
Full sun
Average to sandy soil; drought-tolerant.
Notes: Attracts monarch and swallowtail butterflies. Showy, flat flower heads ripen into 3-inch purple seedpods. In late fall, they split open and reveal silky-haired seeds.

INDIAN PAINTBRUSH

Castilleja spp.
Perennial
Zones 5–9
To 18 inches tall
Blooms summer
Red, purple-red, scarlet, or golden flowers
Full sun
Average to sandy soil; drought-tolerant
Notes: A native prairie plant, which may be semiparasitic on roots of grasses (not lawn grass). Showy bracts and calyxes in terminal spikes above the leaves.

CARNATION

Dianthus caryophyllus
Perennial
Zones 7–10
18–32 inches tall
Blooms summer to fall
Bright pinky-purple blooms; spicy fragrance
Full sun to light afternoon shade
Well-drained, slightly alkaline soil
Notes: Deadhead in summer for repeat bloom in autumn. Doesn't do well in humid heat of the South. Flower petals are edible.

CAUCASIAN LEOPARD'S BANE

Doronicum spp.
Perennial
Zones 4–7
1–2 feet tall
Blooms in spring
Daisylike yellow flowers
Full sun to partial shade
Average soil, prefers loam
Notes: Give it a few years to settle in and it will put on a lovely show. Pair with other early-blooming wildflowers. Goes dormant in summer. Easily propagated from seeds or by division.

PURPLE CONEFLOWER

Echinacea purpurea
Perennial
Zones 3–10
2–4 feet tall
Blooms midsummer to fall
Daisylike purplish-pink flowers with rusty orange centers
Full sun to partial shade
Average to infertile, well-drained soil
Notes: Drought-tolerant; easy-to-grow American native. Flowers attract butterflies; birds enjoy seedpods in fall and winter.

CALIFORNIA POPPY

Eschscholzia californica
Annual that reseeds readily
Zones 3–10
8–12 inches tall
Blooms midsummer
Orange, yellow, or red flowers
Full sun
Well-drained soil
Notes: Sow seed directly outdoors where you want it to grow. Makes a bright accent for border. Flowers close at night.

CRANESBILL

Geranium spp.
Perennial
Zones 4–10
18–24 inches tall
Blooms summer
Red, pink, lavender, blue, white, bicolor blooms
Full sun to partial shade
Well-drained soil
Notes: Not to be confused with the annual geranium (*Pelargonium*). A range of different species from delicate plants to large mounding ones for woodland gardens.

LENTEN ROSE

Helleborus orientalis
Perennial, some varieties evergreen
Zones 3–9
18 inches tall
Blooms winter; late winter; spring (depending on variety)
White, rose, mauve, or mottled blooms
Light to full shade
Moist, humusy, well-drained, fertile soil
Notes: Very desirable plants; many new cultivars and species. Includes Lenten rose, Christmas rose, and stinking hellebore.

PERENNIALS WITH INTERESTING LEAVES

The blooms of most perennials are fleeting compared with the staying power of the leaves. For that reason, look for plants with foliage that provides interest after the flowers have faded. Consider plants with variegated leaves, foliage with undertones of a color besides green (blue, silver, or yellow), and plants with dramatic or delicate foliage.

VARIEGATED OR COLORED LEAVES

Bigleaf ligularia	*Ligularia dentata*
Bronzeleaf rodgersia	*Rodgersia podophylla*
Chameleon plant	*Houttuynia cordata* 'Cameleon'
Hosta	*Hosta* spp.
Kamchatka bugbane	*Cimicifuga simplex*
New Zealand flax	*Phormium tenax*
Sweet flag	*Acorus calamus* 'Variegatus'
Tricolor sage	*Salvia officinalis* 'Tricolor'
Yellow archangel	*Lamium galeobdolon*

LEAVES THAT CHANGE COLOR SEASONALLY

Barrenwort	*Epimedium* spp.
Bergenia	*Bergenia* spp.

DRAMATIC FOLIAGE

Bear's breeches	*Acanthus* spp.
Nippon lily	*Rohdea japonica*
Plume poppy	*Macleaya cordata*
Sea kale	*Crambe cordifolia*
Umbrella plant	*Schefflera actinophylla*

DELICATE FOLIAGE

Fringed bleeding heart	*Dicentra eximia*
Golden feverfew	*Tanacetum parthenium* 'Aureum'
Poppy mallow	*Callirhoe* spp.
Russian sage	*Perovskia atriplicifolia*

Perennials *continued*

DAYLILY

Hemerocallis spp.
Perennial
Zones 3–10
8–60 inches tall
Blooms late spring, summer, early fall
Almost all colors and hues, except pure white and blue; solid colors and bicolors
Full sun to partial shade
Deep, rich, well-drained soil
Notes: Thousands of varieties in a range of sizes, colors, and bloom times. Night-blooming types are fragrant. Edible flowers.

AUTUMN JOY SEDUM

Hylotelephium 'Autumn Joy'
Perennial, evergreen succulent
Zones 3–9
24–30 inches tall
Blooms late summer through fall
Pink to rose tight clusters of flowers
Full sun
Poor to average, well-drained soil
Notes: Neat, succulent foliage with four-season interest. Allow seed heads to remain on plant in winter. Very easy to grow from leaves or cuttings.

EVERGREEN CANDYTUFT

Iberis sempervirens
Evergreen perennial
Zones 3-9
9–12 inches tall
Blooms early spring
White flower clusters
Full sun to partial shade
Average, well-drained soil
Notes: Mounds of white flowers last two months. Cut back by one-third after blooming to maintain shape.

KOREAN YELLOW BELLS

Kieringishoma koreana
Perennial
Zones 5–8
2–3 feet tall
Blooms late summer
Upright, bell-like, buttery-yellow flowers
Partial shade
Moist, humusy soil
Notes: A lovely addition to the woodland garden for its late bloom. The maplelike leaves add interest before flowers appear. Similar to *K. palmata* (down-facing blooms).

PRICKLY PEAR CACTUS

Opuntia spp.
Perennial cactus
Zones 4–9
6–18 inches tall
Blooms midsummer
Yellow flowers
Full sun
Average to sandy soil; drought-tolerant
Notes: A hardy cactus with blooms in July and August. Fruits are edible when magenta to purple; strain out seeds. Be careful of prickly pads. Wear double gloves when handling plants.

CINNAMON FERN

Osmunda cinnamomea
Perennial
Zones 4–9
2–5 feet tall
Blooms midsummer
Rust-colored fertile fronds
Full shade to full sun
Moist, humusy, acid soil
Notes: The best fall color of any fern—fronds turn orange-yellow after first frost. Elegant, formal shape works well in any garden, from woodland to formal.

MONKEY PLANT

Ruellia makoyana
Perennial
Zones 9–10
12–18 inches tall
Blooms summer
Rosy carmine flowers
Full sun to partial shade
Average soil; prefers rich, well-drained loam
Notes: Also known as trailing velvet plant, this is a good perennial groundcover for the South. Purplish leaves are handsomely veined with silvery gray.

GOLDENROD

Solidago spp.
Perennial
Zones 4–9
18–36 inches tall
Blooms midsummer to fall
Panicles of yellow flowers
Full sun to partial shade
Average to sandy soil; drought-tolerant
Notes: Does not cause hayfever. A genus of attractive, durable, long-blooming native plants. Many new hybrids, such as 'Fireworks'.

LAMB'S-EARS

Stachys byzantina
Perennial
Zones 4–10
12–18 inches tall
Blooms late spring
Purple to pink flowers along velvety spikes
Full sun to light shade
Average to sandy soil; drought-tolerant
Notes: This plant is loved for its velvety-soft, furry, silvery leaves. New nonflowering varieties available. Leaves and flowers good for dried arrangements.

ALLEGHENY FOAM FLOWER

Tiarella cordifolia
Evergreen perennial
Zones 4–9
6-inch leaves, flowers to 18 inches tall
Blooms midspring
Clusters of small creamy white flowers
Light to full shade
Moist, humusy, fertile soil
Notes: Long-lasting bloom—six weeks or more. Handsome maple-shaped leaves make a good groundcover. Some varieties have mottled or veined leaves.

TOAD LILY

Tricyrtis hirta
Perennial
Zones 4–8
2–3 feet tall
Blooms in fall
Orchidlike creamy white flowers,
    spotted purple
Full to partial shade
Evenly moist, humusy soil
Notes: A fall eye-catcher with a double row of orchidlike flowers along gracefully arching stems.

TALL VERBENA

Verbena bonariensis
Perennial/self-sowing annual
Zones 7–10
3–6 feet tall
Blooms midsummer to frost; fragrant
Tight 2-inch clusters of purple flowers
Full sun
Average, well-drained soil; drought-tolerant
Notes: Wonderful wiry stems; small, fragrant flowers. Mass plants for effect; self-sows. Good veil plant for front of garden.

SPEEDWELL

Veronica spp.
Perennial
Zones 3–10
To 18 inches tall
Blooms late spring through summer
Spikes of gentian blue flowers
Full sun to partial shade
Moist, humusy, well-drained soil
Notes: Numerous species and cultivars available. One of the best perennials. Prop up with twigs. Cut back after flowering to encourage rebloom.

YUCCA

Yucca spp.
Evergreen perennial
Zones 5–9
2–3 feet tall, 4- to 5-foot flower spikes
Blooms summer
Spikes of bell-shaped, edible white flowers
Full sun
Average to sandy soil; drought-tolerant
Notes: Grown for its architectural form and swordlike evergreen leaves. 'Gold Sword' has green leaves striped yellow.

CHOICE PERENNIALS FOR NORTH AND SOUTH

Some plants perform better in one region of the United States than another. Here are some suggested plants that do well in both areas.

Artemisia	*Artemisia* spp.
Aster	*Aster* spp.
Astilbe	*Astilbe* spp.
Balloon flower	*Platycodon grandiflorus*
Bearded iris	*Iris germanica*
Bee balm	*Monarda didyma*
Black-eyed Susan	*Rudbeckia hirta* 'Goldsturm'
Bleeding heart	*Dicentra* spp.
Chrysanthemum	*Dendranthema x grandiflorum*
Clematis	*Clematis* spp.
Columbine	*Aquilegia* spp.
Common sage	*Salvia officinalis*
Coralbells (alum root)	*Heuchera* spp.
Coreopsis	*Coreopsis* spp.
Cottage pinks	*Dianthus plumarius*
Cranesbill	*Geranium* spp.
Daylily	*Hemerocallis* spp.
False indigo	*Baptisia* spp.
Garden phlox	*Phlox paniculata*
Gayfeather	*Liatris* spp.
Hosta	*Hosta* spp.
Moss phlox	*Phlox subulata*
Peony	*Paeonia* spp.
Showy sedum	*Sedum spectabile*
Siberian iris	*Iris sibirica*
Speedwell	*Veronica* spp.
Spiderwort	*Tradescantia virginiana*
Spotted dead nettle	*Lamium maculatu*
Woodland phlox	*Phlox divaricata*
Yarrow	*Achillea* spp.

Annuals

Because annuals grow, flower, and die in one year or less, it's necessary to replant them every year. Planting different annuals each year allows for experimentation with color, texture, and form. You can even simulate a perennial bed—with annuals of similar shapes, sizes, and colors—to ensure it looks as good as you envisioned it to look before buying the more costly perennials. Most annuals benefit from deadheading. It makes the plant look more attractive, keeps it from going to seed, and encourages more blooms.

Shirley poppy

HONEYWORT

Cerinthe major purpurascens
Annual
To 2 feet tall
Blooms summer
Clusters of nodding deep blue-purple flowers
Full sun
Moist, humusy, well-drained soil
Notes: Best known as cerinthe. Another newcomer—there's nothing quite like it in the garden. Its shrubby habit is appealing; leaves are blue-green and slightly frosted. Flowers have a honeylike scent.

SPIDER FLOWER

Cleome hassleriana
Annual
3–4 feet tall
Blooms summer to fall
White, pink, or violet flowers
Full sun to partial shade
Average soil
Notes: Three- to 4-inch spherical heads. Self-seeds readily. Seedlings come up late in spring, so avoid mulching or cultivating the soil too early. Also called cleome.

CHINA ASTER

Callistephus chinensis 'Fireworks'
Annual
6–36 inches tall
Blooms midsummer to fall
Hybrids with blue, pink, peach, red, or white semidouble and double flowers
Full sun to partial shade
Rich, well-drained, neutral to basic soil
Notes: Range of hybrids with spidery to pompon blooms. Makes a good cut flower. Fills in color in the late-season garden.

LARKSPUR

Consolida ambigua
Annual
9–48 inches tall
Blooms late spring to early summer
Lightly scented blue, white, lilac, pink, or peach flowers
Full sun to partial shade
Rich, well-drained soil
Notes: Also known as annual delphinium. Flower spikes are held above a mass of lacy dark green foliage. Grows best in areas with cool summers. May self-sow.

MELAMPODIUM

Leucanthemum paludosum
Annual
10–24 inches tall
Blooms summer to frost
Star-shaped golden yellow flowers
Full sun to partial shade
Well-drained, average soil
Notes: Another new plant for the garden. Looks like a very vigorous creeping zinnia without the black eye. Forms a mound of foliage dotted with flowers. Good at the edge of a flower border.

FOUR-O-CLOCKS

Mirabilis jalapa
Annual
18–30 inches tall
Blooms summer to frost
Fragrant white, yellow, fuchsia, or peppermint-stick flowers
Full sun to partial shade
Well-drained garden soil
Notes: Another plant for the evening garden; four-o-clocks open their 1-inch trumpets in late afternoon. Their perfume is delicate. Self-sows readily.

WOODLAND NICOTIANA

Nicotiana sylvestris
Annual
6–18 inches tall
Blooms summer to frost
Fragrant white flowers
Full sun to partial shade
Average, well-drained soil
Notes: An old-fashioned plant that's making a comeback. Good for an evening garden—it's fragrant only at night. Self-sows. Flowers are trumpetlike with a starburst at the end.

SHIRLEY POPPY

Papaver rhoeas
Annual
1–2 feet tall
Blooms early to midsummer
White petal edges and pink centers in shadings from red to apricot
Full sun
Poor to average, very well-drained soil
Notes: A graceful, airy plant for gardens and meadows. Flowers may be single or double. They look more delicate than they are. Readily reseeds.

FAN FLOWER

Scaevola aemula
Annual
6–8 inches tall
Blooms late spring to frost
Unusual fan-shaped blue flowers
Full sun to partial shade
Moist, humusy, well-drained soil
Notes: One of the new arrivals, its popularity is exploding. Low-growing with a spreading, trailing habit. Can be used as a groundcover in California. Excellent in containers, especially hanging baskets and window boxes.

SIGNET MARIGOLD

Tagetes tenuifolia 'Lemon Gem'
Annual
6–12 inches tall
Blooms late spring to frost
¾-inch lemony yellow flowers
Full sun to partial shade
Moist, humusy, well-drained soil
Notes: This is one of the few marigolds with edible flowers. Delicate-looking plants with mounds of scented feathery foliage.

NASTURTIUM

Tropaeolum majus
Annual
9–15 inches tall; climbing variety grows
  to 72 inches tall
Blooms spring to fall
Hues of orange, yellow, and red flowers
Full sun to partial shade
Light, well-drained soil
Notes: The edible leaves and flowers have a peppery flavor. Use them in salads or as a garnish. Easy to grow from seed. Can self-sow in mild climates.

TALL VERBENA

Verbena bonariensis
Annual; perennial in Zones 7–10
3–6 feet tall
Blooms summer to early fall
Fragrant purple flowers
Full sun
Humusy, well-drained soil
Notes: Wonderful wiry stems topped with clusters of small fragrant flowers. An excellent veil plant that you can see through, even when planted at the front of a garden. Mass for effect. Self-sows readily.

GARDEN VERBENA

Verbena x hybrida 'Peaches 'n Cream'
Annual
8 inches tall
Blooms early summer to frost
Bicolored peach and cream flowers
Full sun; light shade where hot
Fertile, very well-drained soil
Notes: Handsome lance-shaped dark green leaves with serrated edges. Drought-tolerant. Beautiful combined with daylilies or 'Peach Melba' nasturtium.

PANSY

Viola x wittrockiana
Perennial grown as an annual
4–9 inches tall
Blooms spring to summer (fall to spring
  in mild climates)
Single-, two-, or three-colored flowers; hues
  of white, pink, blue, purple, brown, yellow
Partial shade
Well-drained, fertile soil
Notes: Bright and cheery flowers. Fall-planted pansies last through winter in mild climates.

ANNUALS FOR SPECIFIC SITES

Although the soil preparation for annuals is usually not as intensive as for perennials or woody plants, it helps to put the right plant in the right place. Most annuals can grow in full sun, but not all the places you want to brighten with annual blooms are ideal. For tricky areas, plant the annuals that are best adapted to the conditions.

DRY SOIL

Cigar flower	*Cuphea ignea*
Cockscomb	*Celosia argentea cristata*
Cosmos	*Cosmos* spp.
Dusty miller	*Senecio cineraria*
Garden (zonal) geranium	*Pelargonium* spp.
Globe amaranth	*Gomphrena globosa*
Love-in-a-mist	*Nigella damascena*
Matilija poppy	*Romneya coulteri*
Melampodium	*Leucanthemum paludosum*
Mexican sunflower	*Tithonia rotundifolia*
Monkey flower	*Mimulus* × *hybridus*
Moss rose	*Portulaca grandiflora*
Nasturtium	*Tropaeolum majus*
Pot marigold	*Calendula officinalis*
Sweet alyssum	*Lobularia maritima*
Transvaal daisy	*Gerbera jamesonii*
Vinca	*Catharanthus roseus*
Winged everlasting	*Ammobium alatum*

SHADE

Browallia	*Browallia speciosa*
Coleus	*Solenostemon scutellarioides*
Edging lobelia	*Lobelia erinus*
Impatiens	*Impatiens walleriana*
Wax begonia	*Begonia semperflorens cultorum hybrids*
Wishbone flower	*Torenia fournieri*

Bulbs

Technically, not all of the plants listed here are bulbs. However, they all have enlarged underground food storage mechanisms. Unlike other plants, bulbs are above ground only for a short time. The rest of the year they are dormant, slowly feeding off their underground stores.

Grow bulbs hardy to your region to discover a group of low-maintenance plants. Dig the soil well before planting, set bulbs at the proper depth, cover with soil, water, and wait for them to grow. Avoid cutting the leaves; allow them to die back. Bulbs need to store energy from the leaves to make it to the next season.

Tuberous begonia

LILY-OF-THE-NILE

Agapanthus spp.
Tender tuber
Zones 8–11
3 feet tall
Blooms throughout the summer
Dome-shaped clusters of 6-inch-wide lilylike blue or white flowers
Full sun; partial shade in hot-summer areas
Moist, well-drained, fertile soil
Notes: Also known as African lily. Evergreen in hardiness range; otherwise, dig in fall. Good plant for containers.

STAR OF PERSIA

Allium christophii
Hardy bulb
Zones 4–8
15–24 inches tall
Blooms mid- to late spring
6- to 12-inch-wide spheres of star-shaped metallic violet flowers
Full sun
Rich, well-drained soil
Notes: Blooms resemble fireworks. Flower heads dry naturally; color fades to buff. Spray-paint them for dried arrangements.

HYBRID TUBEROUS BEGONIA

Begonia tuberhybrida hybrids
Tender rhizome
Zones 8–10
10–24 inches tall
Blooms late spring to fall
Red, pink, white, yellow, orange, and picotee-edged double flowers
Partial shade
Humusy, well-drained soil
Notes: Good for shade gardens, with heart-shaped leaves and show-stopping blooms.

CANNA

Canna x generalis 'Tropicanna'
Tender rhizome
Zones 8–11
3–4 feet tall
Blooms midsummer to frost
Gladiola-like spikes of orange flowers
Full sun
Moist, humusy, well-drained soil
Notes: Grown more for its broad lance-shaped leaves than the flowers, which some gardeners remove. Boldly dramatic, it brings a lush, tropical appearance to a garden. In colder areas, start rhizomes indoors.

LILY-OF-THE-VALLEY

Convallaria majalis
Hardy bulb
Zones 3–7
3–8 inches tall
Blooms midspring
Loose spike with 12–20 tiny highly fragrant bell-shaped waxy white flowers
Partial shade; sun in cool-summer areas
Moist, humusy, acid to neutral soil
Notes: Makes a charming, low-maintenance groundcover in a naturalistic, woodland, or shade garden. Excellent cut flower.

CROCUS

Crocus spp.
Hardy corm
Zones 3–7
4–6 inches tall
Blooms late winter to early spring; also some fall bloomers
White, yellow, purple, and bicolored flowers
Full sun to partial shade
Well-drained, average soil
Notes: One of the heralds of spring; the snow crocus blooms even in late snows. The larger, well-known Dutch crocus follows suit.

HARDY CYCLAMEN

Cyclamen hederifolium
Hardy bulb
Zones 7–9 (to Zone 5 with winter mulch)
3–6 inches tall
Blooms late summer to fall
Dark-eyed 1-inch pink or white flowers
Partial shade
Moist, humusy, well-drained soil
Notes: Swept-back petals on leafless stalks resemble butterflies hovering over the 5½-inch heart-shaped silver-marbled leaves.

GARDEN DAHLIA

Dahlia hybrids
Tender tuber
Zones 8–11; dig in fall in colder areas
1–7 feet tall
Blooms late summer to early fall
Every color but blue; also bicolored flowers
Full sun; midday shade in hot-summer areas
Humusy, well-drained, fertile soil
Notes: Hundreds of varieties with single and double forms, from ball-shaped pompons and spiky-petaled cactuslike flowers to dinner-plate-size dahlias. Excellent cut flowers.

ABYSSINIAN GLADIOLUS

Gladiolus callianthus
Tender corm
Zones 7–11
2½–3½ feet tall
Blooms late summer to fall
Fragrant 3- to 4-inch creamy white flowers
  with maroon stars at their throats
Full sun
Deeply prepared, well-drained soil
Notes: Also known as peacock orchid.
Exotic-looking; most fragrant at night.

RUBRUM LILY

Lilium speciosum var. rubrum
Hardy bulb
Zones 3–10
3–5 feet tall
Blooms summer
Fragrant star-shaped deep rose flowers with
  white edges and throats
Full sun
Humusy, deep, well-drained, fertile soil
Notes: Classic summer beauty with up to a
dozen 8-inch flowers per stem.

GRAPE HYACINTH

Muscari spp.
Hardy bulb
Zones 2–8
6–8 inches tall
Blooms early to midspring
Spike with grapelike cluster of 20–40
  fragrant intense blue flowers
Full sun to partial shade
Average to poor, well-drained soil
Notes: A diminutive bloomer that makes
charming drifts under daffodils and tulips.
Naturalizes easily. Good cut flower.

DAFFODIL

Narcissus spp.
Hardy bulb
Zones 3–9
6–24 inches tall
Blooms early to late spring
Yellow, white, cream; solid and bicolors
  (also with orange or pink)
Full sun to partial shade
Humusy, well-drained, neutral to slightly
  acid soil
Notes: Hundreds of varieties range from tiny
species to large-flowered hybrids and
fragrant split-corolla (butterfly) forms.

TULIP

Tulipa spp.
Hardy bulb
Zones 4–7
4–30 inches tall
Blooms early to late spring
All colors—single or multihued—except
  true blue flowers
Full sun to partial shade
Humusy, well-drained, fertile soil
Notes: Single- and double-flowered varieties.
Excellent as cut flowers.

CALLA LILY

Zantedeschia spp.
Tender rhizome
Zones 9–11
1½–4 feet tall
Blooms early spring to early summer
  (summer in cold climates)
White, yellow, green, or sunset-hue flowers
Full sun to partial shade
Moist, humusy, well-drained soil
Notes: Exotic-looking with lance-shaped
leaves. Excellent in boggy or damp sites and
around garden ponds.

SUMMER- AND FALL-BLOOMING BULBS

Most people associate bulbs with spring—daffodils,
tulips, crocus, and hyacinths (all hardy bulbs). Bulbs
give color in other seasons as well. Summer-blooming
(tender) bulbs—planted during the spring in
cold-winter climates (Zone 7 and colder) and dug up
in the fall—make a good bridge in the mixed border,
adding splashes of color among perennials that have
finished or have yet to bloom. In warmer regions they
are planted during the fall and remain in the ground
year-round. Fall-blooming bulbs (some begin in late
summer) are noted with an asterisk (*).

* **Autumn crocus**	*Colchicum autumnale*
Blackberry lily	*Belamcanda chinensis*
Calla lily	*Zantedeschia aethiopica*
Canna	*Canna × generalis*
Crocus	*Crocus* spp.
Dahlias	*Dahlia* hybrids
Foxtail lily	*Eremurus* spp.
Giant allium	*Allium giganteum*
Gladiolus	*Gladiolus* spp.
* **Guernsey lily**	*Nerine sarniensis*
* **Hardy cyclamen**	*Cyclamen hederifolium*
Italian arum	*Arum italicum*
* **Japanese anemone**	*Anemone hupehensis* var. *japonica*
Japanese iris	*Iris ensata*
Lilies	*Lilium* spp. and hybrids
* **Lily-of-the-field**	*Sternbergia lutea*
Lily-of-the-Nile	*Agapanthus* spp.
* **Magic lily (naked lady)**	*Lycoris squamigera*
Ornamental alliums	*Allium* spp.
Siberian iris	*Iris sibirica*
Summer hyacinth	*Galtonia candicans*
Summer snowflake	*Leucojum* spp.
Tiger lily	*Lilium lancifolium*
* **Tuberose**	*Polianthes tuberosa*
Wood sorrel	*Oxalis* spp.

Ornamental grasses

Almost unheard of 15 to 20 years ago, ornamental grasses are now grown in gardens throughout America—formal and informal alike. Part of their popularity comes from their ease of care. The only maintenance is cutting them back during the spring.

Most grasses provide four-season interest. Any evening, listen as a breeze rustles through the grasses. In the summer, enjoy the showy inflorescences; birds will savor the seeds later on. As fall arrives, watch the leaf colors change to pale earth tones. Even during the winter, grasses add architectural form to the garden.

Red fountain grass

COMMON QUAKING GRASS

Briza media
Perennial evergreen grass
Zones 4–8
12–18 inches tall (flowers 12 inches higher)
Blooms in spring
Flower spikelets are luminous green, faintly striped purple; golden seed heads
Full sun to partial shade
Average to poor, moist to wet soil
Notes: Also known as rattlesnake grass. Tiny flower spikelets shake and quiver in the slightest breeze but shatter by summer's end.

FEATHER REED GRASS

Calamagrostis x acutiflora 'Karl Foerster'
Perennial grass
Zones 5–9
6–7 feet tall
Blooms early summer
Feathery pink inflorescences turn light purple in summer, then golden in fall
Full sun; tolerates partial shade
Average to heavy, well-drained to wet soil
Notes: Changes alluringly through the seasons. Seed heads remain attractive.

BOWLES GOLDEN TUFTED SEDGE

Carex elata 'Bowles Golden'
Perennial sedge
Zones 7–9
20 inches tall
Blooms late spring to early summer
Flowers not showy; yellow leaves
Partial to full shade
Humusy, well-drained to wet soil
Notes: Grasslike leaves bend at their tips, creating a mound of cascading foliage that turns luminous golden-green in summer.

JAPANESE SEDGE

Carex morrowii
Perennial evergreen or semievergreen sedge
Zones 5–9
12–18 inches tall
Insignificant blooms
Partial to full shade
Moist, well-drained, fertile to average soil
Notes: Forms a dense, arching mound of stiff, ½-inch-wide leaves. Adds winter interest. Variegated forms with gold or white stripes are most popular.

PAMPAS GRASS

Cortaderia selloana
Perennial evergreen grass
Zones 8–10 (grown as annual elsewhere)
10 feet tall
Blooms autumn
Shaggy plumes of creamy white flowers
Full sun to partial shade
Well-drained, fertile soil
Notes: Razor-edged evergreen leaves form dense, weeping mounds. Flowers remain showy into winter. Eye-catching near water and where struck from behind by sunlight.

BLUE FESCUE

Festuca glauca
Perennial grass
Zones 4–9
6–12 inches tall
Insignificant blooms in summer
Evergreen silvery blue leaves
Full sun
Average to poor, well-drained soil
Notes: A garden favorite, forming hedgehoglike mounds of fine-textured pale silvery-blue leaves. Drought-tolerant. Suffers in high heat and humidity.

GOLDEN GRASS

Hakonechloa macra 'Aureola'
Perennial grass
Zones 4–9
1–2 feet tall
Blooms summer to fall
Inconspicuous flowers
Partial shade
Moist, humusy, well-drained, fertile soil
Notes: Also known as Japanese wind grass. Prized for the elegant bamboolike, bright green leaves that cascade toward the light from short, wiry stems. Foliage turns pinkish red in fall, then bleaches to bright tan.

JAPANESE BLOOD GRASS

Imperata cylindrica 'Red Baron'
Perennial grass
Zones 5–9 (Zone 4 with winter protection)
12–24 inches tall
Does not flower
Full sun to partial shade
Moist, humusy, well-drained, fertile soil
Notes: Upright leaves emerge green with red tips and gradually become redder, creating a stunning, two-toned effect by summer. Fall foliage is flaming scarlet; frost turns it bronze, and winter bleaches it straw.

MAIDEN GRASS

Miscanthus sinensis 'Gracillimus'
Perennial grass
Zones 4–9
3–4 feet tall
Blooms late summer to fall
Silvery flower plumes
Full sun (flops in shade)
Moist, average to heavy soil
Notes: Also known as Japanese silver grass. Narrow leaves with white midrib on a vase-shaped plant. Makes an excellent screen planted en masse.

ZEBRA GRASS

Miscanthus sinensis 'Zebrinus'
Perennial grass
Zones 4–9
4–6 feet tall
Blooms late summer
Airy whitish plumes of flowers
Full sun
Average to heavy, moist to wet soil
Notes: Wide leaves banded horizontally with gold. Tolerates wet soil. 'Porcupine' is a better choice in areas with strong summer rains that can beat down 'Zebrinus'.

FOUNTAIN GRASS

Pennisetum alopecuroides 'Hameln'
Perennial grass
Zones 5–8
2 feet tall
Blooms summer
Foxtail-like flower plumes open green and
   mature to rosy silver
Full sun in the north; light shade in the south
Moist, well-drained, average to fertile soil
Notes: One of the smaller grasses, it is at home in any garden. Fabulous in fall; adds volume to an otherwise empty winter garden.

PURPLE FOUNTAIN GRASS

Pennisetum setaceum 'Rubrum'
Perennial evergreen to semievergreen grass
Zones 8–10 (grown as annual elsewhere)
3–4 feet tall
Blooms summer
Foot-long foxtail-like reddish-purple blooms
Full sun to partial shade
Moist, humusy to sandy soil
Notes: Valued for its arching clumps of burgundy-bronze leaves that bring a long season of color to the mixed border.

RIBBON GRASS

Phalaris arundinacea
Perennial grass (evergreen in mild climates)
Zones 4–9
18–24 inches tall
Blooms summer
Insignificant lacy white flowers
Full sun to full shade
Average to poor or heavy soil
Notes: Also known as gardener's garters. Longitudinally striped green-and-white leaves produce a beautiful flash of white in the garden. May become invasive.

BLUE-EYED GRASS

Sisyrinchium angustifolium
Perennial grass
Zones 3–8
6–18 inches tall
Blooms summer
Star-shaped blue flowers with yellow center
Full sun
Average, well-drained soil
Notes: A native American prairie plant that has become familiar in flower gardens. It is fairly inconspicuous unless planted in a mass. Dainty flowers are charming.

GRASSES FOR CUTTING AND DRYING

Many ornamental grasses make excellent cut flowers, adding movement to an otherwise static flower arrangement. Many of them are also suited for use in dried arrangements or wreaths. Those that are used only as dried grasses are noted with an asterisk (*); the ones suited only for fresh use are indicated with a double asterisk (**).

CUT & DRIED

Annual wild rice	*Zizania aquatica*
Bottle-brush grass	*Hystrix patula*
Cloud grass	*Agrostis nebulosa*
Common quaking grass	*Briza media*
* Common reed	*Phragmites australis*
European feather grass	*Stipa pennata*
Fountain grass	*Pennisetum alopecuroides*
Foxtail	*Setaria italica*
Giant reed	*Arundo donax*
Golden top	*Lamarckia aurea*
Hare's tail grass	*Lagurus ovatus*
Indian grass	*Sorghastrum nutans*
Love grass	*Eragrostis* spp.
Maiden grass	*Miscanthus sinensis*
* Melic	*Melica ciliata*
Northern sea oats	*Chasmanthium latifolium*
Ornamental corn	*Zea mays* cvs.
Pampas grass	*Cortaderia selloana*
** Ravenna grass	*Saccharum ravennae*
Switch grass	*Panicum virgatum*
Tufted hair grass	*Deschampsia caespitosa*
Vetiver	*Vetiveria zizanoides*
* Wheat	*Triticum* spp.

Herbs

Among the oldest group of cultivated plants, herbs have played a significant role in gardens and garden design through the millennia. The first formal gardens may have been the monks' cloistered herb gardens during the Middle Ages.

Today herbs are divided into several use groups—culinary, medicinal, dye, and cosmetic. Although there are significantly more medicinal herbs than culinary ones, culinary herbs are more widely grown in modern gardens. Some gardens are strictly for herbs (usually a formal herb garden), whereas kitchen, perennial, and mixed gardens include herbs among other plants.

Calendula

CHIVES

Allium schoenoprasum
Perennial herb
Zones 3–9
12–18 inches tall
Blooms early summer
1-inch spheres of lavender flowers
Full sun
Moist, humusy, well-drained soil
Notes: Harvesting is good for the plant, which looks best if cut back occasionally. Use the edible blossoms to make a pale-lavender herb vinegar. Grow from divisions or seeds.

FENNEL

Foeniculum vulgare
Perennial herb
Zones 4–10
4–5 feet tall
Blooms summer to fall
Flat heads of edible yellow flowers
Full sun
Well-drained garden soil
Notes: Mildly anise-flavored flowers, seeds, leaves, and stems. Attracts butterflies and beneficial insects; favorite host plant for the swallowtail butterfly in the West.

ENGLISH LAVENDER

Lavandula angustifolia
Evergreen shrub, herb
Zones 5–10
6–18 inches tall
Blooms summer
Spikes of small, fragrant lavender flowers
Full sun
Very well-drained, poor to average soil
Notes: Silvery foliage. Flowers useful when dried; cut while fresh to maintain color. Heat- and drought-resistant; not good for humid South.

ANISE HYSSOP

Agastache foeniculum
Perennial herb
Zones 6–10
3–5 feet tall
Blooms summer
Spikes of pale purple flowers
Full sun
Well-drained garden soil
Notes: Anise-scented leaves and 4-inch spikes of flowers. Good in borders or herb beds. Licorice-flavored edible flowers. Reseeds but is late to come up in spring.

BORAGE

Borago officinalis
Annual herb
Zones 3–9
2–5 feet tall
Blooms spring through fall
Star-shaped sky blue flowers
Full sun
Moist, well-drained soil
Notes: Leaves are edible but have soft bristles. To eat the cucumber-flavored flowers, remove the stamens first. Readily reseeds.

BEE BALM

Monarda didyma
Perennial herb
Zones 4–9
3–5 feet tall
Blooms summer
Clusters of tubelike bright-red flowers
Full sun
Humusy, well-drained soil
Notes: Also known as Oswego tea. Attracts butterflies and hummingbirds. Edible flowers with a spicy mint flavor.

POT MARIGOLD

Calendula officinalis
Annual herb
Zones 3–9
12–24 inches tall
Blooms late spring through summer
Daisylike yellow or orange flowers
Full sun
Any well-drained soil
Notes: Perfect for an edible landscape. In the kitchen, use the petals to brighten a salad or sprinkle over soup. Easy-to-grow, cool-season plant. May reseed.

BASIL

Ocimum basilicum
Annual herb
6–24 inches tall
Blooms late summer to early fall
White or lilac flowers, depending on variety
Full sun
Moist, well-drained garden soil
Notes: One of the basic culinary herbs. Can be dried but loses flavor. Edible flowers have milder flavor than the leaves. Cut stems will root in a glass of water on the windowsill.

PARSLEY

Petroselinum crispum
Biennial herb
Zones 5–9
12–24 inches tall
Blooms spring of second year
White flowers
Full sun to partial shade
Moist, well-drained garden soil
Notes: Attractive in the garden. Use as a border or mix with pansies or other low-growing annual flowers. Nutritious; use in the kitchen as more than a garnish.

ROSEMARY

Rosmarinus officinalis
Evergreen shrub, herb
Zones 7–10 (depending on variety)
3–4 feet tall
Blooms winter to spring
Edible blue, lavender, white, or pink flowers
Full to partial sun
Well-drained, poor to average soil
Notes: A tender perennial; may be grown as an annual or in containers. Needs moderate to little water once established. Leaves and flowers edible.

COMMON SAGE

Salvia officinalis
Evergreen shrub, herb
Zones 3–10
6–18 inches tall
Blooms late spring to early summer
Edible lilac to blue or pink flowers
Full sun
Well-drained garden soil
Notes: Aromatic gray-green leaves. Not good in humid heat of the South. Protect with mulch in cold-winter areas. Favored for stuffings, sausages, and poultry.

PINEAPPLE SAGE

Salvia rutilans
Perennial herb
Zones 8–10 (grow as annual elsewhere)
3–6 feet tall
Blooms summer to fall (winter in mild climates)
Spikes of edible tubelike bright-red flowers
Full sun
Well-drained garden soil
Notes: A treat for its bright flowers and scented foliage. A delicious garnish.

COMFREY

Symphytum spp.
Perennial herb
Zones 3–10
3–5 feet tall
Blooms spring to frost
White to red flowers
Full sun to partial shade
Moist, humusy, well-drained soil
Notes: Ornamental only—not recommended for culinary or medicinal use. Easy, fast-growing background plant. Can be invasive; contain in pots.

THYME

Thymus spp.
Evergreen perennial herb
Zones 4–9
6–12 inches tall
Blooms late spring to summer
Edible pink, lavender, or white flowers
Full sun (partial shade in very hot areas)
Well-drained, poor to average, alkaline soil
Notes: Flavor is fuller when grown in poor soil. Cut thyme back in spring by one-third to keep it lush. In cold regions, protect with a winter mulch. Pest- and disease-resistant.

HERBS FOR CHALLENGING LOCATIONS

Most herbs grow best in full sun and ordinary soil. The Mediterranean herbs (including thyme, lavender, and rosemary) do best in lean, relatively dry soil. The following herbs will grow well in other conditions—shade, moist soil that is well-drained, and wet soil. They are designated as follows: (s) partial shade, (m) moist but well-drained soil, (w) wet soil.

Angelica	Angelica archangelica	s, w
Bee balm	Monarda didyma	s, m
Black mustard	Brassica nigra	m
Catmint	Nepeta × faassenii	s
Chervil	Anthriscus cereifolium	s, m
Coltsfoot	Tussilago farfara	m
Comfrey	Symphytum spp.	w
Coriander	Coriandrum sativum	s
Horseradish	Armoracia rusticana	m
Lemon balm	Melissa officinalis	s, m
Lemon verbena	Aloysia triphylla	m
Licorice	Glycyrrhiza glabra	s, w
Lovage	Levisticum officinale	s, m
Marsh mallow	Althaea officinalis	w
Mint	Mentha spp.	s, m
Pennyroyal	Mentha pulegium	s, w
Soapwort	Saponaria officinalis	s, w
Sweet violet	Viola odorata	s, m
Sweet woodruff	Galium odoratum	s
Tarragon	Artemisia dracunculus	s
Valerian	Valeriana officinalis	w
Wall germander	Teucrium chamaedrys	s
Water mint	Mentha aquatica	w
Wintergreen	Gaultheria procumbens	s

Groundcovers

Groundcover defines a function rather than a specific plant type. As the name implies, the plant covers the ground. Contrary to popular belief, a groundcover need not be low to the ground. In fact, height can range from several inches—a moss, for example—to 5 feet or more, such as any of the shrub or beach roses.

Although different in some ways—annual, perennial, deciduous, or evergreen—all groundcovers provide enough cover that once they are established, mulching and weeding are unnecessary.

Spotted dead nettle

RED BARRENWORT

Epimedium x rubrum
Perennial groundcover
Zones 5–8
8–12 inches tall
Blooms midspring
Delicate sprays of small red-and-white-spurred rosy flowers
Partial to full shade
Moist, humusy, fertile soil; tolerates poor, dry soil in full shade
Notes: Also known as bishop's hat. Heart-shaped red-tinged spring foliage turns green in summer. Plant under trees and shrubs.

HOSTA

Hosta spp.
Perennial
Zones 3–9
6–30 inches tall (flower stalk to 48 inches)
Blooms summer to early fall
Loose spikes of white to lilac (sometimes fragrant) flowers
Full sun to full shade (depending on variety)
Moist, humusy, well-drained soil
Notes: Grown for the mounds of heart-shaped leaves that range in color from deep green to golden, many with variegations.

BAR HARBOR JUNIPER

Juniperus horizontalis 'Bar Harbor'
Evergreen shrub
Zones 4–9
2 feet tall
Inconspicuous flowers
Grown for its fragrant gray-green needles
Full sun
Well-drained garden soil
Notes: Tough plant that grows in most soils. A good barrier groundcover; people and animals can't walk through it.

AJUGA

Ajuga reptans
Perennial
Zones 3–9
3 inches tall; flowers rise 4–12 inches
Blooms late spring
Spikes of tiny orchidlike violet-blue flowers
Light to full shade (sun if soil is moist)
Moist, well-drained, fertile soil
Notes: Gardeners love this ground-hugging, rapidly spreading perennial for its beautifully textured foliage and short flower spikes.

SALAL

Gaultheria shallon
Perennial
Zones 5–8
12–18 inches tall
Blooms late spring to early summer
Clusters of waxy white flowers
Full sun to full shade
Moist, humusy, well-drained, acid soil
Notes: Prized for its leathery dark green leaves. Commonly grown on the West Coast. Edible purple-black fruit in summer.

SPOTTED DEAD NETTLE

Lamium maculatum
Perennial
Zones 3–8
6–8 inches tall
Blooms midspring through summer
Spikes of small orchidlike white, pink, or purple flowers
Full sun to partial shade
Moist, average to rich, humusy soil
Notes: Handsome heart-shaped scalloped-edged green leaves with silver or white spotting. Vigorous, sprawling plant.

EUROPEAN WILD GINGER

Asarum europaeum
Evergreen perennial (only in warm areas)
Zones 4–8
4–6 inches tall
Blooms under leaves in spring—rarely noticed
Grown for its round to heart-shaped 2- to 3-inch glossy green leaves
Light to full shade
Moist, humusy, acid soil
Notes: Spreads slowly by underground rhizomes to form a beautifully textured, dense mat. Drought-tolerant once established.

HEUCHERA

Heuchera 'Pewter Veil'
Perennial
Zones 3–10
18–22 inches tall
Blooms spring to summer
Dainty loose spikes of bell-like white flowers
Partial shade to full sun
Humusy, well-drained soil
Notes: Prized for its show-stopping silver foliage that is flushed and veined with purple and green.

VARIEGATED LILYTURF

Liriope muscari 'Variegata'
Perennial
Zones 5–10
8–12 inches tall
Blooms late summer to early fall
Spikes of purple flowers
Partial shade to full sun
Moist, humusy, well-drained soil; tolerates
  dry soil once established
Notes: Cream stripes fade in sun.
Dependable.

BLACK MONDO GRASS

Ophiopogon planiscapus
'Nigrescens'
Perennial
Zones 6–9
6 inches tall
Blooms midsummer
Pink-tinted white flowers
Full sun to partial shade
Moist, humusy, fertile soil
Notes : Flowers followed by clusters of black
berries. Spreading clumps of dark purple—
almost black—leaves. Contrasts well with
brighter flowers and foliage.

PACHYSANDRA

Pachysandra terminalis
Evergreen perennial
Zones 4–9
6–12 inches tall
Blooms in spring
Creamy white spires of fragrant flowers
Partial shade
Moist, humusy, well-drained soil
Notes: One of the "big three" groundcovers
with ivy and periwinkle. 'Variegata', with its
white-margined green leaves, stands out in
the shade.

DWARF SWEET BOX

Sarcococca hookeriana humilis
Evergreen perennial
Zones 5–7
30–36 inches tall
Blooms late winter to early spring
Fragrant white flowers
Partial sun to full shade
Moist, humusy, well-drained soil
Notes: Attractive, glossy evergreen leaves are
accented with white flowers. Their sweet
scent fills the air.

IRISH MOSS

Selaginella involens
Evergreen perennial
Zones 6–8
3 inches tall
Inconspicuous blooms
Grown for its tufted pale green foliage
Partial to full shade
Moist, humusy, well-drained soil
Notes: The softest-looking groundcover,
it is surprisingly tough, although it won't hold
up to constant foot traffic. Slow to spread but
worth the wait.

HEN AND CHICKS

Sempervivum spp.
Evergreen succulent perennial
Zones 3–7
6–12 inches tall
Blooms summer
Spikes of star-shaped rosy red, purple,
  yellow, or white flowers
Full sun
Well-drained soil
Notes: Handsome rosettes of foliage in
various colors—shades of green to deep
purple. Easy to grow.

GROUNDCOVERS FOR SEASONAL INTEREST

The characteristics of groundcovers—flowers,
fruits, or evergreen leaves—add another dimension
to their utility and gives them multiseasonal
interest. Evergreen varieties are indicated by (e),
flowers by (f), and fruit by (o).

Bearberry	Arctostaphylos uva-ursi	e, o
Bunchberry	Cornus canadensis	e, o
Capeweed	Arctotheca calendula	f
Chamomile	Chamaemelum nobile	f
Chilean pernettya	Gaultheria mucronata	o
Cotoneaster	Cotoneaster spp.	e, o
Creeping mahonia	Mahonia repens	e
Creeping phlox	Phlox stolonifera	f
Daylilies	Hemerocallis spp.	f
Galax	Galax urceolata	e
Goldenstar	Chrysogonum virginianum	f
Ice plant	Delosperma spp. & Lampranthus spp.	f
Lady's mantle	Alchemilla mollis	f
Leadwort	Ceratostigma plumbaginoides	f
Moss phlox	Phlox subulata	e, f
Partridgeberry	Mitchella repens	e
Pussytoes	Antennaria spp.	f
Trailing rosemary	Rosmarinus officinalis 'Prostatus'	e
Salal	Gaultheria shallon	e, f, o
Scotch heather	Calluna vulgaris	f
Snow-in-summer	Cerastium tomentosum	f
Sweet woodruff	Galium odoratum	f
Dwarf sweet box	Sarcococca hookeriana humilis	e, f
Wild strawberry	Fragraria virginiana	f, o
Winter creeper euonymus	Euonymus fortunei	e
Winter heath	Erica carnea	e, f

Vines

True vines climb by means of adaptive parts, and all need support. On their own, their stems are not strong enough to hold them upright.

Some vines, such as clematis, twine their stems around a support, which must be sturdy enough for the vine. Beware, they will twine on living supports; wisteria or wild honeysuckle can strangle a plant.

Others, such as sweet peas, have tendrils that require a thin support—string or wire.

Ivy holds itself up with aerial roots that may damage mortar.

Boston ivy's tiny suction pads cling to a smooth surface.

Clematis 'Carnaby'

BIG-LEAF WINTER CREEPER

Euonymus fortunei 'Vegetus'
Evergreen perennial vine
Zones 4–9
6–18 inches tall
Blooms late spring to early summer
Inconspicuous creamy white flowers
Full sun to full shade
Well-drained average soil
Notes: Grown for its 2-inch oval leathery dark green leaves. Can form a 5-foot-tall shrub, but will also climb higher if given the opportunity. Fruits heavily.

ENGLISH IVY

Hedera helix
Evergreen perennial vine
Zones 7–10
8–18 feet tall
Blooms summer only when plant is mature
Bottlelike creamy green spikes of flowers
Full sun to full shade
Moist, humusy, well-drained soil
Notes: One of the most common groundcovers, it also climbs well. Roots easily along stem. Many variations of heart-shaped and bird's-foot leaves. Invasive.

MOONFLOWER

Ipomoea alba
Tender perennial grown as an annual vine
Zones 9–11
10–15 feet tall
Blooms early summer where hardy, late summer to frost elsewhere
Fragrant 5-inch funnel-shaped iridescent white flowers; night blooming
Full sun
Humusy to sandy, well-drained soil
Notes: Flowers open slowly at dusk. Perfect for an evening garden. Twiner.

CLEMATIS

Clematis hybrid 'Henryi'
Perennial vine
Zones 6–10
5–8 feet tall
Blooms summer
Large white to pale pink flowers
Full sun to partial shade
Moist, humusy, well-drained soil
Notes: Young foliage appears bronzed. Flowers have brown accent. Reblooms readily. Slow to become established, but worth the wait. Mulch well to keep the roots cool and moist.

GOLDEN HOP

Humulus lupulus 'Aureus'
Perennial vine
Zones 5–9
To 20 feet tall
Blooms summer
Unusual, conelike green flowers
Full sun to partial shade
Moist, humusy, well-drained soil; tolerates clay soil
Notes: Grapelike, 3- to 5-lobed golden to yellow-green leaves. Fast-growing twiner.

SWEET POTATO VINE

Ipomoea batatas
Perennial vine, generally grown as an annual
Zones 8–11
3–18 feet tall
Insignificant flowers
Grown for the brightly colored leaves—deep purple, chartreuse, or tricolor (pink, cream, and green)
Full sun to partial shade
Moist, humusy, well-drained soil
Notes: Attractive vines used in containers or as groundcovers.

COMMON MORNING GLORY

Ipomoea purpurea
Annual vine
To 8 feet tall
Blooms summer to frost
Funnel-shaped single or double flowers in hues of white, blue, pink, purple, or red
Full sun
Well-drained, fertile, average to dry soil
Notes: Three- to 5-inch heart-shaped leaves. Flowers unfurl as the morning light hits them; they close by midday and love heat. Twiner.

CYPRESS VINE

Ipomoea quamoclit
Annual vine
To 20 feet tall
Blooms summer to fall
Star-shaped tubular bright red flowers
Full sun to partial shade
Moist, well-drained, fertile soil
Notes: Morning glory relative with
1½-inch flowers that open in the afternoon.
Red flowers are ablaze in late-day sun.
Delicate, fernlike leaves.

GOLDFLAME HONEYSUCKLE

Lonicera x heckrottii
Perennial
Zones 5–9 (Zone 4 with winter protection)
8–12 feet tall
Blooms early summer (sporadically
   throughout the rest of summer)
Spikes of tubular rosy red (outside) and pale
   yellow to white (inside) flowers
Full sun to partial shade
Moist, well-drained, fertile soil
Notes: Also known as everblooming
honeysuckle. Handsome red fruit in autumn.

MANDEVILLA

Mandevilla x amabilis
Woody perennial vine
Zones 8–11
To 20 feet tall
Blooms summer
Fragrant funnel-shaped 2-inch white to
   cream flowers in clusters
Full sun to partial shade
Well-drained, fertile soil
Notes: Also known as Chilean jasmine.
Grown as an annual where it is not hardy.
Gardenia-scented blooms. Twiner.

VIRGINIA CREEPER

Parthenocissus quinquefolia
Perennial vine
Zones 3–9
8–20 feet tall
Inconspicuous flowers in summer
Full sun to partial shade
Moist, humusy, well-drained soil
Notes: Needs a smooth surface to climb.
Will not destroy masonry as English ivy does.
Gorgeous fall color as leaves turn orange, red,
or purple. The skeleton of the vine in winter
is handsome.

PASSIONFLOWER

Passiflora spp.
Perennial vine
Zones 7–11 (depending on variety)
4–12 feet tall
Blooms early summer to early fall
Showy red, blue, white, purple, or blue
   flowers with prominent stamens
Full sun to partial shade
Humusy, well-drained soil; tolerates clay
   and alkaline soil
Notes: Climbs by tendrils; support with string
or wire. Some varieties have edible fruit.

BLACK-EYED SUSAN VINE

Thunbergia alata
Annual vine
To 6 feet tall
Blooms summer through fall
Golden, yellow, or white flowers, usually
   with dark throats
Full sun to partial shade
Moist, well-drained, fertile garden soil
Notes: Fast-growing, twining vine. Excellent
as a container plant. Easily hides a chain link
fence or climbs a pillar.

CANARY CREEPER

Tropaeolum peregrinum
Annual vine
8–12 feet tall
Blooms summer to frost
Edible, frilled, bright yellow flowers that
   resemble tiny birds
Full sun to partial shade
Moist, humusy, well-drained soil
Notes: A dainty relative of nasturtium,
also with pungent, peppery flavored flowers.
Needs support. Quickly can hide a wall or
fence. Attractive leaves.

USEFUL VINES

The uses for vines are many. Included here are
fast-growing vines that will quickly screen out an
undesirable view (s), those that make good
groundcovers (g), and those that are evergreen
and provide year-round interest (e).

American bittersweet	*Celastrus scandens*	g, s
Bengal clock vine	*Thunbergia grandiflora*	e
Bougainvillea	*Bougainvillea glabra*	e
Cape honeysuckle	*Tecomaria capensis*	e, g
Carolina jessamine	*Gelsemium sempervirens*	e
Chinese matrimony vine	*Lycium chinense*	g
Cinnamon vine	*Dioscorea batatas*	e
Clematis	*Clematis* spp. & hybrids	g, s
Confederate jasmine	*Trachelospermum jasminoides*	s
Coral vine	*Antigonon leptopus*	e, s
Creeping fig	*Ficus pumila*	e, g, s
Cross vine	*Bignonia capreolata*	e, s
Cup-and-saucer vine	*Cobaea scandens*	s
Dutchman's pipe	*Aristolochia macrophylla*	s
Glorybower	*Clerodendrum* spp.	e
Golden hop	*Humulus lupulus* 'Aureus'	s
Golden trumpet	*Allamanda cathartica*	e
Gourds, melons	*Cucumis* spp. & cvs.	g
Grape	*Vitis* spp.	g
Kangaroo vine	*Cissus antarctica*	g, s
Moonseed	*Menispermum canadense*	g, s
Nasturtium	*Tropaeolum majus*	g
Rosary pea	*Abrus precatorius*	e, g
Trumpet vine	*Campsis radicans`*	s
Virginia creeper	*Parthenocissus quinquifolia*	g, s
Wax vine	*Senecio macroglossus*	g
Winter creeper	*Euonymus fortunei euonymus*	e, g
Wisteria	*Wisteria* spp.	s

Roses

There are about 10,000 varieties of roses in cultivation. Knowing a little about the types of roses can help you select the right one. Old Garden roses are any rose introduced before 1867 (unless a species). After that date—when 'La France', the first Hybrid Tea rose was introduced—roses are referred to as modern. Hybrid Teas have the classic pointed bud and long stem with a single bloom. Floribundas have clusters of flowers and are often shorter, making them useful in landscaping. Grandifloras are a cross between hybrid teas and floribundas and have properties of both—long-stemmed flowers that tend toward clusters.

Rugosa rose

LADY BANK'S ROSE

Rosa banksiae banksia
Shrub, Climbing rose
Zones 8 and 9
To 20 feet tall
Blooms late spring to early summer
Clusters of small lightly fragrant double soft-yellow flowers
Full to partial sun
Moist, well-drained, fertile soil
Notes: Romantic color and durable good looks. Evergreen leaves and thornless stems. Essential in period Southern gardens.

CECILE BRUNNER

Rosa 'Cecile Brunner'
Shrub, Polyantha rose
Zones 4–9 (Zone 4 with protection)
To 3 feet tall
Blooms late spring to early summer
Lightly fragrant pale pink flowers
Full sun
Moist, well-drained, fertile soil
Notes: An old-fashioned rose that is still popular—the Sweetheart Rose. Clusters of delicate flowers. Available as a climber.

CRESTED MOSS ROSE

Rosa x centifolia 'Cristata'
Shrub, Old Garden (Centifolia) rose
Zones 3–9 (Zone 3 with winter protection)
5–7 feet tall
Blooms early summer
Fragrant very double medium pink flowers
Full sun to partial shade
Moist, well-drained, fertile soil
Notes: Not a true Moss rose, but named for the mossy-looking fringe on the sepal margins that are most obvious in bud. Blooms profusely but does not rebloom.

CHRYSLER IMPERIAL

Rosa 'Chrysler Imperial'
Shrub, Hybrid Tea rose
Zones 5–9
To 5 feet tall
Blooms profusely early summer; reblooms
Fragrant velvety double deep-red flowers
Full sun
Moist, humusy, well-drained, fertile soil
Notes: Beloved for its rich, spicy fragrance and elegant, long-stemmed blooms. Opens to very full flowers. Semiglossy, dark green leaves. Good in warm climates.

CRIMSON RAMBLER

Rosa 'Crimson Rambler'
Shrub, Pillar rose
Zones 6–9
6–8 feet tall
Blooms late spring through summer
Double bright red flowers
Full sun
Moist, well-drained, fertile soil
Notes: Handsome trained on a pillar or an arbor, this rose will continue to provide color through the summer if deadheaded.

EUROPEANA

Rosa 'Europeana'
Shrub, Floribunda rose
Zones 5–9 (Zones 5 and 6 with winter mulch)
2–4 feet tall
Blooms late spring to fall
Deep crimson flowers in clusters
Full sun
Moist, well-drained, fertile soil
Notes: Handsome dark purplish stems and leaves. Attractive bushy plants look good in a formal or mixed border; also good as hedges or mass plantings.

FLOWER CARPET ROSE

Rosa Flower Carpet Red
Shrub, Landscape rose
Zones 6–9
18–36 inches tall
Blooms late spring to frost
Clusters of small red flowers
Full sun to partial shade
Moist, well-drained soil (grows in most soils)
Notes: A new introduction that is winning favor everywhere. Nonstop blooming; deadhead or shear plant. Graceful, arching habit makes it a good groundcover.

GERTRUDE JEKYLL

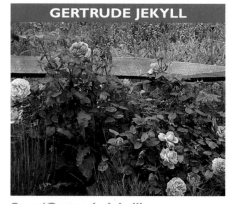

Rosa 'Gertrude Jekyll'
Shrub, David Austin rose
Zones 5–9
36–48 inches tall
Blooms late spring through fall
Fragrant fully double pink flowers
Full sun to partial shade
Moist, well-drained, fertile soil
Notes: One of the series of new English roses that have many of the attributes of Old Garden roses—very double flowers, fragrance, strong stems. Unlike the old varieties, these rebloom if deadheaded.

GRAHAM THOMAS

Rosa 'Graham Thomas'
Shrub, David Austin rose
Zones 5–9
6–18 inches tall
Blooms late spring through fall
Fragrant very double cheery yellow flowers
Full sun to partial shade
Moist, humusy, well-drained soil
Notes: The graceful growth habit makes it ideal for a mixed border or cottage garden.

JACOB'S COAT

Rosa 'Jacob's Coat'
Shrub, Climbing rose
Zones 5–9
8–10 feet tall
Blooms summer to early fall
Multihued double flowers change colors daily, starting yellow and maturing to red
Full sun
Moist, well-drained, fertile soil
Notes: Vigorous, upright climber is handsome on a fence or an arbor. Disease resistant; good rebloom; light fragrance.

MISTER LINCOLN

Rosa 'Mister Lincoln'
Shrub, Hybrid Tea rose
Zones 6–9
4–5 feet tall
Blooms late spring through fall
Highly fragrant velvety deep red flowers
Full sun
Moist, well-drained, fertile soil
Notes: A vigorous, well-branched shrub with continuous blooms (deadhead spent flowers). Rich fragrance and elegant flowers make this a good choice for cutting and exhibition.

WHITE RUGOSA ROSE

Rosa rugosa 'Alba'
Shrub rose
Zones 2–9
To 4 feet tall
Blooms late spring to summer
Lightly fragrant edible white flowers with prominent yellow stamens
Full sun
Well-drained soil; tolerates poor, dry soil
Notes: Large glossy red rose hips cling to the stout, thorny stems from fall into winter. Disease-resistant. Crinkled leaves.

WINGTHORN ROSE

Rosa sericea pteracantha
Shrub, species rose
Zones 6–9
5–8 feet tall
Blooms late spring to early summer
Single pale pink flowers
Full sun
Moist, well-drained, fertile soil
Notes: Grown for its thorns rather than its flowers. Triangular (up to ¾ inch) translucent crimson thorns are prominent on year-old branches. Site where sun can light the thorns.

SPARRIESHOOP

Rosa 'Sparrieshoop'
Shrub rose
Zones 4–8
To 5 feet tall
Blooms late spring through summer
Single light pink flowers
Full sun
Moist, well-drained, fertile soil
Notes: Despite its tough look, this is a good performer in the garden. Unlike Old Garden roses, it continues blooming throughout the season.

DISEASE-RESISTANT ROSES

Roses are thought of as tempermental plants—susceptible to black spot and mildew. However, there are resistant varieties listed below: black-spot resistance (b) and mildew resistance (m).

'Alchymist'	b, m
'Angel Face'	b
'Apothecary's Rose'	b, m
Apple rose	b, m
Beach rose	b, m
Bonica	b, m
'Carrousel'	b
'Cecile Brunner'	b, m
'Charisma'	m
'Chicago Peace'	m
Crested moss rose	b, m
'Duet'	b
'Europeana'	b
'Evening Star'	m
'Felicite Parmentier'	b, m
'First Edition'	b, m
Flower Carpet Red	b, m
'Futura'	m
'Gene Boerner'	b
'Ivory Fashion'	b
'Miss All-American Beauty'	b, m
'Mister Lincoln'	b, m
Pascali	m
'Peace'	b, m
'Pink Leda'	b, m
Pink Peace	b
'Pristine'	b, m
Queen Elizabeth	b, m
'Razzle Dazzle'	b, m
'Sarabande'	b
'Seashell'	m
'Souvenir de la Malmaison'	b, m

Shrubs

Shrubs may be evergreen or deciduous, needled or broad-leaved. Some are grown for their flowers or fruit, others for their foliage, form, or bark. Shrubs add height and depth to a garden beyond what perennials can provide.

Shrubs differ from trees in several significant ways. Shrubs are shorter—usually less than 20 feet tall. Shrubs generally are multistemmed, with their branches lower to the ground. Shrubs are easier to maintain because they are low enough to prune easily with a pole pruner or saw.

Butterfly bush

GLOSSY ABELIA

Abelia grandiflora
Semievergreen shrub
Zones 6–9
5–6 feet tall
Blooms midsummer to frost
Clusters of small funnel-shaped white flowers with red calyxes appearing pink
Full sun to partial shade
Humusy, well-drained, fertile, acid soil
Notes: Lovely as a specimen or massed in a mixed border combined with trees and broad-leaved evergreens. Glossy leaves.

BUTTERFLY BUSH

Buddleia davidii
Deciduous shrub
Zones 5–9
5–10 feet tall
Blooms summer to frost
Long clusters of fragrant purple, pink, magenta, or white flowers
Full sun to partial shade
Humusy, well-drained soil
Notes: Butterfly magnet. Flowers on new wood, so cut to 6 inches in spring. Remove spent flowers to promote continual bloom.

CHINESE BEAUTYBERRY

Callicarpa dichotoma
Deciduous shrub
Zones 5–8
4–6 feet tall
Blooms summer; berries in autumn
Pale purple flowers are not significant
Full sun to partial shade
Moist, humusy, well-drained soil
Notes: Bright purple berries appear in fall. Prune to 6 inches high every spring; it flowers on new wood. 'Leucocarpa' has white berries.

CALIFORNIA LILAC

Ceanothus spp.
Deciduous shrub
Zones 8–10
2–10 feet tall
Blooms in spring
Clusters of blue or purple flowers
Full sun to partial shade
Moist, humusy, well-drained soil
Notes: The warm climate, West Coast substitute for the true lilac (*Syringa* spp.). It has no fragrance, but it provides similar color in the spring garden.

CHINESE REDBUD

Cercis chinensis
Deciduous shrub
Zones 3–9
10–15 feet tall
Blooms late winter to early spring
Edible bright pink flowers are borne directly on the branches
Full sun to partial shade
Moist, well-drained soil
Notes: Spectacular in flower. Multistemmed. Good in the South and Midwest.

FLOWERING QUINCE

Chaenomeles spp.
Deciduous shrub
Zones 4–9
3–10 feet tall
Blooms early to midspring
Round 1½-inch flowers are scarlet, red, pink, or white with yellow centers
Full sun
Light to heavy soil
Notes: Its thorny branches zigzag and form a dense, twiggy mass that is showy in winter. Colorful leaves. Drought-tolerant.

REDTWIG DOGWOOD

Cornus alba 'Sibirica'
Deciduous shrub
Zones 2–7
7–9 feet tall
Blooms late spring
Clusters of small white flowers
Full sun
Moist, humusy soil
Notes: Use massed or in shrub border. Red twigs look striking against snow. Prune the branches yearly or every other year; brightest color is on new wood.

HARRY LAUDER'S WALKING STICK

Corylus avellana 'Contorta'
Deciduous shrub
Zones 4–8
8–10 feet tall
Blooms late winter to early spring
Pendulous creamy green catkins
Full sun
Moist, humusy, well-drained, acid soil
Notes: More attractive in winter without leaves to hide the crooked branches.

PURPLE SMOKE TREE

Cotinus coggygria 'Royal Purple'
Deciduous shrub
Zones 3–9
8–12 feet tall
Blooms summer to fall
Large puffs of tiny purplish flowers
Full sun
Moist, humusy, well-drained soil
Notes: Even after flowering, the structure holds interest. Regular pruning encourages deep color.

CAROL MACKIE DAPHNE

Daphne x burkwoodii 'Carol Mackie'
Evergreen to semievergreen shrub
Zones 5–8
To 3 feet tall
Blooms mid- to late spring
Loose clusters of fragrant small pale pink
flowers
Full sun to partial shade
Moist, well-drained, sandy soil
Notes: Slow-growing, short-lived shrub that
deserves a place in every garden. Handsome
oval cream-edged leaves.

WHITE ENKIANTHUS

Enkianthus perulatus
Deciduous shrub
Zones 5–8
8–15 feet tall
Blooms spring
Clusters of dainty bell-shaped
creamy yellow flowers with red stripes
Full sun to partial shade
Moist, humusy, acid soil
Notes: A slow-growing shrub with slender
layered branches with a graceful upturn;
makes a pretty silhouette in winter.

BURNING BUSH

Euonymus alatus
Shrub
Zones 4–8
10–15 feet tall
Blooms late spring to early summer
Clusters of small chartreuse flowers
Full sun to partial shade (best color in sun)
Moist, average to humusy, well-drained soil
Notes: Also known as winged euonymus and
winged spindle tree. This shrub puts on a fall
foliage display with bright red leaves that is
unrivaled by any other shrub.

FORSYTHIA

Forsythia spp.
Deciduous shrub
Zones 5–9
5–10 feet tall
Blooms early to midspring
Small yellow flowers along the branches
Full sun to partial shade
Moist, humusy, well-drained soil
Notes: Blooms on second-year wood. Prune
after it finishes flowering for optimal bloom
next year. Avoid shaping like a lollipop. Many
cultivars, some fragrant.

DWARF FOTHERGILLA

Fothergilla gardenii
Deciduous shrub
Zones 5–9
3–5 feet tall
Blooms early to midspring
Fragrant 2-inch-long creamy white
bottlebrushes at the ends of branches
Full sun to partial shade
Moist, humusy, well-drained, acid soil
Notes: Fall leaf color is a bonfire of bright
yellow, orange, and red. The dense mound of
crooked stems gives character in winter.

WITCH HAZEL

Hamamelis spp.
Deciduous shrub
Zones 5–9
To 15 feet tall
Blooms mid- to late winter
Fresh-scented ribbonlike yellow flowers
unfurl on warm, sunny days
Full sun to partial shade
Humusy, fertile, acid soil
Notes: Cut a small branch and bring inside
when blooming—it will scent a room.

FRAGRANT SHRUBS

Many shrubs are known for their lovely flowers,
some of which are delightfully fragrant. Add
fragrant shrubs that bloom at different times
to your garden. Space them at least 20 feet apart
so their scents don't clash.

American elder	*Sambucus canadensis*
Barberry	*Berberis* spp.
Butterfly bush	*Buddleia davidii*
Carolina allspice	*Calycanthus floridus*
Clove currant	*Ribes odoratum*
Dwarf fothergilla	*Fothergilla gardenii*
Exbury hybrid azalea	*Rhododendron* Exbury hyb.
February daphne	*Daphne mezereum*
Firethorn	*Pyracantha* spp.
Fragrant wintersweet	*Chimonanthus praecox*
Holly	*Ilex* spp.
Japanese skimmia	*Skimmia japonica*
Knap Hill azalea	*Rhododendron* Knap Hill hyb.
Korean forsythia	*Abeliophyllum distichum*
Korean spice viburnum	*Viburnum × carlcephalu*
Lilacs	*Syringa* spp.
Mockorange	*Philadelphus* spp.
Oregon grapeholly	*Mahonia aquifolium*
Privet	*Ligustrum* spp.
Rose daphne	*Daphne cneorum*
Scotch broom	*Cytisus scoparius*
Summersweet clethra	*Clethra alnifolia*
Swamp azalea	*Rhododendron viscosum*
Tatarian honeysuckle	*Lonicera tatarica*
Viburnum	*Viburnum* spp.
Winter daphne	*Daphne odora*
Winter hazel	*Corylopsis* spp.
Winter honeysuckle	*Lonicera fragrantissima*
Witch hazel	*Hamamelis* spp.

Shrubs *continued*

SEVEN-SON FLOWER

Heptacodium miconioides
Deciduous shrub
Zones 5–8
To 15 feet tall
Blooms late summer
Loose panicles of fragrant white flowers
Full sun
Moist, humusy, well-drained soil
Notes: A relatively new plant introduction in North America. Vase shape; multistemmed habit. Pink capsules follow flowers.

BIGLEAF HYDRANGEA

Hydrangea macrophylla
Deciduous shrub
Zones 6–9
2–8 feet tall
Blooms summer
Large flat-topped blue or pink flower clusters
Partial to light shade; protect from hot afternoon sun
Moist, humusy, well-drained, fertile soil
Notes: The more acidic the soil, the bluer the flowers; alkaline soil yields pink blooms.

JAPANESE HOLLY

Ilex crenata 'Convexa'
Evergreen shrub
Zones 5–8
To 9 feet tall
Blooms midspring
Dioecious—separate male and female plants each bear small fragrant creamy white flowers
Full sun to partial shade
Moist, humusy, well-drained, acid soil
Notes: Also known as small-leafed holly. Dense shrub; easily pruned to shape.

WINTER HONEYSUCKLE

Lonicera fragrantissima
Deciduous shrub
Zones 5–9
6–10 feet tall
Blooms late winter
Small lemon-scented creamy white flowers are not at all showy
Full sun to partial shade
Moist, well-drained, fertile soil
Notes: Also known as fragrant honeysuckle. An understated shrub, it is grown solely for its perfume in winter.

OREGON GRAPEHOLLY

Mahonia aquifolium
Evergreen shrub
Zones 5–8
36–48 inches tall
Blooms early spring
Pendulous clusters of sweetly fragrant yellow flowers
Partial sun to partial shade
Moist, humusy, well-drained soil
Notes: Handsome large hollylike leaves. Spring flowers are followed by small deep blue fruits that resemble Concord grapes.

RUSSIAN CYPRESS

Microbiota decussata
Evergreen shrub
Zones 3–8
24–36 inches tall
Insignificant bloom
Small (¼-inch), scaly cones
Full sun to partial shade
Moist, humusy, well-drained soil
Notes: Also known as Siberian cypress. Prostrate habit makes it a good choice for a groundcover or edge for garden or border. Aromatic, resinous foliage.

FIRETHORN

Pyracantha spp.
Evergreen shrub
Zones 6–9
6–12 feet tall, depending on variety
Blooms late spring
Clusters of small lightly scented creamy white flowers
Full sun
Moist, humusy to sandy, well-drained soil
Notes: Dense clusters of red, orange, or yellow berries from fall through winter.

INDIAN HAWTHORN

Rhaphiolepis indica
Evergreen shrub
Zones 8–10
To 3 feet tall
Blooms early spring
Small white flowers fade to pink at their centers
Full sun to partial shade
Humusy, well-drained soil
Notes: Rich green leaves give this shrub a lush look, even in driest weather. Excellent plant for low hedges.

AZALEA

Rhododendron spp.
Deciduous or evergreen shrub
Zones 5–8
2–6 feet tall
Blooms early spring to summer, depending on variety
White, pink to scarlet, yellow to orange, red, and purple to lilac flowers
Partial sun to full shade
Moist, humusy, well-drained, acid soil
Notes: Showy flowers, some scented, make these plants desirable for a shady place.

RHODODENDRON

Rhododendron spp.
Evergreen or deciduous shrub
Zones 5–8
3–10 feet tall, depending on variety
Blooms early spring to early summer, depending on variety
Large clusters (trusses) of flowers in hues of white, red, pink, lavender, yellow; some are fragrant
Partial shade
Moist, humusy, well-drained, acid soil
Notes: Striking woodland plant.

STAGHORN SUMAC

Rhus typhina
Deciduous shrub
Zones 3–9
12–18 feet tall
Blooms early summer
Conelike green flowers on females ripen as 8-inch seed-bearing fuzzy red clubs
Full sun to partial shade
Well-drained, average to rocky or sandy soil
Notes: A native shrub, it is best in informal or natural settings. Fall leaf color is outstanding red and scarlet.

VANHOUTTE SPIREA

Spiraea x vanhouttei
Deciduous shrub
Zones 3–8
To 7 feet tall
Blooms midspring
Cascades of 2-inch clusters of white flowers
Full sun
Moist, well-drained, fertile soil
Notes: Also known as bridalwreath. With its fountain shape and branches dripping with flowers, it deserves a place of honor in the garden.

COMMON LILAC

Syringa vulgaris
Deciduous shrub
Zones 4–8
To 20 feet tall
Blooms in spring
Clusters of fragrant lavender, white, pink, magenta, or violet flowers
Full sun
Moist, humusy, well-drained soil
Notes: Well-known for its heady fragrance and voluptuous blossoms.

WEEPING ENGLISH YEW

Taxus baccata 'Repandens'
Evergreen shrub
Zones 5–8 (Zone 5 with winter protection)
To 3 feet tall
Blooms late spring
Inconspicuous flowers
Full sun to full shade
Moist, well-drained, fertile, acid to alkaline soil
Notes: Excellent, gracefully arching habit. Flat needles are arranged in spirals around the stem. Good groundcover.

DOUBLE-FILE VIBURNUM

Viburnum plicatum f. tomentosum
Deciduous shrub
Zones 5–8
8–20 feet tall
Blooms late spring to early summer
Double row of single creamy white flowers along branches
Full sun to partial shade
Moist, humusy, well-drained soil
Notes: Horizontally spreading shrub that is elegant and eye-catching all year. Birds eat the bright red fruit in summer.

SHRUBS FOR MULTISEASON INTEREST

As much as we enjoy the blooms of many shrubs, they are fleeting. Look for shrubs that will provide interest for more than one season. This list includes shrubs with showy flowers (f), fruit (b), colorful fall foliage (l), interesting bark (i), a unique or pleasing form in winter (w), or those that are evergreen (e).

Azaleas	*Rhododendron* spp.	e, f
Barberry	*Berberis* spp.	b, l
Beautyberry	*Callicarpa* spp.	b, l
Camellias	*Camellia* spp.	f, e
Cotoneaster	*Cotoneaster* spp.	b, e, w
Enkianthus	*Enkianthus* spp.	f, l
Firethorn	*Pyracantha* spp.	f, b, e
Fothergilla	*Fothergilla* spp.	f, l
Glossy abelia	*Abelia × grandiflora*	f, l
Harry Lauder's walking stick	*Corylus avellana* 'Contorta'	f, w
Heavenly bamboo	*Nandina domestica*	b, l
Holly	*Ilex* spp.	f, w, e
Japanese skimmia	*Skimmia japonica*	f, b, e
Jetbead	*Rhodotypos scandens*	f, b
Oakleaf hydrangea	*Hydrangea quercifolia* (flowers dry on plant)	f, l, w
Oregon grapeholly	*Mahonia aquifolium*	f, b, l, e
Peegee hydrangea	*Hydrangea paniculata* 'Grandiflora' (flowers dry on plant)	f, l
Rhododendron	*Rhododendron* spp.	e, f
Smoke tree	*Cotinus coggygria*	f, l
Sumac	*Rhus* spp. (colorful seedpods persist)	l, b
Summersweet clethra	*Clethra alnifolia*	f, l
Viburnum	*Viburnum* spp.	f, b, l
Witch hazel	*Hamamelis* spp.	f, l

Small trees

Arbitrarily dividing trees into the catagories of small and large makes it easier to give you a sense of their full-grown size. Trees may be deciduous or evergreen, needled or broad-leaved. They are generally single-stemmed; branching begins up on the trunk.

Small trees are those less than 35 feet tall; large trees range from 40 to 80 feet or higher. A word of caution about dwarf conifers: Dwarf is relative to the size of the original tree.

Consider the space before choosing a tree. Select one that will fit the available space when mature without constant pruning.

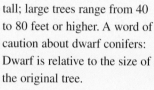

Kousa dogwood

JAPANESE MAPLE

Acer palmatum
Deciduous tree
Zones 6–8
5–25 feet tall
Blooms early to midspring
Airy, pendulous clusters of inconspicuous burgundy flowers
Full sun to partial shade
Moist, well-drained, humusy soil
Notes: Delicate foliage in shades of red. Numerous cultivars available.

SNAKEBARK MAPLE

Acer pennsylvanicum
Deciduous tree
Zones 3–7
20–30 feet tall
Inconspicuous flowers in spring
Partial to light shade
Moist, humusy, well-drained soil
Notes: Also known as striped maple or moosewood. Young trunks and branches have smooth dark green bark with prominent bright white stripes. Handsome bold-textured leaves.

PAWPAW

Asimina triloba
Deciduous tree
Zones 5–8
15–20 feet tall
Blooms midspring
1- to 2-inch inconspicuous purple flowers
Full sun
Moist, fertile, deep, slightly acid soil
Notes: Produces 2- to 5-inch-long edible yellow-green berries that ripen to brownish black. Fruit is fragrant and has a custardlike flavor and texture.

HORNBEAM

Carpinus spp.
Deciduous tree
Zones 3–9
20–30 feet tall
Blooms late spring
Inconspicuous flowers
Partial shade
Moist, well-drained, humusy, acid to alkaline soil; tolerates flooding
Notes: Also known as ironwood. This multitrunk native tree makes an excellent shade tree for small gardens.

CHINESE FRINGE TREE

Chionanthus retusus
Deciduous tree
Zones 6–9
15–20 feet tall
Blooms late spring
Clusters of honey-scented snow white flowers with hanging 1-inch petals
Full sun to light shade
Moist, rich, acid soil; tolerates average to dry conditions
Notes: Attractive, peeling gray-brown bark. Makes a good screen.

KOUSA DOGWOOD

Cornus kousa
Deciduous tree
Zones 5–8
15–20 feet tall
Blooms late spring to early summer
Four pointed white bracts give a starlike look
Full sun to part shade
Well-drained garden soil
Notes: A stunning all-season performer: showy raspberry-like red fruit in late summer; scarlet leaves in fall; attractive winter branching.

FRANKLIN TREE

Franklinia alatamaha
Deciduous tree
Zones 6–7
20–30 feet tall
Blooms late summer to fall
Large, camellia-like white flowers
Full sun to light shade
Moist, humusy, well-drained, acid soil
Notes: Now extinct in the wild, this southeastern native woodland tree was named after Benjamin Franklin. Fall foliage is gorgeous wine red and gold.

VIRGINIA SWEETSPIRE

Itea virginica
Semievergreen tree (evergreen in mild climates)
Zones 5–9
3–5 feet tall
Blooms summer
Racemes of fragrant white flowers
Full sun to partial shade
Moist, fertile soil
Notes: Breathtaking fall foliage—reddish purple to scarlet and crimson. Blooms when not much else does.

CRAPE MYRTLE

Lagerstroemia indica
Deciduous tree
Zones 7–10
15–25 feet tall
Blooms summer to early fall
Large clusters of small white to pink to red flowers
Full sun to partial shade
Humusy, well-drained soil
Notes: Attractive, sinuous bark adds winter interest. Can be trained in either shrub or tree form. New varieties are hardier.

STAR MAGNOLIA

Magnolia stellata
Deciduous tree
Zones 5–9
15–20 feet tall
Blooms late winter to early spring
Fragrant many-petaled starry white flowers
Full sun to partial shade
Moist, humusy, rich, deep, acid soil
Notes: Gray-barked branches are decorated with furry silver buds in winter. Early flowers are often blasted by frost, turning brown.

PERSIAN MEDLAR

Mespilus germanica
Deciduous tree
Zones 5–8
To 20 feet tall
Blooms late spring to early summer
1- to 1½-inch white to lightly blushed pink flowers
Full sun
Any well-drained soil
Notes: Also known as showy mespilus. Edible fruit, good for jelly. Ripens late; requires cold weather or frost for flavor.

SOURWOOD

Oxydendrum arboreum
Deciduous tree
Zones 5–8
40–75 feet tall after many years
Blooms midsummer
Hanging panicles of small white flowers
Full sun to partial shade
Well-drained garden soil
Notes: Slow-growing with a pyramidal shape; remains a small tree for many years. Beautiful in autumn as the leaves turn scarlet and highlight the dangling clusters of small dried fruit capsules.

DWARF ALBERTA SPRUCE

Picea glauca 'Conica'
Dwarf evergreen tree
Zones 3–7
6–10 feet tall
Insignificant blooms
Full sun to light shade
Moist, humusy, well-drained soil
Notes: Slow-growing evergreen; perfect for a large container or a small garden. Silvery blue needles. Protect from harsh wind and winter snow.

CHERRY PLUM

Prunus cerasifera
Deciduous tree
Zones 5–8
15–30 feet tall
Blooms early spring
Fragrant pink flowers
Full sun
Humusy, well-drained, fertile soil
Notes: Also known as purple-leaf plum. Deep-purple foliage holds all season. Prune after it finishes flowering.

FLOWERING TREES

Trees are valuable additions to any property—for their size, the shade they provide, and their elegant form. Some trees also have showy flowers, which add interest in spring or early summer. Those that are fragrant are noted with an asterisk (*).

* Acacia	*Acacia* spp.
Beebee tree	*Evodia danielli*
* Black locust	*Robinia pseudoacacia*
Bottlebrush buckeye	*Aesculus parviflora*
Camphor tree	*Cinnamomum camphora*
Carolina silverbell	*Halesia tetraptera*
Catalpa	*Catalpa* spp.
Dogwood	*Cornus* spp.
Dove tree	*Davidia involucrata*
* Empress tree	*Paulownia tomentosa*
Flowering cherry, plum, peach	*Prunus* spp.
Flowering crabapple	*Malus* spp.
* Fragrant snowbell	*Styrax obassia*
Franklin tree	*Franklinia alatamaha*
Goldenchain tree	*Laburnum* × *watereri*
* Golden rain tree	*Koelreuteria paniculata* *
Hawthorn	*Crataegus* spp.
* Japanese tree lilac	*Syringa reticulata*
Japanese snowbell	*Styrax japonicum*
Leatherwood	*Dirca palustris*
* Linden	*Tilia* spp.
* Magnolia	*Magnolia* spp.
Mountain ash	*Sorbus* spp.
Palo verde	*Parkinsonia florida*
* Russian olive	*Elaeagnus angustifolia*
Serviceberry	*Amelanchier* spp.
Silk tree	*Albizia julibrissin*
* Snowbell	*Styrax* spp.
*Virginia sweetspire	*Itea virginica*
White fringe tree	*Chionanthus virginicus*
*Yellowwood	*Cladrastis* spp.

Large trees

Large trees are usually used as specimen or single plants placed to show them off to their best advantage. Many properties are not large enough to support a large tree—physically or aesthetically.

However, large trees have been planted in many new housing developments. Perhaps that is for the immediate appeal of something more than a sapling. If one is on your property, consider the eventual size—height, spread, and root zone. You may find that the time to remove it is now, and plant a more appropriate size tree instead.

Black gum

BOX ELDER

Acer negundo
Deciduous tree
Zones 2–8
30–50 feet tall
Blooms early spring
Dioecious—yellow-green male and female
    flowers develop as pendulous clusters on
    separate trees
Full sun to light shade
Wet or dry, alkaline soil; tolerates flooding
Notes: A picturesque, craggy tree suited
to difficult sites.

OHIO BUCKEYE

Aesculus glabra
Deciduous tree
Zones 3–8
To 30 feet or more
Blooms midspring
4- to 7-inch spires of greenish yellow to
    pink flowers
Full sun to light shade
Moist, humusy, slightly acid soil
Notes: Also known as buckeye. Prickly fruits
open to reveal brown (poisonous) nuts. A
striking shade tree.

NORFOLK ISLAND PINE

Araucaria heterophylla
Evergreen tree
Zone 10
30–40 feet tall
Inconspicuous bloom
Full sun
Moist, well-drained soil
Notes: Grown as a houseplant in many
areas, it is spectacular in the outdoors in its
full glory. Tiers of branches with upfacing
needles give an unusual effect. Related to the
hardier monkey puzzle tree.

HERITAGE RIVER BIRCH

Betula nigra 'Heritage'
Deciduous tree
Zones 4–9
30–40 feet tall or higher
Catkins in early spring
Full sun to partial shade
Moist, humusy, acid soil; tolerates clay and
    wet, or periodic flooding.
Notes: Often has multiple trunks. Bark peels
off in curling, papery sheets. Especially
handsome when planted in groupings.

AMERICAN YELLOWWOOD

Cladrastis lutea
Deciduous tree
Zones 4–8
30–50 feet tall
Blooms mid- to late spring
Pendulous panicles of fragrant white flowers
Full sun
Moist, well-drained soil
Notes: Multiseason interest. Leaves open
bright yellowish green, change to bright green
in summer and golden yellow in fall.

AMERICAN PERSIMMON

Diospyros virginiana
Deciduous tree
Zones 4–8
To 75 feet tall
Insignificant blooms
Orange fruit, edible after frost
Full sun to partial shade
Well-drained soil
Notes: Dioecious—fruits only on female
trees. Majestic, especially mature trees
with pendulous branches. Lovely yellow
foliage in autumn.

GREEN ASH

Fraxinus pennsylvanica
Deciduous tree
Zones 3–9
50–60 feet tall
Blooms midspring
Inconspicuous clusters of green to
    reddish-purple flowers
Full sun
Adapts to most soils; tolerates infertile soil,
    drought, salt, and alkaline conditions
Notes: Foliage turns a brilliant yellow
in early fall.

GINGKO

Gingko biloba
Deciduous tree
Zones 4–8
To 80 feet tall
Inconspicuous flowers
Full sun
Deep, well-drained soil; pH adaptable; tolerates road salt
Notes: Fan-shaped leaves turn brilliant yellow in late fall. The tree is open and airy, a picturesque framework of massive, irregular branches that casts only light shade.

CAROLINA SILVERBELL

Halesia tetraptera
Deciduous tree
Zones 4–8
30–80 feet tall
Blooms midspring
Pendulous clusters of bell-shaped white flowers
Full sun to partial shade
Moist, well-drained, rich, acid soil
Notes: Also known as silverbell. Dark yellowish-green leaves turn yellow in early autumn.

EASTERN RED CEDAR

Juniperus virginiana
Evergreen tree
Zones 4–8
To 90 feet tall
Insignificant blooms
Bluish berries on female plants
Full sun to partial shade
Most soils; performs in poor, gravelly soil
Notes: Dioecious. Wood is highly fragrant, used to make pencils. In the South, trees are broadly pyramidal; in the North, they are more narrow and do not grow as tall.

GOLDEN RAIN TREE

Koelreuteria paniculata
Deciduous tree
Zones 5–9
30–40 feet tall
Blooms midsummer
Panicles of showy yellow flowers
Full sun
Adapts to most soil types, even very alkaline; drought-tolerant
Notes: Attractive seedpods resemble Japanese lanterns. Leaves turn golden-orange in autumn.

TULIP TREE

Liriodendron tulipifera
Deciduous tree
Zones 3–9
70–90 feet tall; can grow to 150 feet
Blooms late spring to early summer
Unique tulip-shaped green, yellow, and orange flowers are often not seen because the branches are high up the trunk
Full sun
Humusy, well-drained, slightly acid soil
Notes: Excellent fall color—yellow to golden yellow. An aristocrat among trees.

KOBUS MAGNOLIA

Magnolia kobus
Deciduous tree
Zones 4–8
30–40 feet tall
Blooms early spring
Slightly fragrant 4-inch white flowers with a faint purple line at outside of base
Full sun
Moist, humusy, well-drained soil
Notes: Can bloom as early as star magnolia. Easily propagated from cuttings.

BLACK GUM

Nyssa sylvatica
Deciduous tree
Zones 5–9
30–50 feet tall
Blooms late spring to early summer
Inconspicuous flowers followed in autumn by blue berries that by blue attract birds
Full sun to partial shade
Moist to wet, humusy, acid soil
Notes: Also known as black tupelo, sour gum, and pepperidge. Excellent fall color.

TREES FOR FALL COLOR

Many trees have leaves that change color in the fall. Plan your autumn palette with this list.

YELLOW

American yellowwood	*Cladrastis lutea*
Birch	*Betula* spp.
Bottlebrush buckeye	*Aesculus parviflora*
Dove tree	*Davidia involucrata*
Hedge maple	*Acer campestre*
Red horsechestnut	*Aesculus carnea*

ORANGE

Crape myrtle	*Lagerstroemia indica* (may be red or yellow, depending on variety)
Paperbark maple	*Acer griseum*
Stewartia	*Stewartia* spp.

ORANGE TO YELLOW

European hornbeam	*Carpinus betulus*
Red maple	*Acer rubrum*

RED TO ORANGE

Amur maple	*Acer tataricum ginnala*
Black gum (tupelo)	*Nyssa sylvatica*
Downy serviceberry	*Amelanchier arborea*
Flowering dogwood	*Cornus florida*
Japanese maple	*Acer palmatum*
Kousa dogwood	*Cornus kousa*
Sassafras	*Sassafras albidum*
Sourwood	*Oxydendrum arboreum*
Sugar maple	*Acer saccharum*

RED TO YELLOW

Katsura tree	*Cercidiphyllum japonicum*

PURPLISH

White ash	*Fraxinus americana*

GLOSSARY

accent - the use of a plant or object to draw attention to or punctuate a space. This type of feature is usually in contrast with its surroundings, which helps it stand out.

annual - a plant that germinates, grows, flowers, and dies in a single season. Annuals need to be planted anew each year.

baffle - a built structure or planting that slightly obstructs the view into or out of an area. It can also be used to hide objects such as a utility meter.

balance - the visual weight of the garden as measured on either side of a real or imaginary line in the garden.

ball and burlap - also balled and burlapped. The wrapping of the root ball of a field-grown tree or shrub in a single piece of burlap, usually held together with twine. The organic nature of the material allows it to be left in the hole when planted. However, synthetics that look very similar to burlap but don't decompose should be removed completely.

base map - a scale drawing of a piece of property that includes all important fixed objects, such as setbacks, easements, and plantings. It is best drawn to scale on graph paper.

beam - the unit of lumber upon which decking or roofing is typically attached. May be a 2×10 or 4×12, used in building large structures.

beneficial insect - an insect that has positive value in the garden because it preys upon harmful insects, pollinates plants, or does both.

biennial - a plant that germinates and grows vegetatively during its first year, then sets seed, flowers, and dies during the second growing season.

bubble diagram - crudely shaped drawings on a base map that indicate general use areas of a piece of property. This part of the design is created between a site inventory and analysis and the preliminary designs.

building code - rules, regulations, and laws determining exactly where and how a structure or feature is to be built, who is allowed to do the work, and whether any inspections are required along the way.

bulb - a fleshy underground plant structure that contains the nutrients, energy, and "seed" to produce a plant. Also any plant (perennial) that grows from a bulb. Bulbs are typically buried in the ground at least one season before they emerge. Tulips, daffodils, and lilies are common examples of bulbs.

canopy - a solid or nonsolid overhead covering. The woven scaffold of tree branches or the open lattice of an arbor are two examples of a canopy.

catch basin - a grated structure used to capture surface drainage, which is then channeled elsewhere.

color - a design element. Color is broken down into warm and cool, as well as complementary and contrasting. The warm colors are orange, red, and yellow; the cool colors are blue, green, and violet. Complementary colors are adjacent to each other on the color wheel. Contrasting colors are opposite each other on the color wheel.

compost - decayed organic material. Healthy compost comprises a variety of green materials (grass clippings, foliage, and weeds) and brown material (dead leaves, shredded limbs, and thatch).

contour - the line created when traced along the base map or site plan at a specific elevation (height above sea level).

contrast - a principle of design that emphasizes the difference between a plant or an object and its surroundings.

deciduous plant - a plant that has a dormant season (most often winter) that is preceded by a shedding of all foliage. New foliage grows back each year. Deciduous trees and shrubs are the primary sources of fall color.

decking - wood planking placed on top of beams to form a solid surface, such as a deck or path.

detention pond - a lined or unlined hole in which surface drainage is captured, held temporarily, and then released steadily.

drainage - the movement of water across a piece of property. Drainage is divided into two basic types: surface drainage, which is visible and aboveground or on top of surfaces such as a roof, patio, or drive, and subsurface drainage, which occurs belowground.

drain field - the configuration of surface swales and subsurface drain lines necessary to adequately gather and direct all the drainage on a piece of property.

drip irrigation - an irrigation system that uses low volumes of low-pressure water emitted drip by drip at the base of a plant. This is the most economical and efficient way to water.

easement - the right-of-way claimed by a municipality or utility, usually described as a number of feet from the edge of a road or property line within which the owner of the easement has certain rights and limitations.

edging - a permanent, hard material set in place to create a crisp edge between areas of the garden. Most typically it is used between a lawn and a flower bed.

espalier - pruning and wiring woody trees and shrubs against a surface to create a specific shape; also the shape itself.

evergreen - a plant (perennial, tree, or shrub) that does not lose its leaves seasonally. Most evergreens have foliage the entire year.

final design - the culmination of a site analysis, site inventory, program, conceptual designs, and preliminary designs. The final design is a plan-view drawing for the entire project.

finial - a decorative piece that goes on top of a post. Commonly used on fences, it can also be used on arbors and pergolas.

fire ring - a circle of stones or brick set on the ground or a terrace and used in the same manner as an outdoor fireplace.

footing - a concrete foundation that extends below the frost line of the soil upon which a masonry structure is built.

form - an element of design; form is the general shape of a plant or object.

formal design - also known as symmetrical design; involves balance in a planting plan with equal parts on each side of a real or an imaginary axis. Formal designs usually incorporate geometric shapes and straight lines.

foundation planting - plantings along the base of the house that help tie the structure to the garden or mask an unsightly foundation.

fountain head - an attachment to a submersible pump that regulates the volume and shape of the spray.

framing - framing creates solid borders for a structure such as a deck or terrace. In landscaping, it is the establishment of visual boundaries that direct or frame a view.

frost depth - the depth below the soil line that will freeze in winter. This is typically the depth at which a footing must be poured.

grid - a series of equal-sized squares used to create a base map. Each square of a grid can be scaled to a certain size.

hardiness zone - Established by the U.S. Department of Agriculture. The United States and Canada comprise 11 zones, based on average to low temperatures in winter. The hardiness of a plant—the range of zones in which it will grow most successfully—is listed on plant labels and in mail-order catalogs, books, and most gardening magazines.

harmony - a principle of design achieved by having a pleasing combination of all the elements of design. It is synonymous with unity.

header - a row of bricks that crosses a path or drive perpendicular to the direction in which the path is headed. Used to slow design movement along a walk or drive and to add visual interest.

informal design - an approach to design that does not require equal parts on both sides of a design. It uses asymmetrical balance and curving, natural lines instead of geometric shapes.

IPM - the acronym for integrated pest management— a holistic approach that includes chemical controls, but only as a last resort.

joist - lumber—usually a 2×10 or a 2×12—attached to beams to form the area for a deck or roof and on which decking is attached.

knot garden - a type of formal garden design in which lines of different-colored or -textured shrubs appear to weave in and out of each other. The spaces between the plants are often filled with colored stone, mulch, or seasonal annuals.

labyrinth - a design that is created on the ground. Unlike a maze, a labyrinth has a single meandering path that leads to the center and back. There are no dead ends and no walls or hedges. The path is delineated by low-growing plants, bricks, or another material that contrasts with the path.

landscape architect - a formally trained and licensed professional whose expertise includes residential design. As a rule, a landscape architect is the best-equipped professional for designing large garden projects such as drainage, driveways, large decks, or terraces. They work with contractors on the implementation of the project.

landscape contractor - skilled craftsperson who implements the design that you or a landscape architect develop.

landscape fabric - a synthetic material that allows water to pass through but blocks light, soil, and weed roots from penetrating. An ideal base for mulch or a gravel bed.

lath - thin strips of wood attached to the beams of an overhead structure in a manner that creates dappled shade on the surface beneath it.

light - an element of design used to create patterns and accent an area. Shadows, another function of light, can also be used to create patterns.

line - an element of design used to lead the eye, define shapes, and create different areas of the garden.

line level - a device—about the thickness of a fountain pen—that you can hook onto a taut horizontal piece of string to see if the string is level. Useful in maintaining straight lines when attaching pickets on a fence or when pruning a hedge.

low-voltage lighting - a lighting fixture (or system of fixtures) that operates on 12 volts instead of the standard 120-volt household current. Compared to standard light fixtures, low-voltage fixtures are easier to install and less expensive, and there is no risk of electrical shock.

master plan - the fusion of the program and the final design. A master plan is the most important key to a successful garden. It is the road map by which you will implement the final design.

maze - a formal garden planting, usually of evergreen shrubs, that forms a matrix of paths that lead from the outer entrance to the center of the square, rectangle, or circle. Unlike a labyrinth, which has one path, a maze includes wrong turns and dead ends, so the route to the center is not self-evident. Typically, a maze has walls or hedges at least head height that make it impossible to see the destination.

mulch - a covering for soil used to retain soil moisture, prevent erosion, maintain soil temperature, and prevent weeds. Mulch can be organic (compost, shredded bark, leaf mold, straw, nut hulls), which breaks down in time and adds nourishment to the soil, or it can be inorganic—gravel, sand, stones, or even bits of broken clay pots.

nitrogen - one of three essential nutrients (phosphorus and potassium are the others) for healthy plants. Nitrogen fuels vegetative growth. On fertilizer packages, it is the N in N-P-K.

organic - materials that are or once were living and are free of chemicals.

pattern - an element of design that refers to repeated shapes or forms, whether on the ground plane (two-dimensional) or in upright structures and plants (three-dimensional).

percolation test - a simple test to check the rate at which water is absorbed by or percolates into and through soil.

perennial - an herbaceous or semiwoody plant that comes back every year. Most perennials are flowering plants; others rely on foliage for their value.

pergola - a freestanding structure with a roof or lath canopy designed to cast shade.

pH - a term used to describe the ionic balance of soil that affects the availability of plant nutrients. The ideal pH for most plants is between 6.0 and 7.0.

phasing - the order in which a master plan is implemented. Phasing can vary from the order of work in a given week to over several years.

phosphorus - one of the three essential nutrients plants require. Phosphorus promotes fruiting and flowering. On fertilizer packages, it is the P in N-P-K.

plat - a legal document that shows the property lines and any fixed structures. This serves as a starting point for developing a base map.

potassium - one of the three essential nutrients required for plant growth. Potassium promotes root growth and disease resistance. Also known as potash. On fertilizer packages, it is the K in N-P-K.

preliminary design - crude designs used to try different approaches to solving garden design challenges. Typically three or four preliminary designs are drawn; then the best is selected to develop a single final design.

program - a list of specific features, activities, or other attributes you want your garden to have.

repetition - an element of design achieved when the same materials or elements of design are used over and over.

retaining wall - a structure made of wood, stone, or masonry used to hold back soil, usually for the purpose of creating a level area in front of or behind the wall.

retention pond - a hole dug to capture and hold surface drainage.

rhythm - a principle of design similar to repetition. It refers to how the various elements of design are combined.

rise - the term used to describe the height of an individual step in a set of stairs.

rod - part of a rod and transit system, the rod is an expandable pole (typically ranging from 8–20 feet) with feet and inches clearly marked for measuring slopes and grades.

run - the term used to describe the length from the front edge of a step to the back edge of a step in a set of stairs.

runnel - a long, narrow channel, typically lined with stone and containing still or moving water.

scale - a principle of design referring to the relative size of an area or object in relation to its surroundings.

screen - a built structure or planting designed and placed to block the view into or out of an area or to block the view of a specific object or structure. Screens can be solid, or open to allow some light and wind through.

setback - the required distance from a property line to the point where a structure or planting can be placed. A guideline established by each municipality that should be verified prior to any work.

shape - an element of design similar to form in that it refers to the general outline of a plant or structure.

site analysis - the study and evaluation of existing site conditions. This follows a site inventory and includes nonphysical features such as views, smells, and sound.

site inventory - a listing of all physical aspects of the property.

slope - the difference in height between two points, usually given in a ratio such as 1:4, which means the ground drops 1 vertical foot for every 4 feet of horizontal distance.

soil polymer - a synthetic material typically made of silica that is mixed into soil and absorbs and holds water until the surrounding soil dries out. This is useful in containers and small beds but is not practical for large areas.

soil structure - the physical texture and content of the soil independent of nutrition. Structure impacts the way a soil drains and holds onto moisture.

soil test - a simple process by which the basic nutrients, elements, and pH of a soil can be determined. You should test soil prior to amending it.

specimen plant - an individual tree or shrub that is selected, tended, and placed to be viewed as a sculptural form.

staking - the securing of a tree or large shrub using rope or guy wires and wood stakes to hold it in place after planting and usually left in place for one year.

sucker - a volunteer offshoot of a tree or shrub that arises from the base of the plant. Sometimes called a water sprout. These should be removed to maintain a strong main trunk.

terracing - creating one or a series of level areas on a sloped site. Terracing usually involves building retaining walls to hold the soil in place.

texture - an element of design that is both tactile (the way a plant or other object feels) and visual (whether it looks fine, medium, or coarse).

transit - a tool used in conjunction with a rod to measure slopes and grades. A transit resembles a telescope and is mounted on a tripod from which you take readings marked on the rod.

trellis - a structure that is freestanding or attached to a wall or other surface that has an open form upon which plants are often grown.

trompe l'oeil - otherwise known as "fooling the eye," this technique involves false perspective or mirrors arranged to create an illusion. This is frequently used to make a space feel bigger than it really is or to create the element of surprise.

unity - a principle of design that refers to the overall harmony of the landscape and how well the various components work together.

weep hole - small drainage outlet at the base of a retaining wall that allows water to seep out and prevents the buildup of water pressure that may damage the wall.

xeriscape - a seven step approach to landscaping that is designed to reduce maintenance and the need for resources such as water and insecticides.

Metric conversions

U.S. Units to Metric Equivalents

to convert from	multiply by	to get
Inches	25.400	Millimeters
Inches	2.540	Centimeters
Feet	30.480	Centimeters
Feet	0.3048	Meters
Yards	0.9144	Meters
Square inches	6.4516	Square centimeters
Square feet	0.0929	Square meters
Square yards	0.8361	Square meters
Acres	0.4047	Hectares
Cubic inches	16.387	Cubic centimeters
Cubic feet	0.0283	Cubic meters
Cubic feet	28.316	Liters
Cubic yards	0.7646	Cubic meters
Cubic yards	764.550	Liters

To convert from degrees Celsius (C) to degrees Fahrenheit (F), multiply by $\frac{9}{5}$, then add 32.

Metric Units to U.S. Equivalents

to convert from	multiply by	to get
Millimeters	0.0394	Inches
Centimeters	0.3937	Inches
Centimeters	0.0328	Feet
Meters	3.2808	Feet
Meters	1.0936	Yards
Square centimeters	0.1550	Square inches
Square meters	10.764	Square feet
Square meters	1.1960	Square meters
Hectares	2.4711	Acres
Cubic centimeters	0.0610	Cubic inches
Cubic meters	35.315	Cubic feet
Liters	0.0353	Cubic feet
Cubic meters	1.308	Cubic yards
Liters	0.0013	Cubic yards

To convert from degrees Fahrenheit (F) to degrees Celsius (C), first subtract 32, then multiply by $\frac{5}{9}$.

HARDINESS ZONE AND FROST DATE MAPS

The three maps shown here will help you determine the right plants for your garden. The first is the hardiness zone map, established by the United States Department of Agriculture. On this map, the United States and Canada comprise 11 zones, based on average low temperatures in winter. The hardiness of a plant—the range of zones in which it will grow—is usually listed on plant labels and in mail-order catalogs, gardening magazines, and books. If you live on the edge of two zones, use the lower numbered zone to be safe.

The other two maps show average first and last frost dates. This is useful when planning beds for cold-sensitive annuals and vegetable gardens.

Every site has a microclimate created by a range of factors, so your garden may not exactly match the zones shown here.

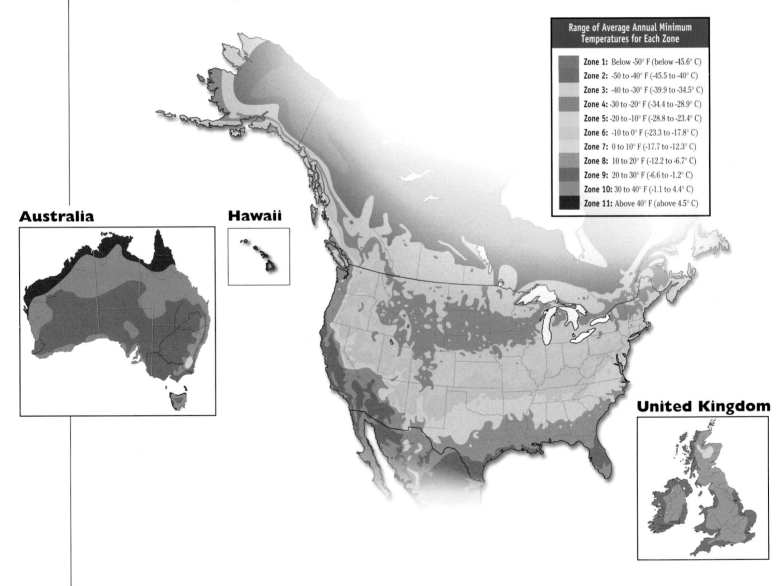

Australia

Hawaii

United Kingdom

Range of Average Annual Minimum Temperatures for Each Zone

Zone 1: Below -50° F (below -45.6° C)
Zone 2: -50 to -40° F (-45.5 to -40° C)
Zone 3: -40 to -30° F (-39.9 to -34.5° C)
Zone 4: -30 to -20° F (-34.4 to -28.9° C)
Zone 5: -20 to -10° F (-28.8 to -23.4° C)
Zone 6: -10 to 0° F (-23.3 to -17.8° C)
Zone 7: 0 to 10° F (-17.7 to -12.3° C)
Zone 8: 10 to 20° F (-12.2 to -6.7° C)
Zone 9: 20 to 30° F (-6.6 to -1.2° C)
Zone 10: 30 to 40° F (-1.1 to 4.4° C)
Zone 11: Above 40° F (above 4.5° C)

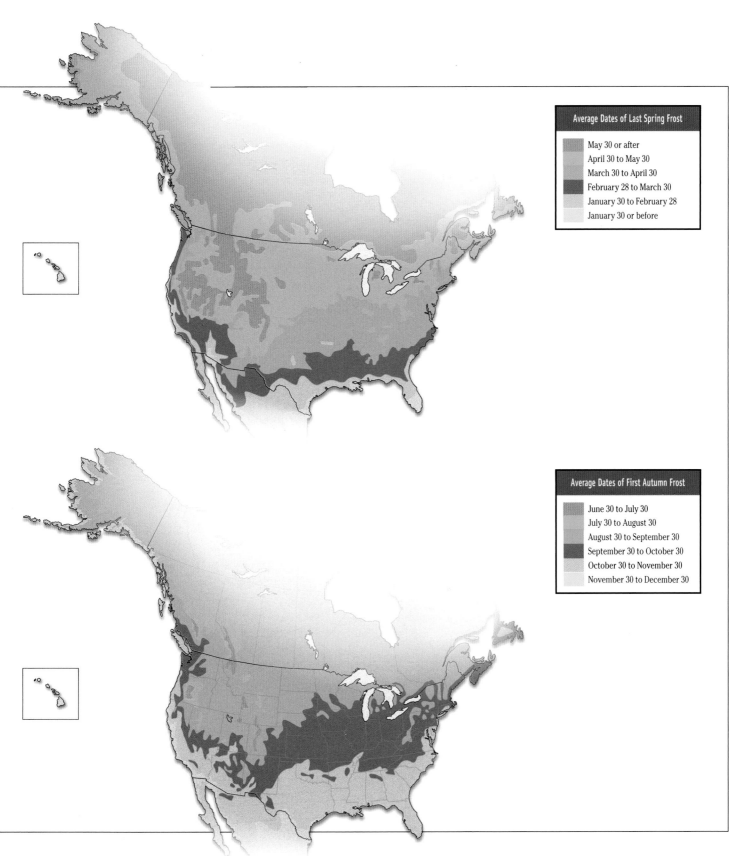

Average Dates of Last Spring Frost

- May 30 or after
- April 30 to May 30
- March 30 to April 30
- February 28 to March 30
- January 30 to February 28
- January 30 or before

Average Dates of First Autumn Frost

- June 30 to July 30
- July 30 to August 30
- August 30 to September 30
- September 30 to October 30
- October 30 to November 30
- November 30 to December 30

RESOURCES

American Association of Botanic Gardens and
Arboretum (AABGA)
351 Longwood Road
Kennett Square, PA 19348
610-925-2500
www.aabga.org
A source for the location and collections found at
botanical gardens and arboreta across the country.

American Concrete Institute (ACI)
38800 Country Club Drive
P.O. Box 9094
Farmington Hills, MI 48333
248-848-3708
www.aci-int.net
A source for information on concrete
products and techniques.

American Horticulture Society (AHS)
7931 East Boulevard Drive
Alexandria, VA 22308
703-768-5700
www.ahs.com
A good source for information about plant hardiness,
new plant releases, and other horticultural information.
Their website has an excellent list of gardening
websites and other resources.

American Nurserymen and Landscape Association
(ANLA)
1250 I Street NW, Suite 500
Washington, DC 20005-3922
202-789-2900
A source for locating certified growers and purveyors
of plants in your area.

American Rose Society (ARS)
P.O. Box 30,000
Shreveport, LA 71130-0030
318-938-5402
www.ars.org
The source for information on growing roses.

American Society of Landscape Architects (ASLA)
636 Eye Street NW
Washington, DC 20001-3736
202-898-2444
www.asla.org
A source for locating licensed professional garden
designers in your area.

Associated Landscape Contractors of America (ALCA)
150 Elden Street, Suite 270
Herndon, VA 20170
703-736-9666
www.alca.org
A source for locating landscape contractors.

Association of Professional Landscape Designers
(APLD)
1924 North Second Street
Harrisburg, PA 17102
www.apld.org
An alternate source for garden designers.

Bedding Plants International
525 S.W. 5th Street/Suite A
Des Moines, IA 50309
800-647-7742
A source for information on annuals.

Environmental Protection Agency (EPA)
Ariel Rios Building
1200 Pennsylvania Avenue, NW
Washington, DC 20460
202-260-2090
www.epa.gov
Good for checking the latest data on the safety of
various products, such as insecticides and pesticides.
This site also has links to the U.S. Department of
Agriculture, which offers information on climate
and soils.

National Arborist Association (NAA)
3 Perimeter Road, Unit 1
Manchester, NH 03103
800-733-2622
www.natlarb.com
The source for locating certified arborists.

National Garden Clubs, Inc.
4401 Magnolia Avenue
St. Louis, MO 63110
314-776-7574
www.gardenclub.org
A source for locating garden clubs
in your area.

National Gardening Association
1100 Dorset Street
Burlington, VT 05403
800-538-7476
www.garden.org
A good, general-purpose source for information
related to gardening.

National Pond Society
4627 Summer Oak Avenue E., Apt. 1028
Sarasota, FL 34243
941-358-1755
www.pondscapes.com
A source for products and the latest methods for
creating a backyard pond garden.

Netherlands Flower Bulb Information Center
30 Midwood Street
Brooklyn, NY 11225
www.bulb.com
A source for information on flower bulbs.

Perennial Plant Association
3383 Schirtzinger Road
Hilliard, OH 43026
614-771-8431
www.perennialplant.org
A source for the latest information on how a
specific plant performs in your region and where
to acquire plants.

Seed Savers Exchange
3076 North Winn Road
Decorah, IA 52101
www.seedsavers.org
A source of seeds for heirloom plants.

Turfgrass Producers International (TPI)
1855-A Hicks Road
Rolling Meadows, IL 60008
800-405-8873
www.lawninstitute.com
A source for information on various turfgrasses.

INDEX